IRONIC OUT OF LOVE

IRONIC OUT OF LOVE
The Novels of Thomas Mann

by IRVIN STOCK

McFarland & Company, Inc., Publishers
Jefferson, North Carolina, and London

British Library Cataloguing-in-Publication data are available

Library of Congress Cataloguing-in-Publication Data

Stock, Irvin, 1920–
    Ironic out of love : the novels of Thomas Mann / by Irvin Stock.
      p.   cm.
    Includes index.
    ISBN 0-89950-890-1 (lib. bdg. : 50# alk. paper) ∞
    1. Mann, Thomas, 1875–1955 — Criticism and interpretation.
  I. Title.
  PT2625.A44Z852   1994
  833′.912 — dc20   92-51091
                                                        CIP

Manufactured in the United States of America

McFarland & Company, Inc., Publishers
  Box 611, Jefferson, North Carolina 28640

To Jack Davis

ACKNOWLEDGMENTS

Thanks are due to the following periodicals in which early versions of certain chapters of this book appeared: *Accent* (the chapter on *The Holy Sinner*), *Salmagundi* (the one on *Reflections of a Non-Political Man*) and *Modern Fiction Studies* (the one on *The Magic Mountain*).

A number of people have helped me. I want especially to acknowledge my debt to Professors Henry Hatfield, Stuart Atkins and the late Erich Heller, whose comments on those published studies encouraged me to write this book. I am also grateful to Stanley Eskin and to Al Rosen for useful criticism of various chapters; to Professor Robert Spaethling, not only for such criticism, but for wise counsel that went beyond matters of literature and scholarship; and to Anne Marie Weisner for valuable help with Mann's language.

But once again my greatest debt, for criticism and support, is to my friend Jack Davis, to whom this book is dedicated.

TABLE OF CONTENTS

"'There is no fixed point outside of life,' Nietzsche says, 'from which it would be possible to reflect upon existence; there is no authority before which life might be ashamed.' Really not? We have the feeling that there is one after all, and if it is not morality, then it is simply the spirit of man, humanity itself, assuming the form of criticism, irony and freedom, allied with the judging word." (Mann, *Last Essays,* 161)

"[Thomas Mann] was a man misunderstood in spite of many honors and much success. His heart, fidelity, responsibility, and capacity to love, which stand behind the irony and virtuosity,... will give to his work and memory a liveliness far beyond our disordered times." (Hermann Hesse, *Chronicle,* 265)

"Even in these times it is possible for a man to construct out of his life and work a culture, a small cosmos, in which everything is interrelated, which, despite all diversity, forms a complete personal whole, and which stands more or less on an equal footing with the great life-syntheses of earlier ages." (Mann, *Letters,* 642)

CHAPTER ONE

The Book's Subject: A Bird's-Eye View

"I have sometimes had visions of a volume of essays that ought to be written: a critique of those dear and precious great old books, the ones toward which we have special relations of love and insight. The treatment should be fresh and immediate, untrammeled as though the works themselves had just appeared in print." (*Essays*, 203)[1]

Mann's novels have long been among my own "dear and precious great old books": for me they are the supreme achievement of our century in the art of fiction and the richest source of the pleasure and wisdom that art can give. This will account for the approach I take in what follows.

To begin with, I have assumed that what Mann was implying in the above remark is true. To write chiefly out of one's own experience of art that matters to us deeply may also add something useful to the ongoing criticism of our subject, whether we offer novelties or only confirm, with new emotion and from a new perspective, what has been seen by others. I have therefore tried, as much as I can, to be "fresh and immediate"; any engagement with the rich body of Mann criticism has been kept to my footnotes and bibliography.[2] But something else follows from my feeling about Mann's novels. It is that I value them far above theories about the artist and his work. For this reason, my book is not an exposé of Mann's unconscious compulsions, whether in his psyche or his culture or his social class or his gender or the nature of language. Indeed, though my chief interest is the philosophical novels that begin with *The Magic Mountain,* I rarely discuss Mann's ideas alone, detached from their contexts of character, feeling and drama. The novels themselves are my subject. I have tried to make clear their essential character—what they are about, what constitutes their beauty and power, and what they lead us to understand.

To speak of what novels lead us to understand is, of course, to oppose outright one currently fashionable theory, the one that denies we can find a

1

writer's meaning in what he or she has written. In fact, I still hold with Words-
worth that "a poem is a man speaking to men" and saying something about our
common lot he has a right to expect us to grasp. This principle, though it applies to Mann's earlier work as well, is especially important for the appreciation
of his novels from *The Magic Mountain* on.

More than any other novelist of the first rank, Mann was given to seeking
and showing the general significance of his individual experience. "To stand
for many in standing for oneself," so he defined the "small kind of greatness"
(Winston, 214) to which he aspired when he was writing, in his first novel *Buddenbrooks,* about his own family's "decline" into the artist. Later, exulting in the
"manifold associations" that enriched the actual details of a holiday described
in *Death in Venice,* he wrote: "I love that word *associations.* For me, that which
is full of associations is, quite precisely, that which is significant" (*Sketch,* 61).
What he loves about associations, of course, is that they are the perceived or
felt kinship that makes one thing a symbol of others, a bearer of meaning. Then
there was the grandiose ambition that, from his youth on, spurred him always
to go "all the way" in exploring what his subjects were teaching him. "My mania
for treatment *ab ovo*" (*Sketch,* 69), he called it, explaining why the Joseph story
became the story of Jacob, a mania that drove him all the way in the other
direction as well, to far-spreading consequences, for that epic also points forward, toward Jesus. Finally, there is the fact that both the protagonists and
the narrators of his novels are always versions of himself: they are given to
thinking.

The result is that though Mann's novels arose out of a self-absorption that
may be called narcissistic, they are also an amazingly rich account of his world
and his culture. Each is about the artist, or the artist-type, or, in the case of
The Magic Mountain, someone who becomes the artist-type; and each is rooted
in his personal experience as the artist-son, born in 1875, of a stern north–German businessman father and an indulgent, "southern," musical mother. But
each was an exploration too of the large general meaning he found in his small
personal subject, and of the way his own understanding of it shifted and deepened in different stages of his development, and the world's.

So that first novel about the end of his confident and successful capitalist —
or "bourgeois" — family in an artist for whom the life of business is impossible
became a picture of the conflict between two ways of being, one that accepts
the struggle of life and the obligation to do well in it, and another that withdraws from the struggle into the realm of feeling and awareness. In this first
novel, it's true, ideas remain buried in the realistic story. But from then on the
unfolding meanings of Mann's fiction are more and more part of the stories
themselves, the central concern, not only of the author, but of his protagonists.
In *Tonio Kröger* and *Death in Venice,* which show what the sickly Buddenbrook
artist would have become if he had lived and written novels like their author,
we find that the conflict between those two ways of being is within the artist,
the artist-as–Thomas Mann, and that its painful rise into consciousness is the

core of the drama. Then, though the protagonist of *The Magic Mountain* begins as an ordinary bourgeois, we see his mind taking on the character and contents of his author's, while that same conflict out of *Buddenbrooks* becomes a key to the opposing ways of thought which underlay 19th century Western culture and erupted into World War I. And as with this first of Mann's three greatest novels, so with the other two. With some version of his own divided self at their center, both the Joseph tetralogy and *Doctor Faustus* became studies of culture extraordinarily rich in ideas pertinent to their time. *Joseph and His Brothers,* written in a period when the humane values of Western culture were being increasingly violated in German anti–Semitic politics, shows how those values were created in the religion of the Jews. *Doctor Faustus,* written after World War II, exposes the kinship between the Nazi horror and a great German artist's career, setting before us their common roots in German culture since the time of Luther, and, by way of music, the equivocal character of art. And though Mann's last two novels are lighter and livelier than all the others, *The Holy Sinner* links his ideas about the artist to the essential character of Christianity, and in *Felix Krull* they become the basis of a vision, not only of the nature of man, but of "Being" itself, the "Being" that emerged — in the "Big Bang" — out of the void.

Of course, this wealth of conscious thought in Mann's later work is exactly what some readers (for instance, Nabokov) find wrong with it. Nor can we deny that there is truth in the old notion that ideas may replace a story's drama with inert and reductive abstractions. But the fact is, they don't do this in Mann's fiction — not enough to matter — and the reason they don't will bring us to the center of his art.

To begin with, Mann was never the kind of writer who regards stories chiefly as vehicles of meaning. "In the final analysis," he wrote in 1951, "accuracy, authenticity, the striking resemblance to real life , is always what gives pleasure in art, in the rendering of psychological states as well as objective states. We may stylize and symbolize as much as we like — without realism it doesn't do. What else have I done in *Joseph* and *The Holy Sinner* if not real-ize?" (*Letters,* 633–634). This means too, as the word "pleasure" suggests, that he never forgot what we go to stories for. "My desire and goal," he wrote me in 1954, "is to entertain."[3] So his novels are not merely ironic, they are often funny; he loved to make people laugh. And they are always organized and narrated in a way to ensure the greatest dramatic effect. Amid the loftiest intellectual discussion in *The Magic Mountain,* he can let slip, with a comic pretence of inadvertence, a hint of story developments to come that keeps his unfolding idea rooted in good old suspense. And what the suspense promises is always fulfilled, first in exciting crescendos of feeling and action, and then in climaxes positively theatrical.

But even this realism and love of stories — in short, even Mann's art — has meaning. For in fiction which lives up to its best possibilities the story is a living demonstration of what the writer finds latent in his subject, that is, of how he understands it. This is not to say that the understanding he brings us to is simply an idea. What we get in such fiction is an experience in which insight is one with feeling: we know because we feel, and we feel because we know. Granted, Mann's novels, being about people who think, give us a lot of ideas along the way. Those three greatest are so full of ideas, in fact, that one must sympathize with readers who prefer stories made of less complex materials. But that, in the main, is what their ideas are: *material*. Their meaning lies elsewhere. It is to be found, as I say, in their stories, in their art, in the way their intellectual material stays alive and serves the drama. I will touch in what follows on some of Mann's methods of pulling off this feat, but let me suggest here what underlies them all.

It is that Mann's deepest concern was not ideas, but his artist-self. This could, it's true, have been a narrowing and by now dated preoccupation, since the prestige of art and its creators has diminished in our culture. But if Mann's artist is indeed the familiar misfit, the dreamer and maker of beauty, what keeps him interesting to us is that his dreaming and making are shown to be the human enterprise in its purest form. "Always," he said, "I have seen in art the pattern of the human, in the life of the artist human life raised to its highest power" (*Order*, 90). For Mann the artist is most of all the human being in love with himself and given over, often impractically, to his own inner life; his "making" is a gifted version of the human mind's attempt to impose its own sense of things on the world. At bottom Mann's subject, like Freud's, was the drama of that inner life. To this subject he brought Freud's awareness — nurtured in him by Schopenhauer and Nietzsche, as well as Western literature in general, long before he read Freud — of the role of feeling in consciousness. For him too it was feeling that drives us to thought and undermines or complicates our ideas, and for him too the strongest and most pervasive of our feelings was the longing born in the body. "Longing — *sehnsucht!*" Mann wrote to his fiancée in 1904 — and it seems clear he was emphasizing the word's sexual meaning. "You don't know how I love that word. It is my favorite word, my holy word, my magic formula, my key to the mystery of the world" (Hamilton, 101). Hans Castorp will arrive at the same key, and after him Felix Krull, but in fact, sex is at the bottom of almost all the stories of this most philosophic of novelists. Mann's subject, in short, is the vicissitudes of consciousness, of mind (or "spirit") driven by feeling — what it opposes and is opposed by, what it costs and what it can win.

This subject opens the way to that special wisdom of fiction in which Mann's work is so rich. For to say that the ideas in his novels belong to their material is to say they are only parts of the whole. As he put it in *Joseph*, they are stations in a journey. What Mann stands behind are the meanings of the journey itself. It is in such meanings — in his grasp of life's complexity, ambiguity, contradictions and open-endedness — that his wisdom resides. Of course, Mann's tendency to smile at ideas that claim to be final truth, his famous irony, is the basis for the recurring charge against him of nihilism. But in fact, it is the reverse of nihilism. He smiles at ideas because he is loyal to what is deeper and richer than they, the human being and human experience.

How he discovered his subject and how it grew as he and his world unfolded what was in them is the story told in this book. But since that subject is first of all himself, we begin with a sketch of his life.

Notes

1. I quote from Lowe-Porter's translations, except where others are named, and silently correct any errors I have found. About Lowe-Porter as a translator, it may be worth noting that, though she has been justly criticized for her occasional inaccuracies, Mann himself valued her gift for conveying his "tone." Thus, expressing regret that she may have grown too "feeble with age" to be given the job of translating *Felix Krull,* he went on to say, "On the other hand, she is the only one who can translate certain passages of the book, verses, doggerel, and altogether strike the tone" (*Letters,* 670).

2. Needless to say, this doesn't mean I haven't learned a great deal from the distinguished predecessors I list in my bibliography. In particular, I want to mention the writings on *The Magic Mountain* by E. Heller, P. de Mendelssohn, M. Swales, and H. Weigand; on the Joseph novels by J. Bab, R. Cunningham, K. Hamburger, T. J. Reed, M. Swales, and M. Van Doren; on *Doctor Faustus* by G. Bergsten, E. Heller, E. Kahler, G. Lukasch, P. de Mendelssohn, T. J. Reed, and M. Swales; and on Mann's work in general by all the above, as well as by H. Hatfield, P. Heller, F. Kaufman, R. H. Thomas. See too the individual critics named after the three essay collections in the bibliography, especially P. Heller (whose "Thomas Mann's Conception of the Creative Writer" in the Ezergailis collection is the best single essay on Mann I've read), E. and K. Mann, M. Price, and N. Rabkin. It should be equally needless to say that though I learned from these writers or was heartened by their support, they are not to be held accountable for my final views, which in some cases differ markedly from those of critics I admire.

3. From Mann's letter to me of May 23, 1954. See note 1 on page 199.

CHAPTER TWO

The Life

"Truly, when I consider the amount of blood and tears, misery and doom, that prevails on earth today, I have every reason to be grateful to my destiny; it has always tried to turn thing well . . . for me." (*Letters*, 376)

Thomas Mann was born on June 6, 1875, in the north-German (Baltic) seaport of Lübeck, one of the free or self-governing mercantile towns which, in the 13th century, came together for mutual support in the Hanseatic League. In the writer's childhood Lübeck was still medieval in atmosphere, with its narrow streets and ancient gabled houses. It was also still thriving, and the Mann family owned one of its most substantial and respected firms. They had been prominent grain merchants in the town since 1790, when the business was begun by Johann Siegmund Mann, and this founder initiated not only the family fortune, but its honorable public repute. "My son," he once instructed Johann Siegmund, Jr., who was to take his place as head of the firm — the advice is preserved in family records — "work hard by day, but be sure only to undertake such business as will allow us to sleep soundly at night" (Hamilton, 6).

The recipient of this advice entered the business himself in 1823, kept it growing, played a minor role in the town government and became the Brazilian Vice-Consul, and after the death of a first wife, he married a second and acquired the substantial Lübeck house that was to grow famous as the home of the Buddenbrooks. Of his five children with the first wife two lived past childhood. With his second he had five more, one of whom was Thomas Johann Heinrich, the father of the two writers, Heinrich, his first-born and Thomas, four years younger. An elder sister of this father, being twice married and divorced, and an eccentric and irresponsible younger brother became the family burdens we would smile at in *Buddenbrooks*, but the father became the model for the most impressive of the Buddenbrooks, Thomas. He joined the family business at fourteen and at twenty-two, when his father died, he took his place at its head. Under his leadership the business expanded into railroads, insurance, banking and shipping, and having been made Royal Netherlands Consul soon after taking the business over, he went on to become a town

Senator in 1877. In 1869 he married Julia da Silva-Bruhns, the Brazilian-born daughter of a German planter and a Portuguese-Creole Brazilian, a young woman who was "Latin" in type, beautiful and "extraordinarily musical" (*Sketch*, 3). In 1890, shortly after building a new house for his growing family, he was honored at a great public celebration of the Mann firm's 100th anniversary.

It's not surprising that Mann felt himself obligated all his life to be worthy of such a family, or that the obligation was intensified by the way it was embodied for him in his father. Mann later spoke with pride of his father's "dignity and common sense, his energy, his industry, his personal and spiritual elegance." Though not "simple," the son goes on, but "rather nervous and sensitive," he was "a self-restrained, successful man who early achieved respect and honor in his world" (*Chronicle*, 1). But the influence on Mann of his businessman father was matched by that of his dark, musical mother. Like Goethe, he said, "I took from my father '*des Lebens ernstes Führen*,' but from my mother the '*Frohnatur*' — the sensuous artistic side, and in the widest sense, the '*Lust zu fabulieren*' (*Sketch*, 4). And though that double influence was eventually to serve him as a clue to the doubleness, not only of his own nature, but of almost everything else, he experienced it for a long time as conflict. In 1932 he wrote that Goethe's "bourgeois" celebration of the "life-worthy," his idea that what made for natural "aristocracy" was not a "sublime incapacity and lack of vocation for ordinary life" but "to be solidly planted in life," to be "positive" and "affirmative," gave him at first "the strange impression of paradox" (*Essays*, 83). For his own journey of self- realization began with the feeling — half guilty, half proud — that those father-virtues were alien to the artist-nature he got from his mother, and that to become what he wanted was to leave them behind.

So he was a poor student, given to dreaming, private reading and writing (poetry), and since his elder brother had already turned away from the family business, he, with his equal disinclination for it, became the final disappointment of his father's hope that a son would take it over. When, a year after that resounding centenary celebration, the father died, life itself began to abet Thomas's estrangement from the regular, respectable life of his forebears. The business was sold, and Julia Mann moved with her three younger children to Munich. (In that Mecca for artists, we may add parenthetically, Mann's two sisters, Carla and Julia, became what he was to regard as victims of the worship of art and its scorn of bourgeois life. Carla, who spent years as an untalented, unsuccessful and dangerously free-living actress, and then hoped for rescue in a "good" marriage, was thwarted when a sadistic former lover betrayed her to her fiancé, and killed herself. Julia, though she began by fleeing the Bohemian life in a regular marriage, with children, also rebelled at last, sank into misery, and took her own life. We will meet them both again, along with their artistic mother, in *Doctor Faustus*). The young Thomas remained in Lübeck to complete his education, and by the age of nineteen had carried it far enough to entitle him to serve in the army for only one year instead of three, and as an officer.

But again his studies were far less important to him than the pursuit of his own interests, which in this period meant the writing he did for the school paper and the concerts he attended in the Lübeck City Theatre. His musical education had been initiated by his mother's piano-playing and singing—her repertoire included works from all the 19th century masters—and it now culminated in an experience of Wagner's operas which not only overwhelmed him as music, but gave direction and scope to his ambition as a writer of fiction. It was to Wagner, he later wrote, that he owed "what I know of economy of means, of effect in general—in contrast to sensationalism, that 'effect without cause'—of the epic spirit, of beginning and end, of style as the mysterious adjustment of the personal to the objective, of the creation of symbols, of the organic compactness of the single, vital unity of the total work" (*Reflections*, 55).

In 1894 he had his first and last experience of conventional servitude: he spent six months as an unpaid apprentice in an insurance company. But even this was a partial fraud because at his desk he secretly wrote the short story "*Gefallen*", which was published and won him a letter of encouragement from the poet Richard Dehmel. Then came a pretence at getting ready for a practical career in journalism by auditing some courses in the Technische Hochschule in Munich. But he was also writing and, since he later acknowledged the influence of Nietzsche on his earliest stories, finding in Nietzsche's work still further "liberation" from the attitudes of his forebears. For, as he said later, "it was Nietzsche who . . . first questioned the highest moral ideals, even truth itself, in their usefulness to life, as he placed the most radical psychology in the service of an anti-radical and anti-nihilistic will." In Mann's view Nietzsche's "rebellion against morality [was] . . . more the rebellion of an artist and lover than that of a truly philosophical nature." And he slyly hints that it is this Nietzsche who is to be found in his own work. "I have always felt that Nietzsche's philosophy could have become a stroke of luck and a happy discovery for a great poet . . . the source, that is, of a most highly erotic-crafty *irony* that moves playfully between life and intellect" (*Reflections*, 58). Mann was to arrive, as we will see, at a very different opinion of that Nietzschean opposition between life and truth, life and morality. But in this early stage of his self-discovery, his estrangement from the bourgeois had still further to go.

In spite of her own predilections, the young man's mother remained loyal enough to her husband's ideas to keep urging Mann away from a literary career. But his resistance prevailed. And when she began to give him, as she already gave Heinrich, a small income that set him free to devote himself to the life he wanted, this money turned out to mean more than the freedom to write. It meant the freedom to go "south" and to give himself up to what he would think of forever after as a "southern" sensuality. In 1895 he spent three months with his brother in Palestrina and Rome, and shortly afterward went alone to Vienna, Venice and Naples. Winston guesses that it was in one of these cities that he had the experience of which he writes, in a kind of recoil, in a letter of the time: "How I hated it, this sensuality which claims that everything fine and good is its consequence and effect. Alas, it is the *poison* that lurks in everything fine and good" (Winston, 97). He "hated it," and yet when he discovered and fell in love with Schopenhauer's great book in 1899, the experience had an odd connection with that youthful sensuality and became another of the anti-bourgeois influences on his thought. His feeling for Schopenhauer, he was to write, "was essentially a metaphysical intoxication, closely related to a late and violent outbreak of sexuality (I am speaking of my twentieth year) and in its nature less philosophic than passionate and mystical. . . . What did concern me, and that in a sensual and suprasensual way, was the element of eroticism and mystic unity in this philosophy. . ." (*Sketch*, 25). It was precisely as a seduction like that of sex toward relaxation of the will and so toward the unity with all creation promised by death that he gave his thrilled discovery to the older, the life-weary Thomas Buddenbrook.

In the young man's disgusted recoil from sexual self-abandon we catch a glimpse of the father he carried within him. But we know now that this stern inner judge had more than ordinary sensuality to deal with. It seems that Tonio Kröger's infatuation with blond, blue-eyed Hans Hansen was based on Mann's feeling for a schoolmate called Armin Martens, of which he wrote in his seventies to a friend: "A more delicate, more blissfully painful love was never again to be granted me" (Winston, 27). His *Diaries* speak of his schoolboy "passion for Willri Timpi, later elevated into Pribislav Hippe" (245) (who is loved by the schoolboy Hans Castorp); of "the youthful intensity of feeling, the wild surges of exaltation and deep despair" of his love at twenty-five for Paul Ehrenberg, which he calls a "central emotional experience" (210); and of his "passion" in 1927 at the age of fifty-two for "the [nineteen-year-old] boy Klaus H." (274). In fact, though this homosexual tendency was surely tamed and muted by his genuinely happy marriage and the demands of his career, it was not only a part of his nature forever, but a part he cherished. Commenting on that change from the "youthful intensity" of his love of Paul Eherenberg to the "benign fulfilment" of his "more mature, more controlled and happier" love of "the boy Klaus H.," he made a striking observation: "This is doubtless the normal course of human affections, and owing to this normality I can feel more strongly that my life conforms to the scheme of things than I do by virtue of marriage and children" (*Diaries*, 210). He is saying, surely, that it is in his homosexuality that he shared most completely in the sexual life of human beings.[1]

But though Mann traveled so far from his forebears in his inner life, there was one characteristic in which he very soon began to resemble them. He addressed himself to his life's vocation as they had to theirs: he became a good worker, industrious, conscientious, persistent against obstacles. The Bohemian life he despised. "It was a youthful romantic illusion and youthful fancy," he was to write, "if I ever imagined I was sacrificing my life to my 'art'. . . . In truth, 'art' is only the means of fulfilling my life ethically . . . so little is the likes of me . . . an esthete in the Bohemian sense, and so very much one in the burgherly sense" (*Reflections*, 73-74). When the early stories appeared in 1898 as his first book *Little Herr Friedmann*, he had already begun (in Palestrina in 1897) to take notes for *Buddenbrooks*. In 1900, as he was starting his army service, the book was accepted for publication. (The army was a hateful interruption to his writer's life; he got out of it in three months by carefully emphasizing a genuine, but minor foot disability.) That faithful work paid off in his life as it had in his forebears'. *Buddenbrooks* appeared in a slow-selling two-volume edition in 1901, and in 1903, reprinted in one volume, it began its triumphant career as an acknowledged German classic, so widely read and loved that in his old age Mann expressed the rueful suspicion that it might keep his name alive when all the vastly more ambitious later novels were forgotten.

The same return to his father's values can be seen in his marriage to Katya Pringsheim. For the marriage made him happy as a husband and father in the good old bourgeois way (he was to have six children), and it provided him for the rest of his life with an irreproachably conventional shelter for his wild adventures at his desk. Nor was this "regular" love a mere expedient. There can be no doubt that his courtship of the girl was also "passionate," and brought its own "exaltation" and "despair." The Pringsheims were a wealthy, highly cultivated Jewish family.[2] The father was a university professor of mathematics and an ardent lover of music—an early champion of Wagner, and even a friend, until the master's anti-Semitism parted them. The mother, herself from a well known literary family, was devoted to literature. Mann entered the family circle in 1903 as a guest at one of the Pringsheim's intellectual gatherings and was received there as already a novelist of brilliant promise. Katya, however, was less interested in marriage than in her own life, in her freedom to make the most of the wealth and culture by which she was surrounded, and in particular in her studies at the university, where she specialized in mathematics. It took Mann two years to draw her "down" from those heights into the ordinary life of human beings he himself was so eager to enter. He persevered because he felt that it was only with this uniquely privileged girl that marriage was possible for him. "Do you know why we suit each other so well?" he wrote her. "Because you, in your own way, are ... as I understand the word, a *princess*. And—you may laugh now but you must understand me—I have always seen myself as a kind of prince, and in you I have found, with absolute certainty, my destined bride" (Hamilton, 100- 101). The genuine intensity of his love, expressed in a series of passionate letters that have been preserved, won her over; they were engaged in 1904 and married in 1905. That the artist too can be happy and can even, without betraying his "high calling," join with and serve his fellows, is precisely the idea of Mann's second novel *Royal Highness* (1909), the "comedy" about a prince and a kind of princess he based on his courtship of Katya Pringsheim and its happy ending.

But after *Royal Highness* came *Death in Venice* (1912). As we will see when we go over these early works, Mann had not yet finished with the artist as outsider. To complete the tale of his self-realization *against* the bourgeois, we must now turn to one more of his early and lasting influences, the relationship—the conflict — with his brother Heinrich. In 1917 Thomas called this relationship "the real or at least the most important problem of my life" (Reich-Ranicki, 21). In fact, Heinrich played a role as great as their parents' in shaping Mann's view of himself and of his life's central issues.

Conflict was not the whole story. In certain periods we find the brothers encouraging, defending and supporting each other. Nevertheless, until Thomas rose to world fame with *The Magic Mountain*, he often felt a distaste for Heinrich verging on hatred. Rivalry was naturally part of the reason. Heinrich was already known as a novelist when Thomas was just beginning, and he kept pouring our novels, plays, stories and essays with a speed that made the other gasp. "Good heavens," Thomas wrote him in 1907, "you've finished another book!" (Reich-Ranicki, 10). In spite of the success of *Buddenbrooks*, Thomas never ceased to work slowly and painfully and often in a state of doubt. ("I believe I am played out," he actually wrote to Heinrich in 1913, "and should probably never have become a novelist. *Buddenbrooks* was a bourgeois book and not fitted for the twentieth century. *Tonio Kröger* was merely maudlin, *Royal Highness* vain, *Death in Venice* full of half-baked ideas and falsehood" [Hamilton, 150].) But if rivalry with Heinrich added a certain intensity to Thomas's distaste, its real cause, and the real source of the "problem," was the genuine and profound difference between them. For Thomas, who always ended by seeing the personal as symbolic, this difference became a clue to the general meaning of the conflict — and also to the doubleness — by which he understood first himself, and then the world.

To begin with, the difference showed itself in their attitudes to art. We can see how Thomas wrote in the "grinding torments" undergone by his *alter ego* Tonio Kröger, as that young novelist's "ambition" and "persistent industry . . . joined battle with an irritable fastidiousness of taste" (*Stories*, 100); or in his account of the daily labors (no doubt on *The Magic Mountain*, already begun) of the narrator of his autobiographical tale *A Man and His Dog* (1918): "I have had to grit my teeth and tussle with a single detail, while at the same time holding a more extended and complex context firmly in mind, concentrating my mental powers upon it down to its furthermost ramifications" (*Stories*, 477). What this martyr to "perfection of the work" saw in his brother's practice he let him know in an unusually open outburst in 1903 against Heinrich's novel *The Hunt for Love*. He complained of its "wild, garish, hectic, convulsive deformation of truth and humanity, its desperate attacks on the reader's interest," its "grotesque world of crass effects," and its lack of "any stringency, any unity, any linguistic stance. . . . Everything that can exert an effect," he went on, "is brought into play without any regard for appropriateness." And in 1904, in a letter to the critic Ida Boy-Ed about his reactions to Heinrich as a writer, he rejected the word "disdain" because "the feeling his artistic personality awakens in me is closer to hatred" (Reich-Ranicki, 7, 10).

But of course, their difference as artists came from a difference more fundamental. Thomas shows what this was in a letter of January 8, 1904, that seems to set his brother above himself, and may well have been sincere (given his ups and downs), but that for us must mean something else. "[You are] superior to me," he tells him, "in human refinement, in spiritual purity and clarity, beyond all errings and confusions." For "I am not capable of looking at a sequence of thought in isolation ... the sense of the complexity of the world overwhelms me" (Reich Ranicki, 9).[3] In fact, that "spiritual purity and clarity" made possible by rising above the world's complexity and leaping straight to the effects and ideas desired began around 1904 to take its classic political form. Writing to Heinrich a month later about his novel *Fulvia*, Thomas remarks on the development it shows, "for me still a little implausible ... toward Liberalism." Though he sees in this a kind of "maturity" far beyond his own, for himself "freedom" is "a moral and intellectual concept, meaning the same as 'Truthfulness'. . . . I have absolutely no interest," he goes on, ". . . in political freedom." And concluding from the emergence of the great Russian novelists out of oppression that "the fight for freedom is better than freedom itself," he declares that for him the blood spilled in freedom's name gives it a character "strangely un-free" and "medieval" (Hamilton, 86-87).

This political aspect of their difference came to an explosive climax during the first days of World War I. Heinrich had become increasingly a champion of France and democracy, and Thomas found himself gripped by a sudden passion of loyalty to Germany. When certain patriotic articles by Thomas were greeted with outrage among European artists and intellectuals, he found it impossible to go on with *The Magic Mountain* until he had explained his position — to himself as well as to them. In November, 1915, he began the series of essays that became *Reflections of a Non-Political Man* (1918). Since this long, arduous self-exploration opened up to him the connection between his own nature and the central issues of Western Culture and so laid the groundwork, not only for *The Magic Mountain*, but for all the novels that followed, it will require a chapter to itself. Here it is enough to say that Heinrich was the adversary that work was aimed at from its inception. When, two months later, Thomas read Heinrich's essay "Zola," the attack it contained on Germany's intellectual defenders in general, and, as he felt, on himself in particular, put his life-long hostility to his brother into the work's center. His brother became for him a kind of extension of their right-thinking father, of the "bourgeois," into the realm of art and intellect, where that Other could be rejected without guilt. For as a liberal Heinrich was a champion of virtuous action, the kind that brings about what ought to be, and so of ideas which, in their "purity" and "clarity," make such action seem easy. It now became for Thomas a matter for pride, not apology, that he himself belonged among those who are slow to welcome change or the action that brings it about. It meant he was closer to reality, to the world's complexity and the inextricable mingling in every action of good and evil. The tendency of his brother's type to regard its own simplemindedness as moral superiority only intensified his scorn.

In 1917 Heinrich made an attempt at a reconciliation. Thomas angrily rejected it as the patronizing gesture of one whose cause seemed to be winning, and at this Heinrich replied—though the draft of his letter which survives is headed "not sent"—with his own rock-bottom view of what kept them apart. The real reason for Thomas's rage against him, he wrote, was "[your] furious passion for your own 'I'." He grants that this passion did produce "several narrow but private works." But he goes on: "You also owe [to it] your complete lack of respect for anything which doesn't suit you . . . your inability to grasp the real seriousness of anyone's life but your own. Around you are arranged extras who signify 'the people' to you, as in your . . . *Royal Highness.* . . . The hour will come, I hope, in which you will see people, not shadows, and then perhaps me" (Hamilton, 184-185). There is truth in this. Thomas did, and always would, seek the world and what it means to be human in himself; he did make the cultivation and exploration of his own ego his life's work. But though Heinrich, in his justified anger, emphasized the way such egotism can blind one to others, Thomas's career would show how it can also lead one back to them.

The fact is, in writing *Reflections* Mann did not end where he began. As we will see, his self-exploration led him to a new awareness that his brother's concern for what ought to be was as necessary to the human enterprise as his own for what is. We catch a glimpse of this development in what he says of Schiller in his 1922 essay "Goethe and Tolstoy." Calling Schiller's "Naive and Sentimental Poetry" the "classic essay which comprehended all others [in its 'sphere' of German thought] and makes them all superflous" (*Essays,* 95), he reminds us that its subject was a version of his own inner conflict and had influenced his view of it. For Schiller the "naive" poet, being at one with nature, "functions as an undivided sensuous unity." The "sentimental" poet, on the other hand— and it should be clear that the word is not being used in its pejorative current sense—has "passed into the state of civilization, and art has laid its hand on him [and so] that sensuous harmony in him is withdrawn, and he can express himself only as a *moral* unity, i.e., as striving after unity." For him inner unity is "only an idea," and what he gives us is "the elevation of actuality to the ideal, or, amounting to same thing, the representation of the ideal" (Schiller, 111-112). It is not surprising that Goethe, as a "son of nature," saw Schiller's essay as a defense against himself, and that he regarded his own "classic" way of being as healthy and the other's "romantic" way as sick. But Mann also points out the "mutual character of the sentimental longing—of the sons of spirit for nature, of the sons of nature for spirit." Not only Tolstoy, he tells us, but Goethe too was haunted by and at last affirmed the claims of spirit, of the moral. And as Schiller spoke of "the higher concept under which both [types] can be subsumed . . . the idea of humanity," Mann concludes that "there is no deciding which of these lofty types contributes more and better to the highly cherished idea of a perfected humanity" (175). The personal relevance of this "higher concept" grew explicit when he wrote to a friend in 1922 of his sense that something even deeper than what divided him from Heinrich was bringing them together. "I feel that may have happened," he added, "when I realize that the thought which dominates my mind these days is of a new and personal fulfillment of the idea of humanity..." (*Letters*, 117).

It's true that that last sentence goes on, "in contrast, to be sure, to the humanitarian world of Rousseau" (*Letters*, 117). But even such modest bows to his old skepticism were soon abandoned. For the rise of German fascism after World War I made him more and more aware of the danger of his old attitudes to what mattered to him—and indeed had always mattered to him—most deeply. In his work the result of this development is that Hans Castorp ends his education on the mountain by coming closer to its Heinrich-figure Settembrini and then by rejoining the human community in the flatland, and that the artist-heros of the novels that followed—Joseph, Goethe, the great Pope Gregory—all rise above their initial estrangement from their fellows and become teachers and saviors. The same development turned the non-political man into a passionate political leader.

Before we go into Mann's politics, however, it's worth noting that his assumption of that leadership role reflected a new assurance of his leadership in German culture, and in fact, of his identity with the greatest of German writers, Goethe. In spite of his propensity to self-doubt, he had always felt himself destined for such lofty rank. While at work on *Royal Highness*, which he tended to take lightly, he began to plan a novel about Frederick of Prussia in which, as he wrote to Heinrich in that year (1906), he would be "undertaking to portray *greatness*" (his emphasis), and to do so as one who had his own experience in the subject. "I am thirty now," he said, too. "It is time to start thinking of a masterpiece" (Hamilton, 124). Of his thoughts about Frederick, nothing survives in print but his fine essay on the King, but there is no doubt that *The Magic Mountain* took its place as the masterpiece his pride required and his bid for identification with Goethe. In fact, the vast increase in its scope led to by *Reflections,* and his acknowledgement as a master by the world, as it were, in the Nobel Prize in 1929, brought his native narcissism to a point that can sometimes make even an admirer smile—or wince. Of the Nobel Prize he wrote that it "had, I knew, hovered over me more than once before and found me not unprepared, with calm if not uninterested insight into the character of my destiny, of my 'role' on this earth, which has now been gilded by the equivocal brilliance of success and which I regard entirely in a human spirit, without any great mental excitement" (*Sketch*, 73-74).

But the truth is, his sense of kinship with Goethe is entirely justified by the striking similarities in their work and their careers. Both won fame in their youth with novels that were nakedly autobiographical. For both their own artist-nature and its problems became their obsessive subject. And both grew vastly in stature, not only as artists, but as teachers, as sages, with novels of education that enlarged the scope of their self-regard until it took in the whole of human life. (Mann was even to match—in the Joseph novels—Goethe's extension of scope in *Faust* Part Two from earth to heaven.) For Mann, whose

admirations were always creative, such similarities became a clue to what he was
and a guide to what he could become. So, in that essay, "Goethe and Tolstoy,"
which he has called an offshoot of his own *Bildungsroman The Magic Mountain*, he
speaks of Goethe in a way that obviously, pointedly, applies to himself. "[T]he
pedagogic element [of Goethe's writings] resides...," he says, "in the autobio-
graphic; it follows from it, it grows out of it." And later: "Nobody has ever loved
his own ego, nobody was ever egocentric, in the sense of conceiving of his own
ego as a cultural task and toiling early and late in pursuance of it, without reap-
ing almost as though by accident educational influence in the outer world, and
the joy and dignity of a leader and former of youth" (*Essays*, 159-160). Then, in
the essay "Goethe as a Representative of the Bourgeois Age" (1932), we are clearly
given by way of Goethe (who, however, is set brilliantly before us) a picture of
Mann's own evolution during and after his work on *Reflections*.[4]

But it is not only Mann's right to identification with Goethe that mitigates
the unattractive effect of his occasional parade of it. There is also the fact that
he shouldered, and fully discharged, the obligations that go with the "greatness." We see him doing so all through the disaster that overtook the world during the second half of his life, the rise and near-triumph of totalitarianism.

Soon after World War I and the Versailles Peace Treaty that made Germany pay so heavily for its dreams of conquest, the fragile Weimar Republic
was shaken by gangs of militaristic thugs. From then on such gangs played an
increasingly important role in German political life. In the Reichstag election
of 1930 Hitler's National Socialist Party went from 12 seats to 107, and in 1933
Hitler became chancellor and, on the death of President Hindenburg a year
later, president as well. For Mann the danger of this revival of German force-
worship was clear from the early twenties. Beginning with his 1922 speech "On
the German Republic," he kept interrupting his work to speak and write
against it, and in 1933 he aroused the Nazis' anger by his speech "On the Sufferings and Greatness of Richard Wagner." Wagner, he said, far from being a
forerunner of the new chauvinism, was in his essential nature a champion of
values that transcended national boundaries, his work "soaked in the currents
of European art," he himself repudiating "all his life long ... power and
money, violence and war"—and in short, he was a man "no retrograde spirit
could claim for its own" (*Essays*, 350). Traveling in Switzerland with his wife
after the speech, Mann learned in a phone call from his daughter Erika that
the weather was bad at home, and his time of exile began.

Now it must be admitted that Mann did not, during his first three years
of exile (he had settled in Kusnacht, Switzerland), openly attack the Nazi
regime. Though the Nazis had confiscated his Munich home, from which
Erika had to steal his Joseph manuscripts at great personal risk, they had not
yet banned his books. In order to be able to publish the Joseph-novels in Germany, he limited himself to expressing, in the occasional essays that accompanied that work, his general hostility to the anti-human forces of the time. He
went so far in his prudence as to withdraw his public support for the emigre

magazine *Die Sammlung* edited by his son Klaus when its first issue turned out to be more openly anti-Nazi than had been expected. All this was painful to him and for some has remained a blot on his reputation. But even Heinrich supported him in his attempt to keep intact his link with the German people.

Tales of *Jacob* and *Young Joseph* were in fact published in Berlin — in 1933 and 1934. But *Joseph in Egypt* appeared in Vienna in 1936, and in that year Mann spoke out at last. His publisher had hoped to open a new publishing house in Switzerland, taking with him all his distinguished writers, but the neutral Swiss refused him permission, and Edouard Korrodi, the literary editor of the *Neue Züricher Zeitung*, defended the decision on the grounds that it was only Jewish writers who were leaving Germany. Mann wrote to that paper in February, 1936, that its emphasis on Jews was mistaken because the Nazis were the enemy not simply of the Jews, but of "all lofty Germanism," of Europe, of Western morality, and of civilization. On December 2, 1936, some weeks after he was made a citizen of Czechoslovakia, he, his wife and their younger children were deprived of German citizenship. (Heinrich and the older Mann children, Klaus and Erica, had already lost theirs). On December 19 the University of Bonn revoked the honorary doctorate it had awarded him. His prompt reply to the Dean of its Philosophical Faculty, printed as a pamphlet and translated into many languages, spread his views of Nazi Germany throughout the world. In 1937 Mann became editor-in-chief of the short-lived refugee periodical *Mass und Wert* (*Measure and Worth*). Though it was intended "not to be polemical, but constructive" (*Letters*, 259), Mann's introductory article spoke up pointedly "for human decency and for freedom, reason, and justice," and from then until the end of the war, and even after it, he produced a steady stream of political speeches and essays, including a series of passionate attacks on the Nazis broadcast into Germany by the BBC.

His political writings and speeches, most of them collected in *Order of the Day* (1942), were mainly called into being by the pressures of the time. But two ideas, or clusters of ideas, run through them all. The first is the confession that the Nazi horror had been made possible by a habit of mind which had been his own until *Reflections* enabled him to move beyond it. (An essay about Hitler is called "My Brother"!) He had been guilty of the German "romanticism," the German "inwardness," which on the one hand regarded culture as above politics, and therefore despised democracy and its "social freedom" and valued "moral freedom" alone; and on the other set life and art above ethical considerations. He could not, of course, repudiate that "inwardness" altogether. But what he had learned from his agonizing reexamination of his own culture, and then from developments after the first World War, was that in the sphere of action it was dangerous. When Germany ceased to be "non-political," its politics became clumsy, brutal, the kind to be expected of a people who regard the realm of action as outside of moral considerations, and whose history has left them with a sense of inferiority and a hunger for greatness. Just as Goethe once said the Germans should be forbidden for thirty years to use the word "*Gemüt*,"

Mann was to say they should give up using the word "profound," until they had learned to use the word "'decency,' simple decency" (*Order*, 254). For him democratic politics, which united culture and thought with action instead of keeping them apart, became the politics of decency. If not the whole of life, it was a vital part of it, with which artists and intellectuals must concern themselves to safeguard the rest. For "the problem of humanity is one problem," he wrote, "whose varied forms and spheres of expression are inseparable from each other." And: "Totalitarian politics are of the devil. The true totality we would oppose to it is that of the human being" (*Order*, 262-263).

Then, the rise of the Nazis added something else to his political education and to the message he felt driven to deliver. He had seen Hitler being secretly, and sometimes openly, welcomed by the "propertied classes" as a bulwark against communism, and he came to believe that the social change they feared was an inescapable requirement of the times. Political democracy must now be social, he declared, and, as had happened in the United States under President Roosevelt (whom he met and admired), it must "adopt in the economic as well as the spiritual domain as much socialist morality as the times made imperative and indispensible" (*Order*, 147). Mann has been called naive as a political thinker, and there is indeed a certain vagueness in his use of the word "socialism." (He also shared the common delusion that Stalin's Russia, though its internal politics could not be defended, was a natural ally of the democracies because she shared their desire for peace and human progress.) But what he meant by "socialism" was simply the idea that social justice (which meant also economic justice) must from now on be part of the political agenda, both within nations and among them. The fact is, what is naive in the essays in *Order of the Day* is peripheral. In their essentials, they are not only realistic and wise, they have a certain nobility, a passionate commitment to "decency." Indeed, these essays remain a pleasure to read (on the whole) because his political message, for all its urgency and simplicity, is always accompanied by his characteristic complexity of thought and his loyalty to "the human being." So he insists that in his political concerns he has not in the least abandoned his commitment to the artist's vision, as he understood it. For "humanity, as it were, in its essence" (*Order*, 90) is precisely what the artist's life represents; and a key requirement of his vocation is "conscientiousness," conscientiousness in moral matters as well as in craft. The artist is above all "the careful human being," who pays "profound and sensitive attention to the will and the activities of the universal spirit; to change in the garment of the truth; to the just and needful thing; in other words, to the will of God, whom the man of mind and spirit must serve heedless of the hatred he arouses among stupid or frightened people, obstinately attached by their interests to obsolete or evil phases of the age" (*Order*, 163-164). This, written in 1938, comes straight from the center of *Joseph*.

Mann had made several triumphant visits before the war to the United States, where the translations of his work by H. T. Lowe-Porter had won him a large and lucrative public and many honors. In 1938 he decided to accept the offer of a position at Princeton and to make his home in this country. From 1938 to 1941 he taught at Princeton, where he completed *The Beloved Returns* (1939). In 1941 he moved into a new house he had had built in Pacific Palisades, California. There he wrote, among lesser things, the last volume of the Joseph story, *Joseph the Provider* (1943); *Doctor Faustus* (1947); his account of the writing of that work, *The Story of a Novel* (1949); and *The Holy Sinner* (1951). But in the late '40's the rise of anti-communist hysteria began to remind him disturbingly of what he had lived through in Germany. In 1950 the Library of Congress cancelled his speech "The Years of My Life" because a recent visit of his to Europe had included a stay in East Germany and the acceptance of honors from that country. He and his wife returned to Europe in 1952, and two years later they settled in Kilchberg, on the Lake of Zürich in Switzerland, where he completed *Felix Krull*, which appeared in 1954. He died in Zürich on December 8, 1955.

One last word is in order. The rise of the Nazis, Mann's exile and his often anguished involvement in politics — to say nothing of personal tragedies like the suicides of his sisters and later of his son Klaus — might well be supposed to have darkened his life. But the fact is, what mainly determined his life's quality was that he continued, even amid the uprootings of exile, to work at his desk every morning from nine to twelve. Moreover, in spite of the doubts and difficulties that never ceased to accompany the work, he had the supreme joy of remaining at his best as an artist right to the end. That the world kept assuring him of this by a steadily increasing stream of honors was of course part of the fun. But most important was the work itself. So, when his American friend and patron Agnes E. Meyer ventured in 1941 to sympathize with his "hard life," he emphatically demurred. "In such a life," he granted, "all sorts of anguish, darkness and perils quite naturally occur," but "in principle I feel it, with gratitude, to be a happy, blessed life," a life in which "the foundation" has always been "serene" and "so to speak, sunny." What he had written about Joseph, he told her, could be applied to himself, that though the world and circumstances were powerful, he believed in their "plasticity," especially for the "Sunday child," the lucky individual who had the gift for turning all that happened to him to good. "A hard life?" he repeated. "I am an artist. That means a man who wishes to entertain himself — and this isn't a matter to pull a long face about. To be sure — and this is again a quotation from Joseph — what counts is how high one carries the entertainment: the higher it goes, the more absorbing the story becomes" (*Letters*, 375-377).

We turn now to that life-long daily entertainment of his and, to begin with, to the way each of his early works, as they advanced toward *The Magic Mountain*, carried it "higher."

Notes

1. Reich-Ranicki quotes this odd sentence from Mann's diary of 1919: "I am in no doubt that *Reflections* are also an expression of my sexual inversion" (19). A teas-

ingly suggestive remark that I'm not sure how to understand. Perhaps part of what it means is that Mann's feeling for hard, military German *Kultur* grew out of his attraction to blond, blue-eyed German manliness.

2. The wealthy, aristocratic Jews in Mann's 1905 story "The Blood of the Walsungs" are based on the Jewish family he married into, the story's twins, whose names and forbidden love are the same as those of Wagner's incestuous brother and sister Sieglinde and Siegmund, being modeled on Katya and her twin brother. Since the story is satirical, it's strange that Mann needed others to tell him it would cause offense, though he then promptly withdrew it from publication. But I don't think we have to add this to the many distasteful examples of the anti-Semitism of otherwise intelligent writers. In fact, I agree with Winston that Mann's attitude to Jews was the reverse of anti-Semitic. Though he objected to those Jewish "artists at repression" who see anti-Semitism in "the mere fact that someone does not overlook so striking a phenomenon as Jewishness," he was always drawn to Jews, both because he found them especially gifted in the realm of intellect and art and out of a "hedonistic" pleasure in Jewishness as "a picturesque fact calculated to add to the colorfulness of the world" (Winston, 24-25). As we will see, his novels fully bear this out.

3. In 1910 Mann wrote an essay on "The Litterateur and the Creative Artist," in which the same positive view is taken of the way Heinrich differed from himself. "He [the Litterateur] is radical because radicalism means purity, nobility and pro-fundity. He despises half-way thinking, cowardice in logic, compromise; he lives in protest against the corruption of the idea through reality" (Hamilton, 139). That Mann would mainly reject such loyalty to the idea which reality opposes doesn't mean he couldn't honestly praise it, too, when life's changes brought its value before him.

4. Such "childish identification with a father-image elected out of profound affinity," Mann said in his essay "Freud and the Future," underlies the artist's career. "The *imitatio* Goethe, with its Werther and Wilhelm Meister stages, its old-age period of *Faust* and *Divan*, can still shape and mythically mould the life of an artist, yet playing over — as is the artist way — into a smiling, childlike, and pro-found awareness" (*Essays*, 426).

5. As Mann's brief delay in speaking directly against Hitler bothered some of his fellow Germans, his lasting anger against those who remained in Germany, silent and comparatively safe to the end, incurred the resentment of others. This feeling grew especially intense after 1945 when he refused the invitation of Walter von Molo, formerly President of the literary section of the Berlin Academy of Arts, that he return to Germany "like 'a good doctor,' to help in the reconstruction" (Hamilton, 334). As Mann put it in a letter to Karl Kerenyi dated September 23, 1945: "No sooner has judgment day broken over Germany than I am to throw back my citizenship to the United States, sell my house, leave my children and grand-children, abandon my work, and hurry back to Germany in order to take my part in a state of misery against which I warned tirelessly for twelve years. Something about this call seems less than just to me" (Kerenyi, 124). Mann said more or less the same thing in the open letter with which he replied to von Molo himself, and with regard to those writers who had stayed in Germany and gone on with their

work, he added: "It may be superstition, but in my eyes any books that could be printed in Germany from 1933 to 1945 are worse than worthless, and I am reluctant to touch them. A stench of blood and disgrace clings to them, they ought all to be pulped" (Hamilton, 335).

CHAPTER THREE

En Route to
The Magic Mountain

"Every piece of work is ... a realization — piecemeal if you like, but each complete in itself — of our own nature; they are stones on that harsh road which we must walk to learn of ourselves." (*Stories*, viii)

"The whole life work of the author has its leading motifs, which serve to preserve its unity, to make that unity perceptible to the reader, and to keep the whole picture present in each single work. But just for that reason, it may be unfair to the single work to look at it by itself.... For instance, it is almost impossible to discuss *The Magic Mountain* without thinking of the links that connect it with other works, backwards in time to *Buddenbrooks* and to *Death in Venice*, and forward to the *Joseph* novels." (*Mountain*, 718)

1. *Buddenbrooks*

Most serious novelists, we know, tend to make their stories out of one obsessive preoccupation which, amid life's changing perspectives, they keep seeing in different and deeper ways. What is unusual about Mann's career is the wealth of meaning he found in his one subject. And though the philosophical novelist who is this book's chief concern didn't fully emerge until *The Magic Mountain* (1924), each of the works that preceded it can be seen as a step toward that spectacular debut. Between the age of twenty-one, when he wrote the earliest stories he chose to put into *Stories of Three Decades*, and thirty-seven, when he began *The Magic Mountain*, he produced a novel and two novellas that would have kept his name alive by themselves, as well as a second novel, a play, and a number of short stories that I would place almost as high. Taken together, these works present a clear picture of a novelist continually extending his grasp of his subject and, as his ideas grew more complex, continually developing the craft required to keep them alive as fiction.

We see him discovering that subject in such early stories as "Little Herr

Friedmann" (about a hunchback), "Tobias Mindernickel" (about a man paralyzed by self-doubt) and "Little Lizzie" (about the abnormally fat husband of a beautiful unfaithful woman). These stories, all from 1897, are not quite directed against the artist, but "Disillusionment" (1896) is about a man permanently disappointed in life because he grew up believing in art's "lies and poltroonery" (*Stories*, 17); and the hero of "Dilletante" (1897), whose small literary talent leads him to scorn the workaday life of ordinary people and who spends his youth as a connoisseur of art and of his own feelings, discovers at last that he has no life at all, and even no self. In short, the young author seems to be making stories out of the experience of being shut out of life by some crippling defect and of art as a compensation poisoned by shame and guilt.

The same experience underlies Mann's amazingly precocious first novel, *Buddenbrooks* (1901). This narrative of four generations of a family of north-German grain merchants (based on his own family in Lübeck) is a triumphant example of the realism he had learned, chiefly from the Scandinavians and the Russians, but also, he has said, from the French and the English, and of the patient, inch-by-inch mastery of execution — each part utterly convincing and vivid in itself and at the same time serving the unity of the whole — which is to be the hallmark of his novels for good. But Mann's animating source was still his sense of inferiority as an artist to the normal healthy others.

The novel once began, Mann has told us himself, with an autobiographical sequence now near its end, the picture of the last of the Buddenbrooks, sickly little Hanno, shrinking from the harshnesses of an ordinary day at school and escaping when free into the passionate expression of his feelings at the piano. In fact, that sequence can be regarded as the seed of the whole work. The great dinner with which it now opens, a celebration of the family's success in business, sets before us exactly the Buddenbrook gift for life so conspicuously lacking in the little artist, and shows it *ab ovo*, early in the 19th century, in the time of its vigorous and confident youth. And though the white-haired Johann Buddenbrook who presides over the dinner is a witty 18th century skeptic, and Johann his son, who is there with his three children, is an example of humorless 19th century religiosity, their differences are trifles beside the devotion to the family business that unites them. This is the real faith by which they live, for it is the business which draws them into the world, uses and develops their abilities, and rewards them with what the world has to give, wealth, power, and the respect of their fellows. Their faith even has its bible, the gilt-edged family notebook in which the important events of each generation have been recorded. Here we once read with the religious Johann a maxim of the founder that, as we know, came from Johann S. Mann, and that will recur as the heart of the Buddenbrook ethos: "My son, attend with zeal to thy business by day, but do none that hinders thee from thy sleep by night" (42).

But in the life stories that follow of those three children (portraits of an aunt in Tony, an uncle in Christian, and his father in Thomas), the young author's tribute to his bourgeois forebears grows more and more mixed.

True, the portrait of Thomas begins as a powerful demonstration of the high gifts that family faith could engage and develop. He gives up a shop-girl mistress and devotes himself to the Buddenbrook firm not because his vision is small, but because it is large. He is drawn by a dream "far sweeter" than love, "the dream of preserving an ancient name, an old family, an old business . . . and adding to it [the business] more and more honor." And he has the intelligence, skill and self-discipline to realize the dream. Then, the portrait of Christian is comic because he goes too far in the "opposite" direction: he is incompetent at business because he is obsessed by the artist's compulsion to observe and describe his own inner life — and even his bodily sensations — to the point of clownishness. ("That is your character," Thomas says once in what is surely a sly dig by the author at himself. "If you can only see a thing and describe it and understand it . . ." [249].) On the other hand, in the story of Tony the family faith has a different look. What makes her childlike and touching is the way her stubborn pride in the business must keep bobbing up out of pain at the sacrifice it demands. And then there is the great confrontation scene in which we learn that Thomas is also fighting that inner battle. Stung by his elder brother's extremity of exasperation into a sudden dignity of pain and insight, Christian charges him with a hostility inhumanly pitiless, and elicits the confession: "I have become what I am because I did not want to become what you are. If I have inwardly shrunk from you, it is because I needed to guard myself — your being and your existence are a danger to me" (453–454).

In fact, the power of heroic self-denial which makes Thomas so successful is also, at last, the reason for his failure. Even as the town is congratulating him on his firm's triumphant centenary, he is aware of a certain weariness. He finds the business world demanding ever more sacrifices — of moral scruples as well as happiness. When he takes little Hanno on his rounds to interest him in the Buddenbrook role that awaits him, the sharp-eyed child sees his father painfully steeling himself for each encounter and is confirmed in his sense that for him that role is impossible. At last, having found the Buddenbrook faith powerless against the despair brought by thoughts of death, Thomas stumbles on Schopenhauer and learns with rapture that death will be a release from the body's, and the self's, limitations. He and his frail son have come together. As his death soon afterward only completes his withdrawal from the demands of life it was once his pride to meet, the little artist succumbs to typhoid because — we learn this from a dramatically icy account of his illness — he lacks the will to live that might have saved him.

Thus the simple polarity of the early stories has been complicated in a way that foreshadows the rich developments to come.[1] Those developments begin in *Tonio Kröger* (1903), where the conflict between artist and bourgeois becomes a conflict of the artist with himself.

2. *Tonio Kröger*

In this beautifully wrought novella Mann's protagonist is again the son of a respected businessman, head of an old family grain business, and a woman from "down there" — the south — gifted in music. But he is no longer the single-minded devotee of art for whom life is impossible. One might say, indeed, that the tale was written to show how, instead of shrinking from life like little Hanno, or, for that matter, soaring absurdly above it like the protagonist of "Tristan," Mann found in his love for life the power to write *Buddenbrooks* and to see even greater works looming ahead.

Moreover, as his subject deepened into his actual artist-self, his art altered too, to convey the drama of his own developing self-awareness. This story is full of ideas, and chief among his methods of turning them into art was his use of the Wagnerian leitmotif. Mann's interest in "'the novel as architecture of ideas' . . . goes back," he said himself, "to *Tonio Kröger*," where "the linguistic leitmotif was not handled as in *Buddenbrooks*, purely on an external and naturalistic basis, but was transferred to the more lucent realm of ideas and emotions and thus lifted from the mechanical to the musical sphere" (*Sketch*, 32). There will be more to say in later chapters about the use and effect of the leitmotif in Mann's fiction. The point to make now is that in *Tonio Kröger* the repeated phrase serves not, as in *Buddenbrooks*, to remind us of what we already know about a character's appearance or behavior, but to convey the steadily deepening idea — or idea-feeling — that links together the tale's key experiences, here the protagonist's recurring experiences of inner conflict. Its function is thus to dramatize exactly what this story is about, which is the growing self-awareness that reconciles Tonio Kröger to his own dividedness.

What divides him are the contradictory influences of his mother, from whom he received what he is, and his father, from whom he learned what he ought to be. For even as a schoolboy given to neglecting his studies for poetry and to emotional excesses in general, he approves of his father's disappointment in him more than he does of the indulgence he gets from his mother. "After all," he thinks, "we are not gypsies in a green wagon; we're respectable people, the family of Consul Kröger" (88). The heart of the experience he will keep reliving is a mixture of yearning and scorn in the presence of those who are different from himself — blond and blue-eyed where his coloring is dark, at home in their lives as he is not because they are untroubled by the awareness in which he takes pride. In fact, the tale's chief leitmotif is what wells up out of the schoolboy's love of Hans Hansen and the adolescent's of Ingeborg Holm — the "longing" in his "richly beating heart," the "gentle envy," the "faint contempt," and the "innocent bliss" (92, 97). And what lifts the work high, both as fiction and as a stage in Mann's inner growth, is the way this ambivalence keeps widening in scope, becoming at last Tonio's clue to the meaning of his life.

Thus the emerging artist gives himself up, on the one hand, to "fantastic adventures" of body and mind — to loveless sensuality under "southern suns," and later, as he settles down to his life's work, to "the power . . . of intellect, the power of the Word," which isolated him not only from ordinary people, but even from the "small fry" among his colleagues. For the latter were still too close to those ordinary others: they regarded their talent as a "social asset" and didn't know that "he who lives does not work, that one must die to life to be utterly a creator" (98-100). On the other hand, Tonio often despised the way he lived ("as though I had a wagon full of traveling gypsies for my ancestors!"), and, as he tells his Russian painter-friend Lizabeta Ivanovna, he finds in himself "all the scorn and suspicion of the artist-gentry — translated into the terms of the intellect — that my upright old forebears there on the Baltic would have felt for any juggler or mountebank" (109). Moreover, his target here is not merely the "small fry," but the best, artists like himself. For he knows very well the questionable sources of their lofty productions, the moral freedoms that make them inwardly more akin to the criminal than to the decent bourgeois. To the Russian's reminder that literature can be "the guide to understanding, forgiveness and love," he replies that it is so indeed in her country, but that in his own "*Tout comprendre, c'est tout pardonner*" is a false promise; knowledge merely overstimulates, saddens and at last sickens, as it did Hamlet, "that typical literary man." Where she sees "the redeeming power of the word," he sees the power of literature to kill our feelings by analyzing and formulating them, by "putting them on ice and serving them up chilled," or else, with the non-literary, the way it spoils "health and innocence." But "I am not a nihilist," he declares as this conversation approaches the climax that defined Mann for good. He really does "love life" — and not as "extraordinary and daemonic," as "savage greatness and ruthless beauty," but "the normal, the respectable," life "in all its seductive banality . . . the bliss of the commonplace" (106-108). When his tirade is over, his friend gently but firmly applies to him the now famous formula: "You . . . are, quite simply, a bourgeois. . . , a bourgeois on the wrong path, a bourgeois manqué" (110).

In the tale's charming final scenes both the "*manqué*" and the "bourgeois" are poignantly confirmed, and Tonio's letter to his Russian friend completes the drama of his self-understanding. As an artist with a "bourgeois conscience," he does suffer, he admits, from standing "between two worlds" and being "at home in neither." But he doesn't envy the "proud, cold" lovers of "daemonic beauty" who "despise mankind." He knows that what will make him a "poet," what already fills his imagination with figures who will lift his work higher than it has yet reached, is precisely his "*bourgeois*" love of the human, the living, the usual. "Do not chide this love," he writes, and here, as more than one critic has noted, he reveals his identity with his author by repeating that leitmotif: "It is good and fruitful. There is longing in it, and a gentle envy; a touch of contempt and no little innocent bliss" (132).

With the conclusion of *Tonio Kröger* Mann took full possession of his subject. Instead of the inferiority of the artist, crippled by his gifts, to the healthy,

ordinary bourgeois, it became his own conflicted way of being an artist, which
meant also the two on-going questions: what was the real nature of the
polarities that divided him, and what was his doubleness telling him about the
human condition? His next important work, the play *Fiorenza* (1904), took up
the subject precisely as Tonio Kröger had come to understand it at the end of
his story. The personal had acquired large general meaning, and Mann's great
philosophical journey had begun.

3. *Fiorenza*

Fiorenza is also an "architecture of ideas," and many of its ideas are amply
expressed. No doubt this makes it a closet drama. But even as a drama to be
read it deserves more attention than it has received, and I suspect that, with
the help of its eloquence and wit, the right production would hold a theatre audience, too. For the play's subject is itself dramatic. It is the Renaissance version of that conflict between the lovers of "savage greatness" and "ruthless
beauty" Tonio Kröger admired but didn't envy and the moralists who oppose
them. And since this version pits the humanist ruler of 15th century Florence
against the ascetic Dominican who was Prior of San Marco, each position goes
all the way and is strikingly embodied. Then, though every speech and action
serves the unfolding theme, it is the conflict which remains in the center. The
first two acts richly prepare us for a confrontation between the opposing positions, and in the third, where they clash, the play's deepest meaning emerges
out of the living passion of their great champions.

That meaning has often been missed because the play is the first fully
worked-out example of Mann's characteristic irony. "I had a feeling even then
[while writing it]," he notes in his diaries in 1919, "that I was developing the
Betrachtungen and the conflict with Heinrich" (701), that is, the conflict in which
he ended by agreeing with his adversary, as well as differing with him. And
in a response to the charge that he was himself an "ascetic": "I gave at least as
much of myself to Lorenzo as to the Prior" (*Letters*, 51). But in fact, the play
goes further than that. It teaches us to smile, not only at singlemindedness, but
also at the irony which smiles at it too easily.

This is hinted at the start, as the luminaries of Florence gather outside the
palace of the dying Lorenzo. The poet Politian, hotly defending humanist
culture against the fulminations of its enemy, celebrates the city's learning, its
art ("nude and unfettered"), the freely developing "personality," and even
"great and ruthless deeds." To him the morality that denounces all this is "the
most exploded idea in the world." But it turns out that his pupil Giovanni,
Lorenzo's 17-year-old son, and the boy's friend Pico della Mirandola, carry
humanist tolerance further than he likes. Giovanni admires the monk's eloquence and experience in religious matters and observes that the fanatical
moralist himself could not improve on his tutor's "singlemindedness." So

various has the boy's mind become that he can praise his tutor, too, and when asked if he is mocking, replies, "I never know when I am mocking and when I am serious" (200). As for Pico, this patron of art declares that religion and morality should be welcomed in Florence because, in this town full of atheists, they are so rare. "Sin has lost much of its charm," he says, "since we got rid of our consciences." Moreover, with "beauty . . . crying aloud in the street, the price of virtue has gone up" and "morality is possible once more" (212). These liberated spirits assent to both sides because they can be serious about neither.

Then there are the artists who, though they have come to Lorenzo to complain about the monk, are also indifferent to the conflict between them. What concerns these free spirits is color and form, not "opinions"; they are content to leave "law and judgment . . . to Fra Giralomo" (226). Mann too, in other contexts, will insist that the artist must be free of the pressure to deal in "opinions." But it tells us something that these artists are presented as entertaining children, in each "something of the fool and the vagabond" (220), rather than as adults worthy of respect.

With the appearance of Lorenzo's mistress Fiore, whose mask-like beauty, learning and wit make her an emblem of the city, the play's deeper meanings begin to emerge. She too has been denounced by Savonarola, and she has called the monk to her lover's sickbed because she wants to see him confronted and defeated. But she has another reason in keeping with her lively intelligence. She knows that the monk is her lover's equal in what matters most, his "glowing . . . spirit" (235), and that the two will be worthy of each other.

In fact, the Lorenzo we find on his deathbed as the last act begins despises the complaisant priest who recently absolved him and hungers for "a confessor who would be as priest what I have been as mocker and sinner" (240), that is, for his notorious antagonist. Having gone all the way in the other direction, the "frightful Christian" may possess a defense against death unavailable to humanist culture. At the same time the ruler hates to relinquish the power he shed blood to win, and the glorious treasures of art and learning it put into his hands; he hates to think that "that wanton" Florence is abandoning him for the new hero because he has become less than he was. "Longing," he reflects, "is a giant's power, owning unmans" (251). Sure enough, he now learns that that power has been bestowed on his enemy. Fiore reveals that Savonarola and she grew up as neighbors in Ferrara and that it is because she took delight in tempting the ugly boy and then cruelly rebuffing him that he fled into the Church. "You," he says, "have made him great." At this point Mann is thought by some to have betrayed his own theme with reductionist psychology. But he has not. [2]

For it is Lorenzo's "enlightenment," not Mann's, which pretends to undermine the monk's moral position. When the humanist — broadminded, conciliatory — asks why the other opposes "spirit" to "beauty" and dreams of a "divine fire" to destroy this "fair world," the answer comes in a "parable" at which we are not permitted to smile. Long ago, in the castle of the Estes, the monk saw dungeons full of groaning prisoners and found that not one among all the cultivated spirits feasting up above was troubled by shame or uneasiness of conscience. "And I saw a great bird in the air," he adds, "beautiful, bold, and blithe of spirit.... And my heart was gripped by pain ... [and] a gigantic resolve: could I but break those pinions!" (266). To the moral passion in this parable Lorenzo responds with the humanist's classic weapons: psychology, pride, and many-sided awareness. Under their apparent differences, he says, they are "brothers." For both are ugly and sickly and were driven to their greatness by pain and need; and both sought power to mold to their visions, like artists, the ordinary masses who never suffered the pain and never had to rise above themselves. (In fact, the monk echoes the ruler's contempt for those ordinary others and his pride in the power to shape them.) Most tellingly, Lorenzo asks if the other isn't aware that what has made his greatness possible in Florence is precisely the culture he denounces: its tolerance, its civilized relish of variety, its readiness, after so much freedom, to see "limitation" (and hence morality) as "genius" (268). In short, he invites him to go beneath his moral ideal, to recognize the hidden motives that fueled it and his secret complicity with his enemy.

But the monk's reply is the answer to such shallow profundities. "I may know and still do it," he proudly declares. And: "God performs miracles. You see the miracle of detachment regained" (269). Though he speaks in his own religious language, his words, translated, are a reminder that greatness is not to be reduced to its origins, and that some of us have the power to rise, not only above the wounds that start us going, but even above the knowledge that would lead us away from what matters most. In fact, the monk's "Christian" rage against the inhuman callousness of the powerful is never mocked by the play. On the contrary, it remains the basis for Mann's deeper irony, which, as we saw, turns against all easy smilers at life's serious concerns. But a second reference to that "great bird," as it opens the ruler's eyes and reawakens his defiance, carries us deeper still.

Lorenzo has asked his adversary what he hopes to gain by replacing him as master of Florence. The terrible answer is, "Eternal peace. The triumph of the spirit. I will break those great wings" (271). These two are brothers indeed! Not only was each driven upward by mastered pain; each was driven too far, too purely, in his own direction. Lorenzo shed blood to fulfil that hunger for beauty, pleasure, glory. But since, in one form or another, such hunger is the motive power of life, it is life whose "great wings" the singleminded moralist would break, and the "peace," the "triumph of spirit" he would bring is death. So, when Fiore warns him at the end that the "divine" fire will one day destroy him too, the monk is not dismayed. In the play's last words he accepts death as the price, the meaning, of what he brings: "I love the fire" (272).

After such an exploration of the aesthetic and the moral positions in their purity, *Royal Highness* (1909), which came next, could seem a descent into frivolity. But though it is a kind of fairy tale, and a cheerful one — Mann called it a "comedy" — it is also a serious answer to such murderous absolutes, and it anticipates later developments in Mann's career. For at bottom it is a celebration of life.

4. *Royal Highness*

Mann's youthful *alter ego* had found that he must "die" to life to be utterly a "creator." True, Tonio Kröger ended by reaffirming his "*bourgeois* love of the human, the living, the usual." But he did so as an artist yearning over a gulf he knows he can't cross and accepting the yearning itself as his greatest gift. What was the young artist to do when he fell in love with Katya Pringsheim and "bourgeois" happiness became a real possibility? What he did was marry the girl and then, to show why he could do so without betraying his high calling, he wrote *Royal Highness*.

But though the novel is indeed a love story with a delightfully happy ending, it was also, he has told us, the solution found by an artist, "ever eager for new things (*novarum rerum cupidus*)," to a problem of his art: "how to take the serious and weighty naturalism I had inherited from the nineteenth century and faithfully practised, and loosen and lighten, heighten and brighten it into a work of art which should be intellectual and symbolical, a transparency for ideas to shine through." He grants that *Royal Highness* doesn't compare to *Buddenbrooks* in "scope and significance," yet "without it," he says, "neither *The Magic Mountain* nor *Joseph and His Brothers* could have been written" (vii-viii). In fact, the novel becomes a kind of allegory. But Mann's "naturalism" — and indeed the realities of his own personal experience — were to be made transparent, not abandoned. What the allegorical Mann used as a vehicle for his ideas became in the hands of the realist a solid and vivid world, characters complex and alive and a story that issues convincingly out of both. As for the fairytale ending, this turns out to be a moving version of the happiness that *is* to be found — sometimes, for a while — in the life we actually live. Though we must call the novel "minor," we should, I think, add the word "masterpiece."

Students of Mann will not take long to recognize the novel's protagonist. For Prince Klaus Heinrich, the second son of the Grand Duke of Mann's fictional German state, was born with a defect — a withered left hand — that cuts him off from his people just as his "highness" does, while his own life-long yearning to know them better, given concrete form, as it were, in his physical resemblance to the national type, keeps drawing him to them and winning their affection. We will find something familiar too in the difference between him and the elder brother he regards as more truly a "highness" than himself. Albrecht abdicates the throne in his favor because, being sickly and austere, he hates the royal duty of mingling with his inferiors. So the political idealist Heinrich soared above the muddy complexities of reality in which Thomas sought "the human, the living, the usual." Finally, Mann's *new alter ego* discovers, like Tonio Kröger, that for all his longing to get closer to his people, it is not really safe for him to do so.

But it will turn out to be significant that he learns this first from his gloomy tutor. Raoul Ueberbein's wretched beginnings and hard life have not only driven him to rise in the world, but have taught him that to be true to a high calling one must renounce happiness. "[M]ind," he tells his pupil, because it "insists inexorably on dignity, indeed actually creates dignity," is "the arch-enemy and chief antagonist of all human good nature." So Highness, which is dignity itself, must cast off all good-natured assent to the fiction of equality and with it the happiness of easy, natural relations with people and life. It must accept instead its difficult role as the "representative . . ., the exalted and refined expression of the multitude." For: "Representing is naturally something more and higher than simply Being . . . and that's why people call you Highness" (77). And when Highness descends, those who had been offering it reverence will promptly take revenge for having done so. That his tutor is right so far the Prince discovers himself when he goes to his first public ball at seventeen, is made drunk, not only by wine, but by the thrill of dancing with the daughter of a bourgeois and being one of her crowd, and ends on the floor with a soup-tureen for a crown, the butt of their spiteful mockery.

But if that reminds us of Tonio Kröger being laughed at in dancing school, Mann's new artist-figure rejects the implied identity. We see this in his response to the poet whose prize-winning poem celebrates the joys of life, while he himself, being frail in health, never touches wine or women and is always in bed by ten. The Prince feels a certain fellowship with one so cut off from life's joys. But he finds the other's resignation to mere poetry a bit repulsive. For *this* artist-figure believes in happiness, and to show that he is right to do so is the point of the novel's "romance."

The gulf between "highness" and the people remains, however, and the girl must be his own kind, must be a "princess." The condition is met. An American millionaire settles in the country and his daughter Imma lives the same life of wealth and privilege as Katya Pringsheim, and though, like Katya, she is devoted to the study of mathematics, and reluctant for a time to be drawn down from her own "clear and frosty sphere" to a zone that is "warmer, more fragrant, more fruitful" (280), his courtship goes well. Still, "I'm waiting for the tureen lid" is the comment of his skeptical tutor. The Prince explains why he thinks he can now be happy without betraying his calling, but Ueberbein shakes his "ugly head." "It cannot be," he says, and for proof tells his pupil of his own great love-renunciation and how it spurred him to become "what he was" (245).

Unhappiness did indeed make the tutor "what he was" and is the key to his wisdom. But in this artist-story such wisdom is pointedly undermined. The Prince once observes that, being "hostile to happiness," his tutor would have made him "sin" against something "nobler than propriety," that is, we must surely understand, against life. And Imma remarks that the tutor is "an unhappy sort of creature," who will probably "come to a bad end" (241-242). Sure enough, when he fails to get the promotion he had counted on as the fulfilment of his pain-engendered compulsion to rise, he kills himself. Unhappiness may well spur one to succeed, but it may also make life seem worthless if one doesn't. It is life that matters to our artist-prince. Nor does this mean his life is free of pain, only that even the pain is seen as good. So, when a sister expresses the hope that his new adventure outside the castle (his love of a commoner) won't lead to a "horrible experience," his answer is that "every experience is fine, whether it be good or bad" (250). For this "Sunday child," as the envious Albrecht calls him at the end, "everything turns out trumps" (322).

But our artist-prince has his own problems, and we learn what these are from his beloved's resistance. Having begun by mistrusting his ordinariness, his wish to draw her down from her heights into the happy common life, Imma later mistrusts his "highness." She finds it hard to have confidence in the love of one whose whole life has been lived for "show." Describing how he performs for his people — always "representing" a personal interest he doesn't feel — she sounds like her author on his favorite subject. "You question," she says, "but you don't do so out of sympathy . . . you don't care about anything. . . . You express an opinion but you might just as well express a quite different one, for in reality you have no opinion and no belief," and so inspire "not confidence . . . but coldness and embarrassment" (284). The Prince begs her to be patient. Her love will be his remedy, just as his may be hers, for they have both been guilty of chilling aloofness from the people and what matters to them. In fact, the rest of this final chapter, which is called "The Fulfilment," shows how love enables them both, in spite of their highness, to join and serve their fellow human beings.

Love's agent is the Prince's Minister of the Interior, who convinces him that he must make an effort to understand the country's economic problems and cease to linger over the necessary conclusion: that these problems can be solved only by Mr. Spoelmann's millions. The Prince's personal happiness "has become a condition of the public weal," and his country's weal "the indispensable condition of his own happiness" (300). Upon which, asking the mathematical Imma to help him, the Prince gives himself up to the study of a formidable packet of books on political economy. His author here slyly remarks that "serious actuality" turns out to be "by no means so difficult to get hold of as he in his Highness thought. The role of representation, in his opinion, was harder" (301). Still, their labors end in a conversation "of a palpably bourgeois tenor and practical result." What they tell each other is the serious meaning of the comedy's happy ending and the love-born wisdom of the young married man who is writing it. The Prince says they must no longer think of their happiness "in a selfish and frivolous way, but . . . from the point of view of the Mass, the Whole." Imma says, "[W]ithout our studies . . . I should have found it difficult to have confidence in you." "And without you, Imma," he says, "to warm my heart, I should have found it difficult to tackle such difficult problems" (313). Thus, though he doesn't cease to be a royal highness given to "representation," love has forced him into real feeling, real need, real fellowship with his people, and taught him that, whatever the difference between them, his fate is bound up with theirs.

The artist-Mann will in fact be more inclined henceforth to look on the personal "from the point of view of the Mass, the Whole" and to make his work useful to his fellows by much laborious study of "serious actuality." But honeymoons don't last forever. As ordinary life returned, he was bound to find his self-criticism returning with it and continuing to expand in its implications and its fictional possibilities. This became evident first in a delightful comic version in the opening book of *Felix Krull* (1911), which I will discuss along with the rest of the novel later on. There his artist is a narcissistic swindler driven by lust for the "sweets of life." But then the settled family man, already the father of four children, took a Venetian holiday with his wife. The result was a "temporary" interruption to *Felix Krull* (in fact it lasted forty years) and the novella *Death in Venice* (1912), which was, until *Doctor Faustus*, Mann's blackest exposé of the artist-nature.

5. *Death in Venice*

Death in Venice is a realistic story, Dostoevskian in its subject — the shattering emergence of the repressed — and also in its psychological insight and its dramatic power. But once again Mann united the drama of feeling with a drama of thought. The story is also a tissue of symbols, foreshadowings, echoes, and commentary that suffuses every time-bound detail and episode with timeless meaning. What the writer-protagonist calls the artist's supreme joy — "thought that can merge wholly into feeling, feeling that can merge wholly into thought" (423) — becomes the reader's joy too, both feeling and thought mounting to their dazzling climax as one.

Though the realistic story is well known, it will be useful to recall here its key elements. It begins with a kind of overture in which the tale's hidden theme will turn out to have been darkly suggested. A recently ennobled novelist in his fifties, taking a walk after a morning of work, pauses beside a cemetery and sees in the portico of a mausoleum a red-haired, snub-nosed, pilgrim-like figure, with a prominent Adam's apple and teeth bared in a grimace, due perhaps to the sun. This apparition, though it is soon forgotten, starts up in his still active imagination, a "vaulting unrest" and a fantasy of steaming tropical jungles, strange birds, a crouching tiger that brings throbs of both "terror" and "longing" (380), and he decides after a moment that a holiday might restore to his work some of the freshness of feeling increasingly drained from it by his tyrannical fastidiousness.

Mann's wife has said that the model for Aschenbach was Gustave Mahler. But Mann himself has told us not only that "nothing is invented in *Death in Venice*," but that all its key details, including even the beautiful boy on the beach, were taken from a Venetian holiday of his own.[3] When he adds that, once arranged, "these details became in the oddest way . . . elements of composition," and that as he worked, he had "the clearest sense of transcendence . . . of being borne up," it is impossible not to suspect that this was because those details were charged with personal meaning from the start and were enabling him to go thrillingly far in self-realization. He had only to take as his donnée the feeling aroused in him by the boy he calls Tadzio, assign it to the great writer he felt certain (in good moments) of becoming and, as in a laboratory experiment, set it free from the inhibitions and scruples that would always keep his own life safe and productive. Then, there are the familiar details of Aschenbach's life and career. He too comes from "strict, decent, sparing" people on his father's side ("servants of state and king" this time, not businessmen), and a mother who adds "ardent, obscure impulse" (382) to the mixture, being the daughter of a Bohemian conductor. He too achieves fame early with works of fiction remote from both the banal and the eccentric. Finally, our narrator's brilliantly plausible critique of the works shows them to be a celebration of the heroic self-control which, since Thomas Buddenbrooks (and in spite of what that character had revealed of its cost), had remained Mann's own ethical ideal. It turns out that Aschenbach wrote the "prose epic on the life of Frederick the Great" which his author abandoned, adopting as his motto the king's famous command, "Hold fast." Then, like the Mann of *Tonio Kröger* and *Fiorenza*, he dazzled the young with his "cynic utterances on the nature of art and the artist-life," turned away from "knowledge . . . lest it lame his will or power of action," rejected (in his novel *The Abject*) "the excesses of a psychology-ridden age" as well as "the flabby humanitarianism of that phrase: '*Tout comprendre, c'est tout pardonner*'" and set forth in one of his dialogues "the miracle of regained detachment" (386).

At this point our judicious narrator-critic interposes two questions about the moral stance that rejects knowledge and justifies itself by the production of art, questions that foreshadow far more than the thirty-seven-year-old Mann could possibly have imagined. "Does it not result in its turn in a simplification, a tendency to equate the world and the human soul, and thus to strengthen the hold of evil, the forbidden, the ethically impossible? And does not form have two aspects? Is it not moral and immoral at once"—the first as "the expression and result of discipline" and the second because it is "indifferent to good and evil" (361)? Mann has stated the principle underlying not only the story about to unfold, but the more extreme "confession" of his old age. In his novel about Nazi Germany he will show how the world was simplified to reflect the souls of monsters, and expose the artist as an agent of the devil.

But even here, in spite of this artist's self-discipline and the lofty honors it has won, we have been alerted to danger. Those throbs of "terror" and "longing" have already hinted that he has been holding himself heroically firm— against himself. In fact, when the elderly writer finds himself dazzled by the beautiful boy on the beach, he responds as one keeping a mask in place: he acts out (for himself) the cool, esthetic pleasure of the connoisseur. Then, when an early departure he has planned becomes increasingly painful and he is thrilled to hilarity by a mistake with his luggage that forces him back to the hotel, the sight of Tadzio through his window brings a "rapture of the blood" that strikes the mask away. Upon which, in a fine touch, he spreads wide his arms in "calm and deliberate acceptance of what might come" (408-409).

Thus the realistic story. But in the very next sentence it takes a strange leap: "Now daily the naked god with cheeks aflame drove his four fire-breathing steeds through heaven's spaces" (409). With this advent of Apollo, announced in language that itself evokes the world of pagan Greece, the deepest secret hinted in the pilgrim-like figure at the start begins to emerge. It is that the soul of our artist is the battleground of Apollo and Dionysus as Nietzsche had described them: Apollo the god of the "*principium individuationis*,"[4] of the individual tormented by separation from the "Primal Unity" and its creative and destroying chaos, the god whose light casts over that intolerable chaos the "illusions" of measure, of beauty, of art; Dionysus the god of the "Primal Unity" and of the orgiastic self-abandon in which we can temporarily rejoin it. For that figure in the cemetery had the physical attributes of a satyr, the Hellenic representative of lust, and the suggestion that death belongs to the mixture of "terror" and "longing" he stirred in the writer has been repeated, as is well known, in two more versions of that satyr-figure.[5]

Of course, the writer clings as long as he can to the "Apollonian illusion." Just as the "naive" art of Homer comforted the Greeks, according to Nietzsche, by showing the Olympian gods as their own self-glorifying "mirrored images," the increasingly enraptured connoisseur on the beach flattered himself with the idea that the exquisite boy was a product of art like his own, and "the mirror and image of spiritual beauty." Then, speaking as that other elderly lover Socrates to youthful Phaedrus, he tells his beloved (in his mind) that it is "impious and corrupt" not to revere beauty because, as "the sole aspect of the spiritual which we can perceive through our senses," it is "the beauty-lover's way to the spiritual." From this follows the idea which is the "source of all the [lover's] guile and secret bliss," that "the lover was nearer the divine than the beloved; for the god was in the one but not in the other" (412-413). Thus he would persuade himself and the other that what he seeks is something more "spiritual" than the brute actuality named by the four-letter word!

But Dionysus is not to be mocked. The intoxicated man dogs the boy's footsteps; he sinks into complicity with the city's venal authorities, who deny the plague, by keeping the secret from Tadzio's unwitting mother ("his art, his moral sense, what were they in the balance beside the boons that chaos might confer?"); and his terrible unmasking is completed by a dream out of *The Bacchae*. Amid a crowd led by a "stranger god" and savagely coupling and feasting on living flesh, he soon finds, though he struggles against it, that "his own god" (430-431) has been replaced by the other, and he has become one with the howling crowd.

So the great writer's degradation — and the story — arrive at their brilliantly painful climax. His hair dyed and his face painted like those of the old lecher who had disgusted him on the boat to Venice, Aschenbach trails the boy through the streets, loses him and sinks down exhausted beside a fountain. "There he sat, the master," our narrator pitilessly declares. And as the "master" babbles to Phaedrus what he can no longer pretend not to know, Mann's darkest view of the artist-nature issues from his "rouged and flabby mouth." Because "we poets," whose "path to the spirit must lead through the senses . . . cannot walk the way of beauty without Eros as our companion," and so cannot cease to be "wanton . . . exult in passion . . . rove at large in the realm of feeling . . . our magisterial style is all folly and pretence . . . our honourable repute a farce." Nor is there any safety in shunning knowledge, with its debilitating tendency to understand and forgive, its dangerous sympathy with the "abyss," and returning to the "discipline" and "detachment" of form. For form too leads to "intoxication and desire" and so at last to "the bottomless pit" (435). As for what is waiting *there* — the final goal and meaning of the artist's irremediable slavery to desire — this comes to Aschenbach in his last sight of Tadzio on the beach as he is dying. The boy standing in the water appears to him a "lovely Summoner" (in the German, *"liebliche Psychogog,"* i.e., Hermes, the summoner and guide to the realm of the dead), and "points the way outward into an immensity of richest expectation" (437).

And yet Mann didn't cut his throat, either then or after the still worse realizations that came later. He lived and, as we know, took joy in his life and his work to the end. How, in spite of its attraction to Eros and death, the artist-nature can love and serve life will be seen in the great novel that came next. But first Mann will have to defend himself against his brother Heinrich, for whom the problem had always been easier to solve because he had never had to struggle with its actual complexity. The defense will make him a conscious master of that complexity and the greatest philosophical novelist of our century.

Notes

1. Fifty years later Mann was to underline the complicating idea by speaking up for the little "prince of decadence" he had sternly killed off in his youth. "[W]ithout that exacting frailness which cannot bear reality as it is, and as it pleases those equipped to face it . . . neither humanity nor society would have advanced one single step since diluvial times. It is infirmity which intensifies life because it is allied with spirit" (*Best*, 759-760).

2. I here venture to differ with the late Erich Heller, who gives this as the reason for the play's failure. And since I will differ with him elsewhere as well, I want to say now that his book on Mann seems to me, on the whole, brilliant, wise, and beautifully written. What comes between us is chiefly his sense that Mann has no right to make use of religious ideas without having

a religion to back them up—he issues checks with no money in the bank. As may already be clear, and will grow clearer, I don't agree that Mann's secular humanism must rule out religious ideas or condemn him to nihilism. I think his checks have quite sufficient backing in his love of human beings and his grasp of life's complexity.

3. "[N]othing is invented in *Death in Venice*. The pilgrim at the North Cemetery, the dreary Pola boat, the gray-haired rake, the sinister gondolier, Tadzio and his family, the journey interrupted by a mistake about the luggage, the cholera . . . the rascally ballad singer, they were all there; I had only to arrange them, when they showed at once in the oddest way their capacity as elements of composition" (*Sketch*, 46).

4. This and the following quotations from Nietzsche come from *The Birth of Tragedy* (183-186) in the old Modern Library collection of *The Philosophy of Nietzsche*.

5. The first is the unlicensed gondolier who ferries the writer to the Lido in a black, coffin-like gondola which invites him to unparalleled relaxation; and the second is the itinerant singer whose troupe entertains the hotel guests while cholera rages in the city, who assures Aschenbach there is no cholera, and who completes his performance with a song in which every stanza ends in shrieks of laughter. Another figure that is at once realistic and "transparent" is the elderly "rake" whose painted face and leering coquetry disgust Aschenbach on the boat, an early hint of "the daemonic power whose pastime it is to trample on human reason and dignity" (420), and a foreshadowing of what the great writer will become.

CHAPTER FOUR

Reflections of a Non-Political Man

"No one remains precisely what he is when he knows himself."
(*Sketch*, 53)

1

As World War I began Mann abandoned his work on *The Magic Mountain*, underway since 1912, for a personal version of "serious actuality," that is, for a long, agitated defense of his sudden patriotism. This patriotism shocked not only his brother, but Romain Rolland and many other European colleagues, and it is easy to understand why the book that resulted has had a bad reputation and was not translated into English during Mann's lifetime.[1] Nevertheless, it was his breakthrough into greatness. By the time it was completed, he had grasped and richly explored the connection between his own life-long dividedness and the conflict at the heart of European culture. The "egocentric" subject of his interrupted novel had become the nature of man.

Mann's defense of Germany first appeared in 1914 in three articles which became the book's point of departure: "Thoughts in Wartime," "Frederick the Great and the Grand Coalition," and a letter to the Swedish periodical *Zvenska Dagbladet*. German militarism, they argued, is the legitimate self-assertion of a nation grown too powerful to submit to a European status quo — and to "bad borders" — created by the Western nations when she was still weak. Rejecting these, she had stoically resigned herself to the appearance of guilt imposed on her by the necessities of European development. But "Germany is warlike out of morality," he declared. And if her military behavior offended against the values of "Western civilization," those of "reason, enlightenment ... good breeding, skepticism," it was the expression of others that had their own justification, those of the German "soul," of German "culture," which seem "offensive and wild" to "less profound peoples." He does say that the "element of the daemonic and the heroic" in German "military morality" arrives at "civil 'spirit' ... as the last and most humanly worthy ideal" (Hamilton, 161-162).

But it will do so only after a German victory, and never as a yoke imposed on her by others.

The book itself, while it moderates and sometimes contradicts the militarism of those articles, struggles to defend the more fundamental position out of which it arose. This position has two parts. The first is a rejection of politics, with its tendentious simplifications, as inferior to the complex human realm, which Mann sees as the special concern of German culture. Since he regards democracy as the great politiciser of human life, this means also a rejection of democracy. The second, entailed by the first, is a willingness to accept the rule of those whose calling it is to run the country and the war. And — at the time of the book — more than willingness. Stung by the world's hostility to Germany, this despiser of politics expresses pride in the empire created by Bismarck, quoting more than once the dictum that Bismarck had put Germany into the saddle, and now she must ride and not fall off. And though he often admits he is thus contradicting his truest self, he attempts to reconcile the contradiction by Dostoevsky's theory that the state is a spiritual as well as a political entity, and as such the preserver and the champion of a nation's culture.

It was after he had begun to work on *Reflections* that Mann read his brother's essay on Zola, and though his book had been an answer to Heinrich from the start, the essay no doubt accounts for the pain and rage that fills the book's early chapters and its all but open references to the personal quarrel between them. For Heinrich treated Zola's defense of Dreyfus against the lies and brutalities of the French military establishment as an allegory of the current situation, in which the reader was to see the German government in the French, Heinrich in Zola, and Thomas in Zola's opponents. But the anger soon gave way to something else. "This book is self-explanation, self-enlightenment, not polemics," he wrote in the book itself, and its style — freely pursuing every clue of feeling, thought, or association — bears him out. And in 1950 he repeated that it was "not a political manifesto," that its real subject was not the day's political issues. "I had never done anything but defend humanity," he said. "I shall never do anything else" ("Years," 256-257).

In fact, *Reflections* is the work of an artist who, in that attack by Heinrich and others, felt his nature "shaken in its foundations, endangered in its vital dignity, and called in question" in a way that made it impossible for him to go on with creative work until he had succeeded in "clarifying and *defending*" what he was. The book is fascinating because it does set forth — explicitly, and with all his powers — what he was. And though this means it often sheds light on his earlier writing, its chief importance is that it underlies all the philosophical novels that came after it. Exploring the mind about to produce a novel unparalleled in its combination of emotional and intellectual wealth, it is the work which lifted Mann into the company of Goethe, Tolstoy and Dostoevsky, artists whose life-addressing thought is part of their effect and their stature. What he leads us to does involve something he calls a "dangerous-harmful element." But this is not really his "bad German" opinions, though it would be easy, by quoting these, to make points against him. "Opinions do not confer rank" (336), as he says more than once. The fashionable "right" opinions lie in the gutter in every era for fools and hypocrites to pick up, just as the "wrong" ones may emerge from thought and art that have to be respected. Our concern ought surely to be, not with his book's opinions as they sound in our ears when quoted alone, but with the complex web of thought that is their context, that determines how *he* means them, and that enables us to distinguish between what comes from his culture's characteristic errors and what comes from its wisdom, and his own.

In spite of which, since those "bad German" opinions will be quoted against him, it may be useful, before turning to the book's real center, to see how far he is from the simple German "patriotard" he can be made to appear.

2

First of all, this passionate loyalist of German culture turns out to believe that to be German means precisely to be cosmopolitan, European, and that the work of all the most distinctively German artists and thinkers — Goethe, Schiller, Schopenhauer, Nietzsche, Wagner and, lastly, himself — inextricably mingle European and German elements. Similarly, though he is proud of belonging to the class of German burghers, he sees its Germanic traditions as ways of safeguarding and expressing a "suprapolitical" (96) humanity. Lukács's description of "the burgherly calling as a life form" — that it means "the primacy of ethics in life" and that it puts duty, order and the lasting and regular work above desire, mood, the momentary and "sensation" — is for him a description of his own life as an artist, and not only of his way of working but of what he produces, which is "an ethical form of expression of my life itself" (72-73). And since, in the German burgher, this Protestant ethical tendency is combined with a long tradition of interest in intellectuality and mastery in the arts, as well as of indifference to politics, the burgherly nature, loyal to "the . . . part of human nature . . . not consumed by state and society" is "almost human nature itself" (97).

Mann grants that in Germany too the hard "capitalist-imperialist bourgeois" is replacing the humane burgher as he knew him in Lübeck and depicted him in Thomas Buddenbrook. But even in this character he had shown a trace of the "new burgher," and of the "heroism" of the "overburdened, overdisciplined moralist of accomplishment, 'working at the edge of exhaustion'" (103). It was his sympathetic "insight of feeling into the connection between the capitalistic neoburgherly character and Protestant ethics" which made him a German patriot. "My 'patriotism' of 1914," he says, "was . . . a sudden and probably quite ephemeral politicizing of this sympathy" (105). What the world hated as German "militarism" was to him simply that burgherly heroism in a people not born to action, but, like Hamlet, called to it tragically by the times and their own new strength. His sympathy for his people was indeed "anti-intellectual," he admits, but it was also "human and poetic" and "I will never be ashamed of it" (106). Note that there peeps out of this self-defense the recognition that it is based on an error, that of an "ephemeral politicization." In my view, this is the chief error of the book, an error he will later, as we have seen, take more seriously and repudiate. It is the same error, though he makes it on behalf of the "right," that the book will accuse his brother of making on behalf of the "left." To "politicize" an idea is to transfer it from the realm of thought, where it can be modified by opposing ideas and kept flexible and tentative, to the realm of action, where it tends to grow rigid and tyrannical. In this case Mann gave the sympathy he felt for the German people to a government that was putting its most dangerous tendencies into action.

About democracy as theory he is equally double in his views. He does indeed express a shocking contempt for "the people," whom he sees (quoting Shakespeare's *Coriolanus*) as exhibiting all the faults of human nature uncurbed by honor or the capacity for self-discipline, and as taking to democracy (here he quotes Schopenhauer) because they ascribe to governments the misery of the human condition and swallow democracy's promise, as unrealistic as it is debasing, of a heaven on earth that will enable everyone "to booze and gorge and breed to his heart's content — and then to croak" (392). These pages are admittedly ugly in their zestful asertion of an ungenerous half-truth. But it turns out that he can't help acknowledging what the half-truth omits, that neither faults nor virtues are limited to one social class. We find him calling for "universal suffrage," because, though all human beings are not really equal, "where it is impossible to give each his own, everyone shall be given the same" (184); for the "democratization of the means of education" so all the gifted can rise; and for the "right of self-determination" (241) that necessarily results from the people's increasing importance in both peace and war. In fact, he arrives at an unillusioned acceptance of democracy as the best political system for practical purposes, though imperfect, that many of us would share. And we would share too his sense of its "spiritual-human dangers," of a "complete leveling," of "a journalistic-rhetorical stultification and vulgarization" (187) and of the need for education and culture to counteract these, education as "the formation of human beings" who are more than their social or political roles, and culture as "an end in itself," with goals independent of "utility" or "the state" (196).

As for the actual democracies then opposing Germany, his opinion is not far from what we have long since come to think ourselves, that their "virtue-mouthing" rhetoric veiled the *Realpolitik* they were actually pursuing — England in India, Ireland, South Africa; the United States in her Spanish-American War; Italy in Libya; France in Morocco; and all of them in this "war to end all wars" and to "make the world safe for democracy" (here I quote our phrases, not his). And yet, though he hotly protests that Germany has become a scapegoat for doing as all do without lying about it, he cannot persist in his uncharacteristic support of the German state. To the idea that "each of the great European nations comprises a potential disaster for all of Europe," we find him adding the parenthesis "(Germany no less than others)" (137). Later he supposes "it is quite possible" that the "humiliation of the German state belongs among the intellectual desirabilities" (183). At last he even fears that a German victory would impose an order which was "hard . . . rather brutal, militaristic to the point of pitilessness," and that "the idea of humanity in this German Europe would really have come off badly" (358). We may well believe him when he remarks, "Let no one say I am suppressing my own contradictions" (190).[2]

But—to repeat—we have better things to consider than his political opinions.

3

"One searches in books," Mann wrote in another of his many attempts in *Reflections* to explain what he was doing, "one searches in the distress of the times, for the farthest origins, the legitimate bases, the oldest spiritual traditions of one's hard-pressed ego: one searches for justification." In fact, a good part of the book is Mann's own version of German history and culture, a version which shows them as the continuous development of the idea of the human which underlies his life's work. No doubt one could make a different interpretation of the data, or find that idea growing in other places, too. For those of us interested in Mann, however, this may be less to the point than the nature and quality of the idea itself.

His view of the special mission of German culture comes from Dostoevsky, to whose battle against Western thought he keeps returning with grateful admiration. Dostoevsky saw Germany as "the protesting kingdom" (25), which had always resisted the Western, originally the Roman, ambition to impose on the world one rule and one ethos. For him this ancient Roman dream of "universal unification" is at the bottom of the Roman church's only half spiritual attempt to unify all people under Christ, of the expansionism of the French Revolution, and of the dream's recent development—socialism—to include in that unity the social class still neglected. The ideas and values of this permanent "Roman imperialism," this attempt to force on the world one right way of thinking, Mann calls "civilization." Germany, said Dostoevsky, fighting Rome for supremacy during the era of Roman Christianity, based her protest on "the most spiritual, the most elementary foundations of the Germanic world. The voice of God resounded from her, proclaiming freedom of the spirit" (25-26). And though Mann adds that German culture was shaped by pagan Goethe, as well as by Christian Luther, he assents to Dostoevsky's main point, that the West's political idea of freedom was profoundly different from "the" moral and religious, the *psychological* idea" of it which spurred German protest.

But this difference is itself the fruit of a more fundamental difference between German culture and "civilization," and here we come upon Mann's
characteristic ambivalence. He grants the "good sense" in the Western charge
of "barbarism" against Germany. Germany did not love or believe in words,
she opposed the West only with her "disturbing stubborn will," and courage not
guided by a "well articulated ideal" is "barbaric." More exactly: "To be without
words is not worthy of a human being, is inhumane." For "civilization," on the
other hand, the whole of culture consists of "linguistically articulated intellect."
Indeed, "civilization and literature are one and the same." (Music and poetry,
being less clearly related to "humanitarianism," tend to seem undependable to
"the literary moral sense.") The legacy of Rome is "literary humanitarianism
. . . the classical spirit, classical reason, the generous word to which the
generous gesture belongs, the heart-stirring phrase that is worthy of a human
being and celebrates his beauty and dignity, the academic rhetoric in honor
of the human race" (31-33).

Here we already have Settembrini, the eloquent humanist of *The Magic
Mountain*. But the passage hints too at the ambivalence which will delightfully
complicate the Italian's portrait. For how can a maker of literature — and more,
a spokesman for the human — disassociate himself from beautiful language that
celebrates the human being's beauty and dignity? He can't: Mann confesses
repeatedly that as a literary man he is inevitably a servant and a beneficiary
of civilization. And yet, when that beautiful language shades over into
"academic rhetoric," it reveals a tendency to turn into gratified self-display
which must start up in the subtle psychologist and moralist a corresponding
shift toward ironical resistance. Nor is "academic rhetoric" the worst of its latent possibilities. For it was just that "literary humanitarianism" which "in the
Jacobin hardened into a scholastic-literary formula, into a murderous doc-
trine, a tyrannical schoolmasterly pedantry." It became, in fact, "the political
spirit of the middle-class revolution," and "civilization" is "nothing more than
. . . the propagation of the politicized and literarized middle-class spirit, its col-
onization of the inhabited areas of the globe" (32-35). It is against this spirit,
Mann declares, that Germany is protesting in the war.

One thing more must be understood if we are to grasp the deepest meaning such protest, and Germanness itself, had for Mann. He tells us that Germany had never developed the kind of "national bond" which in England, say,
or France, imposes a national character on intellectual opponents and moderates their differences. "In Germany's soul Europe's intellectual differences are
'carried to the end.'" And in the individual German's too. "I even mean myself
as well." For this reason, "to be the spiritual battleground for European antitheses: this is German; but it is not German to make things easy for oneself. . . Whoever would aspire to transform Germany into a middle-class
democracy in the Western-Roman sense and spirit would wish to take away
from her all that is best and most complex, take away the problematic character
that really makes up her nationality; he would make her dull, shallow, stupid

and unGerman." And later: "What is German is an abyss." Is not Hans Castorp rising into view, the simple German burgher whose Alpine adventure it is to become — as he turns like a comically open-mouthed observer at a tennis match, from the democratic humanist on one side to the bloody-minded authoritarian on the other — that battleground for European antitheses? At any rate, if Mann does err in the book by assuming that his idea of German culture is embodied in the German state and is the reason for its war against the West, it should be clear that it is that idea which is his deepest concern. What he is chiefly defending as German is human nature and experience in all their complexity, and what he means by "civilization" is the literary and political *simplifications* of the Enlightenment, of what we would call "liberalism." This is not a position which an intelligent liberalism will automatically reject, or will even, so long after Lionel Trilling's *The Liberal Imagination*, find unfamiliar.

In fact, the permanent importance of the book lies in the brilliance of its many-faceted, ever-deepening account of that opposition, or, in the form of it to which he obsessively returns, the opposition between the political type he calls the "*Zivilisationsliterat*" (in the English version "civilization's literary man"), represented by his brother and the non-political type he calls the "esthete," represented by himself. His portrait of the former may have been unfair to the real Heinrich Mann, but it went to the psychological and moral roots of a way of being political that always tends to corrupt political and intellectual discourse. In the United States the type has emerged full-blown twice in the twentieth century, as the Stalinist and the Stalinist "fellow-traveler" of the '30's and as the idealistic members of the "New left" (the "PL" — Progressive Labor Party — or "SDS" — Students for a Democratic Society — and *their* fellow-travelers) who closed campuses in the '60's. But, as I say, Mann analyzes the way this type distorts reality in order to contrast it with a kind of thinking that struggles to tell the truth. "The world is deep at every point," he remarks in one of many echoes of Nietzsche. The book goes on to become a dazzlingly rich account of the mind's effort to do justice to that depth (so rich indeed that no attempt like this one to convey briefly its main themes can help omitting many things as valuable as what it reports). And if some of its ideas will make Americans wince, on the whole these are either peripheral to its chief concerns, or else they are the unfashionable, the discomfiting implications of ideas we have to accept.

4

Mann's critique of his adversary's characteristic attitudes is often deliberately shocking to conventional liberalism. Not only does he follow Dostoevsky in seeing the tendency to blame criminal behavior on society, rather than on the criminal, as removing "all seriousness, all dignity and responsibility from life" (328). Like William James seeking a "moral equivalent to war," he dares to suggest that war is less purely evil and peace less purely good than is sentimentally assumed. He reminds us that war may develop supreme human virtues, that its wounds are often healed by life's mysterious powers of adaptation and growth, and that much of the brutality we impute to it can be seen in so-called normal life itself — in sex, in agonizing childbirths, in man's eternal wolfishness to man. "War is atrocious, yes!" he grants. But, "I see how the war has caused tears over mankind to stream from the eyes of fellows whom it would not cost anything in 'peacetime' to tear their neighbor's heart out of his breast and cast it before his feet — and in only a slightly figurative sense." In the political type's readiness to exploit the war to win plaudits for his humanitarianism, Mann sees "the secret of all descendants of Rousseau, who always, in one way or another, put their children into orphanages and write educational novels" (350-352).

To the charge that he is a "doubter" who is skeptical of "such rough concepts as truth and justice," he replies that the real difference between his type and his brother's is that between the devotion to justice at work in his "two thousand printed pages," justice as "the highest form of conscience . . . as *intellectual* passion, as melancholy, and as truth," and the attitudes of one for whom "justice is only a political slogan." The other is "the most secure, the safest, the most virtuous person" because in his "arrogant carelessness," he is never capable of doubt or of "a wakeful conscience." His kind of justice, an ideal "dragged through the political gutter," is "aggressive, dogmatic, unscrupulous, and basically unjust" (149-150). Though he poses as the self-forgetful martyr to unjust power, calling his opponent its self-serving courtier, it is he who courts the power in *their* world — the intellectual mob and especially its younger members — winning easy glory and profit by a humanitarianism which is all chic rhetoric. For his real concern is not the one to which he pretends. On the contrary, he is given to the heart-felt recital of utopian fantasies precisely because of his indifference to the actual difficulties of the human lot, and what his recital means is "Heed me, who loves." This is why, in spite of his loudly proclaimed love of mankind in the abstract, he is capable of the ugliest behavior to individuals, witness the "unconscionable, humanly irresponsible slander" (158-159) in his remarks about his brother.

Thomas Mann, however, though he "did not stand there, one hand on my heart, the other in the air, and recite the *contrat social*," has in fact, as many readers have testified, "*helped* others to *live*." He has done it by choosing "the hard way," by "letting life speak," and if this way was "more bitter than sweet," in his work "humor and music were correlations of pessimism." In short, he has done it as the "aesthete" (159-160) so despised by civilization's literary man. Accepting thus the contemptuous label, Mann goes on to correct the simple-minded Hedda Gabler idea of the aesthetic approach to life as "vine leaves in the hair," and so on. What it really is we see in writers like Goethe and Shakespeare, who, as Schopenhauer observed, resemble "Nature" in showing each of their characters, when the character is speaking, as right, even if it is the devil himself. Best of all it is seen in Tolstoy's *Lucerne*, where the author explains why wisdom must respect and yet remain detached from all convictions. There Tolstoy calls the striving for "positive solutions" the great source of human misery, every human thought being at once incorrect — "one-dimensional" — because "we can never grasp the truth in its entirety," and correct because it "expresses a part of human striving." People create "compartments," draw "imaginary boundary lines" in the "eternally moving, shoreless, infinitely mixed-up chaos of good and evil . . . and they expect the sea to divide itself along those lines. As if there were not millions of completely different points of view. . . . This imaginary knowledge destroys the instinctive, blessed, original striving for good in human nature." Nor is this the "skepticism, relativism, frivolity and weakness" it is often called by the committed, action-oriented man of politics. For such doubt of the formulas of the intellect comes from a religious reverence for the whole, for the complex actuality of human beings and the world. In fact, "the essence of the esthetic world view" is formed by "reverence and doubt, absolute conscientiousness [i.e., fidelity to one's true sense of things] and absolute freedom [from limiting formulas]."

It is exactly this awareness that our ideas can have (at best) only a partial truth which Mann sees in Strindberg's affirmation of the writer's freedom "to *play with thoughts, to experiment with points of view*" (164, his emphasis). (So, the motto of questing, growing Hans Castorp comes to be *"placet experiri"* — "it is pleasant to experiment.") The same awareness underlies the hidden reservation in the title of Mann's 1914 essay "Thoughts in Wartime," which hints that other times would lead to other thoughts, and his grateful quoting of Rolland's "immortal line," "Each one of our thoughts is only a moment of our life. What good is life to us if not to correct our errors, to conquer our prejudices, and daily to broaden us in heart and thought?" (165). Finally, it is the reason Mann finds art, "with its lively ambiguity, its deep lack of commitment, its intellectual *freedom*," superior to "simple intellectuality" (165).

Civilization's literary man, of course, demands that art serve humanity by teaching political "truth," and sneers at the esthete's belief in art for art's sake. But the aesthete's devotion to art is precisely the reverse of an evasion of life and its claims. For he sees "art as life, art as the mastered, liberated, liberating knowledge of life through form" (225). More, he sees it as "a matter . . . of conscience, of protestantism, of God's immediate presence." But art must serve these in its own way. "A good work of art can and will have moral consequences, but to demand moral intentions from the artist is to ruin his work," Mann quotes from Goethe, and then adds himself that art is "a *form* of morality, but not a moral expedient" (228-229). That is, it is not a "weapon" serving a moral position decided on in advance, but is itself moral conscientiousness actively at work and seeking the truth wherever it leads. Hence *"l'art pour l'art,"* translated into German means art in which "morality takes form," art "as a virtue and a religion," (231) art as a paradigm of the moral life in its actual complexity.

His opponent's idea of morality has little to do with the self-knowledge and the honesty of "conscience." It is rather the idea expressed by those Russian radicals who complained of writers like the author of *Fathers and Sons*: "You want to criticize yourselves; we want to criticize others and to break them" (212). To that "Jacobin" tendency to see morality as the self-righteous criticism and changing of *others*, the aesthete replies, "[B]ecome better yourselves and everything will be better."[3] And to the political type's demand for "the solidarity of all intellectuals," meaning their unanimity in political opinions, his answer is that the only solidarity worthy of respect is what results from the experience of life and suffering common to all, from "comradeship in nobility, brotherliness in pain." This is the source of "all tolerance, conscientiousness, all courtesy of the heart and gallantry, in short, of all *morality* of the intellect," which necessarily involves "*the deepest and most unconquerable disgust for dogmatism*" (his emphasis). People like his opponent, however, "have to be right," to exclude from their ranks "what doubts and opposes," to see those who differ as either "villainous or idiotic." Such rigidity they call the defense of "intellectual freedom," and such "stiff and cold pharisaism" (233-235) the preaching of humanity.

5

But there is also that other reason the book is fascinating. In exploring the difference between civilization's literary man and his kind of aesthete, Mann uncovers the sources of the novels to come and illuminates their famous irony. He makes a distinction, for instance, between his opponent's "virtue" and true morality which points straight toward the central irony of *The Magic Mountain*.

Observing that the political type's perfect confidence in his moral "dignity" must shut out the self-criticism and doubt with which "*morality* would really just begin," Mann asks which is "the more humane . . . humanitarianism," to stand on one's "dignity," or to be "free, soft, pliable, approachable, humble and open to the dangerous-harmful element?" (282-283) In fact, "morality," in his view, "is something *completely* different from virtuousness." As the Bible tells us, "the moralist . . . 'does not resist evil'" because the attraction of evil is "the pull to the forbidden, the drive to adventure, to lose oneself, to abandon oneself, to explore, to understand. . ." (292). Exactly this "pull to the forbidden" will seduce and educate Hans Castorp on his mountain, and it is exactly the willingness to abandon themselves — to the point of death — to the forbidden and the dangerous which the Dostoevskean Clavdia Chauchat will declare to be the mark of the great moralists. The path they travel is "bad"; it is a "dangerous-harmful" openness to the passions, to the irrational, and ultimately to the lure of the final, fatal letting-go. But it is also a way "to understand." It leads to knowledge from which we are barred by "regular," healthy, practical bourgeois life.[4]

It is with just such a "yes-*and*-no," a smiling "yes, but," that the aesthete responds to the "beliefs," the ardent "convictions," in which his idealistic opponent takes pride. And what underlies this response, as I have said, is not skepticism or frivolity or nihilism, but an impulse of affirmation. He resists "convictions," not because he wants to say no, but because he wants to say yes — to opposing positions. The tendency to see truth on both sides of an argument makes him slow to pass judgment (or to jump on bandwagons), but it also "creates spirit, creates depth, freedom, and irony; creates personality." For "personality is being, not opining, and if it tries its hand at giving opinions, then it becomes aware that it consists of opposites" (361-362). But to see truth in opposing positions suggests that the world and our experiences are richer than our contending ideas about them, itself an idea which is on the threshold of religion. Sure enough, the deep-rooted sense of things underlying Mann's irony is identical, he tells us, with what underlies the religion discovered by Pierre — again Mann turns to Tolstoy — when he gives up his intellectual faith in "principles, words or ideas" (Mann's words) for the belief in a "living, constantly perceived God" (Tolstoy's). To Mann, who is clearly not a literal believer, this God is "the universal, the forming principle, omniscient justice, encompassing love," and belief in Him is "belief in love, in life, in art." That is, it is belief in the creative powers of the human mind as it addresses itself — and precisely with love, with relish — to the limitless complexity of the world. To such "religion" it is "convictions," with their inevitable one-sidedness, which are "impious" because they are "inadequate and hostile to life." He grants that, as Goethe put it, "at the moment of speaking a person must be one-sided." But though it may be useful to utter one's thought freely "for the moment," to cultivate it "defiantly," and even with "the gesture of fanaticism," one can avoid "actual stultification" by retaining a private awareness of "the grain of salt on one's tongue," the sense that it is "all just two steps away from an artistic game" (371-372).[5]

Mann's "religion" must of course do without the Utopian social dreams and promises of his opponent. Where society is concerned it is closer to "despair." But for him this is not a defect. Not only does he predict that the "rhetorical faith of revolutionary optimism" will itself lead to despair (as Dostoevsky put it, the attempt to impose human brotherhood politically where the feeling of brotherhood is lacking would turn the slogan "liberty, equality and fraternity" into "liberty, equality, fraternity or death," and would lead to a new "Byronism," that is, to a despairing rejection of all social action), but he even says that this is a change he will welcome. For despair "is a better, more human, more moral — I mean more religious — condition than the rhetorical faith of revolutionary optimism" (381-382). Indeed, "it is despair that frees the path to salvation." How it can do this emerges when he adds: "I believe in humility and in work — work on oneself, which, in its highest and most moral, its strictest and most cheerful form seems to me to be art" (392). Giving up the hope of attaining, not only final, unshakable "beliefs," but a social organization

that can infallibly guarantee "happiness," accepting the humbler task of working on ourselves, we are set free from rigid ideas, free to honor and be enriched
by the unforeseeable wealth of actual experience. This is "the freedom that is
a path, not a goal; that means . . . tenderness, openness for life, humility; a
searching, probing, doubting and erring. . ." And he completes his account of
his faith with a quotation from Lessing: "Not the possession of truth, but the
search for it expands the powers of the human being; in it alone lies his continually growing perfection" (394-395).

Having thus disclosed the affirmation underlying his irony, Mann concludes with a bold, blunt reversal of the formula he had ironically accepted
from his opponent, of himself as the "aesthete" thinking only of art and the other
as political out of concern with morality. To begin with, he declares that in fact
it is the other who is the esthete and he who is the moralist. For the other's
morality is really an applause-seeking "cult of gestures," radicalism as "*bellezza*,"
while what Mann has always demanded from his own work, as well as other
people's, is precisely "ethics," "morality," "art that had a moral emphasis" (398).
(So Tonio Kröger turned away from the Italian bohemian crowd, "all those
frightfully lively people" who "have no conscience in their eyes," as well as from
the "proud and cold" lovers of "demonic beauty" [400].) Mann grants, with his
unresting ambivalence, that it is an unanswerable question whether the artist
cares more for the moral effect of his art than for the artistic effect of his morality; that under his facade of dignity the artist remains an "adventurer of feeling"; that educating youth through art is a risky undertaking; and that, in any
case, art's criticism of life is always that of little Hanno, the "nervous excep-
tion." But this means only that the artist must be content to express "the conscience of the race" without "the insufferable pose of virtue." Such "irony as
modesty" is itself a "form of morality," of "personal ethics" (424-425).

Then Mann dares to assert a further paradox: that the so-called esthete,
with his irony, is also the more truly, because the more realistically, political!
Citing Hans Blüher's definition of eros as "the affirmation of the human being
apart from his *worth*," Mann explains that "irony is eroticism"; it is intellect loving life *with* all its flaws — as Tonio Kröger, we may add, loved Hans Hansen.
In politics it follows that the ironist is conservative because "intellect that loves
is not fanatic, it is ingenious, it woos, and its wooing is erotic irony." Thus,
"conservativism . . . [is] the erotic irony of intellect," and its politics is "ironic
politics." But this is just what politics ought to be, for it is "necessarily the will
to mediation and to a positive result"; it is "cleverness, flexibility, politeness,
diplomacy." This means it is precisely the opposite of the "destructive absolute
of radicalism," which, demanding that "the intellectual must act," must impose
the mind's blueprint without compromise on resisting reality, is "immediately
at the point of political murder" (426-427).

At last, as he ends his book, Mann says "yes, but" even to his own conservativism. Not only does he grant that conservatives may be as one-sided and
simpleminded as their progressive opponents; he also believes that when con-

servativism is at its best, when it is intellectual and ironic, it "may promote democracy and progress in the way it fights them" (430). For literature — Dostoevsky in his time, Mann himself now — is given by its nature to "analysis, intellect, skepticism, psychology," and must therefore work on the side of "democracy," of criticism and change. "In cases such as mine, destructive and conserving tendencies meet, and as far as one can speak of effect, it is just this effect which takes place." So, though Mann is an intellectual critic of life who, unlike his opponent, also has the Nietzschean view of life as "health and innocence" which need protection from art and intellect, his work, too, is part of the "moral-political-biological process behind which civilization's literary man is standing with his agitating whip" (431-432).

"No one remains precisely what he is when he knows himself." Mann said he would have added this maxim to the book's epigraphs if he had found it in time. In fact, as he remarked more than once, the book was written not simply to explore, but to enable him to pass beyond his own war-time one-sidedness. That it succeeded we will see in the novel he went back to next, where the ideas of *Reflections* will be given to Naphta in a way which exposes their dangerous possibilities (as well as their partial truth), and where Settembrini, the novel's version of Heinrich Mann, will at last be honored above his reactionary opponent because at bottom, and with all his limitations, it is he who is the human being's truer champion.

But such regained detachment appeared even earlier. In a letter of April 18, 1919, the younger Mann deplores the judgment of a reviewer that *Reflections* shows his superiority to his brother. The "antithesis" it describes, he says, is "too important and symbolic" to be made a question of "rank and worth." That in him the "nordic-Protestant element is uppermost," with its emphasis on "conscience," and in his brother the "Roman-Catholic element," emphasizing "the activist will," is "'significant' in the Goethean sense, an opposition of principles — but based on a deeply felt brotherliness" (*Letters*, 93). What this suggests is that his brother's way of thinking is after all as legitimate as his, to which, amid the changing needs of life, it can be the necessary counterweight. For readers today, however, Mann's attempt to do justice to his brother's position can be a reminder that his own in *Reflections* is entitled to the same justice. We must be willing to distinguish between what is "ephemeral" in the book and what is not. That done, it should not be hard to grant that, as a contribution to the eternal dialogue between "left" and "right," *Reflections* is not only brilliant, but permanently useful.

Notes

1. An English version by Walter D. Morris appeared in 1983 which conveys very well the book's personal tone and the subtlety of its thought. Professor Morris has also provided an intelligent and useful introduction.

2. George Lukács also saw that this work contained its own contradictions and that "from the standpoint of Mann's career it constituted a *reculer pour mieux sauter*" (*Essays*, 119).

3. Let me anticipate here, since Mann does not, the political man's objection that this can be a seduction away from necessary protest against clear injustice. That is true. But it is also true that to oppose evil without conscience can bring worse evil, and has done so in our time.

4. You don't have to be German to see the possible value of a "dangerous-harmful element." It was seen by Matthew Arnold too, and by Lionel Trilling, who wrote of Arnold's recognition of "elements that for fullness of spiritual perfection were wanted," but that also "belong to a power which in the practical sphere may be maleficent" (*Beyond Culture*. New York, 1965, 28.).

5. This hint, one of many, that Mann is aware of the one-sidedness of his book is another reminder of its basic error. For if such a defiant one-sidedness helps us forward in the life of the mind, in the life outside of the mind, where German power was then at work, it was leaving a trail of corpses no "grain of salt" could revive. But again, this error born of his war-time emotions does not cancel the truth of what he says in its *appropriate context*.

CHAPTER FIVE

The Magic Mountain

"It is essential to break with all so-called idealism of the kind
that broods over how the world ought to be and would
lovelessly impose on the world the result of its thinking....
A labor of Sisyphus, for the antinomies of the world are inherent in existence itself; they are existence, the very fullness
thereof.... An intellectual leader may be expected ... to step
outside the interplay of contraries, recognize the inherent
polarities, and find their equilibrium, but not to postpone the
attainment of the equilibrium by putting more weight on one
side than on the other." (*Letters*, 113)

"Odd entertainment, which had really nothing in common with a novel
in the usual sense of the word" (*Sketch*, 61). So Mann described the novel he
began in 1912 and completed, after the three-year interruption by *Reflections of
a Non-Political Man*, in 1924. He was exaggerating, but he was pointing toward
a truth. In this account of the intellectual development of a "simple-minded,
though pleasing young man" (ix) to a condition very like genius, he permitted
his interest in the drama of thought to carry him "all the way." And though the
novel was enormously successful when it was first published, it has tended since
then to meet with two objections. Some find that as a work of fiction it sinks
under its heavy freight of ideas. Others, who don't disapprove of ideas in art,
consider it unsatisfactory because Mann believes in none of them himself, the
complaint already referred to that his eternal irony is at bottom nihilism.

It will be understood that my own view is different. What seems to me
remarkable about the novel is precisely the fact that all (or almost all — *enough*)
of its ideas, and even of Hans Castorp's dangerously explicit scientific studies,
turn into living fiction, into a narrative that is absorbing, dramatic, moving,
funny (to the point of making us laugh out loud), and often lyrically beautiful.
To convey as human drama the working and growing of intelligence, just this
is the achievement of Mann's art. Moreover, the novel's intellectual scope also
belongs to its artistic effect. For a major source of our pleasure in the parts is
the sense of the complex whole they darkly promise, which means, too, of the

51

partialness of the parts, the one-sidedness of all its contending ideas. This not only keeps us smiling amid the intensities and profundities; it provides its own kind of suspense. It is always a dramatic as well as an intellectual climax when, in scene after scene, those promises of a deeper illumination are increasingly fulfilled. Finally, there is the supreme artistic effect of the grandeur and the moral beauty of that deepening illumination.

As for where the novel is leading us, we find in Hans Castorp's education what we found in *Reflections*, that Mann's smile at all ideas doesn't mean "no"; it means "yes, but." He seems a nihilist only to those who look for ideas in which they can come to rest. The fact is, the novel will at last say its own "yes." But this will not be to one or another of its "counterpositions," but to man, who is "the lord of counterpositions." "I have made a dream poem of humanity" (496), Hans Castorp says after the dream which shadows forth all he has learned on the mountain. He is speaking for his creator. This time Mann's "alter ego" ("Theme," 18) is not an artist but an ordinary human being. And his story is not a drama of tragic conflict but a *Bildungsroman*, an account of how we can learn and grow. Or, to put it in the story's terms, of how Hans Castorp makes his way safely through the dangers of the magic mountain. For, appearances to the contrary notwithstanding, our hero is saved at the end.

1

Reflections of a Non-Political Man made a painful break in Mann's work on *The Magic Mountain*, but it vastly enriched the novel. For in uncovering the sources of his war-time patriotism he was also, as we have seen, going deeper than ever before into the conflict at the center of his life, which was again his subject. The old opposition between the bourgeois and the artist now showed itself to be a conflict between ideas or ideals and the complexities of experience which defy them, and so between great polarities of Western thought. The result was that the "humorous companion piece to *Death in Venice*" he had envisaged, a brief tale of "a simple-minded hero in conflict with bourgeois decorum and macabre adventure," began to draw him into "shoreless seas of thought" ("Making," 720). His simple hero became the "German" his essay had called "barbaric, . . . problematic, an abyss" (32,36), in short, a representative of the abyss of human nature. *The Magic Mountain* became the realm of experience, of the "dangerous-harmful element" that seduces and educates. And as in Germany's soul European intellectual differences are "carried to the end," (39), the novel became the story of his hero's seduction away from the life-reducing safety of bourgeois attitudes and of an education by which his "simple" mind grew identical with that of the Mann who had written *Reflections*—and transcended it.

As for the esthetic risk in such traffic with ideas, Mann met the challenge in many ways, as we will see, but two are worth mentioning at the start. One came from the freedom he had gained from his own one-sidedness by writing *Reflections*. Having performed the war-time duty of expressing it — and done so, as he has said, with frequent feelings of self-betrayal — he could come back in his fiction to the smiling ambivalence in which, as a loyalist of reality, he was most at home. He could turn the novel into what Goethe had called *Faust* and Mann himself regarded as art's essential character, a "serious jest" (72). Then there was the discovery he had made in writing *Royal Highness* of how to combine the play of story-telling with the fullness of his thought. Though this *Bildungsroman* is as solidly and spaciously realistic as if it had been written in the 19th century, the realism is again a "transparency for ideas to shine through" (*RH*, vii), and in fact the novel is also an allegorical fairy tale. Our youthful hero, who comes to the Alpine sanitorium for a rest and a three-week visit to a sick soldier-cousin, gets Room 34 to stay in, eats at one of seven dining room tables, is placed under a spell by an enchantress who admits him to her bed after seven months and, having been diagnosed as tubercular in his seventh week, remains on the mountain, helpless to return, until the "thunderbolt" of war awakens him — the "Seven-Sleeper" — after seven years. And this play with the magic number[1] is the least of the novel's subversions of its own realism. The fact is, almost every development and each of the major characters is symbolic as well as real, and the feeling of larger meaning, if not meaning itself, keeps flashing through the realistic surface like the intermittent colors of some iridescent material.

All of the foregoing — the vast new scope of Mann's "egocentric" subject and the mixture of realism and fairy tale by which it will be dramatized — is planted in what Hans Castorp is when he arrives on the mountain and in what he finds there in his first days.

Our hero is introduced as a typical scion of the Hamburg burgher class, sharing its tastes and attitudes and about to enter, at the age of twenty-three, the respectable profession of naval engineer. But we are also told, in an echo of Mann's account of his own pre-literary work, that his choice of a profession was lightly arrived at and "might quite as well have been decided in some other way" (33). Moreover, his character grows "problematical" because it contains elements which tend to resist "bourgeois decorum." For instance — another echo from Mann's reports on himself apart from his literary vocation — though he accepted his world's "religious" regard for work as the "principle by which one rose or fell" (34), he did not love it, but preferred to sit dreaming, smoking, and listening to music. Then, orphaned early, he was brought up by an aristocratic, progress-hating grandfather who, reciting over the family christening bowl the names inscribed before the child's own, impressed on his mind a respect for the past and for the dead not quite suitable for a future engineer. Most important, there is the "defense" of his hero by the concerned but "candid" narrator, an old-fashioned literary device which here gives life to the weightiest exposition because it bathes everything in the mock-solemn playfulness, humor and innuendos of a particular living voice. He claims that the young man's "mediocrity," though it can't be denied, is not altogether his fault. If Hans Castorp saw "no reason . . . for exertion," it was because a man lives "the life of his epoch," as well as his own, and "in an age that affords no satisfying answer to the eternal question of 'Why? To what end?'" exceptional achievement requires a "moral remoteness" and a "vitality" (32) that are very rare. Thus shallowly rooted in his bourgeois life, our hero is not only open to the temptation of something else, the something else he will find on the mountain, but is ready to listen to the competing answers he will hear there to those fundamental questions.

One more detail is needed to complete this picture of Mann's new "alter ego." We get it from the humanist Settembrini, who grows interested in the young man because he sees him as "life's delicate child"[2] (308), that is, as the human creature in its essential vulnerability, exposed to life's dangers (which will appear on the mountain in concentrated form) by his gifts, his youthful "indecision," and his inclination to play with all possible points of view. "*Placet experirí*" (98), the Italian grants — "it is pleasant to experiment" — and this motto, which will keep recurring to Hans Castorp as the formula for his most deeply characteristic response to life's multiple possibilities, is an echo of Mann's view of the willingness to "play" with ideas of the non-political "esthete" — that is, himself — in *Reflections*.

What Hans Castorp finds at the International House Berghof is exemplified by the two kinds of noise he overhears on his first morning and evening there, from one room a horrible cough that seems to open to his shrinking imagination death's intimate workings on a patient's lungs, and from another a young Russian couple's shamelessly lively love-making. And more significant than either alone is their similarity to each other. For we are told that he listens to the Russian couple as one "practicing a seemly obscurantism" (39), and this is an echo of the "seemly air of absent-mindedness, of obscurantism, as it were,"[3] adopted long ago by his grandfather's servant as he brushed a fly off his master's corpse, which was "no longer anything but body" (28). Sex and death are akin, the echo is telling us, in that each is an utter yielding to the body, a yielding which, in the bourgeois "flatland," tends to be hidden. Moreover, the way this mountain retreat serves the diseased bodies of its patients has the effect, precisely, of intensifying the body's influence on the mind. Not only does the well-fed idleness which is here prescribed become openness to sexual temptation. The hearts of even healthy visitors experience palpitations on this height, "as if," Hans Castorp observes, "the body was going its own gait without any reference to the soul, like a dead body," so that "you keep trying to find . . . an emotion to account for them" (71-72). The emotion the patients tend to find results in a brisk traffic along the joined balconies at night and much gossip at meals the next day.

Our bourgeois hero is of course shocked at all this. But the transforming spell begins, and with it an unconscious desire to stay on the mountain, when the slanty eyes and broad cheekbones of Frau Clavdia Chauchat, also a member of the Russian group and also offensively "slack" in her behavior, stir in him a memory he can't for a while quite grasp. So, when a dying young patient theatrically asserts that he feels like a schoolboy who has learned he won't be promoted and can now stop working and "laugh at the whole thing" (80), our hero dimly realizes that "though honor might possess certain advantages, yet shame had others . . . that were well nigh boundless in their scope," and imagining himself in the other's place, "free of the infinite realms of shame," he shudders at "the wild wave of sweetness which swept over him at the thought" (81). That night he dreams he is a schoolboy borrowing a pencil from Frau Chauchat, and some days later, after a violent nosebleed in a "blue dell" which will ever after be the place for his "stock-taking," he remembers whom Frau Chauchat reminds him of. It is Pribislav Hippe, a schoolfellow with "Kirghiz eyes" and broad cheekbones, whom at thirteen he had adored in silence until one day he dared to borrow his pencil and then return it. "How remarkably like her he looked — like this girl up here!" he thinks, still lightheaded from his nosebleed. "Is that why I feel interested in her? Or was that why I felt so interested in him? What rubbish!" (123). But it is not rubbish. It is a cryptic hint of something the narrative will later make clearer — for instance, when it turns out that the shadow on his lungs discovered by the sanatorium's doctor, a discovery freeing him to stay, is the recurrence of a disease which, unknown to himself, he had had as a child about the time of his passion for Pribislav Hippe. His love each time is a fever of desire rooted in and affecting both the body and the mind, like the libido of Freud. (This is why it will now acqire an intensity beside which the conventional romance celebrated in a flatland love-ditty he keeps remembering will seem to him insipid.) He loves them both in the same way because they are two versions of the same thing. Moreover, that his love is roused each time by a face which speaks of Asia and is accompanied each time by moist spots on the lung are clues, as we will learn, to the nature — the sinister nature — of what so powerfully attracts him, which means also to the conflict between this place of enchantment and the respectable bourgeois world he has left below, the central conflict of the novel.

We get an early glimpse of this conflict in the sick cousin's explanation of the goings-on of his fellow-patients. "They are so free," Joachim says. "I mean they are so young, and time means nothing to them, and then they may die — perhaps — why should they make a long face? Sometimes I think being ill and dying aren't serious at all; just a sort of loafing about and wasting time; life is only serious down below" (51). A casual, "realistic" remark, and yet it reaches so far in its implications that it prepares us for the fairy-tale portentousness of suggestion which this place and those who serve it or live by its values or oppose them will soon take on. For what Joachim is saying is that the people up here have been set free from the great imperatives of normal healthy life in our culture. In fact, the spell our hero falls under is a fever of body and mind which will seduce him away from work, duty, dignity, uprightness and respect for time, the obligation to make time pay in progress for ourselves or our community. This last point is a point to emphasize because the novel will do so. For Hans Castorp to become indifferent to time and progress, to yield to the sense conveyed by the Berghof's regimen as well as by sexual passion, of living in a timeless present, in "eternity," is the same moral dereliction as his desire for the freedom from responsibility and shame conferred by fever. To be indifferent to time and progress is to be indifferent to life. And though our hero seems to himself, and to begin with is, an ordinary bourgeois, he is a bourgeois with old scars on his lungs and a tendency, which the mountain will activate, to new ones, or, as Clavdia Chauchat will later put it, he is a *"joli bourgeois à la petite tache humide"* (342). He is therefore vulnerable to the disease of this place and all its psychic concomitants, which means to becoming, like Tonio Kröger himself (also according to a Russian lady-friend!), a "bourgeois *manqué*." The stage has been set for the great drama of his love-induced mountain journey, with all its adventures of body and mind. And where such journeys lead is openly stated in Settembrini's reference — in a most serious joke — to the newly arrived Hans Castorp as an "Odysseus in the kingdom of the shades," of the "vacant and idle dead" (57).

But what our hero is to learn on this journey is not simply that there is a conflict between loyalty to life and the seduction of death, but something more complex. "There are two paths to life," Hans Castorp tells Clavdia after he has come to understand what has happened to him on the mountain. "One is the regular one, direct, honest. The other is bad, it leads through death — that is the *spirituel* way"[4] (596). Even the bad, the deathward path can serve life! The Jesuit Naphta teaches this when, making fun of Settembrini, who is a Freemason, he tells Hans Castorp how the medieval origins and real meaning of the rituals of Freemasonry mock its current liberal, bourgeois character. The Freemasons began, he says, as an order of alchemists who sought not only to change lead into gold, but in general to transform the lower into the higher; their primary symbol for such transmutation was the sepulcher, the "place of corruption," which "comprehends all hermetics, all alchemy," and in which "the material is compressed to its final transformation and purification." That is the reason their rituals still imply "the neophyte . . . is youth itself," seeking "the miracles of life" on a path that led "through the kingdom of dissolution" (511-512). And because at this our hero remembers how his Hamburg housekeeper's "hermetically" sealed jars kept food fresh for years by withdrawing it from the effects of time, he and his author will from then on join the terms "hermetic" and "alchemy," as Naphta has done, to convey their view of the spiritual effect of Hans Castorp's mountain experience. Thus, near the end, the narrator will describe that experience as a "hermetic enchantment to which he had proved so extraordinarily susceptible that it had become the fundamental adventure of his life, in which all the alchemical processes of his simple substance had found full play" (708). It is precisely because love has led our hero astray through "the kingdom of dissolution" and so set his spirit free from the demands of healthy, honorable, "regular" life that his simplicity will become genius.

2

Mann's *Bildungsroman*, then, is a modern version of the medieval education by love. In this version, however, love is "unmasked" as the most insistent expression of our physical nature, of that hungering, digesting, dying body civilization tends to conceal; it is from this that our spellbound hero will be learning on his "bad path." And as it is "life's delicate child" who is engaged in that risky education, and as Clavdia Chauchat is its sexual lure and the Berghof is the place where it is heightened by disease and encouraged by death, so the four major characters Hans Castorp meets in those first days, as well as the other two he meets later on, will each symbolize — and express — some relation to it. (It should be added at once that if the individualizing features of Mann's characters turn out to be *appropriate*, this doesn't mean they are any the less realistic. What they represent and say arises, like any realistic action, out of their history and temperament, out of what they vividly are and feel.)[5] Moreover, all of these first four will strengthen the mountain's spell, two as its champions, and two by a resistance which, though it also helps our hero's education along, shows itself as limited and blind.

The Berghof's chief medical officer, Hofrat Behrens, knows "what death is," as he jokingly says, because "I'm an old retainer of his" (536). His field is man's physical nature, and sure enough, he is a physically robust man, doing his job with a hearty straightforwardness — except when he sinks into equally hearty and straightforward depression. "Our Rhadamanthus" (60), according to Settembrini, he sentences most of those who come before him to lavish terms in his realm, silences with indignation all frightened last-minute rebellion against dying, and is quick to devalue the world of action, time and progress. ("But what's the use of it?" he asks of the lieutenancy Joachim achieves on his brief return below. "The good Lord sees your heart, not the braid on your jacket" [501].) And though Settembrini ascribes his ideas to commercial greed, they are in fact the sincere expression of what death really, immemorially teaches. Like the protagonist of Hans Pfitzner's music-drama *Palestrina*, which Mann was deeply stirred to find was also about "sympathy with death" (he reports this in *Reflections*), Behrens was led to his life's work by love for a dead wife — she died on the mountain, and he remained there, grieving, to minister to other victims of her illness — and he is still periodically incapacitated by bouts of crippling melancholy, that is, of disgust with life. Then, not only does he have a fellow-feeling for illness because he has been ill himself, he is also that spiritual product of illness (in the world of Mann), an artist: it is his painting of Clavdia and its remarkable skin tones, thrilling Hans Castorp to a comic frenzy of interest in his medical knowledge of what goes on under the skin, that initiates our hero's studies of the human body and thereby of the whole world of nature. And what he teaches is what death's representative would teach. To the young man's "rhapsodic" climactic question "What is the body? What is the physical being of man?" he replies that the body is mainly water and "white of egg" or albumen, and though "you flow away" only in the grave, the body's putrefaction there is exactly the same oxidation of cellular albumen which constitutes its life — in short, that "living consists in dying" (266-265).

As Behrens oversees the body in this lofty "underworld," Dr. Krokowski, an "idealist of the pathological, not to say a pathological idealist" (654), is in charge of the soul; and, again appropriately, he is pale, unhealthy-looking, and faintly repellent. The first of his lectures our hero attends, its import dramatized by the bloody stains (from his nosebleed) on the young man's clothes and the disturbing effect of Clavdia Chauchat seated in front of him, offers shocking revelations about the nature and power of love. Love, he says, arises out of a mass of "perversities" hiding under "the innocence of sucking babes" and "the dignity of silver hairs" and made respectable only by opposing "bourgeois" impulses of shame, disgust, chastity. When those opposing forces are strong enough to "suppress" it, love emerges as illness: "all disease is only love transformed" (127-128). Add to this the speaker's doubt "whether the two conceptions, man and perfect health, were consistent with one another," and the implication is clear that to be sick and driven by love is to be human in the highest degree, and that love is therefore a power it is inhuman, as well as futile, to resist. Thus Dr. Krokowski, like Behrens, is no mere objective scientist of his subject but its subtle champion, forever insinuating titillation while playing the bland teacher; and it is as a fateful going over to the enemy that Joachim sees his cousin entering one day "the half-darkness of Dr. Krokowski's analytic lair" (367). For though Behrens makes easy the way to death and the psychoanalyst does the same for love, the latter's role as the other's subordinate is clearly a metaphor for the relationship of their two spheres, sexual abandon being, as we saw in *Death in Venice*, a preliminary version of our final letting-go.

Joachim and Settembrini are the two who staunchly resist this underworld's seduction. In the former such resistance is not intellectual but a matter of character, for, as Hans Castorp is, in Behrens's shrewd judgment, a "civilian" through and through, his sick cousin is entirely a soldier. That is, he is one who does not ask "Why? To what end?" but finds his fulfilment in accepting without question the authority in his world and by fidelity to duty and discipline. Observing the Berghof's medical rules with military firmness in order to hasten the moment when he can rejoin his regiment, he keeps his eyes firmly on his plate in the presence of *his* Russian charmer Marusja. And when illness forces him back after a brief, defiant return to "the colors," he "expressed the greatest contempt at this cursed slackness." It's true that the increasingly learned Hans Castorp refers to his slackness as the *"rebellio carnis"* (506) man cannot avoid and adduces St. Anthony's experience as proof. And this hint that in Joachim too the slackness of illness is related to the psychic and moral kind which originates in sexual desire is borne out by his self-betraying joy at seeing Marusja again. Yet the question of whether his will to get well has been altogether pure is raised by our friend the narrator with a pointed delicacy. For in spite of the inevitable mixture of motives that goes with being human, Joachim is sufficiently the faithful loyalist of the world of health and duty to justify the affectionate respect of all who know him, including the author, who was happy to find the soldier a favorite of his readers. Still, his resistance is too clearly bound up with intellectual simplicity to give pause to his thoughtful cousin.

It is in the overpoweringly articulate Italian who offers himself as Hans Castorp's guide amid the dangers of this region that the mountain spell is most formidably resisted. The spiritual heir of a "carbonaro" grandfather and a humanist-lawyer father, Settembrini understands that the lack of "seriousness" Joachim finds distasteful up here opposes — and must be opposed by — nothing less than the dominant ideas and values of Western civilization. In what reads like a page from *Reflections*, we are told that for this "independent man of letters," writing well, thinking well and acting well are all at bottom the same; literature is the source of moral perfection and "the moving spirit of both humanity and politics," and "all of them could be comprehended in one single word . . . civilization" (159). Moreover, he sees the world as divided between two principles. On one side is force, tyranny, superstition, quiescence and immobility; and on the other justice, freedom, knowledge, rebellion and "ceaseless fermentation issuing in progress" (157). Because the first is the "Asiatic" principle and the second the "European," those Kirghiz eyes which lure our hero begin to expand in what they suggest, from moral slackness as sexual promise to slackness in matters intellectual, spiritual and political as well. Finally, for his own progress-serving action, Settembrini is collecting literary data on suffering for a work to be published by The League for the Organization of Progress and to be called *The Sociology of Suffering*, a work which will offer enlightenment on two points: "first, that given effects become void when one first recognizes and then removes their causes, and second, that almost all individual suffering is due to disease of the social organism" (246).

The champion of civilization keeps calling the young cousins "engineer" and "lieutenant" as reminders of their proper life duty. Coming oddly near to Dr. Krokowski's view of illness as a "secondary phenomenon," he regards it (in others) as a form of immorality which the doctors, those scoundrels, find their profit in encouraging. And of course he soon understands that the real cause of his pupil's dereliction from duty and his intellectual evasions, resistance, obtuseness in their discussions is his passion for Clavdia. So, in an action of which the symbolic meaning is not obscure, he breaks into the young man's musing on Clavdia in his darkened room by switching on the light; he calls a warning to the *"ingegnere"* (in heartfelt Italian) when his pupil goes for the second time in his life to borrow a pencil from a slanty-eyed beloved, and his view of what this love represents is dramatically/playfully underlined by the way he echoes that warning call when Hans Castorp sets out on an even more dangerous flirting with the Other, that is with the Other in its ultimate form, as literal death in the mountain snow.

Our hero is touched at his mentor's concern, and he takes in like a sponge all he has to teach, though he often gives his ideas and phrases a comical twist which had not been intended. But he soon becomes aware that the humanist is not to be taken at his own valuation. In fact, Settembrini turns out to be an embodiment of the tradition of humanist enlightenment so complete that he also displays everything in that tradition, and in the realities of flesh and blood, that undermines it—this is what makes him comic. Our hero dreams of him once as an "organ-grinder," and though he uses the phrase thereafter partly in self-defense, it also hints at what we are led to suspect when the Italian complacently helps his admiring audience to the word "plastic" as a description of his own eloquence: this eloquence is the glib repetition of stale and self-gratifying verbal poses, and his passionate sincerity nothing but the political type's lack of self- awareness. That he can break off a noble period to "chirrup" at passing girls is only the most amusingly obvious of his self-betrayals. A deeper irony arises out of his lofty ideas themselves. Even before the arrival of Naphta, who will express the most serious arguments against the *Zivilisationsliterat* in *Reflections*, we must become aware of how the assumptions of the Enlightenment, at least in the dramatic purity given them by this fictional embodiment of its latest developments, are their own parody. For what is it but parody—the rationalist's way of simplifying reality carried to absurd extremes—to speak of "almost all" human suffering as so many classifiable effects of a wrong social organization, effects we can confidently hope to eliminate by replacing it with the right one?[6]

So encouraged by death's two retainers and so resistant to the two resisters, Hans Castorp is now especially vulnerable to the stimulus of Behrens's portrait of Clavdia and its remarkable skin tones. Hearing from the doctor that "living consists in dying," he happily concludes, in spite of his teacher's warning against the danger of honoring death at the expense of our obligations to life, that "if one is interested in life, one must be particularly interested in death." To the doctor's scrupulous demurrer, "After all, there is some sort of difference. Life is life which keeps the form through change of substance," the young man retorts, "Why must the form remain?" And in an ultimate drunken apostasy from his teacher's humanism, in which feeling is honored only as it is controlled into form, "Form is folderol" (267).

This hilarious scene, in which Hans Castorp lugs the portrait around the room for a better light and shows such lively curiosity about the sitter's lymph glands—located in "the intimate parts of the body" (265)—and so on, is an especially clear example of what gives comic or poignant human interest to the education at the heart of this novel (and, for that matter, to all Mann's uncompromisingly intellectual fiction). It is his steady awareness that our ideas have an emotional basis usually hidden even from ourselves, an awareness encouraged, as I have said, more by Schopenhauer and Nietzsche than by Freud. The inner development of his conventional bourgeois hero, for whom at the start "equivocal and questionable situations were in general repugnant," is therefore shown as a series of betrayals of the respectable values of his flatland home due to the irresistible seductiveness of what is shameful, and the novel's continuous comedy arises out of the young man's attempt (until, utterly intox-icated, he flings respectability to the winds) to conceal this even from himself. (For instance, Hans Castorp "pondered over" Settembrini's moral objections to "illness and despair — which he found incomprehensible, or at least *pretended to himself to find them so*" [227, my emphasis].) And because all ideas are seen by him, whether he knows it or not, as blocking or serving his desire, the loftiest discussion can make his fever rise, involve him in self-deception and duplic-ities, and give the reader (if he is in on the secret) reason to smile.

But Mann's irony is not the "classic," didactic device valued by Settem-brini; it is the ambiguous kind the humanist sternly warns his pupil against. It is irony that goes both ways. If we keep seeing through Hans Castorp's lofty thought to the "low" wishes it comes from and serves, we keep seeing too that such thought develops a legitimacy of its own. Exactly this doubleness characterizes the passionate study of the human body he turns to next. We find that the "image of life" hovering before him during his hours of "research" is a woman with slanty eyes, and that, though he goes deeply into the essentials of anatomy, physiology, biology, the mechanics of reproduction and heredity and finally of the body's physical context, the large universe around us and the small one inside the atom, his conclusions are no more "objective" than those of the two doctors. For he concludes that life is "a fever of matter . . . a stolen and voluptuous impurity of sucking and secreting, a pullulation, an unfolding" (276) in which albumen, salt and fats combine into the desireable, desirous flesh. Because he also studies pathology, which teaches him that the fever of the Berghof patients is due to "soluble toxins" produced by foreign cell bodies in an organism "perversely" receptive to them, he arrives at the intuition that "the original procreation of matter [out of the immaterial was] only a disease . . . [a] pathologically luxuriant morbid growth produced by the irritant of some unknown infiltration; this, in part pleasurable, in part a motion of self-defense . . . was the Fall." And "just as disease in the organism was an intoxica-tion, a heightening . . . of its physical state," so life itself "was nothing but the automatic blush of matter roused to sensation and become receptive for that which awaked it" (285-286). His own desire is now justified as a human version of the central creative process of the universe! And yet, though we are thus led to see through his assumption of scientific authority, we must also recog-nize that his conclusions enforce respect. Not only do they have their own drama and grandeur as they unfold (another reason this "research" is not bor-ing but fictionally alive); they have genuine suggestive power as metaphors for the unity underlying the chaotic variety of nature. Moreover, our hero has done his homework with German thoroughness; he has learned a great deal, and everything he has learned stays with him and works back on the love which spurred his research. So, when he falls to his knees before his beloved on Car-nival Night, his passionate speech is a comic paean to "the marvelous sym-metry of the human edifice" (342), the shoulders, haunches and breasts ar-ranged in pairs, the great branches of the vessels and nerves, and so on.

Then, we see again how the irony goes both ways when Hans Castorp, emboldened by his studies, defies his teacher's "progressive" disapproval of his tendency to overvalue illness and death and begins to stand, "expertly reverential" (293) at deathbeds and to squire about on her last walks a dying girl. True, we smile at how passion dupes him — and Settembrini seems justified — when some of the dying patients he wishes to respect act like frivolous fools and when the silly gossip Frau Stöhr whispers, in a remark which hits home, that the girl is merely his substitute for the woman he dare not yet approach. But then the way he defends himself to Joachim wipes the smiles off our faces. He says that humanity's shared doom justifies "subdued and ceremonial" (295) behavior to each other (a foreshadowing of "the mutual courteous regard" [492] which it will later be seen to produce in the beautiful creatures of his dream in the snow). And scorning Settembrini's view that he and his kind have "a monopoly of morals, as well as of human dignity — with his talk about 'practical life work' and Sunday services in the name of 'progress'" (296) — he reminds us of the realities of the human condition that do indeed call for the "religious" shift to less immediate considerations and a larger perspective.

But we get the novel's most dramatic example of the possible truth in ideas initiated by desire (as well as a rich flowering of the "fairy tale" symbolism which arises out of the tale's impeccably realistic surface) when, on Carnival Night, our hero crosses his "Rubicon" at last and approaches his beloved. This chapter, "Walpurgis-Night," and the later one called "Snow," are the high points of the novel, which places them, in my view, among the supreme achievements of fiction.

3

That the carnival is an occasion for utter yielding to the "bad path" we promptly learn from Settembrini, who describes it in ironical quotations from the Walpurgis-Night scene in which Goethe's Faust attends a bestial orgy of witches and warlocks. Sure enough, our hero thanks the humanist for all his teaching in what is clearly a speech of farewell. Then, ignoring the other's warning cry, though he turns pale himself at the action's "widening circle of associations" (325), he goes up to the dazzling Clavdia to borrow a pencil. Moreover, he is borrowing the pencil to "join the others" in a game introduced by this realm's ruler Behrens, in which the patients try to draw pigs with closed eyes and in fact produce formless "abortions" (329-330). That is, for love of the beautiful representative of Eastern "slackness," he is now abandoning altogether the rational self-control and the humanistic self-respect of Western civilization.

What follows is a quiet explosion of passion long pent up and charging our hero's every syllable, pause and gesture, from that opening request with lips too stiff to sound the labials to his final wild outpouring on his knees.

Moreover, the richly building awareness that is the fruit of his passion, an awareness connecting all he has been with all he has learned, is also released in this explosion, which is therefore as full of meaning as it is of feeling. Finally, Frau Chauchat, too, is realized with all Mann's "Russian" brilliance of psychological detail, and she too is a character who thinks as well as feels; she can express and defend what she is. They meet, therefore, not only as a man wildly in love who is speaking out at last and a woman profoundly stirred and amused at the long-awaited declaration, but as conscious representatives of opposing ways of being, those of "bourgeois," orderly Germany and spiritually unbuttoned Asia. And the drama of their dialogue (a drama intensified by her announcement that he is almost too late, that she is leaving on a journey the next morning) lies in the way her sense of the gulf between them, for her a gulf only to be bridged during the carnival freedom that permits the *tu* to replace *vous*, is gradually overcome by his passionate demonstration that, as a German, he is already closer to her than she knows and that what has happened to him and inside him on the mountain has brought him in spirit to her side. That this is indeed a Walpurgis-Night betrayal of bourgeois decencies he virtually confesses when he insists they speak in French. For him, as he says, "*c'est parler . . . sans responsabilité ou comme nous parlons en rêve*" (336).[7]

So she suggests that Germany is "orderly" and "pedantic" (354, 466); she mocks him as "*un petit bonhomme convenable*" of good family and a docile pupil of his teachers, whose fever is a mere incident and who will soon go home to serve his country with his engineering and forget completely that he ever talked up here in dreams; and by way of climax, she answers his eager question as to what she and a Russian friend concluded about the moral life with what is almost a direct quotation of the humane morality Mann posed in *Reflections* against the shallow, self-righteous virtue of the *Zivilisationsliterat*. For them, she says, "*la morale*" is to be found, not in virtue, reason, discipline, but rather in abandoning oneself to danger, in losing oneself, even to the point of death. "*Les grands moralistes n'étaient point de vertueux,*" she says, "*mais . . . des grands pêcheurs, qui nous enseignent à nous incliner chrétiennement devant la misère*" (340). (Here we remember Father Zossima bowing to Dmitri Karamazov.) And a moment later she removes her paper cap and addresses him with "*vous*."

But he does not yield. He tells her first that Germany is less orderly than she thinks ("We love what we have not" [335]), and that what Europe calls "liberty" may be more pedantic than Germany's need for order. What he means emerges when, boyishly appropriating his teacher's phrase, he adds, "*Nous sommes peut-être des* delicate children of life, *tout simplement*" (336). He is affirming as the deeper truth about the German character (another echo from *Reflections*) that risky openness to the inner abyss of human possibilities which elicited his teacher's concern about him, an abyss untouched by the "pedantic" formulas of the Enlightenment. To this abyss he is now ready to abandon himself, just as, when drawing pigs, one simply leans back and closes one's eyes. For his state, he tells her, is the same as his dying cousin's, which means, as we have learned to understand, that both are in the grip of their bodies — of the dark, complex, death- oriented forces of nature — and thereby equally withdrawn from healthy, normal life and its duties.

His love for her, he now concludes as one who "raved," is not only identical with the illness she makes light of, but is the same love that scarred his lungs in his childhood and that — before he knew her! — brought him to the mountain. For, like Pribislav Hippe in his time, she is now the living embodiment of that Other which his nature and his sex must seek forever, *"le Toi de ma vie, mon rêve, mon sort, mon envie, mon éternel désir."* To her *"Allons! Si tes precepteurs te voyaient,"* he responds with a comic frenzy of repudiation of Settembrini's lectures which makes clear those ultimate implications of his passion already noted, that it is the rebellion of his body's hunger against Western civilization. *"Je m'en ficherais, je m'en fiche . . . de la République éloquente et du progrés humain dans le temps, car je t'aime."* *"Petit bourgeois!"* she now murmurs, caressing his lowered head, and adds — surely to the triumphant joy of her author at thus linking by an echo from *Tonio Kröger* the majestic work of his maturity with that tale of his youth — *"joli bourgeois à la petite tache humide."* And to her question that is already a thrilling promise, *"Est-ce vrai que tu m'aimes tant?"* he replies with a final intoxicated statement of the lesson his passion has taught him. The body, love and death are one and the same, he says, because the body's life *is* desire and dying. But though in these activities the body is obscenely predominant, yet each has another aspect than the obscene. As death lifts us above such transient concerns as eating and money-making and brings us into the solemn realm of history, the eternal, the sacred, so in love we do honor to the miracle whereby organic life produces a *"sainte merveille de la forme et de la beauté,"* our interest in which is a most humane interest, and *"plus éducative que toute la pédagogie du monde"* (342).

Sexual desire is clearly the source of these ideas. But it should also be clear that they have their own truth. There *is* for the human imagination a life-enriching influence in what, seen in its nakedness, is the horror of death ("Death is the mother of beauty," said Wallace Stevens), as well as in the animal seizure of sex. And we must also say yes to Clavdia's morality, as we do to Dostoevsky's. Such a "Russian" awareness of our fellowship with sinners and criminals is surely essential for a humane, an open-eyed morality; the virtue which thinks itself above all that is mere ignorance, if not hypocrisy. Moreover, that his desire has helped our hero grow — has opened his mind to his author's polarities and prepared him for the religious perspective of Naphta, which comes next — we see when he chooses soon after to wait on the mountain for Clavdia's return rather than to go home with his dutiful cousin. Thinking over his past life and all he has recently learned, he realizes that his interest in "the human form divine" is now bound up with problems for which, though they don't matter to the soldierly Joachim, "he had come to feel as a civilian responsible," problems of "form and freedom, body and spirit, honor and shame, time and eternity" (389-390). To go home, he thinks later, would be to give up his contemplation of "*Homo Dei*" — he is now borrowing from Naphta — his "'stock-taking,' that hard and harrowing task, which was really beyond the powers native to him, but yet afforded his spirit such nameless and adventurous joys" (421). What began as an alibi for sexual passion has become a passion of the mind. Though still waiting for Clavdia's return, he will now listen to the debates of Naphta and Settembrini, and at last go impatiently beyond them, as one faithful to a "civilian" duty and to self-justifying spiritual joys he has really come to feel. And they are precisely the duty and the joys of his author!

4

The function of Naphta is to further our hero's education on the "bad path" by opposing to the Italian's democratic, humanistic answer to that question "Why? To what end" the great other way of answering it in our culture. And if their debates are sometimes a bit long or circular (as well as uncompromisingly learned and philosophic), they are, in the main, quite sufficiently dramatic. Not only do the ideas always express character, as I have said; they emerge always in a battle for our hero's tantalizingly open mind, a battle comically ferocious under the intellectual's courtliness and ending, in a way altogether appropriate, in blood and death.

The little Jesuit is the son of a *shochet*, a butcher whose profession among Jews joins religion with blood; he is physically ugly, despising the body and valuing only beauty of "spirit"; and he is a man of intellect and so, as Settembrini observes, is given to "new combinations." What divides him from the Italian is the chief of these new combinations and an example of Mann's prophetic grasp of the essentials out of which the future grows. He is a Catholic communist because, he explains, it is the world proletariat which is now "asserting the ideals of *Civitas Dei* in opposition to the discredited and decadent standards of the capitalitic bourgeoisie." Like the heretic-burning Church of old, which was also "communistic" and condemned "commercial activity," it aims "to strike terror into the world for the healing of the world, that man may finally achieve salvation and win back to freedom from law and the distinction of classes to his original status as a child of God" (403-404).

This justification for the use of "terror" is not quite the same as Mann's (tentative) excuse for German militarism in *Reflections*. But it's clear that in Naphta he is exposing the bloody consequences of valuing any idea of what society ought to be more than human life. It is to become, in effect, another "retainer" of death. Moreover, he shows that Naphta's "salvation" means slavery. The Jesuit claims that "man is the measure of all things" and his "welfare" is the sole criterion of "truth" (398, 551) in order to justify absolute power for those who "know" where that welfare lies. So he not only accepts flogging, torture and the stake, but rejects (like our own still persisting "counter-culture" of the '60's!) the forms and disciplines — and even the literacy — of "bourgeois" culture. He would set people free from those constraints (which in fact develop a sense of individual possibilities and rights) in order to make them malleable for "the absolute mandate" (400), sink them into the "anonymous and communal" (404) and turn them into obedient children of God.

But we also find in Naphta's scorn of Settembrini's bourgeois liberalism what Mann did *not* reject in *Reflections*, a grasp of the dark complexities of existence that liberalism tends to shut out. This is why he keeps answering his adversary — and stretching our hero's mind — in a way we must respect. To begin with his politics, he smiles at the other's belief that the free human spirit will show itself only in "love of one's kind" and that national self-interest will soon submit to ideal justice in "courts of arbitration" (383). Later, attacking his ruling assumptions (which have also been ours), he calls faith in progress "the cry of the patient who constantly changes his position thinking each new one will bring relief" and points out that "justice" and "freedom" are problems, not "beautiful gestures." Not only can the demand for justice lead to "paralyzing doubt" and "unscrupulous deeds" (691). Because God — or nature — is not even-handed but creates human beings with varying gifts, the question arises, *which* justice, the kind that gives differing individuals their own or the kind that treats us all alike? ("One law for the lion and the ox is oppression," we may add from Blake.) Then, just as the "freedom" promised by the French Revolution led to an ocean of blood and after that to inhuman exploitation by the liberated bourgeoisie, so the thirst for freedom often grew out of and led to reactionary intolerance, as when nationalism thereafter asserted itself in its name and ended in tyranny. At last he openly admits he is sowing "seeds of doubt deeper than the most . . . modish free thought ever dreamed of doing" because Settembrini's "humanity is today nothing but a tail end, a stale, classicistic survival, a spiritual ennui . . . yawning its head off while the new Revolution is coming on apace to give it its quietus" (697). All this too is one-sided. Yet it is surely as illuminating a warning as that of Ivan Karamzov in his poem of the Grand Inquisitor.

Naphta is equally telling on the way the mind works in philosophy and literature. He reminds Settembrini (to his pupil's delight) that intellectual progress often requires a withdrawal from life which the bourgeois would consider irresponsible. He calls pure science a "myth" because what we see is determined by what we believe and will — this (Nietzchean) psychological insight is for him the meaning of St. Augustine's maxim "I believe in order that I may understand." Later, following Kant, he goes so far as to call it "an insult to the human spirit" to accept even space, time and causality as "actual conditions existing independently" of our own "forms of cognition," and "blasphemous rubbish" to think the mere multiplication of numbers in astronomy can reveal "the essence of infinity and eternity" (691-692). As for Settembrini's faith that literature is "the path to understanding, forgiveness and love," to this he replies that such "understanding," etc., is "an emasculation . . . of life" (525) and that literature has in fact been the voice of passion and the irrational, vide ancient myth, in which Hermes-Thoth, the inventor of writing, is also "an ape, moon and soul deity, a god of death and of the dead," and, according to the cabalistic Middle Ages, "the Father of hermetic alchemy" (524). (Hans Castorp's brain "reeled" at so sweeping a reversal, but readers of *Death in Venice* will not be surprised.)

Finally, in Naphta's religion, "god and the Devil were at one" in being opposed to the "arch-philistinism," the "ultra-bourgeoisiedom" of "so-called normal life" (463-464), which thinks it can have the purely good. In fact, his religion emphasizes the idea out of Tolstoy's *Lucerne* which Mann quoted in *Reflections*, that of the whole as a chaotic mixture which mocks all human distinctions and categories. This is why he joins Behrens, Krokowski and Clavdia in seeing life as an intermingling of good and evil, health and disease, living and dying, in which bourgeois ethics are complacent simplemindedness, and calls the pursuit of pure health the "dehumanization, the animalizing of man" (465). For him the role of genius is precisely to descend into "disease and madness" to find the wisdom that will enable ordinary men to avoid them. And though Settembrini reacts with passion against the disgusting "*guazzabuglio*" (464) that replaces a world of clear moral distinctions by which youth may be guided with a "morally chaotic All" (408), Hans Castorp's "bad" education has long prepared him—and us—to see the humanist's simpler world as a sentimental dream.

And yet, when the dizzying contradictions of these two intellectuals—not only of each other but (amid life's varying contexts) of themselves—impel our hero to leave talk behind and to see what he can learn by a direct encounter with death in the snowy mountain, his teacher's second warning call—against this new danger—makes him aware of a change in his view of him. "You are a windbag and a hand-organ man, to be sure," he now thinks. "But you mean well, you mean much better, and more to my mind than that knife-edged little Jesuit and Terrorist . . . though he is nearly always right when you and he come to grips over my paltry soul" (478). With this observation something discreetly hinted before emerges into the open, and the novel begins a massive shift from the instructiveness of the "bad path" to its dangers, which means also from the limitations of Settembrini's humanism to its permanent claim on our gratitude. What has turned Hans Castorp around in his growing awareness that he does *after all* want to live and his growing appreciation of the fact that, though both of his teachers are one-sided, the Italian is one-sided on behalf of life.

Granted, the young man's love—that is, his anarchic sexuality—and the deep considerations to which it led him have made him sympathetic to Naphta's contempt for life "stupidly conceived as an end in itself" (464). He too has associated death with the higher values, and he has expressed the view (planted in him by his grandfather over the christening bowl) that "ordinary people" seem "fit for life" (465) but somehow unworthy of the dignity of death. But there have been moments when Settembrini, for all his comic blind spots and vanities, has opposed the bias toward death and affirmed the "bourgeois" emphasis on life in ways that seem to be spared his author's usual irony, and it was he to whom Hans Castorp—and the reader—listened with respect. "Death," he has said, "is worthy of homage as the cradle of life, the womb of palingenesis," but "severed from life," it exerts "a vicious attraction" (200), for, he adds later, it "unlooses," it brings "deliverance," not *from* evil . . . but . . . by evil. It relaxes manners and morals, it frees man from discipline and restraint, it abandons him to lust" (412). Our hero has to know from his own mountain experience that this is true. And though the novel has been one long demonstration of the value for life of such "relaxation," it will now show itself as a warning against valuing it for its own sake, *over* life.

As for that "aristocratic" scorn for the cherishing of mere life as "bourgeois" and "Philistine," Settembrini replies to this in words that Mann will echo in the 1932 essay "Goethe as a Representative of the Bourgeois Age." "The respectable, the bourgeois," he will observe, "is the home of the universally human," and he will go on to say that the "license to pessimism," to seeing incapacity for "ordinary life" as "aristocratic," which he got in his youth from Schopenhauer, was counteracted by Goethe's "emotional complex" of "man, love, future" as one and as comprising the "life-worthy" (*Essays* 70, 83). So, "fit for life," Settembrini instructs his pupil, ought not to be used in a derogatory sense because it really means "worthy of life," these conceptions suggesting another "equally beautiful, 'worthy of love,'" and "both together, love-worthy and life-worthy, made up the true nobility" (465). And we also hear Goethe—and Mann—in the Italian's indignant response to Naphta's contempt for humanistic intellectual disciplines.

Then, Settembrini seems to be speaking for Mann even in certain of his political ideas—that is, for Mann's regained detachment from his own Naphta views. Once, for instance, he puts his finger on what is surely the chief danger in Naphta's insistence that prior "belief" is a condition of understanding and usefulness to man is sufficient validation. "Your pragmatism needs only to be translated into terms of politics to display its pernicious character in full force" (395). In fact, it is precisely the major error of *Reflections* that it applies its psychological truths to the sphere of politics, where they are inappropriate and become murderous. And because even in *Reflections* democracy was increasingly accepted in spite of its flaws, there is no reason to think Mann is smiling at the Italian when, to Naphta's idea that we must choose between God in the church or the evil of absolute state power, he offers democracy as a third alternative and declares, "Democracy has no meaning whatever if not that of an individualistic corrective to State absolutism of every kind" (399).

But the novel gives us reasons for Hans Castorp's preference for the humanist that are more dramatic and persuasive than argument. When our hero is struggling against the temptation to rest a little in the snow, a rest he knows is the way to freeze to death, the Jesuit's teaching comes into his mind as an excuse for giving up, for seeing his struggle to stay alive as "a purely ethical reaction, representing the sordid bourgeois view of life, irreligion, Philistinism." But he remembers too Settembrini's warning that illness affects the mind because it "adjusts its man," offering "sensory appeasements" and a "merciful narcosis." And he realizes that the seductive pleasures of lying down now are a "benefaction" only "if you are not meant to get home . . . but if you mean to get home, they become sinister" (485). Though it is by going further than Settembrini would approve and risking the deadly sleep that he will now attain the joy of his "dream poem of humanity," it is the humanist's teaching which keeps him aware all through it that "dream and sleep . . . are highly dangerous to my young life" (497) and which brings him back to his feet to get "home." Thus, "in the clutch," Naphta's subtleties disarm him and the humanist's simpler loyalties keep him strong. Finally, there is Settembrini's startling triumph over Naphta in the duel which caps the frenzy of their mutual hostility. Like Dostoevsky's Father Zossima in his youthful duel, he shows that he prefers to die rather than to kill—he shoots into the air and offers himself to his opponent's bullet. And that Naphta shrieks "Coward!" and fires into his own head, thus "confessing that it takes more courage to fire than to be fired upon" (705), is a climactic demonstration that, "in the clutch," his ideas make death the easier choice.

Still, as we have seen, our hero's shift toward Settembrini is not total acceptance but only grants him his due as a spokesman for part of the truth. It is the dream Hans Castorp attains by going still further on the "bad path" the humanist abhors (but that he returns from alive by rejecting the influence of its champion, the Terrorist) which gives him his vision of the whole.

5

The chapter called "Snow" culminates in what might have been a dangerously explicit statement of the novel's vision, even going so far as to italicize its core idea. What saves it—what puts it among the greatest achievements of the art of fiction—is that it carries all the way Mann's characteristic methods and gifts. For it is an account of a genuine battle against death in an Alpine snowstorm, of the terror of the battle and the gigantic and "uncanny" beauty of the mountains, which could make the fortune of a realist but which is at the same time a "transparency" for the full, accumulated wealth of the novel's meanings. Along with the chapter's densely particularized reality, its gripping and comic drama of character in action (comic even here amid the terror), we get a play of ideas by which, as in music, the hints of meaning that came before are echoed, related and fulfilled and which also provides the special Mann effect of intellectual daring and dexterity and a sort of silent ta-ta! of the consciously triumphant performer.[8] Obviously, the writing has a hand in the triumph, the perspectives taken, the choice and arrangement of details, Mann's mock-solemn manner, verbal drama and eloquence (all these beautifully reproduced in Lowe-Porter's English). But its chief source is a kind of explosion of idea-carrying leitmotifs.

We have seen how Mann made use in his previous work of that trick learned from Wagner, the repetition during later episodes of phrases which arose out of earlier ones. Here, he tells us, it is "the technical device that attempts to give complete presentness at any given moment to the entire world of ideas that it [the novel] comprises" and so to "abrogate time itself" ("Making" 723). It does this by keeping us continually aware, with echoes like the one mentioned earlier of the "seemly obscurantism" practiced by the respectable bourgeois before the body's gross self-assertion, that the apparently different episodes time brings on in the story are merely different versions of a single unchanging reality. It is to be noted that Mann's leitmotifs are a method of conveying ideas which serves rather than violates the art of fiction. For they convey not just ideas, but the living experience, the drama, of their birth. First of all, for the reader, who arrives at insight by way of a small shock of recognition. But more important, whenever it is Hans Castorp rather than the narrator who repeats the old phrases, the echoes become an example of *his* basic experience, which is precisely the stretching, the "heightening," as Mann puts it, of his mental powers. We see him engaged in the very act of understanding. And his returning to those phrases is in this chapter especially dramatic, not only because it is our hero's danger — literally deadly at last — which is thrusting upon him the timeless truth concealed under their originally innocent surface. His thrilled recognition of connections and meanings is now the climactic fulfilment of a growing hunger, the hunger for understanding, which has become the intellectual version, as it were, of the sexual kind that first led him "astray."

We are told that he had two desires in this period. One was "to be alone with his thoughts and his stock-taking projects," and the other, "allied" to the first, was "a lively craving to come into close and freer touch with the mountains in their snowy desolation" (473). These desires are allied because the magnificence and "deathly silence" of the mountains are no more "uncharted and perilous," no more "uncanny," than the heights to which Naphta and Settembrini had brought his mind. Besides, he felt "a kinship with the wild powers" of these heights. They seemed "a fitting theatre for the issue of his involved thoughts, a fitting stage for one to make who, scarcely knowing how, found it devolved upon him to take stock of himself in reference to the rank and status of *Homo Dei*" (477-478). That is, their wildness reflects his own — first manifested in his passion for his "Kirghiz-eyed" schoolfellow — and it is in just this old wildness that he is now seeking the nature of man.

So when he grows aware, on the day of the storm, that he has "deliberately set out to lose his way," and even then does not turn back, our judicious narrator finds that his excuse — that the danger is not yet critical — masks a truer reason which is "blameworthy" and "presumptuous," a desire to issue a "challenge." For "when a young man lives years long as this one had, something may gather . . . in the depths of his soul," discharging itself at last with "a mental, 'Oh, go the devil!' a repudiating of all caution whatsoever, in short, with a challenge" (481). This lets out the secret. Just as he earlier became aware — and we with him — that he had come to the mountain in order to find again the "*toi*" of his nature (its Kirghiz eyes a sign of its otherness and a promise of sexual joy free of the constraints of civilization), we are now led to see that he came, too, out of the impulse to seek the truth of his own — of human — nature in an encounter with that Other, nature itself in its naked destructive power. To embrace the adorable Asiatic and to know what the human creature is are two aspects of one desire, the desire for the forbidden — that is, the danger- ous — which must always be simmering under civilization and its discontents. Our hero's climactic fulfilment of the first occurred on his Walpurgis-Night. Now, in this "icy void" where his heart throbs with exertion and fear and he feels "a naive reverence for that organ of his, for the pulsating human heart up here alone . . . with its question and its riddle" (478), he will fulfil the second.

The realization dramatized by that explosion of leitmotifs is precisely that he is now (amid snow flakes whose crystalline symmetry, we are reminded, is alien to life) in the very heart of the realm to which desire has lured him, the realm of death. This is why he listens to the "primeval silence" of the mountain with "his head on one side, his mouth open" (476), which is how he listened to his grandfather's solemn references to the dead over the christening bowl and how, later, glad to be sick for Clavdia's sake, he looked at a preview of his own death in his skeletal hand under the x-ray machine. Here, too, as on a previous frightening advance on his "bad path," he finds it hard, when he speaks aloud, to pronounce the "labials." And when the color of the light from holes his stick makes in the snow recalls to him "the Tartar slits . . . of Pribislav Hippe and Clavdia Chauchat," he repeats in the stillness, "With pleasure. . . . But don't break it — *c'est à viser, tu sais*," a mingling together of what each said on lending him a pencil, and then "his spirit heard behind him words of warning in a mel- lifluous tongue" (479).

The dream he sinks into while resting against an abandoned hut can be "a dream poem of humanity" because, as he realizes when he comes out of it, we dream the way Naphta's medieval artists work, "anonymously and com- munally," and express in our dreams, if "each after his own fashion" (495-496), what is common to us all. His dream now is a recognition that — to use the words of Mann's letter — "the antinomies of the world are inherent in existence itself" and that we must say yes, not just to one side or another of that doubleness, but to both. For he sees first a movingly perfect Mediterranean people — "children of the sun" — who are beautiful and wise and whose behavior is marked by "mutual courteous regard," a "reasoned goodness conditioning every act" (492). But one of them is gazing, rigid, at a temple, and approaching it through columns that look like a forest of beeches "by the pale northern sea" (493-494) — the sea of his home! — our hero finds within two "witchlike" hags dismembering a child with bare bloody hands and cracking its bones between their teeth. They scream curses at him in the dialect of his native Hamburg —

another sign of home — and it is in his flight from this horror that he awakens, or half-awakens, by his hut in the snow.

What follow, in the thrilled clairvoyance of the half-awake which will not be remembered, is his understanding of the dream. He realizes that "the great soul of which we are a part" has dreamed through him "its own secret dream, of its youth, its hope, its joy and peace — and its blood sacrifice," and that he has earned the right to be their vehicle because in his mountain sojourn he has "known reason and recklessness . . . wandered lost with Naphta and Settembrini in high and mortal places . . . known mankind's flesh and blood" and given back "to ailing Clavdia Chauchat Pribislav Hippe's lead-pencil." Though he has learned that "he who knows the body, life, knows death," he has learned "the other side of the story" too. This side says that "all interest in disease is only another expression of interest in life . . . only a division of the great and pressing concern which, in all sympathy, I now name by its name, the human being, the delicate child of life, man, his state and standing in the universe." And having acknowledged by this use of Settembrini's phrase for him that he himself has been the representative of man and his mountain adventures of man's life, he accepts what the dream revealed, that behind mankind's "enlightened social state . . . the horrible blood sacrifice was consummated." Moreover, he declares that if those "children of the sun" were "so sweetly courteous to each other in silent recognition of that horror," it would be "fine and right," he holds with them and not with Naphta or Settembrini.

What he has grasped is that we can have our lives and all their beauties only on the horrible condition that we be greedy, lustful animals who die. The beauties are all rooted in bodily appetites which, if not controlled, produce also that horror of cannibalism and which curse in the dialect of Hamburg because it is the language ("dog eat dog") of ordinary life. ("That's why there are wars," someone said, pointing to a mother hugging her child.) And to see that the "mutual courteous regard" of those "children of the sun" comes from recognition of the horror is to oppose both Settembrini and Naphta. For the first, "forever blowing on his penny pipe of reason," is "all Philistinism and morality" and "irreligious," that is, shallow in his moralizing because he is ignorant of the horror which is part of the whole. And the second, whose religion is "only a *guazzabuglio* of God and the Devil, good and evil," seeks to lure the individual soul into "mystic immersion in the universal" because to him that soul is as nothing beside his "Absolute." Hans Castorp rejects their pedagogue's "counterpositions," their "disease, health! Spirit, nature!" in which one or the other alone is called "aristocratic." He knows now that "man is the lord of counterpositions, they can be only through him, and thus he is more aristocratic than they. More so than death, too aristocratic for death — that is the freedom of his mind. More aristocratic than life, too aristocratic for life, that is the piety of his heart" (495-496). He means that by the power of our minds, we can see beyond and control those dangerous forces in the body that lead through desire to death, and so can cling to life's goals and get "home." But by the piety of our hearts, our loyalty to that whole we can only feel, we are lifted above the partialness of life's temporal goals to enlarging contact with the eternal.

A final insight remains, however, the peak of our hero's long development and, because the drama also points in the same direction, the answer, once and for all, to those who see Mann's endless irony-that-goes-both-ways as mere nihilism. "Death," he grants, "is a great power," greater than reason, for "reason is only virtue, while death is release, immensity, abandon, desire." And as it is desire — which he next bluntly asserts is "lust, not love" — that goes with death, it is love by which death is opposed. "Only love, not reason, gives sweet thoughts. And from love and sweetness alone can form come: form and civilization, friendly, enlightened, beautiful human intercourse — always in silent recognition of the blood sacrifice." And his soaring thought comes to an end in the italicized resolve: *"For the sake of goodness and love, man shall let death have no sovereignty over his thoughts"* (496-497). What I suggested at the start should now be clear. If Mann is a nihilist with respect to ideas, smiling at the one-sidedness of them all, this irony always implies an affirmation. It is a defense against that one-sidedness of our various humanity and of the creative, form-building power of our loving response to the world.

6

It's true that from now on our hero's story becomes mainly that of the increasing moral decay of one whose "holiday" has lasted too long. But what is often overlooked is that his deathward slide is always resisted — and in the end reversed — by a loyalty to life, a "conscience" he can never quite ignore. And first we see how this saves him from yielding to the last and most seductive of the novel's idea-bearing characters, the great comic creation Peeperkorn.

Hans Castorp is ready to learn from the rich old coffee planter Clavdia brings back as his rival because Peeperkorn is not another reasoner about life but its passionate lover. He responds to all its gifts — food, drink, friendship, women — with an intensity that makes him hilariously incaple of coherent speech but that sweeps everyone along and puts the two brilliant talkers "in his pocket." Moreover, like the other major characters, he knows and can teach the meaning of what he is. So for him those gifts are "holy," and in providing and celebrating them he sees himself doing God's work in a world where such work is surrounded by dangers. These dangers are not only our physical limitations, like the drunken fatigue that puts his fellow revellers to sleep at his great orgy of food and drink and that he rebukes with a breathtaking reference to those other sleepers, who were asked, "What, could ye not watch with me one hour?" (569). They can be subtler and more terrible — they can be whatever diminishes our power to feel. For "life," he says, is "a sprawling female, with swelling breasts close together, great soft belly between her haunches, slender arms, bulging thighs, half-closed eyes" who "challenges us to expend our manhood to its uttermost span" (566). And as feeling is the "masculine force" by which life is awakened, "man is nothing but the organ through which God consummates his marriage with roused and intoxicated life"—in short (of all things!), the penis of God. To feel is therefore our "sacred duty" and to fail in feeling "is blasphemy; it is the surrender of His masculinity, a cosmic catastrophe" (603).

The younger lover's pain at the rival—and even his old passion for the woman—are soon replaced by his student's delight that "hermetic pedagogy" has given him "this too: contact with an out-and-out personality" (575), a complaisance which rather annoys the woman and quite shocks the Italian. "Personality," Mann had observed in *Reflections*, "is being, not opining" (362), and in fact, what this one teaches our hero is that beside the self-justifying vitality of "being," opinions, however clever, are pale reductions of life. But though Hans Castorp is thus liberated once and for all from the bullying of intellect and its formulas, he also learns from the other something he did not mean to teach. The worship of feeling can itself be a danger to life because it stakes too much on what passes. The danger is hinted in the "fear" (591) and "anguish" (597) our hero notices underneath those explosive intensities. And the hints are borne out when, increasingly decrepit and aware at last of Hans Castorp's relationship with Clavdia, the kingly man poisons himself—to avoid "blasphemy," our hero understands, and Clavdia calls it an "abdication" (624), that is, on behalf of the younger lover—and both are right.

But Hans Castorp has alerted us even before this to the one-sidedness of the great man's credo. Once he defends the sad makeshifts of the impotent from the other's wrathful contempt because "I incline by nature to excuses, though there is nothing 'large' about them" (567). Then, having himself attained to irony, he "respectfully" observes of Peeperkorn's resounding declaration about the organ of God that such "theology," though it ascribes to man a "highly honorable, if perhaps somewhat one-sided religious function," has its "alarming side," as does "all religious austerity . . . to people who are built on modest lines" (603). With these "small" remarks Mann's unheroic hero is affirming the allegiance that increasingly defines him—to our actual, ordinary humanity and the endless development which is our actual life. Just as what we are cannot be contained in the rising and sinking formulas of the intellect, neither is it quite the same as the passion by which, from time to time, we are spurred into growth. The reader is thus prepared for the sexless forehead kiss over Peeperkorn's deathbed by which Hans Castorp shows the woman that he is now more a "surviving member of a severed brotherhood" (627) than a lover, and for his accepting without protest, soon after, her final departure.

Still, from this point on, as I say, our hero's condition gets worse and worse. For an essential effect of the mountain spell is what happens, when growth-inducing passion is gone, to those whom it has seduced into abandoning life and its claims. They get bored. And here it must be granted that with the disappearance of the woman who lured our hero onto his "bad path" the novel also suffers a certain let-down. The experience which follows is no longer that of a man drawn by passion toward thrilling prizes of the body or the mind but precisely that of one with nothing in life to care about. It soon appears, however, that this condition too belongs to the story and that it can produce developments sufficiently urgent, dramatic and comic to be worthy of the rest. For boredom is a mild name for something that can be quite terrible, can be "demonic" (627). It is the Devil, we are reminded, who finds work for idle hands. In fact, having lost the strength of will to bring his "holiday" from life and time to an end by himself, our hero falls under the domination of the "demons and ape-headed gods" whose collective name is "The Great God Dumps" (633). While his fellow-patients devise schemes to square the circle or to solve the world's economic problems by collecting old newspapers, he simulates life by a contest with chance—he plays a form of solitaire. And, to his own secret horror, he finds himself justifying this waste of life and time to the shocked Settembrini by a "pert" repetition of that motto *"placet experiri"* which had once served his mind's growing. Moreover, it appears that all the Berghof's patients suffer from the same increasing malaise, wasting energy and feeling first in crazy fads and then in crazy mutual hostility (including crazy anti-Semitism). The Berghof becomes a more and more obvious picture of Europe, a Europe fatally detached from reality and on the eve of the "thunder-bolt" which will, at a fearful price, bring it back.

It's true that when our hero is put in charge of the Berghof's new gramophone and develops a passion for music, this seems a "nobler" way to give vitality and content to the passing hours. But if the evocations we get of his five favorite recordings eloquently convey the self-justifying experience of art, this is only to alert us to its dangers. For we are told that the harmonies "flow over him" from a "truncated little coffin of violin-wood" and that he listens as he has always listened to the enfeebling teachings of death, with "his head on one side, his mouth open" (642). Sure enough, each of those five pieces turns out to be an expression of his own condition, giving spiritual status and beauty to the sinister rejection of life. And though, in the case of Schubert's "glorious song '*Der Lindenbaum*,'" our friendly narrator anticipates the reader's indignant recoil from such "vile detraction" (652), he remains firm. Indeed, he goes further. He suggests that with this music (as can happen with other things) it is precisely uneasiness of conscience that makes for the intensity of Hans Castorp's love. And Mann incorporates into his text here, with a slight but revealing change, a rich passage from his essay "Nietzsche and Music" (1924), which asserts that music is "a fruit, sound and splendid enough for the instant or so, yet extraordinarily prone to decay; the purest refreshment of the spirit, if enjoyed at the right moment, but the next, capable of spreading decay and corruption among men" ("Nietzsche" 144-145). That is, though music *is* an overflow and celebration of life, feeling, of which it is so intimate an expression, has a dangerous tendency to life-scorning excess. This is why, as the passage taken from the essay goes on,

it was a fruit of life, conceived of death, pregnant of dissolution; it was a
miracle of the soul, perhaps the highest . . . sealed with the blessing of con-
scienceless beauty, but on cogent grounds regarded with mistrust by the eye
of shrewd geniality dutifully "taking stock" in its love of the organic [in the
essay: "by the eye of a responsible and controlling love of life"]; it was a subject
for self-conquest at the definite behest of conscience.

It is precisely our hero's inner resistance to the spell that, as he listens, his
"alchemistically enhanced thoughts" soaring "higher than his understanding"
and merging with those of his author, lifts him to a final grasp of the affirmation
which, for Mann, lies beyond all antinomies. He sees that such "soul- enchantment," the seduction by passion most powerfully practiced in music, could, in
the hands of a certain kind of popular "talent," acquire a volume by which it
could subjugate the world, found "earthly, all too earthly kingdoms, solid, 'progressive,' not at all nostalgic," but that the truly "faithful son" of that realm
"might still be he who consumed his life in self-conquest, and died, on his lips
the new word of love which as yet he knew not how to speak" (652-653). This
cryptic observation seems to me an almost explicit rejection of that German
Kultur Mann had struggled to defend in *Reflections*, as well as a prophetic an-
ticipation of its horrible Nazi form. For it is a warning against the political exploitation of inchoate feeling by which that *Kultur* had sought the power to
subjugate the world. Mann's "alter ego" affirms the primacy of "conscience,"
our obligation in matters of feeling to avoid drunken self-abandon and to submit, in the essay's words, to a "responsible and controlling love of life." But of
course, since he lacks the gorgeous confidence of Settembrini, he must end by
granting that this love has yet to find its expression — that "new word" — in
human society.

A "Seven-Sleeper" cannot, however, break out of his enchantment unaided.
Though our hero has thus taken conscious possession of the insight he had
fleetingly grasped in his dream, the "depravity" of that sinister boredom will
lead him to his blackest treason yet. It will culminate in a seance presided over
by the "pathological idealist" Dr. Krokowski, in which Hans Castorp asks the
medium to bring back his late cousin. This "scandalous lying-in" (678) — the
living woman laboring to give birth to the dead — he defends against Settembrini with the opinion Mann himself put forward in "An Experiment in the Occult" (1929), that such things too must be counted among nature's possibilities.[9] Still, it's clear that the attempt to bypass life's normal limits is presented
as an action peculiarly shameful. We see this not only in the humanist's indignant reminder of man's duty and "creative right" (667), to make distinctions
among those possibilities, moral and other kinds, but also in the agony of
remorse with which, when Joachim does reappear in the half-darkness, our
hero leaps up — himself at last his own Settembrini — to end that traffic with
death by putting on the light. And it is because of just this all-surviving allegiance to life that the "thunderbolt" of war can save him.

That he is saved at the end we are virtually told as well as shown. For he is described as a "Seven-Sleeper . . . released . . . from enchantment by exterior powers" that bring about his "liberation," and as raising his arms to "a heaven that however dark and sulphurous was no longer the gloomy grotto of his state of sin" (711). Then, Settembrini embraces him as he departs to join his countrymen, calling him Giovanni for the first time, even though his pupil will now become his enemy. Surely this is because he is going home out of the same life-serving fellowship with the human community the Italian has always preached.[10]

True, we catch our last glimpse of Hans Castorp carrying a bayonet amid exploding shells which leave his survival in doubt. His saving human loyalty has its bloody side! But this final image of the novel is also a final version of the doubleness of his dream in the snow. For as he runs he is singing under his breath some verses from that "glorious song" "*Der Lindenbaum.*" And though on the mountain the song was an example of the deathward lure of the beauty of music, we were not permitted to forget even there that it too has another side. Sure enough, he sings among the bullets of the "loving words" the song's Wanderer carves into the tree. And reminding us of the "dream of love" which came to his hero once before "out of death and the rebellion of the flesh," our narrator ends his tale with the prayer-like question — more than a question it cannot be — whether from this "universal feast of death . . . Love one day shall mount" (716).

So the great work of Mann's prime rises above its own antinomies. Acknowledging the "blood-sacrifice" that belongs to our humanity, it has also reaffirmed the allegiance at the heart of his youthful *Tonio Kröger*, that bourgeois love of the human — of life — which, through the whole of his long career, was the source of both his thought and his art.

Notes

1. Oscar Seidlin, in his excellent essay "Mynheer Peeperkorn and the Lofty Game of Numbers," thus sums up the traditional idea Mann took over and used in his own way, the idea of the combination in 7 of 3 and 4: "3 is the Trinity, the divine and the noumenal; 4 is the earth, with its four corners, seen under this symbol all through the ages" (Bloom, 186).

2. Erich Heller prefers to translate *"ein Sorgenkind des Lebens* as "a problem child of life" (Heller, 174).

3. Lowe-Porter has thus found perfectly adequate duplications of Mann's echoing leitmotif here, for in the original the early phrase is *"mit eine ehrbaren Verfinsterung der Miene"* and the later one, *"physiognomisch drückte es sich aus in einer ehrbaren Verfinsterung seiner Miene."* (*Der Zauberberg* [Germany: S. Fischer Verlag, 1966], pp. 44 and 54.)

4. Hermann Weigand, who accepted Lowe-Porter's version most of the time

in his book on the novel, preferred to translate *"der geniale Weg"* as "the way of genius" (6). But note that the French word *spirituel* points in the same direction.

5. Mann's characters and events should perhaps be regarded as samples of reality rather than symbols of it. As samples of the reality they represent, they are real and symbolic at the same time.

6. Since completing this chapter I have discovered in the work of Mikhail Bakhtin an account of Dostoevsky's "polyphonic" fiction which is applicable to the art of Mann and which issues in a startlingly exact formulation of what Mann satirizes in Settembrini. For Bakhtin, Dostoevsky's fiction succeeds in mirroring the actual complexity of intellectual life in the world because it presents ideas, not as right or wrong, but as expressions of character, and as emerging and developing out of conflict. Moreover, this conflict of ideas also goes on within us. It follows that to do justice to the reality available to the human mind takes many points of view — "dialogue," not "monologue" — and that such justice is a process which never ends. This insight into the "dialogic principle" as required by *"the eternally unfinalizable something in man"* (his emphasis), who "never coincides with himself" (Bakhtin, 58-59), leads to a critique of the life-reducing "monologic principle" which points straight to Mann's own man of reason. "The consolidation of monologism and its permeation into all spheres and [of?] ideological life was promoted in modern times by European rationalism with its cult of a unified and exclusive reason, and especially by the Enlightenment, during which time the basic generic forms of European artistic prose took shape. All of European utopianism was likewise built on this monologic principle. Here too belongs socialism, with its faith in the omnipotence of the conviction" (Bakhtin, 82).

7. Here is an English version of the French on this and the following page,

p. 63: *"C'est parler,"* etc. "It is to speak without responsibility, as one speaks in dreams."

"la morale." "morality."

"Les grands moralists," etc. "The great moralists are precisely not men of virtue, but . . . great sinners, who teach us to bow as Christians before suffering."

"Nous sommes," etc. "We are perhaps, quite simply, delicate children of life."

p. 64 *"le Toi de ma vie,"* etc. "the Thou of my life, my dream, my fate, my longing, my eternal desire."

"Allons!" etc. "My goodness! If your teachers could see you."

"Je m'en fiche," etc. "I laugh at it! I laugh at . . . the eloquent Republic and human progress in time, because I love you!"

"Petit bourgeois," etc. "Little bourgeois . . . pretty bourgeois with the small damp spot. . . . Is it true that you love me so much?"

"sainte merveille," etc. "sacred marvel of form and beauty [which is] more educational than all the pedagogy in the world."

8. There is a passage about the art of Pfitzner's music drama *Palestrina* in *Reflections* which conveys, no doubt deliberately, Mann's own performing magician's ideal of art, as well as his sense of the artistic possibilities of ideas. Mann speaks of the "unification" and "deepening" provided by the "Wagnerian motif," the dazzling effect of climaxes exceeded by greater ones, which have been prepared by the "exquisite, permissable, yes, imperative and enthusiastic cleverness, circum-

spection and politics of art," and the highly "entertaining" effect of showing "life in the light of thought," the detail acquiring "dramatic tension" by means of the idea which "speaks through it" (293-301).

9. Mann allowed himself a departure from strict realism in this scene about which he later expressed certain misgivings. Joachim returns wearing a helmet which Germans were to wear in the coming war, a bit of foreshadowing even Mann's broadmindedness was not ready to accept among nature's infinite possibilities.

10. It now occurs to me that this return of Hans Castorp may be a hidden metaphor for what his author had done when he wrote *Reflections*. Didn't the same impulse of human fellowship draw the non-political man down from *his* mountain to the same community? I wouldn't put it past Mann's bottomless slyness to have intended such a final identification with his "alter ego."

CHAPTER SIX

Joseph and His Brothers

"A man who does not grasp the fact . . . that spirit and matter, soul and body, thought and extension or . . . will and movement are the necessary twin ingredients of the universe . . . have equal rights and may therefore be considered in their togetherness as the representatives of God — he who has not grasped this might as well employ his days with the idle rumors of the world." Goethe (*A Man*, v. 2, 200)

"Religious symbolism is a cultural treasure house wherein we have a perfect right to dip when we need [to] use familiar images to make visible some aspect of spirit." (*The Beloved Returns*, 369)

"Good God, how old they had got!" the 40-year-old Joseph thinks as he looks at the brothers he last saw when he was 17. "It was very moving," we are told by Mann's narrator-guide to the old tale's original or lived version, "as all life is moving" (1059). Then, after the great climax of this reunion, when our narrator suspects his audience of getting restless because "we know how it turns out already" and there is nothing exciting left to hear, "Take my word for it," he assures us, "you are wrong." Jacob will soon put his arms around the best-loved son he had thought dead — "there is nothing thrilling in that?" he demands. "We know already! But that is a foolish thought. Anybody can know the story. To have been there is the thing" (1119). Thus the author himself answers the natural question, What's the excuse for turning the 50-some pages of Genesis, long regarded as beautiful in their economy, as well as in other respects, into a vast epic of four volumes, one of them the size of two, and, in the English version, of 1,207 pages?[1]

Mann's excuse — or a large part of it — is that he wanted to put us there. He wanted to make out of that highly condensed story of the Jewish discoverers and first servants of God a novel that would convince, grip and move us as a story of real people in a real world. He has succeeded. *Joseph and His Brothers*, whatever else it is, is a great realistic novel. In retelling the old story for twentieth-century readers, Mann has revealed between its lines, has drawn

80

from the masses of post-Biblical legends,[2] and has invented outright whatever its portentous developments needed to make us feel they had to happen. They take place in an ancient world that is vividly and solidly evoked, and they rise out of the kind of characters we find most persuasive, characters driven by multiple and contradictory motives, and by motives often hidden not only from others, but from themselves. Then the novel is funny, as well as moving. "Just because it is so solemn," Joseph tells his steward as, like his own author, he artfully sets up the climactic reunion to come, "it must be treated with a light touch. For lightness, my friend, flippancy, the artful jest, that is God's very best gift to man, the profoundest knowledge we have of that complex, questionable thing we call life" (1056). Though Mann thus (indirectly) says it himself, as he sooner or later forestalls his critics by saying everything, he also does it. And finally, the story is powerfully, even theatrically, dramatic. Not only are all the well-known events linked together as causes or effects of one great development. That development, beginning as threats or promises implicit in character and unfolding in steadily intensifying crescendos, passes through a succession of climaxes in which, stage by stage, every threat or promise is explosively fulfilled.

But again Mann's drama of feeling is one with a drama of thought. His chief characters are still highly intelligent and articulate. Then, like *The Magic Mountain*, only more so, this story is told by a friendly narrator who, in spite of his own (comical) tendency to agitation, is forever deepening our awareness of its meaning. And what now carries Mann even further toward the philosophic — one can say the religious — is the shift in his subject from "the middle class and the individual" to "the typical and the mythic" (*Letters*, 231), which is to say, to the great grapplings of Genesis with the fundamental human questions. Of course, Mann's irony persists: a chief pleasure of the novel is the continual shimmer of "diplopy" (*Doppelsichtige*), as he now calls it (601), the double-seeing that brings the low and the lofty together. But again the irony turns out to be ultimately affirmative. In this version of the old tale we are shown how the "thinking out" of God is a way of doing justice to life, the way of genius, and how, through these Jewish myths or "stories," man lifts himself by his own bootstraps, organizing upward, toward life, the dangerous chaos of his possibilities.[3]

As for the novel's protagonist, every reader of Mann will recognize the dreamer whose irrepressible superiority and self-delight divides him painfully from his "regular" brothers, lifts him above them, and bears fruit which enriches their lives.[4] But if Joseph is another version of the artist, the artist is now revealed to be a version of Joseph. In dramatizing again, and more brilliantly and fully than ever before, what the artist is and how he suffers and learns and "cons" the world and serves it, Mann shows him, too, as an heir of Abraham, Isaac and Jacob, and the faithful servant in his own way of the God at the center of their lives. We may well be amazed at how Mann unites his permanent "egocentric" subject and Genesis without violating what is essential in each.

To see how much meaning Mann uncovered in the old story, and this without failing (or rarely failing) to keep it alive as fiction, we will go over certain parts of the novel in detail.

1. "Prelude": The Meaning of Myth

The book of Genesis is about a people who seem remote from us because myth is for them a living language, a language of symbolic events and relationships, of categories and values by which they understand and direct their lives. But the purpose of the novel's thirty-page "Prelude" (its "pseudo-scientific foundation," Mann called it [*Letters*, 157]) is not only to introduce us to that antique language. It is also to remind us that myth is a permanent element in our way of coping with the world.

We are shown first that myth is the inevitable goal of any search for beginnings. For as our guide leads us "downward" toward Joseph and the history that shaped him, it turns out we have entered a bottomless well, in which each apparent beginning becomes a "coulisse" or channel to others more remote, until we find ourselves among legends and stop — since we can't go on forever — at what answers our need. We find too that legends — or myths — live on because the human types and relationships they preserve are rooted in the eternal nature of humanity and continually recur. Since exactly this is true of the "myths" of fiction, we need not be surprised when, in the quickening emotion of our guide's arrival at his "dusty-stony Mediterranean goal," he describes the "hell" into which we have followed him in terms that recall *The Magic Mountain* and other Mann works opposing the abnormal consciousness of the artist to the healthy unconsciousness of those actively engaged in life.

We have descended, he says, into the "the dead-and-gone world" where the "story-teller," tasting of "death and knowledge," confronts "the essence of life," the eternal "presentness" hidden inside "the time-forms of past and future . . . in which life reveals itself to the folk." And what he seeks in this "dead-and-gone world," as "Ishtar there sought Tammuz and Isis Osiris," is "the first and last of all our questioning and speaking and all our necessity, the nature of man." Moreover, the tale told in myth "*is*, it always *is* , however much we may say It was." And as myth is "the garment of the mystery," its "holiday garment . . . is the feast, the recurrent feast which bestrides the tenses and makes the has-been and the to-be present to the popular sense" (32-33). Obviously, this an effect of fiction as well, for instance, of the novel we are now beginning. And here we come on a chief reason for the narrator-guide whom we have already heard breaking into his own story with such comical intensity and whose living voice will lighten the novel's heavy burden of thought. This voice, that of a fellow human being whose emotions keep contending with his story-teller's "objectivity," becomes virtually a character in the novel, or just outside it, in order to dramatize the fact that what we are reading is not Genesis, but Genesis in the "feast," its events being freshly experienced by one of ourselves, though far more learned than we, and that what they teach is still true.

The point is later dramatized and extended in Joseph's teacher Eliezer, who seems to be regarded by himself, as well as Jacob, as identical with the Eliezer whom Abraham begot on a slave woman long ago. And though it is as "clear as day-light" that he is not, yet "daylight is one thing and moonlight is another . . . and it might be the clearness of the moon which would appeal to the spirit as the truer clarity." Speaking of Eliezer in this "lunar syntax," Jacob means not only both Abraham's and the present one, but "*the* Eliezer altogether," that is, the essential Eliezer-type, quite as Eliezer does when he describes experiences which "actually" belonged to another as his own. But "just what do we mean by actually?" our narrator asks, and he goes on to suggest that our current insistence on our individuality is itself only a convention, and one which ignores all that binds "the individual consciousness to the general" (77-78). We have been reminded that we too walk, though unaware, in the footsteps of archetypes and that myth teaches us not only what man was, but also what he may be. The many duplications of type and event in Genesis will in fact be seen as examples of how mankind shapes itself on the past. As for the models that will shape the life of his enormously conceited hero, our guide prepares us for them by a "casual" reference to two myths of resurrection. The first is that of the "World-saving Babe" his story prefigures, Who "every Christmas is born anew and lies in the cradle, destined to suffer, to die and to arise again." The second is the older myth of the god known variously as Tammuz, Osiris or Adonis (he will reappear later as the corn-king Usir) in whose feast the boy Joseph periodically relived "the murder of the lamented Son, the youthful god . . . and his resurrection" (19-23).

But our search for beginnings must carry us to another source than the past and its legacy of archetypes, than the culture into which we are born. That source is the creative human mind. This is the meaning of the mysterious Schopenhauer-like observation in the "Prelude" that the history of man is "older than the material world which is the work of his will, older than life, which rests upon his will" (23). The world we live in could not have existed before us because it is the world as we perceive it, and since what we are and will determines how we see, they must come first. It is because the novel's deepest theme is precisely the connection between the creative power of the mind and the central myth of Western Culture that the "Prelude" virtually begins with the story of Abraham's discovery of God. And the way our narrator presents its defining elements shows how the subject will be treated throughout the novel.

He employs the religious language of the Bible with all due respect, but insinuates at the same time the discovery's psychic origin and secular meaning. So, what drove Abraham out of Ur was "unrest of the spirit" born of a pride that would not bow down to any power lower than "that god upon whose image his spirit laboured, highest among all the rest . . . the God of the Ages." It is in this unrest of spirit that Abraham "heard" God's famous promise, for we are told that when he compared his state with that of "the great majority," he realized that his unrest was "pregnant with the future," that it would "fructify many souls . . . make proselytes like to the sands of the sea," and "give impulse to great expansions of life hidden in it as in a seed" (5-6). We learn finally that Abraham's God, "in whose will inscrutable, great, far-reaching things were in process of becoming . . . was Himself only in process of becoming," and that He was therefore a God "for whom one must at all times keep oneself free, mobile and in readiness" (31). In short, Abraham's "unrest" is that of genius, and it is pregnant with the future not only because the future grows out of the ideas of creative genius, but because his pride refuses to stop at any fixed or limiting conception of the power underlying the whole. The expanding "life" which results from such unrest and such pride and which leads, not to one or another final conclusion, but to ever further "becoming," is the ruling value of Mann's whole career.

"How Abraham Found God," the more detailed account of Abraham's discovery, is put off for good reason to the narrative of Joseph's education. But our guide concludes his foundation-laying "Prelude" by adapting a Kabbalistic myth of God's creation of man and the world which hints at the connection between His nature and Joseph's strangely checkered career. It is a myth, he says, which comes from an ancient tradition of thought "based on man's truest knowledge of himself." But it "obviously . . . requires filling out" because it issues in a contradiction which may conceal an allusion to certain "mysterious decrees of God . . . considered by the teachers and preachers as too holy and inscrutable to be uttered." It is a story of the "first completely human man, the Hebraic *Adam Qadman*, who was created to serve as God's champion in the struggle against the evil penetrating the new creation, but who became enamored of his own image mirrored in matter, descended to it and "fell in bondage to lower nature." Out of pity for this "primevally human soul" (23-27) God created the world of forms on which it could gratify its desire. But after this comes the puzzling contradiction. It seems that when God sent a "spirit" down to draw the soul back to its higher home, the spirit, seduced by the world, betrayed its mission. And what makes this puzzling is first the suspicion that God would certainly have foreseen the betrayal, and then a hint in the story that the "soul" which clings to the world and the "spirit" which is sent to draw it back to God are two aspects of one being. The secret too "holy" to be uttered would seem to be that of God's complicity with the spirit's treason!

Sure enough, we are told that it is not God but His angels who are "the kingdom of the stern." They keep asking, "What is man, O Lord, that Thou art mindful of him?" because they detect in God's creation of a living world of good and evil evidence of "a certain disgust with their own psalm-chanting purity." Now, the polarities of good and evil will be accompanied in this novel, as they were in *The Magic Mountain*, by those of life and death — life involving the human mind's work to shape the future, and death its respect for the "holy" past. In the grand conclusion of the "Prelude," our guide tells us that "these mysteries deal very freely with the tenses," that "the saying, soul and spirit *were* one, really means that they are sometime to become one," and that the spirit, which is "detached from the world"—as moral judge concerned to make it better—is "the principle of the future and represents the It will be," while the "form-bound soul," which is "involved with nature"—i.e., is the lover of what exists and so of the past it naturally came from—represents "the past and the holy It was." And though each claims to be "the water of life" and "accuses the other of dealings with death," the truth may be that "the mystery, and the unexpressed hope of God lie in their union . . . in the interpenetration of both principles, in a hallowing of the one through the other which should bring about a present humanity blessed with blessings from heaven above and from the depths beneath" (28-29). This is the novel's first echo of Jacob's deathbed description in Genesis of his best-loved son, that he would be blessed—which our guide tells us actually means *was* blessed—with "blessings of the heavens above, blessings of the deep which lieth under" (Gen. 49:25). We have been forewarned that Joseph's story, like that of Hans Castorp, will show those opposing "principles"—and again they will also appear as spirit and flesh—as inextricably entangled with each other. And in the doubleness by which they are reconciled Mann has given us the key to both the Hebrew God and the nature of the artist.

To begin with, the Kabbalistic myth has reminded us of a doubleness—indeed, a contradiction—in the Hebrew conception of God. For (to back Mann up with quotations he didn't happen to use) though He calls on His people to be righteous and to "choose life, that both thou and thy seed may live" (Deut. 30:9), He also declares: "I form the light, and create darkness: I make peace and create evil: I the Lord do all these things" (Isaiah 45:7). In fact, the contradiction is inherent in human experience. It is the conflict between the necessary narrowness of the moral impulse, which chooses life but says no to death and evil, and the many-sided awareness which sees them as inter-related parts of the whole. And it is because this conflict will receive its richest embodiment in the relationship between Jacob, who serves God as a moralist, and Joseph, who serves Him as an artist, that the "Prelude" closes with a glimpse of the profound difference between them.

Of Jacob we are told that the temperament and calling bequeathed to him by Abraham—"disquiet . . . a bitterly sceptical laboring over the true and the just, the whence and the whither, his own name, his own nature, the true meaning of the Highest"—has stamped on his brow the "unrest and dignity" which are "the sign of the spirit" and made God Himself seem to Joseph only "a higher replica of his father." Of Joseph we are told that he derived from his mother a nature, "blither and freer . . . conversable, social," while the consciousness of his father's special love, to him a guarantee of God's, resulted in "a sense of consecration, an austere bond, and with it a flow of fantasy which may have been the decisive ingredient of his mental inheritance" (30-31). In short, though Joseph reveres his father's moral "nobility," he is himself too "blithe" to share it, and his sense that he is specially loved by Jacob—and so by God—not only creates in him his own bond with the Highest but sets him free for the play with reality (the "fantasy") of the artist. That blessing from above and below will become Joseph's leitmotif because it is also Mann's formula for the artist's sympathy with both sides of life's eternal antinomies, a doubleness which will give him a deeper understanding of God than Jacob's, but which the father, though he finds it disturbingly seductive, will never approve.

It is in order to put their conflict before us alive and to hint at its deepest implications that Mann begins the novel itself with the great dialogue between Jacob and Joseph at the well.

2. "Overture" at the Well

Jacob's 17-year-old darling, having been driven off by his irritated brothers, is sitting half-naked beside a well, and abandoning himself, to the point of a slight seizure, to incantations and gestures to the moon. When the father discovers him there, his worried question "Is my child sitting there by the well?" (42) has a deeper cause than appears at first. It seems that the tribe's religious leader is given to "association of thought," to seeing the hidden meaning of what is before him. And because his son's pagan behavior beside a *well* has brought into his mind ideas of the "lower world," with its seductive filth, and of the descent of the boar-mangled Tammuz, he soon bursts into horrified warnings against the practices of the "monkey-land of Egypt," where people dress in obscenely transparent clothing, worship beasts, and give themselves up to bestial lusts because "they have . . . neither word nor understanding for that which is sin" (60). With that, like a shaft of light thrown on the road ahead, the idea emerges by which Mann will illuminate the story of Joseph in Egypt and unite it with his own. Egypt will be to Joseph what the magic mountain was to Hans Castorp, the realm of the body, of sex, of death, and Joseph's Egyptian adventure will be the result, not simply of his brothers' anger, but also of an Egyptian tendency of his nature the father does well to rebuke.

But Jacob, we are told, had "two passions in life: God and Rachel," which, we know, became God and Joseph. Indeed, our narrator grants that the partiality for Joseph of this "too-much feeling man" would seem blameworthy if it were not encouraged in him by "God's own intemperance" and a way He had "of preferring this one and that one" which, "humanly speaking, [was] often unjust" (51). It is this partiality that now plunges the man of God into the agonized "muse" or fantasy which, when he confesses it to his son, takes us to the heart of his inner conflict and of the religion that imposes it. He has remembered Abraham's heroic readiness to sacrifice his son to God and has realized that "my love was stronger than my faith" (60), and that he, at such a command, would deny the Lord. His faith will turn out to be stronger than he knows. But his conscious mind is now tormented by the guilt of his conscious weakness. And this climax of the novel's opening presentation of Jacob will lead to another in its first picture of his son, which will place before us the artist's deepest nature and role.

The boy begins by cleverly defending those "sinful" values of the Egyptian "underworld," then shows the same wit in grasping those of his unhappy father, and at last finds a way to interpret Jacob's fantasy that wonderfully heals him of guilt. In that refusal to sacrifice his son, Jacob was not denying the Lord, but obeying him! For it was He Who had substituted a ram for Isaac. Jacob had rejected the human sacrifice, which could only have been demanded by "Melech, the Bull-God of Baalim" (67), out of the humanity which had come to distinguish the Jewish God from His pagan predecessors.

Where, asks the thrilled father, did the boy get this power to utter truth (not the whole truth, only a part, for Jacob has already learned, as we will see, that God is not simply humane), and to do so with "graciousness" and "wit" that make it "a delight to the understanding and a balsam to the heart." In the euphoria of his triumph, Joseph replies to that fundamental question with a flood of astrological and religious lore that conveys plainly enough a fundamental answer. In brief, it is that he got from his parents contradictory blessings — like Tonio Kröger! From the father, who was born when the sun was at its zenith, came the "daylight" blessing of conscious, disciplined reason. From Rachel, who went early into the underworld, came the blessing of the moon, which represents not only the Virgin (a fact that will later join other suggestive hints of the story of Jesus), but also "Thoth, the writer of tablets," who "speaketh between things for their good and promoteth intercourse," and who, because of his own tangled myth, could "play the go-between twixt paternal and maternal inheritance, keep the balance between father- and mother-power, and blithely reconcile the blessings of the day with the blessings of the night." But the intoxication of his father's praise now carries the boy to a prophetic intensity that renews Jacob's uneasiness. Not only does he dare to foresee for himself "a share in the events of the kingdoms of the earth and the administration of authority." He goes on to hint that he will be among those whose "brow drippeth with oil" from the tree of life in the "garden of the world," whose "eyes are drunken with the shining of red wine" from the figs on the garden's other tree, that of knowledge and death, and whose words will be "a brightness and a laughing and a consolation to the peoples, and will show them a ram in the thicket for a sacrifice unto the Lord instead of the firstborn son, so that they are healed of tormenting fear" (67-69).

What we have been told is that it is with the "wit" of the "writer of tablets" — the artist — that Joseph healed the agonizing conflict in his father between his human nature and his aspiration to serve the Highest. And that second echo of Joseph's double blessing helps us see how the artist works. His gift is to promote intercourse between things for their good, between what is "above" and "below" (spirit and body, reason and feeling), and also between the artist himself and the world. It is because Joseph wanted to free his father from life-crippling guilt and also to win his grateful indulgence for himself, and because he had the "wit" to find in the story of Abraham's sacrifice what would serve the "good" of both, that he arrived at his insight into the story's meaning, the new humanity of God. He had seen that the will of God—what is right—changes as human beings change. And here, since Mann has expressed very clearly himself this key idea of the novel, and of his whole career, it may be useful to set it down in his own words.

Speaking in a letter of his sympathy with the call to safeguard "the springs of progress," he notes that this might also be seen as "a kind of religious spirit which consists in obedience to and constant regard for the changing aspect of truth." And he goes on:

> In the still largely misunderstood Joseph novels, I used the term *Gottes-klugheit*—meaning man's prudence in uniting his will with that of God and not insisting on remaining in states "which He wishes us to go beyond." I call such obstinacy *Gottesdummheit*, stupidity before God, a state which necessarily leads to catastrophe, and in which ultimately there is a longing for catastrophe as a way out [*Letters*, 545].

We will see later that *Gottesklugheit* can also require us to resist change when it is too brutal and too fast and so becomes itself a force which cripples rather than liberates. Enough to say here that what Mann means by the word is the power to sense the changing character of reality, that is, of man and his world and the relationship between them, and thereby to free us from inappropriate ideas; and that for him it is precisely this power which is the defining gift of the artist. Joseph's passionate conclusion is thus true insight, not mere magical prophecy. What he has seen is that such power is at bottom an allegiance to life. How would it not be useful to his fellows in the "events of the kingdoms of the earth" and, even more important, in their souls, where it sets "brightness" and "laughing"—sets life—where before was the "tormenting fear" of death? The myth of the ram in the thicket, which is to say, of the new humanity of God, has become a metaphor for the religious—the humane—function of art.

3. Jacob

The novel's first two volumes, about Jacob and his "lamb" and the events that bring about their death-like separation, uncover a shocking secret. It is that father and son "together . . . brought the lamb to the pit," that is, to the dry well into which the dreamer was flung by his raging brothers. And though it will turn out that what impelled them both to the follies that led to the disaster was a persistent fidelity to God, we are never permitted to forget the low origin of their high allegiance. The first-born blessing, for instance, that Jacob finagled away from his elder brother Esau turns out to be merely the brains and industry by which the natural winner profits from opportunities the loser passes by. Even worse, Mann dares to reveal that Jacob's famous encounters with God were fantasy-consolations born of humiliation. Borrowing from the rabbis a legend of how Esau's son Eliphaz pursued his fleeing uncle in order to kill him, Mann added the detail that Jacob saved his "precious covenanted life for God and the future" only by groveling, weeping and begging, that is, by "the loss of the man's whole honor" (90). It was "straightway after the degradation," our guide points out, that Jacob had his great vision of the ladders full of ascending and descending angels with the Lord above promising him what He had promised Abraham, that his seed would be numberless and he would be "blessed before all." This vision was erected, we are told, by a soul "humbled, yet smiling privily in its abasement . . . for its own strength and consolation in the space of its dream." And when he awoke, he wept for joy, "laughing the while at the thought of Eliphaz" (90-92). As for the night-long wrestling match at Jabok Ford by which Jacob later won another blessing and the new name of Israel from a mysterious stranger, this dream came to him, our guide informs us, while he was awaiting his reunion with Esau in "actual bodily fear" (58).

But of course, if Mann's realism comically deflates those "heaven-sent" blessings, it also establishes them anew on a basis the tale's current readers will find easier to accept. It does so even with Jacob's fantasies of God's special favor. For these lift the fearful man to genuine spiritual leadership through his struggle, amid life's worst terrors, to live up to them and to reconcile the contradiction they present between God's love and His cruelty.

The pain of that struggle is real. "Lord, what dost thou?" (257), he asks as Rachel is dying of Benjamin's agonizing birth; and later, in his grief over the loss of Joseph, he turns against God altogether. With the nihilism of despair, he replies to the soothings of Eliezer, that repository of the tribe's God-led history, by ridiculing his servant's claim to be the Eliezer of Abraham, which is to say, by scorning as irrational folly the mythical ("moonlight") ways of thought which for him and his people give meaning to life. But though suffering may temporarily estrange the patriarch from God, it ends by teaching him to know God better. And since in Mann this always means to know better the reality called by His name, the account of Jacob in his agony becomes a demonstration of the secular meaning of God's savage inhumanity and of the Hebrew acceptance of it.

Jacob learns, to begin with, that his is a "jealous God," Who punishes "unbridled indulgence in arbitrary favoritism" because "He regards [it] as His sole prerogative." And if, adds our guide, this idea of God's "petty and passionate" jealousy offends us, we are free to think of it as a "relic, spiritually unabsorbed, of earlier and less disciplined stages in the development of the divine essence" (219-22). He is thus reminding us of certain facts we have already been given about the name Israel. It was originally the name of a savage desert people who worshipped a "fire-breathing, storm-breeding warrior [god]" called Yahu and who, living in terror of their lives, warded off the god's violence by rites which included male circumcision. "Drawn into the orbit" of Abraham's "spiritual speculations," we were told, this people "not only strengthened the physical basis of the Chaldean's religious tradition, but also contributed elements of their own devastating deity to nourish the conception of the divine essence which was struggling toward realization through the spirit of mankind, to which, indeed, Osiris of the East, Tammuz, as well as Adonai, the mutilated son and shepherd of Melchizedec and his Schechemites, had also given colour and substance" (83-84).

It is God's murderous jealousy, our guide now goes on, that makes so terribly binding the covenant between God and man. For "the bond of God with the human spirit active in Abram"[7] rose out of an impulse toward "mutual sanctification" of which it is impossible to know whether its source was man or God. That is, God needed us for this sanctification as much as we needed Him. "God's command to men: 'Be holy, even as I am holy!' . . . really means, 'Let me become sanctified in thee and be thou also sanctified.'" It is because "God only attains His true dignity by the aid of the human spirit and . . . man . . . only becomes worthy by contemplation of the actuality of God and its reference to himself" that there exists between them a "connubial" relation. And it is this relation which accounts for God's insistence that He alone is entitled to the extravagant passion felt by Jacob for Rachel and Joseph, that for human beings to love in this way anyone but Himself is idolatry and forbidden. Nor have we a right to object to a God so passionate in punishment. For "only in passion," our guide concludes, "does the turbulent word of 'the living God' rightly test and fulfil itself." This is why, "after we have heard the whole story, we shall realize that Joseph, however much his weakness injured him, possessed more understanding of the livingness of God, and knew better how to take skilled cognizance of it, than his father who begot him" (210-211).

What we have been told is that the divine is a developing human conception of the nature of reality, of the power which expresses itself in the great whole of which we are a part. As such, it retains among its elements those aspects of reality which were reflected in earlier myths of that region. In particular, it retains the savagery reflected in Yahu, for the universe in its endless unfolding — the "living God" — is no less "passionate," its "word" no less "turbulent," to us than it was to our primitive forebears. So, in entering into that covenant with a God Who does destroy those we love, Who does make us suffer for loving them more than the whole, man has bound himself to accept — revere — that whole in its *doubleness*, as both holy and terrible. This is why, though Jacob's "Lord, what dost Thou?" over the dying Rachel is not answered, the human spirit then shows in him its "glory." For "in this silence, it does not depart from God, but rather learns to grasp the majesty of the ungraspable." While the Chaldean women and slaves chant their litanies over

Rachel, "thinking to bind to human wishes the unreasoning powers . . . Jacob had never yet so clearly understood as in this hour why all that was false, and why Abram had left Ur to escape it. The vision vouchsafed him into this immensity was full of horror but also of power; his labour upon the godhead . . . made in this awful night a progress not unconnected with Rachel's agonies" (257). It is true that Joseph will understand God's "passion and turbulence" better than his father because, as our tale hinted long before, the artist is more open to life in its doubleness than the one-sided, righteousness-seeking moralist. But the "glory" man's spirit does achieve in Jacob—glory still, even if Joseph will go further—is that of realizing what Job too will realize, that the great whole acts for reasons beyond the grasp of man, who is only a part, and that it is due to our own self-respect not to pretend it is smaller than it is, but to say yes to it in all its majesty and terror.

Mann's "midrash" will also find meaning in Jacob's terrible second bereavement. It will not only show us how culpable folly can be one with a deep-lying fidelity to God, but will answer in the process a question Genesis has left us with: Why did the father send his "lamb" off to the brothers in Schechem—and even let him go with that maddening many-colored coat—when he had to know of their murderous hatred? The answer lies in what Mann has "discovered" about the famous coat. As with all his "discoveries," this one illuminates the old story, turns it into a single sequence of related events, and links it to Mann's own life-time concerns. Once a princess's rich veil, the colorful fabric had been bought by Laban for Rachel, and then used to disguise Leah on the night of the deceptive marriage. In this gift to Joseph of so significant a family heirloom, the brothers rightly divined Jacob's secret intentions of making "the first-born of Rachel the first-born of them all" (276) and giving the blessing to him.[8] And it is because the rage that drove them with their sheep to far-off Schechem shocks Jacob into guilt, and even fear, that he sends Joseph on the journey to bring them his greetings.

It turns out, however, that under that motive is a deeper one the father could not have borne to know in full consciousness. The dark truth our guide conveys first in hints and at last openly is that in sending Joseph to his brothers, the remorseful and frightened idolator is actually repeating the sacrifice of Abraham he once thought beyond his strength: he is taking the risk of offering his son up to God. And it is because he remembers well the murderous rage of the brothers he seemed to forget that, until Joseph is restored to him, he will suspect that they, and not the wild beast all agree to blame, destroyed his son.

And yet! "If only the father could have faith beyond death according to the ancient hope," Joseph will later think in the pit where the brothers have thrown him, ". . . the blood of the beast would be taken, as once it had been, for the blood of the son" (391). He means that somewhere in Jacob's mind, in the degree of his faith, the hope of Abraham's last-minute reprieve might well accompany the terror of the sacrifice. If so, though Jacob will never know this consciously, but will have to suffer as people do in the sorrowful days of the "feast," will have to believe that the lost one is gone forever, his act of faith will also be rewarded. He will learn at last that the blood he saw on that coat was indeed the blood of a beast God had taken in place of the son. And as in those pagan myths he remains aware of "not with his mind, but with his feelings" (58), the sacrificed son will return not only alive, but in glory.

4. Young Joseph

We see two contradictory things going on in our hero's early years. On the one hand, his special gifts and the ambition necessary for their fulfillment are being forged. On the other, the self-love that goes with such gifts is bringing down upon him a deserved and eye-opening punishment. The subject of the second volume is the unfolding and interplay of these typical aspects of the artist's boyhood, and its underlying idea is that each is essential to the triumph to come; they are the two sides of one coin.

Genesis has established the fact that Joseph was not only a remarkably prophetic dreamer and dream-interpreter, but also remarkably "well-favored." So in Mann's version the boy reaches a dangerous extreme of conceit and his brothers of envy because he combines in a god-like way the usually separate gifts of beauty and intelligence. Moreover, this combination shapes his inner life. "The "treasured idea" or "secret passion" which "more or less consciously" sustains the "vital sense of life" in all of us is in him the conviction that body and spirit belong together, and that "the consciousness of the body and beauty must be improved and strengthened through the consciousness of the mind and spirit, as well as the other way around." Such devotion to body and spirit as a unit is a "cult," we are told, "prone to degenerate," but for that very reason "intoxicating, because mental and physical emotions were therein so enchantingly mixed" (273-274). We were shown the danger of this enchanting mixture in the story of Gustave von Aschenbach, and its power to educate, as well as destroy, in that of Hans Castorp. When Mann's Joseph goes to Egypt, we will see how the artist faithful to his calling avoids, if only by a hair, the danger of domination by either body or spirit alone, and so becomes a joy-bringing mediator of their conflict in the world.

But natural gifts are not enough. Having been confirmed and directed in his outrageous conceit by those myths of gods who go below and rise in glory, Joseph must also acquire a sense of what to be. This part of his education is recounted in the chapter called "How Abraham Found God." And as we learned about God's savagery along with Jacob, we will learn with the young Joseph how He became Holy. This is the chapter's covert subject, and it comes as the climax of our hero's studies because what Abraham found and Joseph-as-artist took in as the central message of his religion was the world-shaping power of the human imagination.

We were prepared earlier for this view of Abraham's discovery by another idea borrowed from the Jewish mystics, the Kabbalistic idea of earth and heaven as mirroring and reciprocally affecting each other. The search for origins ends in mysteries, our guide has said, because it "has to do not with distance [which we travel in a straight line] but with the sphere." For the sphere consists of an upper and a lower, a heavenly and earthly hemisphere, "which complement each other in a whole, in such a manner that what is above is also below, and what happens in the earthly repeats itself in the heavenly sphere, and contrariwise." Moreover, the sphere revolves, and the heavenly and earthly not only "recognize themselves in each other," but change places, as we see when gods become men, and men gods. And though Osiris was once a king of Egypt and Egypt's kings are now gods as men, "what Osiris was in the beginning . . . remains unanswered, since there is no beginning in the rolling sphere" (124-125). The sphere is a metaphor of the relationship of the mind of man — its "heavenly" side — and the world it seeks to understand — its earthly one — and its meaning is that what we are and what we are looking at are so intertwined as sources of what we see that it is fruitless to ask which came first; for us they came together.[9]

But Joseph's tribal belief was that God had "brooded on the face of chaos and had created a world by the might of the Word." In fact, our guide does at last give priority to the "heavenly" side. He observes that though we can never be sure whether stories like those Eliezer tells Joseph originated in heaven or on earth, still, "in the interests of truth and justice," we must acknowledge that "what is below would not know how to happen and could not, so to speak, occur on its own without its heavenly image and counterpart" (282-282). For "let a thing be ever so present, it was in fact only actually present when man has given it life and called it by name" (274).[10]

Which brings us to the Name by which man has "given life" to his developing conception of the Source of all being. We now learn that Joseph was particularly moved by the idea that had impelled Abraham to his great discovery, that one should "take seriously" the question of whom one should serve, and in fact "serve the Highest alone" (283). It was this idea that had led the Forefather to his rejection of all lesser gods and his concentration of "all the manifold properties of the divine, all blessing and all affliction" (285) in the one Highest, a Being "greater than all His works," the "space in which the world existed," while "the world was not the space in which He existed" (287). And yet Abraham was not thereby diminished.

For though the "mighty properties" which he ascribed to the Deity were probably God's original possession, and "indeed something objective, existing outside of Abraham," yet it was he who "recognized them" and "by thinking made them real." He could do so because "the power of his own soul was at certain moments scarcely distinguishable from them. It interlaced and melted consciously into one with Him." The bond or convenant between the Lord and Abraham was therefore "only the outward confirmation of an inward fact" (285). It was because "He was also in Abraham, who recognized Him by virtue of his own power that Abraham's ego . . . held itself stoutly upright in face of Him" (287). Such oneness with God accounted not only for Abraham's daring expostulation with Him before Sodom, but for God's tolerance of it. And when (in still another legend Mann takes from the rabbis) Abraham "upbraided" God for "double-dealing" in demanding justice from mankind, since He had to know the world and justice could not exist together, God's benevolent silence was, we are told, "the expression of a tremendous fact," a discovery about God which was "prob-ably" Abraham's "creation" too, that "He was not the Good, but the All. And he was holy! Holy not because of goodness, but of life and excess of life; holy in majesty and terror, sinister, dangerous, deadly, so that an omission, an er-ror, the smallest negligence in bearing to Him might have frightful conse-quences. . . . The discretion which He enjoined became piety, and God's living majesty the measure of life, the source of the sense of guilt, the fear of God, and the walking before Him in holiness and righteousness." In fact, as we have already seen, that bond was also, on God's side, an expression of His jealous demand to be worshipped alone, "without the flicker of an eyelash toward those other gods of whom the world was full." This was the reason the new relation of man with the Divine brought about the new, the accursed possibility that the bond might be broken and that one might "fall away from God" (287-288).

Finally, our narrator points out one more peculiarity of Abraham's God which is to become part of Joseph's mind. Though unlike the pagan deities, whose stories identify them with this or that natural process, Abraham's God, being the Power which expresses itself in the All, has no mythical history, yet it is also true that "He lay in bonds and was a God of waiting upon the future." God has a future because He is still known only to a few. Not till the day Abraham's knowledge of His "boundless kingship" is shared by all the world will He come into His "apotheosis" and "fulfillment." It was because Abraham was the one through whom He had begun to make Himself known that, to the "private re-sentment of His angels," God declared, "'verily, I will anoint him!'" (289-290).

As usual, Mann has employed the language of religion in a way that enables those of us whose language is secular to translate it into our own. The pride of Abraham which would worship nothing less than the Source of All is the sense that man must keep himself open to all to do justice to his own possibilities. Moreover, because "excess of life," an endless fountain of life, is what characterizes the universe, it is a betrayal of life, as we first saw in the "Prelude," to blind ourselves to its endless becoming by static or limiting con-ceptions of what it is. Of course, being part of the whole, man had better heed its "commandments" (as far as he can know them) with the "piety" which is "discretion" lest he suffer "frightful consequences" for breaking them. But Abraham showed too that the man of genius can do more than accept the universe and its apparent necessities (though it was to be Jacob's glory that he could do so much). He can stand upright before them, contend with them, and even induce them to yield to his own sense of what is right. He can do so because "the power of his own soul . . . [is] at certain moments scarcely distinguishable from them." Interlacing and melting into one with the universe, this power enables him to select among its elements and arrange them to reflect what he is and what he wants.

Abraham's dealings with the All thus exemplify those of the great imaginers — think of Newton and his kind — who, in part creating, in part perceiving, turn the chaos of nature into an order we find beautiful and useful. By the power of his imagination, he stamped upon the universe-as-man-engages-with-it, a universe hitherto merely savage, his own values. Linking its laws with the moral law, basing on the nature of things the human desire for righteousness, he began a process which would transform, humanize, the community of man. It is because this "sanctification" of the human community is still in progress that God has a "future" and His servants have a goal which gives meaning to their daily lives. (To look ahead, the same orientation toward the future will thrill Tamar in Jacob's story of his people and will draw her into the elaborate schemes by which she enters the story and becomes the ancestor of Jesus, the next great Agent in the humanization of the world.) As for the new danger Abraham brought into being, that of falling away from God, it would be the loss suffered by those who, taking a part for the whole, cease to feel themselves part of a whole worthy of reverence. Just as the feeling of belonging to that whole makes life's difficulties bearable for the truly adult, its loss makes us victims of pure chaos and our suffering that of the bewildered child.

Eliezer's teaching, then, has prepared our artist for his career. Having acquired a Highest to serve and a holiness to safeguard, and having understood them as creations (in part) of the aspiring human mind, Joseph is ready for the painful process by which the talented child grows into the man of genius, or, in our story's terms, for the "sacrifice" that will lead him through "death" to glory. The downward spiral begins when our hero, in the novel's second great father-son dialogue, wheedles Jacob into giving him the mysterious present he had once mentioned. And now again we are shown how "Jewish" wisdom issues out of the distinctly mixed nature of the artist. To begin with, Joseph's behavior is that of a deliberate charmer twisting a helplessly doting parent around his finger. But that the father gives in and the spoiled brat is soon drawing the lightning down on himself with that coat is clearly due to his gifts, as well as to the self-delight they bring with them. For the clever boy gets his way not only by losing to Jacob at chess, but also by comforting the old man in another of his religious troubles. This time what is bothering Jacob is not a fantasy, it is an idea. But again Joseph answers his father's need by piercing through to the humane, the life-serving core of their religion.

Jacob's new trouble is the reverse of the earlier one. Instead of thinking God has fallen behind His people and still demands a ritual the human heart rejects, he now fears that God has moved ahead of them and must abhor a ritual to which they still cling. Because it is the night of Passover, he has been "musing" on the Hebrew practice of slaying and eating a sheep which, when its blood is daubed on the side posts of each house, becomes a substitute for the "firstling" required by the Avenger "in expiation for man and beast" (316). Jacob has realized that the sheep they eat represents a primitive human sacrifice, and the thought sickens him as he was sickened, he remembers, to learn that Laban had sought a blessing for his house by walling up his first-born in its foundations. Though Jacob grants that such savagery must once have brought blessing or Laban would not have performed it,[12] it had done the unlucky man no good at all.

Joseph begins by suggesting that Laban's sacrifice was vain because it was based on an outworn custom. "For the outworn is repulsive to the Lord; He is beyond it and wishes us to be so, too." Laban would have done better, he says, to do as their own people do and substitute a beast for the child. When Jacob replies that even the substitute would make people vomit during the feast if they knew the significance of what they were eating, Joseph gently demurs again. "Let us slay and let us eat," he says, and he asks his father to consider the tree (Mann borrows the symbol from Nietzsche), whose roots are encrusted with dirt while its "blithe tip," out in the air with the Lord, remains untainted. The parable pleases Jacob, but he confesses that what worries him is the suspicion that the Avenger whom they appease in "the feast Pesach" is probably not God but the murderous pagan deity, "the Red One." At this the boy advises the troubled man to be less "precise in his interpretations" and to avoid the "undue haste" that leads to "destruction." "Let the feast be spared," he goes on, and new and better legends will arise in place of the old. And he not only cites the legend of Isaac and the ram, but, with a prescience that is another playfulness of his author, suggests that God might even provide a new basis for the Passover feast some day in a "great redemption and deliverance" (317-318).

The clever boy has helped his father see that it is precisely because of such dirt-encrusted roots that the tree can produce the leaves, and we the feasts — of myth and art — which comfort and delight us. "Undue haste" in cutting ourselves off from our primitive impulses would mean "destruction" because such impulses are the necessary basis of our human nature; they don't invalidate, they give life and warmth to the more humane forms we find to express them. "Have I . . . spoken consolingly?" Joseph asks, reminding us of the "interested" motive that underlies the artist's wisdom. Upon which, in a second access of grateful joy at Joseph's "balsamic" words, Jacob defines the double nature of that wisdom. What he says is also a formula for the way myth (tradition, culture) remains alive. "Thou spokest of the custom and yet at the same time for the future. . . . And spokest . . . for an abiding which is at the same time a station on the way" (318-319).

That same "diploxy," the sense of seeing Joseph in two ways at once, attends all the rest of this account of his boyhood. He shows off the new coat, for instance, with a blindness to the envy and rage it excites that is as "incredible" in Mann as it is in the Bible. To the warnings of his decent brother Reuben (one of the novel's great creations), he replies with a complacent blindness to the feelings of others that even our partial guide calls "criminal": he says criticism is out of order because his life is a version of a god's! And yet that insufferable reply is symbolically right. Joseph's story will make it clear enough that he is serving God's plan by his folly, but first it is strikingly "proved" in the novel's one deliberate violation of its own realism. Our audaciously playful author has dared to accept the view of certain rabbis of the "stranger" who directs the boy to his brothers. He too shows him as an angel sent by God, though Mann's angel is one of those referred to in the "Prelude," and later in the final volume's "Prologue in Heaven," as impotently resentful of God's interest in human beings.[13]

But it is in this volume's great climax that that doubleness is most fully revealed. We now learn that the blows with which Joseph is greeted by his maddened brothers, and which make him weep and plead, are also his great awakeners from the blind self-obsession of childhood. Out of a dazzling two-layered stream of thought — on the surface, that of the piteous child, and underneath, that of the adult, thrilled by a blaze of insight — emerges the realization that the brothers were *his* victims! It was *he*, with his fatuous assumption that all must love him more than themselves, who had driven them to take on themselves the guilt of his entirely justified punishment. And Joseph realizes something even more shocking: at bottom he had known the assumption was false and that those "innocently" recounted dreams and the flaunted coat were gathering the lightning against him. *Why* had he thus risked his own destruction? Calling this question a "riddle" impossible not only for Joseph to solve, but for anyone, "perhaps because [it contains] . . . so much that is contrary to reason and even perhaps holy" (388), our guide says quite enough to enable us to solve it for ourselves. He remembers that Jacob presented us with the same riddle in his failure to stop Joseph from taking along that coat ("together . . . they had brought the lamb to the pit"), and the hidden motive which solved it then solves it now. As Jacob had duplicated Abraham's sacrifice of Isaac, Joseph went where his father sent him *in order to be sacrificed*, and thereby to enter upon the next stage of his myth-duplicating rise to glory.

It is because the sacrifice they have chosen is part of God's plan that those hidden motives of father and son make a riddle that is "holy." And this, being translated, means that each (unconsciously) knows that it is the way out of error and sterility into life and life's unforeseeable possibilities for good. So Jacob had to abandon the secret wish to make the boy over into a first-born he is not and give him up to life's chances. And Joseph had to face the painful break with childhood that is required for the inner development of genius. But of course, if such awakening is painful, it is also full of joy. "His reason laughed as at a joke," we are told, when he heard Reuben suggest that he be thrown into the "pit." At that word so rich in mythical associations he is "filled with the joy of understanding" because his danger could not "prevent the concentration of his soul upon the wealth of allusion by which the event proclaimed itself as higher reality, as a transparency of the ancient pattern, as the uppermost turning undermost, in short, as written in the stars."

It is true that our narrator, expressing Mann's bottomless awareness, now grants the possibility that the boy's myth-inspired confidence in his resurrection might have been "a device of nature to tide him over the unbearable" and to give him, during his three horrible days in that grave-like pit (over which a "stone" has been placed, as will be done before another grave) the "natural hope to which life clings" (390-391). But he has also told us that in such "playing and dreaming" Joseph showed himself "a true son of Jacob, the man of thoughts and dreams and mystical lore, who always linked his life to God's." Though "less spiritual, more shrewdly calculating," Joseph, too, believed that "a life and activity . . . which does not base upon anything heavenly and recognize itself therein is no life or activity at all." For "the transparency of being, the characteristic recurrence of the prototype—this fundamental creed was in his flesh and blood too, and all spiritual dignity and significance seemed to him bound up with awareness of it" (388). That is, he is one who *makes* the events of his life significant (though to others they would mean nothing) by taking great prototypes as his models. Thus, the god-like greatness men rise to is forever reborn in those who admire and base themselves upon it and so lift their lives—and all our lives—out of triviality and disorder into dignity and meaning.

There is one thing more to be said about the way Mann has made sense of this episode. In discovering that it woke Joseph out of the narcissism of childhood, he has found the answer to a second question Genesis left hanging. Why didn't Joseph, in the Egyptian years that followed, let his father know that he was alive? The answer is that "the insight gained in the pit into the deadly errors" of his former life had driven him to renounce it and to share his brothers' conviction that he must "die" to that life, that his silence was "as logically necessary as the silence of the dead" (449). For if he returned to his father now, he would surely, in his weakness, betray them as he had done before and so heap still higher the wrongs he had done them. In fact, he will shortly take an Egyptian name because, as he will explain much later to Pharaoh, he *had* to be "silent" to Jacob, "and I vowed myself to silence with my name" (957).

5. "Prelude" to Joseph's Egyptian Story

Joseph in Egypt expands a short passage in Genesis (chapter 39, and not all of that) into the longest of the four volumes because the passage gives only in their bare results the two most substantial developments of the old story and requires the greatest wealth of Mann's dramatizing and illuminating invention. In the first Joseph, sold by the Ishmaelites to Potiphar, "found grace" in his sight, and all his master had was put into his hand; in the second the "well-favored" Hebrew slave roused the wild desire of Potiphar's wife, but resisted her plea of "Lie with me" because, being so trusted by his master, "How," he said ". . . can I do this great wickedness and sin against God?" (39:9). The Bible chapter goes past her desperate clinging to his "garment," her cry (in effect) of rape, her husband's wrath and Joseph's imprisonment to the prisoner's rise to a position of trust under the prison's captain. But our canny story-teller ends this volume, too, on a great "curtain scene," in which both the human develop-ment and its theme are dramatically concluded, here that of the woman's desperate fury and the judgment in which her husband gives her, in his own way, the vengeance she demands.

The world of Egypt will now appear before us in brilliant detail, but again all the lore Mann has gathered for his story will be shown as metaphors for eter-nal life-patterns, and again all of these will branch out from one organizing idea. The act of imagination by which Mann uncovers the permanent mean-ingfulness of Joseph's Egyptian story, unifies its episodes, and makes it his own, is to grasp as living reality the drama Genesis gives us in its shorthand: that of young genius on the make in the world of adult experience, and torn between the conflicting temptations of flesh and spirit. And Mann can create an Egypt that is a richly detailed historical construction and that yet serves his idea because ancient Egypt *was* divided between a religion of the flesh and a religion of the spirit and because, though the latter was strikingly akin to that of the Hebrews, Joseph's religion *was* a rejection of both. We are introduced to each by another foundation-laying "prelude": the instruction Joseph receives from his kindly merchant-master as their caravan, having made its way through the hellish, skeleton- littered desert, enters the Egyptian "underworld."

In brief, what he learns about the dominant religion is that it regards "the beast" as "the sacred place" where "man and god find themselves," where "the three are one" (462-463). For its supreme god Amun is periodically reborn not only as Pharaoh, but as a ram who cohabits with a virgin; Osiris, its god of death (known in a related myth as Usir, the corn king), goes below and rises yearly as the bull Hapi, who is called "Provider of the land" (465) because his semen is the overflowing, fructifying Nile; and this very bull, in still another mythical development, is "the living representative of Ptah" (509), "the god who created works of art" (504). Then, from his own sensations as he stands before that religion's monstrous representative the sphinx ("Hor-im-akhet created before time"), Joseph feels it to be "dangerous to the child of God and a snare to the descendant of the promise" because it had "nothing to do with promise," but, "fixed in vacant immobility, endured drunkenly on into . . . [a] future" that was "wild and dead . . . mere endurance and false eternity, bare of expectancy" (501). In short, the people of Egypt celebrate precisely what Hans Castorp was seduced and educated by in his mountain "underworld," the body as animal, with its beauty, its lusts, and its dying, and the illusion these impart that our real existence is in those orgiastic frenzies in which we seem to partake of the eternal, i.e., in an "eternity" which mocks the time-respecting purposes and activities of healthy ("bourgeois") life. This is why Egypt was "Sheol" to Jacob, "the kingdom of the dead," and "utterly taboo," as "the seat of worship of the past, of dalliance with death, and of insensibility to sin" (460-461).

This fleshly religion did, however, engender its own negation — in a brief
return to the worship of a god more ancient than Amun, the sun-god Aton-Re.
In its extreme, revolutionary form, this other religion became the virtual
monotheism of Amenhotep IV, who took the name of Ikhnaton.[14] It will be
in the final volume's great conversation between Joseph and Pharaoh that
Ikhnaton's religion will confront that of the Hebrew and each will be most fully
revealed. But we get a preliminary glimpse both of how they are similar and
how they arc different when the caravan arrives at the seat of the light-bringing
sun-god Aton-Re, the city of On, later to be known as Heliopolis.

Just as the "preferred activity" of the priests of On is "to make out of many
one," so Aton-Re, as "the Horizon-Dweller," who is "world-wide and world-
friendly," is willing to find himself in the gods of other cities and peoples, and
"loved the stranger as himself." In all this, Joseph learns, he differs from the
younger Amun, who incorporated other gods, including Re, the sun, not by
"reconciliation" but by "consuming" them, by "conquest," and whose horizon
"was . . . so narrow that . . . he knew and realized nothing but the land of
Egypt" (494-495).[15] An admirably intellectual and spiritual cult then is this of
Aton-Re. But it seems that it can go too far in its own direction. For the sun's
color, gold, painted on all the temples and monuments of On, reflects sunlight
so glaringly that the eyes of its people are forever blinking and tearing. The
devotees of light, with their passion to find the underlying idea that makes one
out of things apparently different, may have trouble seeing clearly what is
before them.

Such hints of the doubleness of the world Joseph is entering are accompanied by others of the doubleness with which he will respond to it. Thus, the
clever 17-year-old regards his father's horror of Egypt as a "pious prejudice,"
feeling "that sympathetic curiosity which is regularly the product of parental
moralizing and warning," and even a sense of "youthful triumph thus to coquet
with the moral terrors of the underworld." And yet his relation to his father
"was not one of opposites alone." He also senses "in his blood . . . a mute resolve
which must have gladdened his father's heart," that of "the child of Abram" not
to be overawed by the splendor of this other world, a resolve that would be kept
alive in him, moreover, by "a deep and native spirit of mockery," of "contempt"
(461).

Then, there is the "yes, but" in the Egyptian name, the "name in death"
Joseph portentously announces to his merchant-master as the one he has
chosen for his new life. This name startles the merchant, and will startle others
later on, because it suggests Joseph's extravagantly vainglorious idea that his
life is a version of that of Usir-Osiris. Usarsiph, which Joseph will also pronounce Osarsiph, combines a reference to the gods of death and harvest with
another, in the third syllable, to the black swampy depths they go into and rise
out of, depths repeatedly associated in the myths of the region with sex and
fruitfulness. It is because the name thus seems to say yes to the values of the
"underworld" that it will later delight the lustful woman who embodies them,

and later still displease the young Pharaoh who totally rejects them. But what each will fail to grasp, being equally, though differently, one-sided, is that for Joseph the name says yes to the world of death on behalf of the harvest to come in the world of life, a harvest it belongs to the artist to expect, even if he doesn't yet know what it will be.

Finally, this "prelude" gives us two sly echoes-in-advance of Joseph's great refusal of Potiphar's wife that seem to point in different directions. We are told that the reason he didn't try to escape from the Egyptian slavery that lay ahead could be put into words thus: "How could I commit such a folly [*Narrheit*] and sin against God?" (469). Of course, we know he committed follies enough that *served* God's plan. The folly that is sin, however, is that of presuming to be "wiser than God." And this is a "blunder" it is "right native to Joseph [i.e., to the artist] to avoid" because it is the blunder of one who says no to *expanding life*, who fears — presumes to know — where life will take him. But that same leitmotif-in-advance recurs with a significant difference the night after Joseph's encounter with the sphinx has "set his young blood in an unrest." When the monster comes to him in a dream, saying, "I love you," and asking him to name his name, Joseph's reply is, "How shall I commit such a deed [*Ubel*, i.e., evil] and sin against God?" (501). The *deed* is now the sin. This time the familiar words are telling us that the son of Jacob has already sensed in the animal religion of Egypt the temptation of a sexuality held above moral considerations and knows that though it would have been a sin against life to avoid the temptation, it will also be one to yield to it.

It is because our artist can be truly at home only where such opposites come together that this sequence ends with an account of the last city the caravan visits before it reaches its goal. We are told at once that Menfe will become Joseph's favorite city in Egypt, and the reason it delights him is that it is a city of pyramids, of tombs (its full name meaning Royal City of the Dead), whose people carry on amid the tokens of death a bustling cheerful life. Moreover, this doubleness is expressed by the very name Menfe, which is an "impertinent" joking abbreviation of its gloomy full-length form and so especially pleasing to Joseph, who is always drawn to the "jesting spirit" (503) which, as Thoth and the "wit" he inspires, brings together the heavenly and the earthly, a spirit we will see again as the joking god in Joseph's conversation with Pharaoh. It should come as no surprise that our artist's favorite city is full of the "graven images" abhorrent to Jacob because it is the "house" of Ptah, who, as we know, "created works of art" and of whom Hapi the bull is "the living representative." And though Joseph has "recognized that in consequence of his own estate [as one whose high purpose requires his descent into this "underworld"] he belonged thither, and that the forbidden was not forbidden to him, but even oddly appropriate" (505), still, he will have to learn that a certain loss must accompany all that he wins by serving God as an "Egyptian."

But first he finds in Egypt itself a reinforcement against its most powerful temptation. He finds it, as Genesis shows us too, in his new master Potiphar.

6. Joseph and Potiphar

In both versions of our story the temptation of the wife doesn't appear until Pharaoh's "courtier" has put all he has ("save only thee") into Joseph's hands and inspired a loyalty the Hebrew will feel it to be a sin against God to betray. But Mann has made these developments, too, part of the story's unity and meaning by a "discovery" of his own. We learn from him that Potiphar was a eunuch! In spite of rabbinical legends that call him a father, Mann reinstated this buried meaning of the word "courtier" to make possible a situation useful both for the story and its meaning. For the story, it lays the groundwork for the wife's later eruption into her madness of sexual hunger. What it means Joseph learns one day as he eavesdrops on Huia and Tuia, the ancient twins who are the courtier's parents. It seems that when their son was an infant these twins, aware that times were changing and that the once holy union of incest — the utter immersion in the "brewing mother-stuff" of the sexual swamp — would be "hated by the light and the powers of the new order" (508), decided (as our guide puts it later) to "speculate in the hereafter and make him [their son] a courtier of light" (670). And indeed, the spirit-obsessed court of Pharaoh has richly compensated them for their son's loss.

Listening to all this, Joseph understands why "Jacob's inherited thoughts about God might afford the subtlest test one could apply to a possible decline of custom and tradition from the will and influence of the Lord." For those clumsily up-to-date parents show that merely to be aware of changes in "the Lord and the times" can also lead one astray, can lead to bloody sacrifice little different from that of Laban, who sacrificed *his* son because he clung mindlessly to the outworn. He remembers what he had to tell Jacob, that the Passover feast is a tree "which like the Lord has risen out of the earth but must wither if one uprooted it," and that the skillful will always find a way to advance which requires no cruel uprooting. This is why the Lord, "who after all had not always been what He was," had become "a God of sparing and of passing over. . . . Wisdom and passing over: these seemed to Joseph related thoughts, which might exchange their garb and even had a name in common: goodness." And remembering, too, how Abraham had found his son replaced by a ram, he concludes, "The tradition of these people here, in however exalted kingdoms of good taste they moved, was lacking in such good stories. There was some excuse for them, repulsive as they were" (587).

But the desexing of Potiphar also made possible a kinship between Pharaoh's courtier and his Hebrew slave. For being so cut off from the world of the flesh, Potiphar (another of Mann's beautifully realized characters) is devoured by the need to be protected and justified in his lonely eminence. And Joseph has been helped by his tradition of the "rolling sphere" to recognize that the eunuch's need is a version of God's and his earthly master a version of his Master in heaven. True, since God contains both sexes in Himself, He is to the eunuch as "two to nothing." But God is jealous precisely because He is also "wifeless and childless" (588-589). Moreover, the dying old steward Mont-kaw,[17] who has become Joseph's Egyptian father, draws him into a "pact" that drives home the same point. Because Montkaw loves their master and has seen that Joseph can supply better than he what Potiphar needs, he proposes a "pact" by which Joseph will become the "successor and son, who protects and justifies the father in that he protects and justifies the noble master in bond with the dead." "Long have I understood such a bond," Joseph replies, "which one makes with the master as with one another in his service" (605).

In fact, Joseph has already decided to join Montkaw in this service, know-ing he can do the job far better and convinced his success will be useful to God's plan to prosper him in Egypt. And though we smile when our partisan guide warns us here that to call Joseph "coldly calculating" would be "precipitous and censorious," that "the situation was too complicated for such moral judgments," he justifies himself at once in a way that strikes home. He reminds us that Joseph will keep faith with the "cipher" by "loving and sparing," just as he did with the "needy Two" (588-589). A smile may well be in order, but we must also grant that our con-man's calculation *does* coexist with sincerity.

We see exactly this mixture (which also characterizes Joseph's seductive speeches to Jacob, the merchant and Montkaw, and later to the prison's cap-tain and Pharaoh) in the two conversations Mann invented to make clear why Potiphar put all he had into Joseph's hands. For they show the young man deliberately instilling the confidence which in Genesis he tells the wife he will not betray and in Mann we have learned is Potiphar's special need. And because the politic idea at the heart of each is rooted in his religion, they serve too as further revelations of its timeless meaning, as well as of the artist-nature.

In the first we watch the young careerist "improve his chance and prove that he had a right to it" when he is put to work by Montkaw in Potiphar's garden. As soon as the master appears and notices him, Joseph arrests his at-tention by expressing his fondness for trees with an enthusiasm that is artful as well as genuine, slips in a quick sketch of his myth-resembling life-story, and when the eunuch smiles skeptically at Joseph's calling his a "virgin birth" because it occurred in the sign of the Virgin and to a woman whose womb had long been "closed," seizes on this skepticism as his climactic opportunity. He points out that "virgin birth" is a metaphor for the perfectly real and common begetting initiated by spirit! Of this, Joseph says, the creation of "all the manifold shapes of things" by the word of God is the great example, but the commands of the master of a great estate are another, for he makes everything fruitful "by the breath of his nostrils" (599-600). And for a final proof of the superior power of spirit, Joseph asks, Who is more truly manly, the one who knows no fear, or the one who fears and yet commands his body to face the enemy?

The effect of these words on the eunuch is set forth in a key paragraph of the novel, a paragraph rich in both thought and feeling, and all the more moving because of its tone of deliberate self-control amid great epiphanies. We are told that there now streamed through Potiphar the "sense of well-being" which has been thought to signify that the apparently ordinary beggar or wayfarer one has held speech with is also a god in disguise. For "Realities wear each other as disguises. . . . The borderline between the earthly and the heavenly is fluid; and one need only fix one's eyes upon a phenomenon for it to break up in diplopy." Not that our narrator means to call Joseph a god. "There are stages and pre-stages of the divine: half-gods, transitional existences, intimations." But though he grants that some of the youth's hints of his own "deific" nature might be taken "in a literary light," the question remains how much of the effect he produced was due to his deliberate arrangement of the facts and how much rested upon "objective elements: traits which characterized the life of beneficent presences, beings by nature deific, consoling, saving and redeeming" (601).

What we have been shown is that Joseph belongs among those "intimations" of "deific" beings — "consoling, saving, redeeming" — because he has infused the facts of Potiphar's wounded condition with a healing meaning. Though the artist is thus exposed again as a confidence man, we also see again that the "inventions" by which he advances his career do serve the "deific" purpose. In fact, there is finally no contradiction because to give redeeming meaning to the chaos of life is precisely the object of that career, and indeed of the order-making human mind, which the artist, in his special way, represents.

Having celebrated the life of spirit to which the eunuch is limited, Joseph next finds an occasion to reject the anarchic sexuality Potiphar fears — knows — will some day wreck his peace. This conversation is about a tale Joseph reads to his master of a "fowler maid" and a youth who, sick with longing for each other, are restored to health when she goes to his bed and they rove "hand in hand . . . through the flowery garden of their joy." Potiphar presses the young man to admit, as one whose beauty must often open that garden to him, that he finds the tale pleasing. With "a consummately lofty and critical air" Joseph replies that it is "pretty," but "perhaps a little too simple — just a trace" (611).

His reason for thinking so emerges as he explains his people's view of sex. Not only are they wedded to a jealous God and so to some degree "set apart" from its joys. Certain chosen ones among them are especially consecrated to God and are brought to Him as "a whole offering" — if the son's father can't perform the sacrifice, it is "done to him." At Potiphar's expression of distaste for such a doing to sons, Joseph at once assures him that though the sacrifice is commanded, it is also a sin and forbidden, and a beast is sacrificed in the son's place. And since "we, almost alone in the world, know what sin is," and the Egyptian finds the word puzzling, he explains that sin is precisely what is both commanded and forbidden. This "painful contradiction," as Potiphar calls it, is the Hebrews' response to that garden, which they see as "a dread, a daemonic kingdom, where an accursed command has play, full of the jealousy of God. Two animals lie at the gate," Joseph continues, "the name of one is shame, of the other guilt. And out of the branches looks a third, and its name is mocking laughter." We need not ourselves be puzzled by that contradiction, for it is the contradiction between body and mind, or flesh and spirit, and sin is what is commanded by the first and forbidden by the second. The three animals are the punishment visited by spirit on those who abandon themselves to the body's lust. Joseph concludes with an account of how his people's God once punished a man for immoderate love of a woman by taking her away, and how the man then loved the dead woman in her living son, who became one of those "set apart for special zeal" (612-613); and Potiphar grasps at once — as he is meant to do — that the tale is Joseph's own, and that he will be safe with Joseph from the betrayal he most fears.

Such, we are told, were Joseph's "methods of 'flattering' his master and being 'helpful' to him in the sense of the bond which he had made with Montkaw." And the reason the word "method" should no longer chill our sympathies, whether it refers to Joseph's dealings with his earthly master or with his heavenly one, our guide now explains in a way that underlines his artist nature with a sort of comic openness. "Sheer sincerity," he observes, "unassisted by calculation and a good technique," is unlikely to achieve the "practical results" intended, that of inspiring well-being, confidence and trust in another. He then reminds us again that if his hero's calculation in insinuating that promise still seems offensive to anyone, "let him . . . remember that Joseph in the hour of temptation did not betray the confidence so engendered" (614). The technique of the artist, though it *is* the seductive trickery of a confidence man, may be seducing us for our good as well as his own, and toward a vision on which he is honestly staking his life.

Nevertheless, the temptation *will* come to a Joseph full of the sexual vigor of youth, and from a woman who is no mere villain. In fact, our author has discovered that the servant of God is less innocent and Potiphar's wife less guilty than we thought.

7. Joseph and Mut

Mann found his version of Joseph's temptress where he had found his Potiphar, between the lines of Genesis itself. And what he found is that she has been terribly wronged by the brevity of the old report. So our guide speaks up for the woman — here called Mut-Em-Enet — and his agitated defense is an especially effective example of his narrative style, comic in its display of partisan emotion struggling in vain for restraint, and yet rich in reality and power. Mut's shocking "Lie with me," he tells us, could not possibly have been the easy invitation of "a common prostitute" Genesis makes it seem. True, "a light moral attitude" has to be assumed in that animal-worshipping society. But Joseph was a Hebrew slave, and she was the delicately reared wife of a courtier of Pharaoh, who would surely have played a lofty role in that society. "I would put my hand in the fire," our guide exclaims, "staking my whole reputation as a story-teller," and swear to the blamelessness of Mut's life "up to the time when the gods made her a reeling maenad." When she did say those words, "biting her tongue . . . she knew herself no more; she was beside herself, her reason dethroned by agony" (670-672).

The social role Mann gives her to play is also a version of her role in Genesis. As she represents there the animal sexuality by which Joseph is tempted, she belongs here to a religious order of wives of Amun and brides of his divine son. At the same time her position as an honored symbol of sexuality not only arms her against degrading liaisons, but serves as compensation — increasingly feeble, however — for what she suffers as a eunuch's wife. So, when she abandons her "religious honor and everything in the realm of the idea on which her life is based" in a "terrified outburst concerned to save . . . her fleshly honor and her human womanhood" (720), she will do it as one in whom the idea and the flesh have come together, who herself at last embodies, enacts and, as we will see, powerfully expresses the sexuality-as-goddess celebrated in the myth.

No justice can be done here to the psychological brilliance and dramatic power of this episode as a story of sexual passion — its onset, its duplicities, its combination of suffering and bliss and its towering, world-despising egotism.[18] It is enough to say that the woman's three years of agony ("in the first she tried to conceal her love for him; in the second she let him see it; in the third she offered it to him" [722]) culminate in a scene of passion which ranks in intensity and wealth of meaning with the "Walpurgis-Night" chapter of *The Magic Mountain*.

What we now learn is that Joseph drove Mut to the frenzy which again dooms him to the pit by the same narcissistic folly which maddened his brothers years ago. The form it takes this time is the idea that his Hebrew faith in a "living God," his Hebrew detachment from the sex- and death-worship around him, lifts him above the "fiery bull" he is warned against by the knowing little dwarf who defends him. So he justifies the meetings which the woman demands and which it stirs his flesh to think about with the delusion that he can turn them into lessons in the business of the estate, and thus lead her "from the personal to the objective" (732) and cool her passion. The "overweening-ness" of the notion that he can keep the woman's soul in "leading strings" and the self-deception that accepts that "fig leaf" hiding his own lust are an adult version of the boy's fatuous conceit in believing that others must love him more than themselves. Once again our narrator frankly admits that Joseph's conduct "cried out for retribution."[19]

But — since with this narrator there is always a but — "we cannot help smiling," he observes, at the "mental processes" of certain "exalted spheres," whose retribution seems to honor the moral demands of the "kingdom of the stern," but does so in a way that leads the favored culprit to "good fortune much greater and more brilliant than that which had been destroyed" (817). That this good fortune is *also* deserved, that, just as in his boyhood, Joseph is serving God even in his folly and guilt, is made quite explicit in the chapter "Of Joseph's Chastity," in which our guide turns around and defends the ambivalent torturer of Potiphar's wife whose guilt he has been at such pains to make clear.

The chapter is frankly offered as an "explanation" and "summing-up" of all that Joseph's resistance in Genesis had to mean. But though this is another extreme example of Mann's risky explicitness, the parade of ideas remains alive as fiction because it comes to us — in the many-toned voice of Mann's narrator — warm with the feelings it examines and expresses. We find too that developments already convincingly established may be made more dramatic — because more rich in meaning — by the mere statement of their hidden implications.

The seven reasons we are given for our hero's chastity are a further exploration of what makes the artist one with the servant of God. To begin with, Joseph denies himself to the woman because he was "betrothed to God," and to a God by whom he knew himself to be jealously loved. And though our "modern sense . . . may be . . . offended" by ideas about the capricious favoritism of the Unseeable (whatever name He bore)," still, "they have their place in time and evolution," and, in any case, Joseph's sense of his great election is "justifiable" because "its probability rests upon his personal worth" (750). Again we have been told that it is the artist's sense of his own genius which lays on him, so favored by life, the obligation to be faithful to life in its endless unfolding, that is, to resist the seduction of the part in order to be true to the whole.

The six remaining reasons are all particular applications of Joseph's fidelity to God. Together they tell us that he never forgets "of whose spirit he was child and of what father son" — Jacob, above all, though, as we have seen, others play Jacob's role for him in Egypt. This is why the climactic seventh, which "comprehended all the others," is a condensed formulation of the "primeval No" that distinguishes Jacob's religion from Mut's. Since the desperate woman represented for Joseph "the temptation of Sheol," the "combined idea of death and dissoluteness," to yield to her meant "literally to lose all"; it meant to yield to the lusting body's "shameless unreason" against "the inherited dictate of his blood to uphold the claims of reason in this field." Of course, Joseph will *understand* such "sin" because "all spirit is nothing but understanding of sin." That is, it is the no of the free intelligence to what is "commanded" by the body and so it can arise only when those seductive commands have made themselves felt. But it *is* a no. For "the God of Joseph's fathers was a God of the spirit — at least that was the goal of His evolution, for the sake of which He had made a bond with men. Never since He united with theirs His will to salvation had He anything to do with death and the nether world or with any madness rooted in the dark bottom of fruitfulness. In man He had become aware that such things were an abomination unto Him, and in his turn man too had become aware of it in Him." It was to make "a clear divorce between themselves and the corpse-gods of their neighbors" that the Hebrews and their God renounced "any view of the hereafter" (754). *Life* was to be their concern—so Mann gives us his version of that command in Deuteronomy to "choose life, that both thou and thy seed may live." The Hebrew's rejection of the seductive woman is a rejection of the bodily drunkenness which would swamp his mind, his power to shape his life toward lifeserving ends.

And yet he kept going to those phony pedagogic sessions! Why, in view of his seven-fold reason, didn't he stop? Our guide anticipates this natural question, and his answer, as by now we will expect, grants the negative view in a way that makes it part of the defense. Yes, he *was* "coquetting with the world" out of "sympathy with the forbidden thing" and the "arrogant self-assurance" that he could "retreat whenever he liked." But, "to look at it on its good side," this was also the ambition "to push matters to the uttermost in order to carry off a greater triumph," one that would make him "more precious to the father . . . than [after] an easier trial." And to go deeper still, he was led by the feeling that the delicious dangers he toyed with—and the pit that waited beyond them—were his way to the great fulfilment "written in the plan" (757)—or, to translate yet again, that the experience of passion and pain, provided he keep his wits about him, is the artist's way to the fruitfulness implicit in his gifts.

What the high-minded torturer finds when the woman's abject (and inflammatory) plea draws him to her room at last brings him a first glimmer of insight that he has wronged her as he had his brothers. Not only does he become aware that her breasts and thighs are swollen, that an "eruption of sex" has given her "the beauty of a witch." She has bitten her tongue almost through in order to punish herself for the shamelessness she intends and also to make it sound like childlike innocence: he hears her lisping! Our guide "would not seem to mock at her who had death at her heart," and so offers only brief examples of her lisp, but these are quite enough to lend a horrible-comical poignance to the self-abandonment with which she speaks of the "bliss undreamed-of" (767-768) awaiting him in her untouched body. The battle that follows carries us to the heart of both the human drama and what it reveals of the servant of God and the artist.

To begin with, she presses him to admit there is something warmer than conventional respect in his calling her "the sovereign of [his] head and heart," and when he begs her not to pry into the sweetness that inevitably enters into such forms with a master who is also "mistress and lovely woman"—to "show kindness and mercy to the life of the heart"—she tells him he is turning things upside down, for it is she who is pleading for that life. That is, in place of his Hebrew sympathy for the whole person, with its mysterious mixture of spirit and flesh, she wants sympathy for the body alone. We see more of the central difference between them when he begs her to consider how far their brief pleasure would be outweighed by "evil consequences and . . . remorse," and she thrusts aside his prudence with contempt. Her changed body has become a "vessel of love" which will make him feel he is not a man, lying with a "human woman," but a god, satisfying his lust "with mother, wife, sister, for lo, I am she!" To him this is the madness which thrusts us below the human, whose "special property it is to think beyond the moment and consider what comes after." It is not for himself that he fears, but for her, he says, and most of all for her husband. And in a profound novelistic playfulness Mann learned from Cervantes,[20] the character comments on his own story. Joseph warns her that all their words and deeds "can become history and literature," begs her to "take pity upon your story," and then, saying he wants to express all the wealth of what he means in words which are fit for "the people's mouth" and which "every child can understand" (770-774), he utters at last — and Mann gives word for word in italics — his great refusal in Genesis (39:9). It is this reminder of the loyalty to Potiphar which stands in her way that brings the woman to the ultimate meaning of her "Lie with me" and Joseph to the ultimate meaning of his resistance.

She begins with what she had bitten her tongue to screen, the crime that tends to be hiding (however deep and opposed) under every adulterous "Lie with me." She lisps "sweetly, with pouting lips, 'But I might kill him,'" and paints a picture of how easily that mere "tindery mushroom of a man" might be dispatched and Joseph become master of his house and his bed. When Joseph pleads with her to consider that Potiphar is like a father to him, and that to live with her in the house of murder would be like living with his mother, "Fool!" she cries. ". . . With his mother each man sleeps — the woman is the mother of the world, her son is her husband, and every man begets upon his mother. . . . Isis am I, the Great Mother, and wear the vulture hood, and you shall name me your name, sweet son, in the sacred sweetness of the begetting night — " Upon which, out of his horror, bursts his fundamental faith and loyalty: "No, no, not so! . . . The Father of the world is no mother's son. . . . To Him I belong, before Him I walk, the son of my father, and once for all I tell you I will not so sin against God, the Lord, to Whom I belong, to shame my father and murder him and pair with my mother like a shameless hippopotamus" (774-776). Accepting Freud's myth of the Id and the dream of incest and patricide hidden by civilization under all our ordinary lusts, Mann has shown the answer of the Ego as that of the child of Abraham and the artist. The Father to Whom he belongs and will be loyal is "no mother's son" because He comes, as we have already learned, from the spirit. He is the resistance of the free, life-serving intelligence to the deathward-tending compulsions of the flesh.

But Joseph must go into the pit once more because he remains a young man in Egypt and the tormented woman's seductiveness is not likely to be canceled by lofty argument. So she compels him to come to her on that day when she is alone in the house and he knows it. She does so by consenting to certain degrading rites of sorcery which a black slave promises will bring him to her bed a lusting body utterly free of his resisting soul. Even then the loving woman our narrator has passionately defended is not quite dead in her, for she dreams, as she *would* dream, that "if the lust be deep enough, love may blossom from it" (816). But she will take what she can get. Sure enough, the spell-bound youth comes back to the house — and so to his ruin — fatuously pretending to himself that household duties require him. And though to her "moonlight" reasoning the filthy sorcery is what makes him come, we are of course free to recognize it as merely a ritual enactment of the delicious filth of animal sexuality with which she has long beclouded his reason and is now submerging it.

As for what saves him at the last minute, Mann has discovered this in a rabbinical legend, though he adopts the legend with a significant change. The rabbi tells us that Joseph was able to break away from the desperately clinging woman because Jacob's face appeared before him. But our guide insists that the face didn't simply appear. It was Joseph's "spirit [that] evoked the warning image." And just as in his final outburst to the woman he joined "Father" and "father," so the image evoked is one which mingles with the features of Jacob Potiphar's "fatherly traits" and Montkaw's, and "over above all these were other mightier traits" (830). Joseph has deliberately called up the fathers who, with Jacob at their head, have represented for him the Highest. Once again we have seen our artist saved from crippling reduction to the part by his fidelity to the whole, to life, and by his own creative will.

8. Joseph and Pharaoh

"Everything has its time," Mann's Joseph will say to Pharaoh. ". . . When I was a lad I dreamed and my brothers were angry and chid me. Now when I am a man has come the time of interpretation" (936). The immediate goal of this artist-Joseph's development, which we will see him reach in his interpretation of Pharaoh's dreams, is the power to interpret the dreams of others by using what he has learned from his own, which means too from his self-love and the follies and eye-opening punishments it brought down upon him. But such feats are themselves in the service of something more fundamental. What the artist as *master* is chiefly concerned to interpret is suggested in one more foundation-laying prelude, the "Prologue in the Upper Circles" which begins this final volume.

Just as in the "Prologue in Heaven" at the start of Goethe's drama of another man of genius favored by God[21] (and also, of course, in the story of Job), Joseph's fate is shown as proceeding from certain exchanges between God and His adversary, whose "business" is "to realize and bring into the world evil." In the voice, mainly, of one of the cautiously resentful angels, we are told that Shemmael[22] offered two suggestions to make God's life "livelier." One was that He should create man, who, being fashioned in God's image like the angels, but fruitful too like the beasts, would enrich "the world's repertory"

(844) by bringing into it good and evil, and with these the need for pity, mercy, judgment and punishment. The other was that He should exchange His "somewhat anaemic spiritual all-sufficiency for the full-blooded fleshly existence of a corporeal folk-god" (849).

Of course, Shemmael made the suggestions in the hope of enjoying God's "chagrin." But it turns out that, in spite of certain fierce punishments of His mixed new creation, God took the moral world less seriously than the other did. The real reason God adopted the suggestions was "curiosity about Himself." For man, being more like Himself than either angels or beasts, would serve as His "mirror" (845), while the folk whose tribal God He chose to become was one in whom "the quality common to the human race, of being an instrument of God's self-knowledge . . . came out in peculiar strength." He had of course foreseen that the "chosen seed," convinced it knew better than His corporeal tribal Self what He really was, would eventually restore Him to IIis proper rank and to the "beyond-all, all-sufficing spiritual" (850-851).

We have thus been alerted to what it will mean for this child of Abraham to have arrived at his "time of interpretation." He is ready to interpret the nature of God. This is why our narrator will frankly confess that the deepest reason he undertook to tell Joseph's story long ago was to bring back the "famous but almost unknown conversation" of Pharaoh and Joseph recorded in the chapter called "The Cretan Loggia," to bring it back "in all its members." For Pharaoh's "inordinate enthusiasm and favour" seem in Genesis "to lack foundation and motivation" because Joseph's dream-interpretation is only one of its members. What has to be restored is the talk which preceded and accompanied the interpretation and gave it its significance. This conversation was our narrator's goal from the start, and is, in fact, the novel's intellectual climax, because it is (as Pharaoh's listening mother calls it) "a conversation of gods about God" (979). Joseph will rise to glory by bringing to the one-sided God-seeker, who had come near it but could never reach it by himself, the conception of the Highest and of man's relationship to Him which lies at the heart of the religion of the Jews.

But to say that the Hebrew Joseph has become the interpreter of the nature of God, Who is the Whole, is also to say that Joseph-as-artist has become one of those in whom life grows aware of its own nature. And it is of the essence of Mann's idea that this awareness will not be of a "truth" finally grasped and imparted. It is rather the power to stay in touch with life, and to help others to do so. This is what is conveyed in the new Egyptian name Pharaoh gives Joseph when he enters at last on his destined career. The name, translated, is "The god [Aton] . . . says: Life be with thee!" This means, we are told, not only "Live thou thyself," but also "Be a life-bringer, spread life, give living-food to the many . . . in a single epithet, the Provider" (984-985).[23]

Of the prison experience that is to be Joseph's springboard to Pharaoh, it is enough to note here what it reveals of that artist-as-master and his magic-seeming gift. As before, Joseph has wept at his terrible come-down and been

comforted by "the play of allusion" that shows uplifting "correspondences" between his own circumstances and "higher things" (853). But what is new is the
"confidence" he displays as he stands in his bonds before the prison captain.[24]
Though he has certain external reasons for feeling hopeful, his "real confidence," our guide now observes, comes not from these, but from "the happy
mysteries of his own nature" as one of "the children of the blessing." It is no
longer the "blind confidence" of the boy that all must love him more than
themselves. It is rather the conviction that "his ego and the world . . . belonged
together, they were in a way one, so that the world was not simply the world
by and in itself, but . . . his world," and could therefore be "moulded into a
good and friendly one." It is belief in the "plasticity" of circumstances which
"generally speaking" was "trust in God" (861-862). This is not to be the last time
we will be reminded that the self-love of the artist is at bottom one with the
Hebrew's "piety" to God.

    As for Joseph's power to read the future in dreams, Mann finds the way
to make this "real" in an odd foreshadowing of twentieth century depth psychology in the Bible itself. We read in Genesis (40:5) that Pharaoh's imprisoned
baker and butler dream "each man according to the interpretation of his
dream," and so Mann's Joseph explains "the mystery of dreaming" by observing that "the interpretation is earlier than the dream, and when we dream, the
dream proceeds from the interpretation." That is, the dream proceeds from the
dreamer, who is its living interpretation, and it is in our knowledge of him that
we find its meaning. He says too: "Dreamer and interpreter . . . are actually
interchangeable and one and the same, since together they make up the whole.
Whoever dreams interprets also; and whoever would interpret must have
dreamed" (893). It is the humanity we share that makes interpretation possible
and its truth recognizable. Joseph goes on to prove all this in a dazzlingly
plausible version of the two prophetic dream-decipherings in prison, but it will
be his interpretation of Pharaoh's double-dream — of the seven fat kine and
seven fat ears of corn devoured by seven lean of each — that will be the novel's
crowning example of how he operates. Its brilliant success will show us again
that psychological insight is only part of his gift: the rest is his self-serving imagination. Joseph's achievement will be a work, not of science, but of art.

    The sickly, 17-year-old mystic before whom the 30-year-old Joseph must
perform turns out to be another victim of inner conflict. His passion for
"knowledge of the Highest," so intense it leads to fits of rigid unconsciousness
in which he thinks his father Aton sends him instructions, involves not only
an extreme revulsion from the animal religion of Amun, but acute distaste for
the material "black earth" concerns and the military practices required for the
empire's well-being and safety. This gives him "conscience and conflict head-
aches," because he fears his evasion of royal responsibilities will create a danger
to Egypt on its "material side" (913) and so lessen his persuasiveness as a
religious teacher. It is after an especially intoxicating orgy of theological discussion with the priests of On — he arrives at the thrilling idea that there exist

"incorporeal realities, immaterial as sunlight . . . the spiritual" (915) — that his guilt reaches a climax and erupts in his terrifying dreams. And it is because of that altogether justified guilt that he will be able to reject the absurd interpretations of his own soothsayers and recognize at once the truth of Joseph's.

Joseph's fabulous uplifting in his very first meeting with Pharaoh is the tale's climactic demonstration of his seductive power. And conveying, as I have said, the core meanings of the novel, it is an especially brilliant example of the art by which Mann gives dramatic life to his ideas. Not only is the account of Joseph's faith, which is the meeting's chief burden, organized toward a climax suspensefully postponed. His ripened thought remains living fiction because it comes from him, not merely from his author; it is the culmination of a character development — that of a genius — convincingly established. Finally, the talk proceeds from beginning to end as a delicate, but feelingful tug-of-war. For as Joseph pulled back in his earlier dealings with devotees of the animal flesh, he will now have to do so with Egypt's supreme devotee of the spirit.

Thus when Pharaoh asks what sort of seizures will accompany his prophecies, Joseph pleases the boy's worldly mother (placed here by Mann to represent the royal interests he neglects) and turns him "sulky" like "a chidden child" by answering his question with a sly rebuke of Pharaoh's own tendency to fits. Admitting that he did once disturb his father by twitching and eye-rolling, Joseph assures Pharaoh he has left all that behind and now relies on "divine reason" alone. "Divine reason" shows itself, he then firmly instructs the young enthusiast, in a

> composed manner of interpreting [which] is due to the fact that it is an I and a single individual through which the typical and traditional are being fulfilled .... For the pattern and the traditional come from the depths which lie beneath and are what bind us, whereas the I is from God and is of the spirit, which is free. But what constitutes civilized life is that the binding and traditional depth shall fulfill itself in the freedom of God which belongs to the I; there is no human civilization without the one or the other [937].

As he had once rejected the intoxication of the flesh, Joseph now rejects the strangely similar intoxication, not of spirit as his people know it, but of spirit as it is known to the one-sided light-worshipper. It is a lust of the mind to submerge itself in the general (the typical, the traditional, the universal) which is equally of the "depths," equally a compulsion that would make us all alike and all slaves. This is why civilization — and surely we can add art — requires that the general "fulfil" itself in the particular, the concrete, the individual. That takes the sober — i.e., free — life-oriented intelligence of individual conscious minds.

But it is not by rebuke that Joseph seduces. He now repeats word for word his promise in Genesis: "God shall give Pharaoh an answer of peace" (41:16,

938), and we are shown that this means he knew *in advance* he was going to find a reassuring interpretation of Pharaoh's dreams. To our "con-man" the facts are malleable! And the King is delighted. A reference to Joseph's God enables him to bring up another beneficent god, "a brother . . . or other self" of Thoth, the god of writers, with whom the King has already associated the sly and literate Hebrew. After telling a story which shows this god as a "sly-boots" (939), not overly scrupulous about the truth, Pharaoh praises him as "the god of favourable chance . . . of smiling inventiveness; shedding blessing and well-being — whether honestly or even a bit dishonestly won, the way life is" (941). And it is when Joseph reveals that the spirit of this god is familiar to his people, making the King laugh at tales of Jacob's holy trickery with Esau and Laban, and Rachel's with Laban, that he plunges into the long-awaited recital of his dreams.

We will now see in Joseph's interpretation — that seven years of poor harvests will "devour" seven of rich ones unless Pharaoh appoints a wise overseer to prevent it — the essential elements of the artist's work. The version of reality he offers is a mixture of what he perceives and what his imagination does with it, and his driving motive is a selfishness which also serves his fellows. But though we have encountered this artist-work in Joseph's earlier "interpretations," as I have said, the precocious youth is now a master and his work this time will address the world and lift him to greatness as its provider.

The reality our artist perceives in the dream is the guilt that underlies it, the fear that since lean years do occur, famine must threaten the Egypt whose ruler subordinates his "black earth" duties to "higher things." Then the inventer of serviceable fictions seizes on the number seven for the same reason the dreamer did, because it is a convention easy for the minds of their time and place to accept. That the story-book number must be loosely interpreted our guide makes a comic point of emphasizing. Finally, there is the personal, the career motive for the message Joseph finds in the dreams, a motive our narrator will also make explicit after a number of hints. Joseph, he will tell us, "at once brought Pharaoh's dreams and what they foretold into relation with his own plans and purposes," which involved "expecting and preparing the way," that is, expecting Jacob and his people and preparing the way for them to join him in his glory. Indeed, "we cannot deny," he admits for the second time, "that his attitude . . . was a thought too eager, almost enough so to cool the sympathy we would wish to preserve for Rachel's child." But he says too that those "plans" of Joseph are at once "personally spiritual, private, and yet of . . . world-shaking significance" (990). This is why, to the mother's charge that he has manipulated her son for his own purposes, Joseph will be able to answer honestly, "I was without falseness against him, great Queen. . . . And I will remain so" (971). That is, there is no conflict between his two allegiances.

But in Mann's version the dream-interpretation leads Pharaoh only part of the way. It is after the God-talk that follows, inflaming him to the point of a seizure, that he will put Egypt into the Hebrew's hands. This talk begins, naturally enough, with the King's closer look at the brilliant soothsayer. He asks him his name at last and learns it is the self-chosen Osarsiph; and it is that packed bundle of meaning which shifts the talk to God. For though Pharaoh is glad of a precedent for changing his own Amun-name to one celebrating his father Aton, he disapproves of the honor Joseph has done the "dead lord Usir." The "Osar-creed" of the religion of Amun fills him with horror because it sets on the throne of judgment a god "who is only just, but without mercy." "Amun," he says, "would make the world one in rigid service of fear, a false and sinister unity," but "my Father would . . . unite his children in joy and tenderness." Joseph defends his choice of "a name of death" not only as appropriate for one "set apart," but because the depths are the realm of the "holy" and "consecrated," and it is only "when we make offering to the depths" that we "rightly make them to the heights. For God is the whole." But Pharaoh rejects this mixing of opposites. God is "light," he insists. "It is the wicked," like his detestably cruel ancestors, "whose fate is directed from below." And because men "copy whatever picture you make of them [the gods]," he would "purify the godhead" in order to "purify men" (955-957). Upon which, encouraged by a sign from the mother that she would welcome a correction of such impractical high-mindedness, Joseph replies to this Egyptian version of Settembrini's "bourgeois," "philistine" demand for the purely good with the great central "yes, but" of Mann's thought.

It is really a "yes," as well as a "but," for he begins by granting that Pharaoh has spoken the truth. "Yet we know," he goes on—and this is the first of two classic formulations in the final volume of the sense of things which underlies Mann's irony—that

> Pharaoh would not have speech die away and cease at the truth. Rather he desires that it free itself and go on, past the truth and perhaps to further truth. For what is true is not the truth. Truth is endlessly far and all talk is endless too. It is a pilgrimage into the eternal and looses itself without rest, or at most after a brief pause and an impatient. 'Right, right,' it moves away from every station of the truth, just as the moon moves away from each of her stations in her eternal wanderings [958].

In short, because neither the Whole nor its parts are ever still, *what is true in one context may be untrue in another.* And Joseph now demonstrates the point by applying it to the violence Pharaoh abhors. He tells him about the "moon-wanderer" Abraham, whose name means "high father" and whose quest for truth led him to the discovery of God and to the covenant between God and man that they should be holy "the one in the other," but who nevertheless did battle with robber kings to free his kidnapped brother Lot. For the "peace of God" can be brought to the "stupid and bad" only by force. And seeing Pharaoh's annoyance at such apparent compromise with evil, Joseph tactfully murmurs, as if to himself, what he would say to the king if he dared to disagree.

As Abraham's descendant and a "go-between twixt above and below," he would say, "The sword is stupid; yet I would not call meekness wise. Wise is the mediator who counsels courage in order that meekness may not be revealed as stupid in the sight of God and man."

We laugh when Pharaoh replies, "I have heard . . . what you have been saying to yourself." But such laughter is precisely what the king now rejects! Though he grants that "the spirit of the mischievous god" spoke through Joseph, and Joseph adds that this god hates violence, too, but knows "better than anyone else that one may be right and yet wrong," the King again draws back. He remembers how he laughed at Joseph's tale of Esau, that other "wrong right one," and he now admits it made him uneasy. "Perhaps it is true that what is funny is always at the same time a little sad, and that we only breathe freely and happily at the pure gold of serious things." Like Settembrini again, he is speaking for all who demand the pure, and themselves one-sided — and therefore humorless — cannot accept the irony that goes both ways. And since Pharaoh has called God "light," Joseph now puts in terms of light the eternally necessary warning. Light is really "serious and stern," he says, because "power . . . streams up from below into its clarity — power it must surely be and of masculine kind, not mere tenderness; otherwise it is false and premature and tears will follow" (958-959). To this warning, significantly, Amenhotep has not been listening. He is still clinging to his own truth, and a moment later he bursts into a passionate celebration of Aton which is the actual hymn to the sun and its tender nurturing of all life credited to Ikhnaton. But the tug-of-war has been drawing him forward. What completes the seduction is Joseph's answer to the question still hanging between them which the king now bluntly utters: "Your God, who and what is he?" (965). Didn't that ancestor who discovered Him, Pharaoh wants to know, also find He was the sun?

Joseph's answer — that Abraham's pride would not bow down to any mere "witness," however God-like, but only to "that to which it bears witness" — is for the gifted Egyptian a dazzling revelation of the hidden goal of his own thought. He knew it, he cries, his god had told him during a seizure that he was not Aton, but "Lord of the Aton." If he put the message aside, this was only because he was the "King and teacher" of a people incapable of belief in the unseen, and "I may not think what I cannot teach." But in his joy he now rejects his mother's approval of such arrogant "statemanship," for "we must speak what we know and witness what we see." And when Joseph, urged, goes all the way and tells him how Abraham had discovered that though there was something of himself in God, God was nevertheless "greater than His works and outside them," Pharaoh again "recognizes" what he means, that the God Who made all we know and are *must* exist in another realm, outside both. (So modern physics tells us that the universe we know was created by a force which came before it — in this sense exists outside it — and which may have produced, may yet produce, unimaginable other universes.) The King now remembers that he also heard in a seizure that he must call his Father, not "my Father above," but "my

Father *who art in heaven*" (Mann's emphasis). At this, his joy growing ominously intense, he kisses the Hebrew and pours out the final realization to which he has been led. Accepting the vast inclusiveness of Joseph's God, he emphasizes (as he would) God's human side, and his words anticipate those of Jesus and the Gospels.

The love of this Father, Who is in heaven, this "Being of beings," Who "does not become and die," is "in the world," he says, "and the world knows Him not." But though men live in darkness and do evil because they don't understand the light, they will grow blessed through belief in Pharaoh, His son who will teach His word. And where Joseph had spoken of how light must be strengthened by power, Pharaoh emphasizes the opposite truth, that "out of the mother-depths below power strives upward to be purified" and to become spirit in the flame of the "father spirit," that is, the body must be controlled by mind, and animal man become as the son of God. Those who believe will be rewarded, he concludes, for "my words are not mine, but the words of my father Who sent me" (966-969).

With this the ecstatic seer, who is not yet capable of the sobriety of "divine reason," loses consciousness. As Joseph now declares to the mother, on this day Pharaoh has shown the world that "a man can be right on the way and yet not the right one for the way" (971). And in fact, though Pharaoh will remain Joseph's loving and grateful friend, all later references to his religion make clear that he has slipped back from the height where he had briefly grasped that God was the Whole. So, when Joseph brings his father before the King, we are told that the two who stand together in this moment of time are really "ages apart," one a "sickly boy," distilling from past accumulations of religious thought "a tender and sentimental religion of love," and the other a "wise, experienced old man . . . at the very source and fount of widely developing Being" (1162).

9. The Judgment of Jacob

The reunion which brings the novel to an end is another triumphant example of the oneness in Mann's work of thought and feeling. Since the drama is now itself a life-illuminating conjunction of past and present, all the wealth of the tale's meaning emerges in this climax as climactic understanding. And here, too, Mann's version of Genesis seems the mere working out of its own hints, though certain of its details are shown to be needless or contradictory to its evident meaning.

We are prepared for the reunion in many ways. One is our guide's account (which is, one must grant, somewhat "ponderous" in its explicitness) of what Joseph, as the Provider, has become. Having made his headquarters in Menfe, that *lively* city of *tombs*, because its doubleness appeals to his own, he is now best described by the word "Tam." This is an "equivocal" word, we are told, and it means the same as "Thummim" in the "curious formula 'Urim and Thummim,'"25 in which Urim is "yes," and Thummim is "yes-no." Or one can put it that "Tam, or Thummim, is the light and dark, the upper and under-world at once and by turns; and Urim only the light." It follows that the phrase "'Urim and Thummim' does not express a contradiction; it only exhibits the mysterious truth that *when one separates a part from the whole of the moral world, the whole always stands opposed to the part*" (my emphasis, 995-996). This "mysterious truth" is the other perfect explanation of the irony of Thomas Mann, which is precisely the smile of a devotee of the whole at the pretension of the part to completeness.

Of course, the Jew can only succeed among the others — to use the slightly pejorative word — by "assimilating." Hence our guide's funny discomfort at the thought of how this one's father, whom he here sees fit to refer to as Yakob ben Yitzschak, would react to Joseph's behavior during his "time of emancipation" — which, when he marries, becomes a "time of license" (1006). As an Egyptian nobleman, he is soon performing "a priestly office," and "to put it rather baldly, he had an income from idolators" (1003), a knowing reference by Mann to something explicitly forbidden among the 613 commandments which still guide the life of the orthodox Jew. Then, as the Bible also tells us, he marries the daughter of "a priest of On," a *shikseh*! Finally, this heir of Abraham, Isaac and Jacob has two half-Egyptian sons and calls the first Manassah — "forgetting," according to a footnote to Genesis 41:51, and translated here as "God has made me forget all my connections and my father's house" (1009) — and the second Ephraim — "fruitful" in the footnote to the next verse and here "God has made me to grow in the land of my banishment" (1013). So the Jewish boy seems to announce he has "assimilated" and to boast he has thereby prospered.

But no. Our guide insists that in spite of all those embarrassing goings-on, there are extenuating elements in Joseph's situation. For instance, he is at least a priest of Aton-Re, who has lately emerged as "lord of the Aton" — that is, the "goyish" religion he serves is the one which doesn't clash too badly with the beliefs of his people. More important, Joseph feels himself to be "a very special case." Not only does he regard "his own exiled and cosmopolitan existence . . . as that of a man set apart for a special purpose," who will therefore be treated with "forbearance" by "the Master of the Plan" (1004). He believes that the Plan — that he should be sent to Egypt to bring about his people's "deliverance" — was itself a secondary motive for snatching him away from his father. We are reminded that he can "see through" that motive to the deeper one of God's "jealousy" lest Joseph love any of His creatures more than Himself. Our guide grants that the words "see through" may seem "irreverent," but "Is there," he asks, "an activity more religious than studying the soul-life of God?" Indeed, "To meet the politic of the Highest with an earthly one is indispensable if one wants to get on in life." It was such politic that kept Joseph "silent as the grave" to his father all these years. "And his name for his first-born was in the same category. 'If I am supposed to forget,' the name was meant to say, 'then, lo, I have forgotten.' But he had not" (1013).

So we have been told that to succeed in the world of the "others"—the flesh-worshippers—the artist too must to some degree become one of them. For it is only by entering that world, the world of ordinary human experience, that he can win for his fellows his life-serving insight. As for God's jealous love of Joseph, we have already seen that it is a metaphor for the necessary self-love of the artist, for whom the call of life, of his own inner development, does require that he be exiled from his home and his father. Then, if God is the power underlying the whole, what is His "soul-life" if not the endlessly changing relationships among its endlessly changing elements? The religiousness that studies the soul-life of God is the artist's attentiveness to that whole which is never still, and his "politic" is the "tact," a word our guide also uses, that intuits how we too must change to remain in harmony with it.

The drama that culminates in the great reunion is that of the Grand Vizier's tense waiting for reports that the famine has brought his brothers to buy grain in Egypt and his explosive joy when they appear; of his sly tricks to force them to prove their honesty by bringing Benjamin with them on their second visit ("In plain words," Jacob protests when they urge him to let Benjamin go back with them, "you demand from me that I send this last remaining one to join his brother Joseph" [1082], and of course he is right, though only we know in what way); of the additional tricks by which he convinces himself the brothers have changed and will not sacrifice Benjamin for their own interests as they did him long ago; of his astounding disclosure and forgiveness and embrace and the message he sends back with them to Jacob; and finally, of the momentous coming together of father and son. All of this is thrilling; all of it shimmers with innuendos of memory and meaning. But the drama reaches its peak in the scene of the great Egyptian lord feasting the eleven sons of Jacob, whom he has so strangely known how to seat in order of age, with "little Benjamin" (now the father of eight with two wives!) beside him. It is a scene in which the lord's playful talk of their lost brother—startlingly echoing certain talks of long ago—fills Benjamin with a torture-joy of knowing and not knowing, so that a moment comes when a cry "was damned back in his breast . . . or rather . . . it was not yet there" (1102). And that waiting cry exemplifies our own suspense, for as the brothers set out for home, we feel with the wretched, reluctant Benjamin that something of tremendous importance has been left hanging—and feel with him too when, hearing the noise of the lord's pursuing soldiers, he utters that great cry at last, and then not another sound (though the "stolen" cup is discovered in his baggage and they are all brought back) until the noble Egyptian, tears glittering on his face like jewels, confesses the secret he already knows. There are, of course, other ways than this to write great fiction. But really, when we consider that Mann conveys in one sequence the immediate experience of this reunion, the rich past it grew out of and completes, the large myth-idea it embodies, and also, in his manner of telling, the combination of laughter and tears arising out of the consciousness of all this at once — when we consider, in short, how Mann joins the most primitive appeal of story with such complexity of art and thought, the question arises whether the possibilities of fiction have ever been so richly realized.

But it is with meaning that we are here concerned. We get a hint of what Joseph's machinations mean when he commands the brothers, in Mann as in Genesis, to tell their father of his glory. The dearest wish of the assimilated and successful Jew, of the artist triumphant among the others, is to be vindicated by the judgment of the father, that is, of the moral authority of his world. But to say this is not yet to say all. What Joseph wants is not quite what he gets. For Jacob is brought before us again on the eve of their reunion precisely to emphasize that he is not only a loving father; he is also a judge who speaks for God, or at least for the moral aspect of God which has been his life's concern.

Mann found a warrant for this in Genesis (46:1-4), where we are also reminded of Jacob's connection with the Highest when he is on his way to join his son. The Lord pays him a final visit at Beersheba to tell him not to be afraid of going to Egypt, for He will make him a great people there and bring him out again, and Joseph will close his eyes at the end. To be sure, our narrator reminds us that Jacob's earlier encounters with God were dreams born of humiliation and makes it plain that in this one too the nervous man is told just what he needs to hear. But Mann's emphasis now is not on the lowly origins of Jacob's vision but on its truth. God's appearance this time is preceded by an explanation of Jacob's decision to go to Egypt and then by a sermon he makes to his people which, together, boldly forestall that debunking view of the vision and ground it in timeless realities.

Our narrator observes that the reason Jacob gives in Genesis for his great move — to see his son before he dies — can hardly be taken literally. For if seeing Joseph were all that mattered, "his high-and-mightiness" could have come to his "little father." No, the real reason this "expert in God-knowledge" is taking his people to Egypt is his belief that the famine which raised Joseph so high and brought his brothers before him belongs among the "arrangements in a comprehensive plan" to bring them there. Our guide now promptly grants that one might call it "arrogance" and "egoism" in Jacob that he regards in this light what affected so many people other than his own. But he also points out that in Jacob's mythical view, this "descent" into Egypt is a version of others, that is, of eternal patterns of being which he briefly reincarnates. And "where the ego opens its borders to the cosmic and loses itself therein, can there be any thought of narrowness and isolation?" But the defense of those irritating traits goes deeper.

Reminding us of earlier examples of the same traits in Joseph, our guide now openly states their religious import, that is, their value for human life. "Arrogance and egoism are only negative words," we are told, "for a highly positive and fruitful attitude which we might call by the more sympathetic name of piety." For "piety is the subjectivation of the outer world, its concentration upon the self and its salvation," the sense of "God's especial . . . concern," in short, that tendency to "take himself seriously" without which a man, having no reason to aspire and struggle and rise, is "soon lost." What is involved is not mere self-glorification, for in the wide-spread blessing that arose out of Abraham's "presumption" we see "the connection between the dignity of the self and the dignity of humanity." In fact, "The claim of the human ego to central importance was the precondition for the discovery of God; and only together, with the consequence of the utter destruction of a humanity which does not take itself seriously, can both discoveries be lost sight of again."

What we have been told is that the idea of God is a form of the conviction of the value of the self. Man's self-concern is enlarged by that idea to a sense of the whole as friendly to man (in spite of its terrors), as father-like, as *humanized*. Nor is this mere "wishful thinking," for, as we have been seeing all along, it is in fact open to man, as he faces the world, to select, organize, emphasize, according to his needs; half-perceiving, half creating, he does himself make the world he lives in. Moreover, "If piety is the being penetrated with the importance of the self, then worship is piety's extension and assimilation into the eternalness of being" (1139). It is because piety to God is self-respect and self-respect entails respect for the whole, including humanity, that both can only be lost together and, when they are gone, we have the Nazis and the camps.

Jacob delivers his sermon under the "oracle-tree" at Beersheba, and because this tree was originally a "Baal-tree," he reminds his people of a fundamental difference between their God and Baal. It is that Baal is a "true plurality," there are many Baals, representing many things, whereas their own God is all "that they singly were . . . the Being of all being, Elohim, the many as one." Jacob grants — in a bow by Mann to the Christian Trinity which lies ahead — that this One can appear as "three-fold," for instance, as the Father, the Shepherd and the Angel which overshadows "as with the wings of doves." But "all together they were Elohim, the threefold unity" (1146-1148). The idea of a single hidden power as the source of the various universe had of course appeared earlier, even among the polytheistic Greeks. But it may well be that the awful weight assigned to it by Hebrew monotheism underlies the work of Spinoza, of science, in short, of the most characteristic developments of Western thought.

So the father we find leaning on Judah's arm when the great Egyptian lord arrives at their meeting place in his gilded chariot is the same divided soul we met at the well long ago, torn between the melting love of the man of feeling and the suspicions of the man of God. "Who is the fairly thick-set man . . . arrayed in all the splendor of this world. . . ?" Jacob asks — to me this sentence (though also funny) is one of the most moving in the whole story — and when Joseph comes near, his two hands hold him back while he peers into "the Egyptian's face with love and sorrow painted on his own." It is only when the son's eyes grow wet and become as Rachel's eyes that the father "let his head fall on the stranger's shoulder and wept bitter tears" (1151-1152).

This ending of their long ordeal leads at once to what it has taught them, which for this pair has to mean taught them of the nature of God. "Father, do you forgive me?" the son begins. He is thinking, we are told, of the "blind conceit . . . [the] hundred follies, for which he had atoned with the silence of the dead" and for which his father has suffered along with him. The old man replies that God has forgiven them, for He has restored them to each other, and when he adds that the punishment was as terrible as God is mighty, Joseph makes his father smile as he used to do. He defends both God and those, like Abraham and Jacob himself, who have reproached Him for "intemperance." Being so mighty, he ventures, God may strike harder than He knows or intends, and "a friendly and restraining hand . . . as of one whom He loves can do no harm. But now," he goes on, "we will praise His mercy," which is a "wisdom" commensurate with His "greatness." And since this wisdom is to be seen in "the rich meaning of His acts" and in the "manifold action [added] to His decrees," it is clear that though God meant to punish them by the long separation, He meant also that Joseph should become the deliverer of his people in the famine, and "above all" that father and son should be reunited. "We blow hot or cold, but His passion is providence and His anger far-seeing goodness. Has your son," Joseph asks by way of conclusion, "come somewhere near to fit expression about God the Father?" "Somewhere near," Jacob says, and adds, "He is the God of life, and life, of course, one only gets somewhere near."

Jacob's reply is a "yes, but" worthy of Joseph—or of their author. But it is soon clear that he and Joseph are still divided as they were at the well long ago, and that the boy who was already given to "underworld" Egyptian tendencies has, as a man, become half an Egyptian. The judgment Jacob must now pronounce on his dearest son is that of God as *he* knows Him, the God of the spirit Who says No to the deathward-tending flesh. This emerges comically at first. Like an elderly greenhorn, the moralist glances with suspicion at Joseph's gorgeous regalia and asks if the "child" has kept his "purity" among this brutishly lustful people. Upon which the embarrassed Egyptian Jew tells his father that people are really the same everywhere—"in other words, they are so-so"—and he'd better remember he is a guest and not go around criticizing. But it is not at all funny when their talk turns to the first-born blessing the father had once thought to give him. His voice full of heartbreak and love that will persist in all he says to Joseph till the end, Jacob tells him that though he had meant that coat of many colors long ago for "the first-born and the inheritance," God had "torn" it and "admonished [him] with a mighty hand, against which is no rebelling." Joseph, he says, has been "elevated and rejected . . . both in one." The double blessing, endowing him "with blitheness and with destiny, with wit and with dreams," has raised him above his brothers in a "worldly" way. But his triumph is also a defeat. "Through you salvation is not to reach the peoples, and the leadership is denied you" (1153-1155).

Why it must be so emerges in what Mann has added to Jacob's deathbed "testament." We find in his version that the father knows only too well that nothing is "sweeter than the double and the doubtful." Nevertheless, he goes on, "the double is not of the spirit, for which we stand, but is the folly of the peoples." And though beauty was united with wisdom in Joseph and he remained faithful to God amid the world's temptations — even winning, with his "spirit of charm and mediation," the rare blessing that he pleased both God and the world — still, that blessing is "not the highest and sternest.... Play and playing it was, familiar, friendly appealingness, approaching salvation yet not quite seriously a calling or a gift." That he knows he lacks the gift that saves will keep him, the father says, from "presumption" (1194-1195). And Joseph seems to agree with this judgment. On the novel's last page he assures his brothers they need not fear his anger at the old wrong done him, even though their father is no longer between them. Their fear, he says, is a sign that they don't realize as he does the meaning of the story they are in, "God's play," in which he was led to provoke them to evil so that all could at last be turned to good. But "perhaps that is the way it ought to be," he goes on, "and I am to blame myself for knowing far too well what was being played" (1207).

No doubt this concluding modesty is a hint that our author can stand apart from his creation. "It is probable," Mann has remarked, "that I could not have written this success story if I myself were a Joseph" (*Letters*, 509). Mann has to know more than Joseph, and what he knows is what Joseph light-heartedly grants is possible, that the artist's rich awareness, which means (among other things) of the good in evil and the evil in good, must at certain times give way to the moralist's single-mindedness. It will not be long, in fact, before *Doctor Faustus* reveals — confesses — that the artist's openness of mind can be an openness to horrors. And yet. What does it mean to have that calling for spiritual leadership which the "play and playing" of Joseph denies him? The question has already been answered in Mann's portrait of Judah, who has earned the first-born blessing not only be being next in line for it, but by his character. For the lust-harried older brother, who lay with Tamar thinking her a harlot, has been vividly realized by Mann as one of those troubled souls in whom flesh and spirit are in painful opposition. No smiling "Yes, but" comes from *him* to each side in turn. It is precisely because he is forever battling against the flesh within himself that he can be relied on to be the spirit's grimly one-sided champion out in the world. But if we need his "seriousness" in times of struggle, it takes something else to do justice to life and to preserve our joy in it.

This is why Jacob's dying words, for all they take away from his artist-son, end by giving again, and with the extravagance of love. Though the first-born blessing has gone to Judah, still, "I bless you, blessed one," he says to Joseph, "with all the strength of my heart." And: "Higher shall my blessings mount than the blessings of my fathers upon my own head." At last: "Songs shall stream far and wide singing the story of your life, ever anew, for after all it was a sacred play and you suffered and could forgive" (1195).

The fact is, though Mann's concluding reservation about the artist serves his need for detachment and a final irony, the novel has already undermined it. It is true that Joseph's doubleness was often weakness. But not only have we seen that "however much his weakness injured him, [he] possessed more understanding of the livingness of God . . . than the father who begot him." We have seen too that the artist *can* be faithful to the Highest, faithful in his own way, which means to himself as well, and therefore to us. It is precisely by his sympathy with both sides of life's eternal antinomies that he mitigates the pain of their conflict. It is by "play and playing" which are wisdom that he helps us turn the inhuman whole into a human home.[26]

Notes

1. As usual with Mann, when the idea of retelling the Joseph story came to him (in 1924), he thought he would write something short, a novella.

2. There is a five-volume work by Louis Ginsberg called *The Legends of the Jews* which brings together the folk tales about Biblical characters and events preserved by the rabbis in the Talmudic-Midrashic literature from the second to the fourteenth century, as well as "apocryphal-pseudepigraphic" tales rejected by the rabbis and preserved by the Church Fathers in the first few centuries after Christ. In this work, especially in Volumes One and Two, we can find a great many of the scenes and touches by which Mann (adapting them for his own purposes) illuminates and makes real the story of Genesis. But it gives me pleasure to add — with my thanks — that before I encountered Ginsberg I heard many of these rabbinical tales in the study of my cousin Mrs. Emunah Zlotkin in a suburb of Jerusalem. She translated them for me directly from the marginal commentaries in the big tomes of a Hebrew Bible, conveying, by her Talmudic *nigun* (traditional sing-song) and her own reactions, far more than literal meaning. In Jerusalem I was also helped in my search for Mann's sources by Professor Mosheh Greenberg, Chairman of Bible Studies, Hebrew University.

3. Mann's Joseph is, in fact, a twentieth century "midrash." "Midrash" is the name of both the process of interpreting Biblical texts and the resulting interpretations. According to Barry W. Holtz in one of the essays in *Back to the Source*, a fine introduction to the basic texts of Judaism, it emerges where "new cultural and intellectual pressures . . . must be addressed," coming into play "as a way of resolving crises and reaffirming continuity with the traditions of the past" (179). A good description of what Mann has done in *Joseph*.

Mann gives us his formulation of key elements of his own "midrash" in "Freud and the Future" and "The Theme of the Joseph Novels."

4. That this novel is also about that "egocentric" subject, Mann tells us himself in the letter I quoted above. "Basically," he says, "it is once again, like *Buddenbrooks*, the story of a family's development; in a certain sense it is even again a story of decadence and refinement. Young Joseph, an *artistic* personality living in a religious sphere, has approximately the same relationship to his forefathers as Hanno Buddenbrook to his — except that . . . in this mythic book the familial and middleclass element is lifted into the realm of general humanity. At bottom the book aspires to be, so to speak, *an abbreviated history of mankind*."

5. In *Mythology and Humanism: The Correspondence of Thomas Mann and Karl Kerenyi*, there is abundant evidence that Mann received from Kerenyi much data, stimulus and support for his treatment of myth in *Joseph* and later works. A letter by Mann dated September 7, 1941, expresses gratitude for the "joint effort that has developed between us over the years," an effort which, along with the work of Jung, has brought together "mythology and psychology," in order that "myth be taken away from intellectual fascism and transmuted for human ends" (103).

6. Gershom G. Scholem tells us in *Walter Benjamin: The Story of a Friendship* (trans. H. Zohn [Philadelphia, 1981], p. 96-97) that the German-Jewish philosopher Oskar Goldberg was Mann's instructor in Jewish mysticism and that "the first novel of [the] Joseph tetralogy is in its metaphysical sections based entirely on Goldberg's book [*Die Werklichkeit der Hebraer*]" (98). But this is misleading. To judge by Scholem's own account of Goldberg's ideas, they are to be found, not in *The Tales of Jacob*, but in the fascistic speeches of Chaim Breisacher in *Doctor Faustus*. Goldberg regarded the first five books of the Bible, Scholem says, as "a continuum of pure magic." He explained Judaism as a "decline from ancient magical Hebraism, and in so doing shrank from no conclusion and no absurdity. What Goldberg aimed at was a restoration of the magic bond between God and His people. . . ." His ideas were "demonic," Scholem says too and had "a Luciferian luster" (96-97). *The Tales of Jacob*, as we will see, is about how Judaism *humanized* the divine.

It is worth adding that Scholem himself reveals, in *Major Trends in Jewish Mysticism* and *On the Kabbalah and Its Symbolism*, that the ultimate source of many of the Hebrew myths and symbols Mann uses to convey the timeless meaning of the religion of the Jews and its kinship with his own thought is the writings of the Kabbalists, and especially the *Zohar* or *Book of Splendor*. For instance, the first book (p. 215 et. seq.) tells the story of "Adam Kadman," as it is spelled by Scholem. And in the second (pp. 104, 409) Scholem says that Kabbalah transformed the idea of the *Shekhinah*—"literally indwelling, namely of God in the world"—from God's presence in the world to the "feminine element in God" and at last to "*a part of God himself . . . exiled from God*" (his emphasis) because of human sin. This separation is at the bottom of the "cleavage between the upper and the lower, the masculine and feminine," and is symbolized in the separation of the Tree of Life from the Tree of Knowledge, or "of life and death." And it is the restoration of their unity which is "the meaning of redemption."

7. Mann adds innuendos by his ways of naming or referring to a character. So, in place of Abraham, the patriarch's later honorific name, meaning "father of great multitudes," he often uses the original name of the wanderer from Ur, Abram. And our narrator tells us that Abram's other form, "Abiram," means "'my father is exalted' [in the Anchor Genesis 'the father is exalted'] or also, probably just as correctly, 'father of the exalted.' For in a way Abraham was God's father" (285).

8. As I said, that coat also links the episode with the story's deepest meanings and Mann's eternal preoccupations. Not only does it connect Joseph with his dead mother because wearing it he seems to Jacob Rachel herself come alive. Mann has made it into a concrete symbol of the "underworld" element in Joseph's double

blessing. Its famous colors turn out to be pictures of pagan deities that darkly hint at the death and rebirth of gods and of the role of death in life. "A marvelous thing . . . hath Israel given thee," old Eliezer says after seeing the pictures, "for in the veil is life and death." And surely we hear in what he says next an echo of Hans Castorp's discovery on his mountain: "But death is in life and life in death, and he who hath learned this truth hath penetrated the mysteries" (325).

9. For Mann's source for the idea of the "sphere," see Scholem's *Major Trends*, e.g., where it quotes this from the *Zohar*: "'The process of creation . . . has taken place on two planes, one above and one below. . . . The lower occurence corresponds to the higher; one produces the upper world . . . the other the nether world (of the visible creation).' Both differ . . . only in that the higher order represents the dynamic unity of God, while the lower leaves room for differentiation and separation. . . . But . . . 'If one contemplates the things in mystical mediation, everything is revealed as one.'" This is followed by the "formula": "He fills everything and he is everything" (222). All this will be frequently echoed in Mann's novel. See, too, Abraham Kaplan's "The Jewish Argument with God," which tells us that "Kabbalah expounds a parallelism between the Upper World and the Lower World. Whatever is done in the one sphere is reflected by corresponding events in the other. . . . The Lower World, rather than being a shadow of the Upper World, symbolizes it; like other symbols, it evokes the reality it names" (46).

10. From H. D. F. Kitto's *The Greeks* (Middlesex, 1951, p. 187, fn. 1): "'Logos' is usually mistranslated 'word'; it is rather 'speech,' or, the idea which is conveyed by speech. 'In the beginning was the Word' really means 'In the beginning was the Conception'" (187, fn. 1).

Of course, this idea of the role of our own imagination in making the world we live in is also to be found elsewhere than among the Jewish mystics — for instance, in German idealism and English romanticism. And it has been explored in our time in Nelson Goodman's *Ways of Worldmaking* (1973) and Jerome Bruner's *Actual Minds, Possible Worlds* (1986).

11. In the Tamar section Mann's narrator makes the Hebrew orientation in the future explicit by lapsing oddly into rhyme. Asserting that Jacob was not among those "clouded souls" ("pious," not pious) who regard only the past as holy, he thus expresses what he calls his "creed": "Who honours not the future 'one day,' to him the past has nought to say, and even the present he fronts the wrong way" (1027). (In the original: "*Wer nicht das Einst der Zukunft ehrt ist nicht das Einst der Vergangenheit wert und stellt sich auch zum heutigen Tag verkehrt.*") That is, it is what we want our future to be that makes real and productive both our memories of the past and our dealings with the present.

12. When *could* savagery be right? Perhaps at a stage in man's development when it has a "survival value" otherwise unavailable.

13. This creature will reappear twice in the same role. He will meet Reuben at the well, where the big brother has come to rescue Joseph and is in despair at finding him gone, in order to plant a "seed of expectation" that he may yet see him again; and later he will lead the caravan of Joseph's master safely through the desert that guards the approach to the "underworld" of Egypt. Does Mann again get away with this violation of his own realism? Well, why not? Not only does that resentful

agent of God behave exactly as he would if he existed. All he says and does, as with the supernatural elsewhere in the novel, hints at realities. And finally, nothing vital to the story rests on his supernatural powers.

14. To serve his idea Mann has availed himself of the liberty given by the historical uncertainty of Ikhnaton's dates to move him 400 years backward from the period after the Jewish exodus usually assigned to him and made him the Pharaoh of Joseph.

15. For the relevance of all this to the politics of Mann's own time and place see Raymond's Cunningham's book on *Joseph* (1985).

16. The Anchor Genesis note on Genesis 37:36 is "*Potiphar*. An Egyptian personal name, 'One whom (the god) Re has granted.'" This is followed by "*courtier*. Literally, 'eunuch'" (291).

17. Montkaw is one of the characters Mann has invented to help the story of Genesis to come about. The others are Jacob's servant Eliezer; Potiphar's parents, Huia and Tuia; the dwarfs Bes and Dudu, who help and hinder Joseph in his rise in Potiphar's house; the High Priest Beknechons, who represents Amun among the great as Dudu does in his lower sphere; and Pharaoh's mother.

18. But I might mention in a footnote the narrative device by which this development is realistically brought about. Mann embodies in the two comic warring dwarfs the opposing attitudes which the gifted Hebrew slave would naturally have encountered on his way upward in Potiphar's house, an opposition which is a comic version of that between flesh and spirit. The hostile dwarf Dudu, a self-satisfied mediocrity whose pride is in belonging to the dominant religion and people and in the virility befitting a devotee of Amun, hates the rising foreigner and initiates the sexual drama, first by warnings that awaken the interest of his mistress, and then, seeing what has happened, by becoming her pander and promoting the meetings that lead to Joseph's ruin. The other dwarf Bes is a witty jester who not only laughs at the pretensions of Dudu and loves the gifts of Joseph, but who has a horror of sex. *He* plies Joseph with warnings against the "fiery bull" the young man ominously refuses to understand. These dwarfs carry what they represent to hilarious extremes that remind one of Molière. Especially Molière-like is the scene in which Dudu proudly brags to Potiphar how he'd exposed the Hebrew by bringing him and the woman together, unaware, in his blind self-satisfaction, of the retribution he is inciting until it explodes in rain of blows.

Among the scenes that dramatize Mut's passion, I might mention two of the best. There is the great dialogue of Mut and Potiphar in which the struggling woman begs her husband (himself deeply burdened because he knows what she suffers) to get rid of the foreign slave, delights in the praise by which Potiphar defends him, and, when she is finally refused, covers her face to hide her irrepressible joy. In the other, adapted from a rabbinical tale, Mut shows her woman friends why she is suffering by having the beautiful Hebrew serve them wine just as they are peeling oranges with specially sharpened knives. Gazing at him, they bathe themselves in their own blood.

19. That Joseph is guilty to the woman Mann might well have inferred from Genesis itself. For we read there, "And it came to pass, about this time [a time when Potiphar's wife pleaded with him "day by day . . . to lie with her"], that Joseph went

into the house to do his business and there was none of the men of the house there within. And she caught him by his garment, saying Lie with me, and he left his garment in her hand and fled and got him out" (Gen. 39:11-12). Mann would surely be justified in concluding from this not only that Joseph kept putting himself in the woman's way, but that, as chief steward, he must have known that the men had left her there alone and came back to the house *because* he knew it.

20. See Mann's essay "Voyage With *Don Quixote*."

21. Mann has pointed out in his Library of Congress address "The Theme of the Joseph Novels" (and elsewhere) the influence on the novel of Goethe's *Faust*, and especially the Classical Walpurgisnacht of Part II. Clearly, he found in it a stimulus and an encouragement to convey his own playful overview of human culture by means of archetypes and archetypal experiences. And of course, the Faust who says the devil can take him if he asks life to remain fixed at some gratifying moment is a brother of Mann's Joseph, who, as we will see, serves a "God of life" Who is endlessly "becoming." Mann's essay "Faust" is full of evidence of the kinship between them, e.g., "Irony is his [Goethe's] 'second soul'" and the observation that Goethe makes Faust speak with a sigh of "the two souls within his breast: the one the lusty hunger for love, the clinging sensuality; the other his longing for the pure and spiritual." The sigh he breathes is "half-hypocritical," we are told, "for well he knows that dualism is the soil and the mystery of creative fruitfulness" (*Essays*, 21).

22. Spelled Samael, this is the name of the "Prince of Demons" (a development out of the Angel of Death), according to *The Encyclopedia of the Jewish Religion* (31).

23. Though the "living food" Joseph provides is not only for the body, he completes God's plan by saving Egypt (and his own people) from famine. He does this, Mann has said, as "an American Hermes" (xiii). In fact, his policies resemble the "New Deal" of Franklin D. Roosevelt, a president Mann met and admired; he remodels "the property concept into something which was both preservation and abrogation" (1165).

24. In the prison captain Mai-Sachme, a would-be poet of unlived love fantasies who is bored with his prison duties and glad to turn them over to the gifted Hebrew prisoner, Mann has again created a vivid realistic basis for the skimpy facts in Genesis. Moreover, he "discovers" (as a useful move to economy and dramatic unity) that this same captain, having been asked to join Joseph in his time of glory, is also the chief steward who, in Genesis, helps him trick and test his brothers.

25. In Exodus 28:30 in connection with Aaron, and in a number of other books of the Pentateuch in connection with "priests," Urim and Thummim are referred to as things added to the "breastplate" of those who go before the Lord and who "bear the judgment of the children of Israel." The Yale University seal places beneath those words in Hebrew the Latin words *Lux et Veritas*. These are clues to Mann's use of the words as a formula for wisdom, in which pure light is corrected into truth by an admixture of life's darkness, "yes" by "yes-no."

26. That Joseph *is*, on the whole, the way Mann sees the artist in himself he told Agnes Meyer in the letter of 10/7/41 quoted at the end of Chapter Two.

CHAPTER SEVEN

The Beloved Returns
(Lotte in Weimar)

"Sitting at my desk [over this novel] . . . I would perform the
'unio mystica' with Goethe." (*Story*, 5)

The Beloved Returns, which appeared in 1939 between the third and last
volumes of the Joseph tetralogy, is fascinating simply as a living portrait of
Germany's greatest writer. Based on an actual episode of Goethe's old age, it
conveys, along with the significant events of his life, the full range of his mind
as this has been preserved in the works, the letters and the richly recorded conversations. But what makes the novel a characteristic Mann triumph is something else. It is first that, without ceasing to be a faithful portrait of Goethe,
the novel becomes another, and a further, illumination of Mann's eternal subject, the nature of the artist as he found it in himself; and then, that every bit
of its carefully assembled data becomes part of the story, which means too of
its unfolding idea. All of it is brought together in a climactic display of
genius—at work and among others—that the novel foreshadows from its
beginning and that, in the last three chapters, brings dazzlingly to a close.

1

Mann had dreamed of doing a Goethe novel since his work on *Death in
Venice* in 1911. But he was set free to write it, he said, only when "a light and
humorous approach offered itself with the anecdote about the visit of the aged
Charlotte Buff to Weimar" (*Letters*, 417). Charlotte Buff is of course the blue-
eyed Lotte who was the source of Werther's black-eyed Lotte in *The Sorrows of
Young Werther*, which made Goethe famous at twenty-five, and the "return" was
that of an elderly widow with a pathetically nodding head to an old man who
had become the acknowledged monarch of European culture and the literally
ennobled Privy Councillor of the Duchy of Saxe-Weimar. But this is only the
tip of the iceberg.

What gives the anecdote its meaning is the way the "lovers" had come together and parted long before, an episode partly known to us from the shamelessly candid account of it Goethe put into that first novel. The young poet had been introduced to Lotte by her fiancé, who was his friend, and soon he was pressing his love on the girl in the delusion that because she was engaged and honorable, and he was fertile in spiritual names for what he wanted them to share, he could do so without guilt. He knew himself better at last. Though Werther was to leave—of course, by suicide—after forcing on his Lotte a "storm of kisses" and being rebuffed, Goethe claims in his autobiography that conscience drove him away from the real one when he saw he had grown "more passionate than was right" (*Truth and Poetry*, 482). Still, two years later he perpetuated the wrong he had done his two friends by publishing their "three-cornered" love episode—and even Lotte's first name!—to all the world. Then came his letters of explanation and excuse—it was not real life, but art, it had made the world love and honor Lotte as he did, and so on—and the Kestners forgave him. Before their correspondence ceased, they had sent him silhouettes of their children—nine of the eleven survived infancy—to add to one Lotte had given him of herself.

But there is more to the iceberg. The record tells us that before he met Lotte, and during the years before their reunion, the poet had loved, left and turned into literature a number of other women, and Mann reminds us that Lotte would have read about some of them, as well as herself, in the first books of his autobiography, which appeared in 1811. (Oddly enough, the only beloved inspirer Goethe didn't leave was the rather coarse and simple mistress he had shocked his high-class Weimar friends by talking into his home after his liberating Italian journey and, after the birth of a bastard son, shocked even more by marrying.) And in the year of Lotte's "return," he was completing *Faust*, the drama in which a man of genius also loves and leaves a girl (destroys her, indeed), rises high in the world, and is at last forgiven.

Finally, we know that the reunion-dinner *chez* Goethe was not a success. A daughter Clara, who, along with Lotte's Weimar sister and brother-in-law, was also invited, wrote of their host to a brother that "his conversation was . . . commonplace and superficial," his courtesy that of a "courtier" and "there was so little that was heartfelt about it all, that my very soul was wounded" (*A Man*, 260-261). Lotte herself wrote to a son (in a letter the novel quotes) that what had taken place was actually "a new acquaintance with an old man," and though, "in his stiff way he did all he could to show me courtesy," it was not "pleasant" (437). Goethe also felt, apparently, that something more was wanted than he gave. A letter exists—and Mann bases his last chapter upon it—in which His Excellency apologizes for being unavailable in this period, but offers the widow his box at the theatre that evening and his carriage to take her there and back.

Part of the reason the anecdote enabled Mann to write his Goethe novel at last may already be clear. The reunion of the artist with the woman who had resisted him on behalf of normal ("bourgeois") life was another confrontation between the eternal polarities of Mann's thought. But Mann's subject had always to be new as well as old. What this one also offered him was that these "opposites" were brought together by a near-seduction, and that the seducer was Germany's supreme genius, who carried what he was all the way. Moreover, since Lotte had resisted the seduction and forgiven it, her "return" in old age raises two interesting questions: What was she seeking in this attempt ("fantastic," Mann calls it in his first chapter) to "revive the past and connect it with the present" (53-54)? And, What did she find? To give us his answers, Mann did with this anecdote what he was doing with the legends of Joseph; he "discovered" under the events we know the feelings and motives they must, or might well, have come from. And though the actual reunion ended in trivialities, and Mann was too committed a realist to pass up the chance to show why, he didn't in this tale, any more than in his others, let realism prevent the fullest, most "fantastic," unfolding of his idea.

He did, however, make four small changes in the facts. He replaced Clara, the daughter who accompanied his heroine, with the older daughter Charlotte, who had given up her own life to the care of a crippled widower brother and his children. He settled the visitors, not at the home of Lotte's Weimar sister, where they actually stayed, but at a hotel. He enlarged Goethe's guest list for the dinner to include, along with the poet's old friend and her family, certain members of his Weimar circle. And at the end—most audaciously—he brought Lotte and Goethe together for a conversation that never took place. As we will see, these changes don't contradict the actual character of their reunion, but only help to dramatize what it could—and should—have meant to both.

2

Mann's title informs us that the novel is at least as much about Lotte as it is about the overpowering figure at its center. In fact, it is in large part the story of how she herself arrives at the answers to those two questions. Thus Mann chose Charlotte to accompany his heroine to Weimar as one whom a life of self-sacrifice has made sourly observant and who will provoke her mother to blushing, and revealing, self-defense. And he placed them in a hotel in order to make possible three prompt visits by members of Goethe's circle who will reanimate her old grievance against him. By the time these visits are over, the first question—about the reason for her return—has been answered.

We learn, to begin with, that the old lady's view of that far-off love-episode is not what a daughter like Charlotte would approve. Though Lotte is proud that "the great temptation [was] honorably overcome" (27), she is equally proud not only of the glory to which *Werther* lifted her, but of the "deathly sweet" (27) experience it came from, a kind of experience her poor daughter has never

known. It turns out, indeed, that when her agonized bridegroom offered to set
her free to choose the poet, it was "not entirely" out of loyalty to him that she
refused, but because she "feared the mystery of the other's nature," which seemed
to her "inhuman, without purpose or poise" (31). Mann's Lotte even plans to
go to Goethe (when he responds to the note she is writing him) in the kind of
white dress she used to wear and, since she remembers sending the poet a pink
"breast-knot" to mitigate the pain of his departure, with a pink ribbon missing
at her breast as a reminder! Such clinging, as of an "elderly schoolgirl" to
youthful "unwisdom," embarrasses the daughter, but their author defends it.
It is an instance, we are told, of "the blithe and shamefaced secret of our
dignified old age," the "faith of our youth [which] we never . . . relinquish"
(25-26), that under the external changes we remain the same. A "casual"
remark to remember. For the same faith and the same clinging to the feelings
of youth will underlie both the guilt and the greatness of Goethe.

It's true that the talk of the visitors goes on for pages (as some readers complain). But what keeps it quite sufficiently alive as fiction is that all three are
in a state of conflict, first within themselves and then with Lotte. Though they
are all (of course) Goethe's admirers, the two men have been drawn to the
heroine of *Werther* as fellow-victims, and the woman has come on behalf of still
another: they count on her sympathy. And as Lotte finds herself resisting what
they want from her, she begins to understand what she wants for herself.

The first, Goethe's invaluable assistant Dr. Riemer, forces that kinship on
Lotte as a kind of preface to his awed and horrified account of the master's
deepest nature. It seems Goethe has kept him in his service all these years by
the promise — never fulfilled — that he would recommend him for a university
professorship. And the reason the ambitious scholar allowed himself to be ex-
ploited was his inability to give up his thrilling daily contact with such a mind,
"the most winning form that greatness can take on earth, the genius as poet"
(79). Even his eyes are thrilling, the man embarrassingly confesses, and Lotte,
remembering, has to agree. So a barely repressed rage keeps alternating with
his profound appreciation. And while Lotte listens to all this with "half-
contemptuous pity" (59) — that is, as one who had the strength to resist the
powerful seduction — she can't help realizing that what drew the man to her is
the same thing that made her welcome his visit. Both have endured "the life-
long discomfort of an unresolved past," and both hope "their coming together
might help them . . . solve the riddle and lighten the burden" (53).

But it is Riemer's passionate account of the nature of the seductive power
that uncovers the deepest meaning of Lotte's "return." In a playful reference
by Mann to his unfinished portrait of the artist as Joseph, Riemer sees Goethe
as blessed with the double blessing Jacob called down upon his dreamer-son —
"blessings of the heaven above, blessings of the deep which lyeth under" — and
interprets this as Mann does in the longer work: it is "the blessing of humanity
as a whole" (83), that is, of nature and spirit in their unity. While the rest of
us suffer a continual conflict between the nature in which we are rooted and

the realm of spirit toward which we yearn, for "the darling and familiar of Nature" that double blessing is "the formula for a harmony . . . absolutely noble, and an earthy bliss" (84-85). But though this explains one's extraordinary sense of well-being in Goethe's presence, it is also the reason one feels a powerful impulse to run away. For Goethe's "boundless good nature" and "sympathy" imply a "destructive tolerance for everything, a world without end or aim, where good and evil have the same ironic right." To Riemer Goethe's "all-embracing irony," which is also "the neutrality of absolute art," is "nihilism" (85-86). It is this which accounts for his way of alternating, like nature herself, between happy-making brightness and a gloom which chills. For joy comes from taking sides, from enthusiasm. And the poet is devoid not only of the warm political faith of his fellows; he is even cynical about art. "A poem," he has said, " . . . is a kiss which one gives all the world. But no children come of kisses" (90).

There will be more about "kisses" in a moment. Now the remark Riemer reports about their biological fruitlessness leads this mother of eleven to the painful secret of *her* grievance, to that "old, never-settled, tormenting score" (99) she finds she has come to Weimar to settle. It is that Goethe had loved in her a charm of young womanhood someone else had discovered and nurtured, laying his emotions "like a cuckoo-egg in a nest already made" (108). Worse than this, he had become a "parasite" and tempter in "a sort of play," as "an emotional means to an end that was unreal and extra-human" (110-111). For Kestner was to remain the real bridegroom and to shoulder the obligation of marriage and a family. The poet wanted nothing from her but kisses!

Riemer's "defense" of his master actually helps define his crime. Goethe's love was never "serious," he assures her. It was the spirit of poetry in him, enjoying, like Narcissus, its own beauty and "intoxicated by the sense of guilt she has herself invoked" (112). And when he calls "noble" an actual remark of Goethe's to a friend which Lotte now remembers, that he was sure of her loyalty to her bridegroom and counted on her not to "deceive" him, she cries out her continuing agony of bewilderment that the poet could speak of deception while he, with his "god-like power of attraction" (114) and those cloudy promises that committed him to nothing, was deceiving her.

Lotte's first visitor has thus reawakened her old grievance against Goethe, even as he has prepared her (and us) for the greatness she is about to meet. Adele Schopenhauer, the philosopher's young blue-stocking sister who comes in next, will repeat the contradiction. Though she begins by informing Lotte that German society, which "takes pleasure in bowing down" (133), has turned her old friend into a tyrant, a bully and a bore, and will end with an indictment even more shocking, she can't help celebrating the Weimar sage. This emerges as she reports his attitude to her own "romantic" generation.

What characterizes the young these days, she admits, is a taste for unbridled feeling, a sentimental nostalgia for medieval culture and Gothic legend, and a hot "freedom-and-brotherhood" patriotism which is drawing the separate German states together under Prussian leadership to shake off the hated yoke of Napoleon. And the response she reports is the scorn of the classicist who left the cult of feeling behind with his own *Werther* and of the champion of world culture (and especially French literature) against reactionary nationalism. To be sure, she gives us a glimpse of the great man's repellent egotism, so like what Mann was accused of himself. After a French retaliation had destroyed the homes of others but left his own untouched, he had likened himself to the man in Lucretius's poem who takes a certain pleasure in watching from the safety of a cliff how the shipwrecked struggle below him amid the waves. But it is not ego we see in his rejection of that passion for "fatherland and freedom." "The German," Adele quotes from the master, ". . . must take in the whole world in order to have an effect on the world" and cultivate the "social virtues at the expense of . . . inborn feelings and rights." Again (speaking to an ardent foe of Napoleon): "It is not enough to mean well. . . . One must also be able to see the consequences of one's activities. I shudder at yours because they are the first manifestations . . . of something frightful, to be displayed someday by us Germans in the form of the crassest follies" (160-161).

Despite her intellectual's superiority to the times' excesses, however, Adele's unbroken monologue amusingly duplicates, in its clichés of thought, feeling and language, the sentimental romances of the day. Her romance is the story of her dear friend Ottilie von Pogswich, the adoring daughter of one Prussian officer who falls in love with another at the time when she is engaged to Goethe's son. Ottilie and Adele found the young man wounded and, hiding him from the French, nursed him back to health. The contrast between the hero of romance they make of him while he is helpless in their care and the ordinary creature he turns out to be when he is well becomes a comic exposure of the sentimentality that nurtures and gilds this period's bloody nationalism. But it is the way the romantic tale threatens to end that Adele has chiefly on her mind. For she has come to beg Lotte to save her friend from a marriage to Goethe's son that would be another seduction by the father, and a seduction strangely—and significantly—duplicating his crime of forty-four years ago.

For in her view Goethe, who has recently lost his wife, wants Ottilie to marry his son and so to become the new mistress his home requires because she is exacty the slim, girlish Lotte-type he has always preferred. Moreover, "The son loved in her the very type of his father's election. His love . . . was bond-service" (206). As for Ottilie, it is the father by whom she is being tempted. That it couldn't possibly be the son Adele makes clear by describing him as history has in fact brought him down to us, that is, as a debased version of his father—politically in his passion for Napoleon, and morally in his Bohemian rejection of discipline, his drunkenness, his womanizing. In short, he lives by the artist's values without the self-regulating power of his genius. So, in a striking example of Mann's ingenuity, playfulness and wit, Adele concludes by pleading with Lotte to "be a mother to this image of your own youth" and "on the grounds of what you once were to the father save her from being sacrificed to a fascination" like that Lotte herself escaped (218).

When August, reeking of wine, takes Adele's place in Lotte's room a moment later, his official purpose is to deliver his father's invitation to dinner. But what keeps *him* talking is the conflict between pride and humiliation that has dominated his life as the "love-child" of a genius (only belatedly legitimized by his father's friend the Duke), a conflict in which the pride is on the surface and the humiliation — and a furious resentment — undermine it from below. Hotly defending his father's behavior, he not only arouses Lotte's distaste but seems to have intended to do so, whether he knows it or not. On the other hand, what he says out of the resentment he feels far more deeply and that he expects her, of all people, to share moves her to the poet's defense.

So his rage against his father's critics, particularly those who had censured the marriage to his mother, turns out to be a mask for his rage against his father. Such a man, he says, has "the right to live according to his own lights, by the fundamental, classic law of moral self-government . . . the law of free and self-governing beauty," which is a law not only of art, but "of life as well." The "Christian patriots [who looked down on his mother and] moaned over the conflict between genius and morality" know little of art, for they were the same as those who found immoral the *Meister*, the *Elegies*, *Elective Affinities* and even *Werther*. This view of the irrelevance — the philistinism — of moral criteria in art will be familiar to art-lovers. But the overwrought and tipsy son has also pointed out that the artist's freedom is "the freedom to which I owed my very existence" (234) — he might have added his behavior — and so has reminded us of the miseries of that existence and the cost to others of such freedom, which is to say, of the danger of applying aesthetic criteria to life.

It is because this dark side of the artist's freedom is August's real message that all he tells Lotte is suggested by and keeps returning to an episode that led the poet to abandon one of his recent victims. Marianne von Willemer, already immortalized as the elderly Hatem's love Zuleika in Goethe's *East-West Divan*, had been the ward and mistress and was now the wife of an old friend. What August forces his shrinking listener to understand is that it was his father who, enchanted by the girl at their first meeting and eager for more, insisted that his friend marry her. He is telling Lotte that the seducer-parasite was at it again! And the betrayer, too — for he ends the story by informing her that when the carriage taking his father to the von Willemers overturned, he decided this was a sign that his love had served its purpose "as a means to an end." He gave up his journey and never went back.

But it is a predecessor of Lotte's who serves August as the most telling example of the artist's egotism and leads his ambivalence to its deepest insight and pain. After his pride has boasted that his father resembles the great Napoleon as a "tremendous and dominating force" (244), his anger remembers Friederike Brion. This is the girl whom, according to the autobiography, Goethe left weeping when he bade her farewell from the saddle, who "pined away" unmarried and whose grave at Baden August is sure the poet never visited. He now grants that his father could see such miseries in "terms of universal humanity" and convert them into "enduring works of art." But soon after he is declaring that the "*idée fixe*" of Goethe's life and work is that "disloyalty and betrayal" are "renunciation," and then that the thought of Friederike's tears fills him with "dread" because a great poet's life "conditions the character, culture and future of the nation" (246-247). He means that the moral "freedom" which wrung tears from the girl would make countless others weep. At last, his ambivalence reaching its climax, he defends Goethe's behavior as a stout renunciation of the "possible" for the "actual"—love-dreams for work and career—and then invites Lotte to share his "sadness" at the way the "actual" overshadows the "possible, the unfulfilled . . . [the] might-have-been" (248). A moment later he expresses awe at "the mystery" bodied forth by the poem in which Zuleika's love of great old Hatem is compared to the dawn lighting up a mountain—"the universe takes on a human visage and the ego looks out with eyes of stars" (251)—and then makes it clear, without daring to know it consciously, that he finds this expansion of Hatem-Goethe's ego unbearable.

It is when Lotte gently but firmly resists the young man's indictment of his father that we arrive at Mann's most momentous "discovery" about her. The fact that she rose long ago above the pain and self-pity of the victim Mann takes as a clue to how her judgment of Goethe would be complicated forever. In her opinion Goethe is not a "bad emperor," like that "blood-reeking demon" Napoleon, but "one of the good and mild ones" (244). And she not only honors her tempter's achievements; she even believes he is not wholly responsible for the fate of his victims! The tearful girl who "pined away" would have been more "worthy of her lover," Lotte says, "if she had had enough resolution to carve herself out a real life after he was gone" (247). Granting tactfully that it is a kind of "idealism" to honor the "possible" over the "actual," she nevertheless suggests that "perhaps resolve reaches higher on the moral plane" (249). And though she finds it distasteful that Marianne was treated as "a means to an end," the loyal wife and mother concludes by proudly reminding the young man that "any good and resolute means can make an end out of itself" (254).

We have been shown that Lotte is indeed "worthy" of the poet. She has been capable of accepting, even in him, the human mixture, and yet, in spite of that mixture, she has lived the moral life, and is still living it, as "resolutely" as he has lived the life of the artist. This means that if, or when, she confronts him at last with the moral question, it will be as one before whom the great man will feel compelled to justify himself. He will have to reply with his—and Mann's—deepest sense of the human value of the artist's mission.

3

Of course, those two questions, to which Mann's version of Lotte's "return" provides the answers, carried a third along with them. This Goethe, whose effect on others and on her constitutes so much of the story, what was he in himself? Without an answer to this, we can't fully know either the drama or the meaning of her return.

This question is answered in the novel's last three chapters, which set before us one of the greatest of Mann's creations, Goethe himself at the height of his powers. In the first we see him in his morning privacy, luxuriating in his swift and soaring thought and deep into the world-containing second part of *Faust*. In the second, about the painful dinner with Lotte, we see him in his relations with others, awkward and brilliant, hurtful and pathetic. In the third, confronted by his most famous victim in a situation which rules out all evasion, Goethe replies at last to the judgment brought down upon him, even within himself, by his artist-life.

The long chapter of Goethe alone is a kind of miracle. We get his mind by way of a stream of thought that is dramatically motivated at every point, thought and feeling giving birth to each other through leaps of memory, association, awareness, realization, and that is also organized as a crescendo, the ideas introduced at the start growing steadily in scope and fulfilling themselves at the end in a climax of thrilled understanding. But, as I have said, this is only part of Mann's achievement. He shows too how all that intellectual wealth rises out of a doubleness which is the key to both the crime against Lotte and his own kinship with Goethe, the *"unio mystica"* he felt with the great man while entering his mind. To convey more than highlights here is of course impossible. But we can see that inner division at work in Goethe's "casual" opening reflections — another of Mann's theme-stating "overtures" — and then, with the help of certain metaphors, the rich unity in which the division is reconciled.

It is naturally "no accident" that we first meet the poet as he awakens with an erection from a dream of the Venus and Adonis he had seen in a painting. ("What, what? Here's a brave showing, forsooth! Good for you, old man!" [281]) From this union of sex and art his mind moves to his still unwritten poem "Cupid and Psyche," then to the consoling idea that his subjects grow richer while waiting and can't be taken from him, any more than Schiller, to whom he gave the idea for *Wilhelm Tell*, could take from him the subject as he saw it, not the other's "high-flown revolutionary play," but "the real, easy-going, epic, ironic thing." For while he waits he grows "like a tree," and now, "with all my being beautifully opening out," he feels ready to do justice not only to that poem but to his "Reformation Cantata," which will prove "the old pagan got more out of Christianity than all the rest of them put together." (The complacent anti-revolutionary, the ironist, and the pagan all revealed as one.) After a few less pleasing thoughts his "unquenchable friend" droops, he checks the time and he sees he was awakened promptly, as usual, by his "seven o'clock will, calling me to the business of the day," that will which had been "alert down there in the pregnant vale, like a well-trained hound gazing wide-eyed on love-lorn Aphrodite with look both understanding and remote" (282-284). (At this "will" that even in the "pregnant vale" remains "understanding and remote" and poised to return to "business," the great man's "betrayals" stir in our minds.)

Goethe's "paganism" now shows what it is in reflections on Schiller. Led by certain associations from that will-hound to the folk-sayings he has been collecting, he feels again his fellowship with the folk-nature, "part of nature herself, elemental, earthy, pagan . . . fruitful soil of the unconscious, nourishing vale of renewed youth," and soon he is thinking of his great departed friend as an opposite to himself, whom he could never really love. For Schiller had been unaware that "man . . . must take from time to time refuge in his unconscious, [that] there his being has its roots" (284-285). But though Goethe will later refer to his friend as "the great Pthysicky" (352) to make clear that such alienation from nature is illness, he now gladly acknowledges that in him the defect became an element of genius. It made him "childlike," but also a representative of "intellect and free will," which are precisely "not nature"; it made him "nothing else but man." It was this greatness that struggled, though in vain, to lift his fellow Germans up "to himself and the life of the mind" and provided the understanding and encouragement Goethe needed to resume work on *Faust*.

Then, as Goethe remembers that precious support, his thoughts turn to what his fidelity to nature enabled him to produce, first in the realm of art and then in that of science. Soon he is exploding against those who keep pestering him to stick to his "gift for poetry" instead of wasting his time in "dilettante dabbling" in other matters. "As though a man wrote the Werther at four-and-twenty," he thinks, "and then lived and grew another four-and-forty years without outgrowing poetry! . . . How do they know," he goes on, "it isn't the poetry that's the dabbling and the serious work lies somewhere else, namely in the whole of life?" They forget, those "fools," that Napoleon said of him, "'That is a man.' Not 'That is a poet'" (289-290). The memory which follows of those who carped at his color theory[1] reminds him of the equally narrow literary specialists who kept objecting to the improprieties of his poems and plays, and his thoughts become a passionate defense of the ardent amateur against that "sour, unhumorous lot" who lack "understanding of life" and don't know that all men's work is "so much dross" if it is "without love and the stimulus of taking sides" (291). Obviously, this is not the taking of sides Riemer said Goethe was chillingly above, since it has nothing to do with politics or fashionable controversies. His love rises out of his own depths, and the side he takes is nature's—or his own. Moreover, "the guild, the trade, the profession" remain slaves to tradition, while "dilletantism is related to genius," to the "daemonic," precisely because "it is not bound but free" and can "see a thing with new eyes." They scorn him for not submitting to their limiting categories. "As though the universe, the All, were not all one! As though only he who had unity would not be the one to understand it—as though Nature herself would not yield her secrets to him who was of her." And in his excitement he remembers "the Cosmos, the all-embracing history of nature" he once dreamed of writing

("Who can do it, if not I?"), and this sense of all he might yet do stings him into a passionate prayer to "Mother Nature" (295-296) for more time.

It is not, however, this high philosophic climax that concludes the opening sequence, but an odd drop "downward." A moment before he had fought back against a sudden awareness of old age, its aches and itches and the disdain of the young, by reminding himself of the "ever greater spiritual and intellectual strength" age brings, not only to the writer, but to the lover, and then of "the glowing bliss of age when the love of youth confers on it the boon of new life" (292). Now his prayer for time reminds him of the bad effect on his own sense of time of music, of how wisely his recent "little one" (Marianne) spoke of music's power "to compress so much living and experience into a little space" and of the "nonsense" he gave her in reply: "Love and music, both are brief and both eternal." This "nonsense" is not innocent; it is exactly the dangerous illusion — that of contact with the eternal — by which love and music seduced Hans Castorp on his mountain away from his duty in the world, his duty to respect time and make it pay. By promoting that illusion, the champion of nature is revealed as one with the seducer. Sure enough, he now remembers their joy as Marianne sang and he read his poems, while "Albert slumbered, Willemer slumbered . . . and was made a mock" (298). Since "Albert" is the name Goethe gave the bridegroom whom Werther betrayed, we see he knows very well that the episode with Marianne is a repetition, the sweet recent version of his life's recurring pattern of love and "renunciation," i.e. "disloyalty and betrayal." So the great man's living presence forces upon us Lotte's ultimate moral question: how to reconcile his life-enhancing gifts with the ugly self-indulgence of the seducer who sacrifices others to his pleasure or his art.

4

The first of the two metaphors which convey the reconciling principle emerges when the poet shows his servant the cocoon of a milkweed caterpiller. The creature is undergoing "transformation," he says, so "the psyche [can] slip out to live the brief fluttering life it ate so much for when it was a worm." "Marvels of nature" (302), the servant sagely observes, and in fact, all of Goethe's thought can be understood as flowing from one or another of the two aspects of nature this marvel exemplifies. Looked at as it changes, it reveals life as a process of metamorphosis upward, in which the earthy original stuff remains a source of energy. Looked at as a whole, it shows that life is composed of "opposites" which paradoxically require each other. As we know, a sense of the oneness of "worm" and "psyche" underlies Mann's irony as well, which qualifies every judgment of what is by a smiling awareness of its origins and of what it may become.

The other metaphor is a kind of corollary of the first. It is that of the "circle," and it expresses Goethe's "piety" toward the worm, which is to say, his

lifelong need to circle back to the original source of his vitality. As he is reflect-
ing on the mind's—the spirit's—relation to life, the cold water of his morning
sponge bath brings the thought that the celebration of the elements in his "Pan-
dora" will be exceeded in depths and richness by the one planned for Faust's
classical Walpurgis Night. "Life is growth," he tells himself. "What has been
is weak, strengthened of the spirit, it must be lived anew" (308); and later, "In-
spiration, fancy, ideas as gift of physical stimulation. . . . Mind, product of life,
life that again in mind first truly lives. . . . What matter," he goes on, "if the
thought springing from joy of life thinks better of itself than it is. It is the joy
that counts—self-satisfaction makes a poem of it." Out of this view of mind
emerges his view of death. Life's "last thought," the "dread of death," is "despair
of the idea—it is the stream of life run dry."[2] That is, as life's joy excites in mind
those ideas in which life "first truly lives," the "last thought," that life is over,
may be a mere reflex of despair. "Piety," he concludes, "would have faith that
into the black renunciation of the life-forsaken soul might some time break the
joyful ray of higher life" (310).

The piety by which Goethe keeps the stream of life from running dry is
very different, he thinks with scorn, from the new generation's "neo-piety . . .
neo-Christianity" (310). It is a "secret hoping and trusting and honoring of the
mystery"; it is a readiness to "give up existence in order to exist," that is, to give
up existence in and through the old forms because what he venerates is not
forms—Blake's "mind-forged manacles"—but the living experience they come
from. "The beast's life is short," he thinks. "But man can experience recurrence,
he knows youth in age, and the old as youth; it is given him to relive what he
has lived, his is the heightened rejuvenescence that comes after triumph over
youthful fears, impotence and lovelessness, the circle closes and shuts out
death" (314). Later he defends his notorious clinging to old pleasures and
routines as a way of "clinging stoutly to your ego, preserving your personal
unity," for "renewal and rejuvenescence" can be found "only in unity, in the
closed circle of personality, that bids defiance to death" (321). Goethe's "closed
circle" is the pious return to past feeling that keeps the ego and its ideas and
values alive, and the death it prevents is the dissolution of the ego in the outer
chaos, in disconnectedness and drift.

So Goethe realizes that his great "renewal" of 1811 which produced the *West-
Eastern Divan* (about his love of Marianne) arose out of a cluster of events which,
though apparently different from each other, were all akin, were all a reaching
backward to the deep-lying source of his vitality. He himself groups the events
together. In this period there came, he says, his new young friend Sulpice
Boisserée to show him the value of the Gothic romanticism he had opposed
(which means, too, of his own youthful enthusiasm for it), Napoleon the "Cor-
sican Timur, my mighty and sinister friend," his recent mental journey on
behalf of *Faust* to past cultures and "to the partriarchs," a physical journey to
his "motherland" Frankfurt, and at last—it is clearly a culmination—"came
Marianne" (315). And not only are the spiritual events linked to his friendship

with the bloody tyrant and both to the thrillingly seductive and seducible girl. The girl is linked to Lotte! For was not Lotte "already Marianne to the life, or rather was Marianne not Lotte, when she sang Mignon, and Albert sat there, too, sleepy and complaisant. Really, like a recurrent feast" — he is using the word as it is used in *Joseph*, as the periodic reliving of primal life-patterns in religious festivals — "celebration and imitation of the original solemn performance, timeless memorial rite, less life than before, yet more, more intellectualized life" (319-320).

What does the seducer relive in his recurrent feast? It is not the act of procreation, which "God gave to the worm" as well and which is "anonymous, animal, without choice, shrouded in darkness." Though he has "wormed it enough" in his time, "the kiss is more in my line," he thinks, being love's "poetry" and "still discriminating, still individual" (318). His aim is the kisses that delight and revitalize the individual ego — and after that the poems that express it; he leaves it to others to serve the race by making babies. And so when he asks himself later if it is "sheer impudence and *hubris*" to treat as "raw material . . . to exploit as he sees fit" people who have their own "meaning and purpose," his answer is: "No, it is nature and character laid on one, and borne in God's name — enjoy it and forgive it, it is there for your pleasure" (335). Before the story is over we will find "searing pain" under Goethe's easy self-exculpation. But this morning of thought is that of the genius in the fruitfulness of his self-delight, and both the "worm" and the "psyche" in Goethe now fully reveal themselves. To begin with, we are shown how Goethe's egotism undergoes an efflorescence in the realm of spirit that unites his ego with the world. His servant's compliment to his hair leads him to the "joyful and profound" mystery of his own nature, and that to his "passion for autobiography" as an interest in nature's "highest result," in which "the most dangerous tendencies" of the German stock he comes from have "been . . . civilized, purified . . . and compelled to great and good ends by dint of a character springing from somewhere else altogether." Mann's own response to the Nazis now expresses itself in Goethe's well-known distaste for those "dangerous tendencies": the "cloudy vaporing" and "berserker excesses," the self-abandonment of his fellow Germans "to every fanatic scoundrel who speaks to their baser qualities, confirms them in their vices, teaches them nationality means barbarism and isolation" and they grow "great and glorious only when they have gambled away all that they had worth having. . . .[3] They think they are Germany," he declares, as Mann was to do on his own behalf, " — but I am." For he knows that the worm is incomplete without its psyche. *His* Germanness consists in the will "to assent . . . to give both sides play . . . to be the whole, to shame the partisans of every principle by rounding it out — and the other side, too." For "the combination of all forces makes up the world," and what he values above all is "humanity universal and ubiquitous, parody secretly directed against itself . . . world dominion as irony, blithe, both-sided betrayal" which issues in "culture, universality, love" (330-331).

So he regards the "national narcissism that wants to make its own stupidity a pattern and a power over the rest of the world" as a denial of "what in fact they [the Germans] are," a denial for which they will be scattered "over the earth like the Jews." And just as "their best always lived in exile among them," it is "in exile only" that they will "develop all the good that is in them for the healing of the nations and become the salt of the earth" (338-339). Openness to the other, though they do always turn against it, is his people's real gift to the world.

The metamorphosis upward reaches its climax when a spasm of disgust with politics leads him to *Faust*. His secretary John, formerly a revolutionary and made wiser (he claims) by Goethe, interrupts the interior monologue to seek his help; he wants to become a censor hounding revolutionaries for the state. The poet angrily denies responsibility for John's new cynicism about human possibilities and, again alone, grows aware of the real reason for his annoyance. It is that his work is his "objective conscience" and he is uneasy about his plans to lead Faust into this nasty world of public action. And though he reassures himself by remembering that his mocking devil Mephistopheles will expose and deflate the hunger for fame that spurs Faust to "the great deed," we learn next that Mephistopheles, too, will be left behind. In spite of the "bitter irony" in which the scene he is planning must end, what precedes the irony and follows it will reflect his own tendency to side with God as "the Positive Principle, the Creative Goodness" which, in response to man's "human need" and hunger for counsel, always seizes on what encourages and points the fruitful way. Moreover, Mephistopheles and his "hocus-pocus" — inorganic trickery — will be kept out of the Helena scenes in which Faust embraces the ideal beauty of his ultimate longing because that fulfilment can be won only "naturally and humanly," by "the power of his passion alone" (354).

That it is this power which underlies life's metamorphoses emerges when, thrilled by his own invention, Goethe thinks of how his homunculus will provide "the playfully scientific, Neptunian-Thaletic basis and motivation for the appearance of the highest type of human beauty" (355-356). Here it will help us to remember the homunculus and his fate. This glass-enclosed mannikin created in the laboratory by the scholar Wagner, and so a creature of the idea, longs for "true being," for "substance." But, as Thales teaches him, life originated and developed to ever higher forms, not in fiery explosions, but by gradual evolution that began in the sea. Proteus (the master of metamorphoses) therefore fills him with an "imperious craving" for the sea nymph Galatea, and diving into the sea, he breaks his sheltering glass against her throne. "May Eros . . . reign," the Sirens sing as the homunculus disappears, "who engendered all." (*Faust*, 11, 213-214).[4] Immediately afterward, drawn back into being by Faust's "imperious craving" for the ideal beauty he had once glimpsed, Helena arrives out of the sea. So Mann's Goethe now understands that the fate of the homunculus, with Helena as our example of its goal, will show the power of love to bring the "little clot of organic mud at the bottom of the ocean" through "life's lovely metamorphoses" to "its highest and finest form" (356).

But then comes the climax in the other direction. Goethe has assented to Winkelman's view that "the highest product of ever-advancing nature is the human being" and to his lofty affirmation of the "humanism of the senses." But such "humanism" brings into his mind — in a precipitous drop downward — the sensuality in which it originates. There follows at once a meditation on sex and its duplicities which leads him to what "in the whole moral and sensual world" he has dwelt on all his life with most "horror and desire." This is "seduction, inflicted or borne . . . sweet and terrible, like a command laid on us by a god." It is "the sin we sinlessly commit, guilty as tool and victim both . . . the test no one withstands, it is so sweet, even to endure it spells defeat" (357-358). And the long interior monologue comes to an end in his moved reflections on an Eastern tale he dreams of writing that completes this dark confession.

The wife of a Brahmin, a woman who needed no ewer for carrying water from the river because her perfect purity has the power to turn the water into a crystal ball in her hands, sees a "divine youth" mirrored in the river and loses the power. Her enraged husband cuts off her head at the mound of sacrifice, and when he is forced to relent by their son and permits him to rejoin head and body, a terrible mistake is made. The head is joined to the body of a pariah woman recently sacrificed, and there arises a "giant goddess . . . of the impure" in whom the "heavenly tender vision of the youth" in her mind forever kindles in her heart "lust and madness and despair." But the crystal ball is not lost, for it is to be found again in this very poem of seduction! "The poet much seduced, the tempting-greatly-tempted, he has the power and the gift, the pure hand that shall shape the crystal ball" (359).

With this strange boast Mann exposes the identity of Goethe the artist with Goethe the seducer. Each is an agent of nature; it is nature that the seducer yields to in himself and calls forth in his victim, nature as the lawless sexuality which hides under our civilized moral constraints and which the victim can't help finding so sweet ("deathly sweet" were Lotte's own words) that "even to endure it spells defeat." Repression may have its usefulness, but the time always comes when nature in us cries out to be liberated. As advance scout of our fullest humanity, the artist will be among the first to feel this and, by the seductive charm which is his gift, tempt us to feel it, too. And it is in Lotte's experience that we see why this can be a crime. For her tormenting "riddle" came from the fact that the poet who awakened her desire was not "serious." Leaving her to suffer guilt because she was committed to the moral life, he, being committed to art and only "playing" with life, went off "innocent" to shape his crystal ball. And it is he, forsooth — the tempter and betrayer — who gets credit for achievements of the spirit!

But the metamorphosis upward, not the worm, is the chapter's final word. When Goethe's son interrupts his morning of thought by bringing him Lotte's disturbing letter, the great man changes the subject with amusing abruptness.

Showing August a perfect crystal he has found, he launches into a lecture on the nature of crystals that is clearly a screen for his discomfort at his victim's "return." It need not surprise us, of course, that it is also a lightning-quick response to the moral challenge she threatens him with. The crystal, he explains, has "no inner time, no biography"; once formed, it is already "at the goal"; its perfection is that of death. "The true kind of being," on the other hand, belongs to what has "time within itself . . . making its own time" and "moving in its own circle." It entails "working in and on oneself, so that being and becoming, working and work, past and present, were one and the same thing and produced a permanence that would be endless progress, growth and perfectionment" (364). This is a version of that tree described by Joseph, whose roots in darkness and dirt are only one aspect of a living whole and whose leaves wave in the bright air. Though Goethe has not quite freed himself from guilt, his defense is that what matters most for the artist is life, and the "work" inside his "own circle" by which he assists its "endless . . . perfectionment."

5

The last two chapters give us two encounters with greatness. The first, about the reunion dinner, shows us the disappointing mixture it has to be in the flesh, entangled in the normal web of human relationships and the pride and pettiness that come with them. It was in part to serve this realistic purpose that Mann enlarged Goethe's guest list to include, along with Lotte and her daughter, Dr. Riemer, the art-historian Professor Meyer, their wives and a visiting geologist. The second encounter will show what it might be like to meet that same greatness outside the web, in its purity.

Thus Lotte's feelings during the dinner are painfully divided. To begin with, her old friend's courtier-like politeness, his "almost deathly" look of "avoidance and gravity" at her nodding head, the "purposeful vagueness calculated to regulate the situation from the first word on" (395-396) — all this is distressing to the "elderly schoolgirl" with the "lacking ribbon" who hoped to connect the present with the past. Then, too, she finds it unpleasant that Goethe and his fawning friends seem to identify his spiritual with his worldly distinction. "The spiritual," she thinks, "needed to be poor, ugly and bare of earthly honor, in order to test aright the capacity of men to honor it" (415). But it is soon clear that if their common worldliness unites Goethe with those other guests, the fact that, as artist, he defiantly represents spirit keeps provoking a hidden hostility that puts Lotte on his side.

What divides him from his fellow Germans again leads Mann's Goethe to the Jews. This emerges first in the great man's comment on the dinner wine: "Our dear Germans are a crack-brained lot and have always worked their prophets as hard as the Jews theirs, but their wines are the noblest gift of God" (404). A moment later he recalls how, in the Middle Ages, a barefoot friar brought about a massacre of the Jews as "the source of all evil" (411). Then, though he seems to join his guests in their polite German anti-Semitism by making them laugh at his imitation of a harried Jewish pedlar, he suddenly shifts into a paean to this people "smitten by God" that acts on his listeners like a slap in the face. The Jews, he says, are "pathetic without being heroic" because their experience has made them too "wise and skeptical" for heroism, "wisdom and irony" — his own traits! — being audible in the accents of the "simplest Jew" (412-413). And not only does this "extraordinary stock" possess special gifts for "medicine, music, literature (most German Jews writing a purer German than most Germans)." They arouse the expectation that they will play a "role in the shaping of the future on earth" because their "qualities as human beings and their moral convictions . . . [were] secularized forms of the religious." It is in this sense that they are "the people of the Book." He concludes that there is an "extraordinary likeness" in the "destined role" of the Germans and the Jews and that there may some day come an outburst of world hatred against this "other salt of the earth, the German stock" (416-417), worse than that medieval massacre. (One winces, perhaps, at an identification of the Jews with their most savage persecutors. But if the Germans are "the salt of the earth" in their prophets and will be "scattered" because they reject them, the idea is not absurd.)

Observing in silence Goethe's effect on the others, Lotte finds herself moved in contradictory ways. When his monologue shows him in his ordinary humanity — for instance, in his delighted account of a crystal he found — they respond with a love that brings tears to her eyes. But when his cutting, imperial judgments leave them behind, the hostility she senses frightens her and brings a sudden sympathy for her old friend. The fear is brought to a climax by Goethe himself. First he quotes a Chinese proverb: "The great man is a national misfortune," and she imagines that under their laughter, his guests want to scream, "The Chinese are right!" Then, as in retaliation, he quotes a remark of Frederick the Great in his old age: "I am tired of ruling over slaves," and her sense of what they are feeling rises to "horror" (419-420).

But if Lotte sides with Goethe as the representative of German spiritual gifts against German hostility to spirit, the anecdotes about art and the artist that end his monologue bring back the Goethe she must oppose. Speaking of a great singer whose art was for her only a means to make life easier for her father, he seems to approve of "the artist's contempt for his art." Not for the first time Lotte is "chilled and frightened . . . for his sake as well as her own" (423). This belittling of art, for which the artist once sacrificed her and by which he lifted her to compensating glory, diminishes them both. Then, half-tipsy with liberal wine-drinking, Goethe tells them about the imprint of a kiss that was seen one day on the glass covering the "sweet, melancholy mouth" of a da Vinci painting of *Charitas*, and how the culprit was found to be a young man with "very kissable lips." For Goethe (so shockingly responsive to the lips of a young man) this episode shows that it is "through the senses [art] . . . works on the spirit" and constitutes a "touching allegory . . . of hot-blooded emotion" aroused by "icily unresponsive matter . . . a sort of cosmic jest" (426-427). Lotte may well feel entitled to her mild boast (in the carriage on the way back to her sister's house) that in honoring Goethe's greatness, she shows her own goodness. For this time the drunken poet has confessed not only that his art embodies and arouses passion — and passion shot through with "perversity" — but that it does so while remaining as indifferent as the nature for which it speaks.

7

When, in the novel's concluding chapter, Mann's Lotte accepts the offer received by the real one of Goethe's theatre box and his carriage and after the play finds the great man seated in the carriage's shadowy corner, she is not surprised. She calmly accepts it too that they speak for a bit in the play's high-flown rhythmic language, which is still sounding in her ears. But the obvious explanation — that the meeting is her fantasy — won't do because Goethe will soon begin to speak as if the fantasy were his own. As we will see, he expresses ideas she could not have imagined and even includes her among his own "dear visions" when he says his final goodbye. The solution to the puzzle (of course) is that the fantasy is their author's. Having "discovered" that the unfulfilled, unfulfillable motive for Lotte's Weimar visit was to charge Goethe with that crime against her, Mann understood that a defense of his crime — against her and all the others — must have been awaiting its occasion in the poet's mind. What they both dreamed of saying — or at least should have dreamed of saying — they have been enabled to say by the fantasy of fiction, in which life's fragments are completed and its hidden meanings revealed.

But though the episode's unreality is slyly exposed, it is also a climactic last meeting of characters who remain realistically, enjoyably, themselves to the end. So, when Goethe refers to the "faded allusions" of Lotte's attire at dinner, her "touchingly nodding head" (495) and the comfort she might take in the preservation of her lost youth in *Werther*, she bitingly retorts that "the stiff-legged Excellence saying grace to your sycophants" (447) is not the youth preserved in his *Egmont* either. Still, the "resolute" woman who is "worthy" of him is there along with the elderly schoolgirl. It was she who dismissed the boyish idea of this evening's play that great men are either greatly good or greatly evil because she knows that greatness is a mixture of good and evil. Now, breaking in on Goethe's pretense that she came to Weimar to see her sister, she confesses what Mann "discovered" and Mann's Goethe soon shows he understood, that she came to complete the "fragment" left by their encounter long ago and to give their story "a tolerably redeeming close" (443).

As for her old friend, he too appears at last in what Mann has showed us is his deepest reality. Instead of the merely realistic Goethe of the dinner, Lotte now encounters the man he might have been if he had decided to face the music and speak to her from the heart. This one smilingly grants that, in spite of his objections, she did right to come back. For "any life that has significance has also unity." And since it is "spirit . . . that lends significance in art and life," her attempt to bring past and present together is as much an action of the spirit as his own recent rereading of "our" book *Werther*, which was "no chance," he says, but belonged to "a phase of renewal and recurrence" (444-445). What he means is that both his old crime (recently "renewed" with Marianne) and Lotte's desire to confront him with it testify to the spirit's hunger to give meaning to life. So, at her angry response to his claim that his book should compensate her for what she suffered, he sympathizes with her anger, "or the pain that expresses itself as anger," and then confesses that he has come to her now precisely to face it "and perhaps to soften it by a heartfelt plea for forgiveness." Nor can we doubt that the plea is genuine. For when Lotte, still hurt, pretends with a laugh that she is too grateful for the honor he has done her to feel entitled to apologies, his reply is shockingly bare of irony. Her laughter is a refusal that "stings" he says, and he actually speaks of the "craving for forgiveness," the "searing pain" a man feels when a "justified reproach" pierces "the darkness of his self-esteem" (447).

This from the Weimar Goethe gives her pause, as well it might, but her jealousy brings back the schoolgirl in one last outburst. She reminds him that according to his autobiography, it was not for her he felt that burning guilt but for the earlier one with whom "the pattern" began, the one he said goodbye to from his horse. Though she is proud that she didn't pine away like Friederike Brion, but did her duty and now rejoices "in honourable widowhood," she can almost weep to think the other might one day be given her place "in the temple of humanity." The Goethe who is speaking from his center smilingly reassures her. His loves were all proof of his fidelity, he declares, because under the changes of form the beloved has always been an "other you." At this the schoolgirl disappears for good and the woman who is "worthy" of him says what she came to say.

It was, after all, not vanity that brought her back to him. It was her desire to see "the might-have-been, the possible," and to ask if he, in all his "glory," ever thought of the "impairment and loss" that resulted when he gave it up for his lofty actuality. For she knows that "all reality and achievement are nothing but the impaired possible." True, "we humbler folk must . . . brace ourselves against [this] . . . till our heads quiver from the strain" (so the old lady's tremor fills with meaning: it is her symbol of the price exacted from us by the moral life), while his "actual" looks "not like renunciation or unfaithfulness, but like a purer fulfilment and a higher faith." And though she can't repress ironic congratulations at the way he thus eats his cake and has it too, she doesn't really begrudge him "the incense" he breathes. What she cannot accept is the smell of "sacrifice" in the place where he is, which looks "almost like a battlefield" and "the kingdom of a wicked emperor," and she names the wounded: Riemer, his son, the "little person" who will soon "fly into your upper rooms like a moth to the candle," and even includes Marie Beaumarchais, the abandoned heroine of his *Clavigo*, as a figure representing all his abandoned women. "Ah, it is wonderful to make a sacrifice"—as Goethe does when *he* renounces for his art—"but a bitter, bitter lot to be one" (448-451).

This rock-bottom reproach of his victim and his own conscience brings the artist to his rock-bottom self-defense, the answer he makes "from my heart in expiation and farewell." It is a great answer, and in it the worm that becomes a psyche joins Lotte's image of the moth and the candle as Goethe-Mann's ultimate symbols of the artist's life.

Sacrifice, he says, "is a mystery indivisible, like all else in the world, one's person, one's life and one's work. Conversion, transformation is all. They sacrificed to the god, and in the end the sacrifice was God." That is, what began as sacrifice for a god still crudely imagined became, as man developed, the Christ in whom the human has risen to the divine. So with the "conversion" of art. As artist-seducer, he is indeed the flame that sacrifices the moth. But as the artist who expends his life on his work, he is also the candle, sacrificing himself to produce the flame, and, as one who is himself drawn irresistibly to art, he is "the drunken butterfly that falls to the flame—figure of the eternal sacrifice, body transmuted into soul, and life to spirit . . . the sacrifice, and he that offers it. . . . Once I burned you," he goes on, "ever I burn you, into spirit and light." For the deepest craving of his life is "the play of transformation," as when the young grows old, yet with "youth like a miracle shining out in age, age out of youth." And this unity of worm and psyche, of that which is and that which, inside the "circle" of our own ego and its dark creative hunger, it is burned into becoming, is the law of all life and culture. "Unity in change and flux, conversion constant out of and into oneself . . . life showing now its natural, now its cultural face, past turning to present, present pointing back to past, both preluding future and with her dim foreshadowings already full. Past feeling, future feeling—feeling is all." Feeling is all because it is by feeling, born and ever renewed in the sexuality that unites us with living nature, that we make an endlessly developing unity out of the world's chaos and drift. This is why he can end, "Let us open wide eyes upon the unity of the world—eyes wide, serene and wise" (451-452).

If his victim wants him to repent, the time for that will come, he says, at the hour of death, which will appear as the reality foreshadowed by all leave-takings and the moment when faith in one's own sense of the world—that unity-preserving "circle"—receives its most terrible blow. Still, "Death, final flight into the flame—the All-in-one—why should it too be aught but transformation?" And he concludes with an echo of the end of *Elective Affinities*: "In my quiet heart, dear vision, may you rest—and what a pleasant moment that will be, when we anon awake together." What Mann elsewhere scorned as a sop to the simple-minded here becomes a hint (put kindly into Lotte's language) of how far Goethe's faith in metamorphosis could go, his idea that even death may not bring our developing to an end.

"Peace to your old age" (452), Lotte whispers, absolving him. Though a moment later the servant helps her out of a carriage that holds only herself — the fantasy confessed — Goethe's self-defense and her benediction have acquired a quite sufficient reality. For us, if not for the real Frau Kestner, her story has at last received "a tolerably redeeming close."

Notes

1. As a scientist Goethe dared to do battle with Newton in his theory of color, and he actually discovered a bone (the intermaxillary) hitherto unknown to anatomy. It's interesting, by the way, that Goethe has lately been championed against Newton by Mitchell Feigenbaum, one of the creators of the new science of "chaos." ("Where Newton was reductionist, Goethe was holistic," as James Gleick puts it in *Chaos: Making a New Science* [Viking: New York, 1987], 165.)

2. "Energy is the only life, and is from the body; and reason is the bound or outward circumference of energy." In this maxim from *The Marriage of Heaven and Hell* Blake anticipates Goethe's view of the bodily source of the energy — or "joy" — which is "the stream of life," as well as his view of reason as what takes over when energy dies away.

3. "Perhaps you have heard the story that the British prosecutor in Nuremburg quoted Goethe on the Germans, thinking that the quotation was authentic, when it was really from *The Beloved Returns*," Mann wrote in a letter, and added that "everything Goethe says in my novel might very well have been thought and said by him, so that in the higher sense the prosecutor had quoted correctly after all" (*Letters*, 508).

4. "Nereus. Was flammt um die Muschel, um Galatees Füsse . . .
  Als wär es von Pulsen der lieve gerührt . . .
  Thales. Humunculus ist es, von Proteus verführt —
  Es sind die Symptome des herrischen Sehnens . . .
  Sirenen. So herrsche den Eros, der alles begonnen!"
  (*Goethes Werke in Zwei Bänden*. Erster Band, 912)

CHAPTER EIGHT

Doctor Faustus: The Life of the German Composer Adrian Leverkühn as Told by a Friend

"How much *Faustus* contains of the atmosphere of my life! A radical confession, at bottom. From the very beginning that has been the shattering thing about the book." (*Story*, 154)

"In the final analysis there are only two basic attitudes ... : the aesthetic and the moral." ("Nietzsche," 172)

1. The Idea and the Method

Though *Doctor Faustus* (1947) ranks with Mann's greatest novels, it is often painful to read and it gives a sense (which Mann has abundantly confirmed) that it must often have been painful to write. The reason for this is that it comes from a vision of hell, and a hell we have to recognize as real. The place is described for Mann's artist-hero by the Devil himself in the dialogue which exposes the novel's darkest secrets. It conveys at once, he says, the feeling that

> "*here everything leaves off.*" Every compassion, every grace, every sparing, every last trace of consideration for the incredulous, imploring objection that "You cannot do so unto a soul": it is done, it happens ... in soundless cellar, far down beneath God's hearing ... unrecorded, unreckoned, between thick walls [245].

That this is the hell created by the Nazis is clear enough, even without the later reference to the "thick-walled underground torture chamber" (481) Germany had become. But one thing more must be said to account for the novel's core of anguish. The idea-feeling expressed in its rich unfolding is the same as that implied in the title of Mann's essay on Hitler, "A Brother." It is his sense of kinship with the Nazi torturers. This is why he tells his story as a version of the medieval German legend of the man of genius who accepted hell as the

150

price for superhuman powers. Like Marlowe's and Goethe's, Mann's version of the old tale shows it to be a mythical expression of certain devilish possibilities of human nature, possibilities that emerge when it seeks greatness in freedom from moral restraints. And what Mann reveals, or confesses, is that those devilish possibilities, though they of course belong to human nature in general, have been especially encouraged by German culture, the culture which nourished him.

In *Doctor Faustus* Mann's one "egocentric" subject, the artist as he found him in himself, thus continued to expand in its scope. It now took in what he had learned from twentieth-century Germany about the "bad path to life," the "Egyptian" path, the artist's path that led Hans Castorp and Joseph to life-serving wisdom by way of the forbidden and the dangerous. Of course, Mann had not been unaware of how bad that path could be. Hans Castorp's dream in the snow of the witch-like hags devouring a child and screaming curses in the dialect of his native Hamburg was a symbol of the "blood sacrifice" that accompanies humanity's fairest virtues. But in view of what was done by the Nazis, the familiar idea took on terrible new force. This exacerbated a persistent problem of his art. Like Joyce and other sufferers from "the crisis of fiction" in our time, he had been finding traditional story-telling increasingly banal. Now the usual indirection of fiction began to seem to him a kind of evasion. "Far be it from me to deny the seriousness of art," his narrator says—and the point will recur in a way that shows he speaks for his author, "but when it becomes [that is, when things become] serious, then one rejects art and is not capable of it"[1] (176). Mann's artist-story became a study of Germany too, and his work became a gigantic enterprise of "montage," as he calls it in *The Story of a Novel*, a mosaic of facts, ideas and quotations from all the spheres of life touched on by that double subject.

To begin with, he now wove into his story what was happening in Germany as he wrote it, as well as his own shame and rage at the acquiescence of so many of his fellow Germans. Then, along with the devilish character of the Nazi "blood state," he sketched its roots in the past and the "innocent" foreshadowings that appeared early in our century of what was to come. As for the artist-story itself—that of a contemporary German composer of genius—in this we are given not only the composer's personal life, as the source and consequence of his career, but what reads like a musicologist's account of the way such a career must develop: *its* roots in the past, in the evolving traditions of Western music; the rich thought that would underlie the work; and detailed descriptions of many of the protagonist's compositions based on actual or possible twentieth century music.[2]

Mann knew well that such cold-blooded "construction" in art was a danger to both unity and vitality. But he was an old hand at finding the one in the many and drama in the undramatic. Though the problem had grown extreme (and the novel does give its readers more trouble than any of his others), he solved it now as he had done before. Here too everything comes to us through a narrator feelingly related to his subject and aware of all its implications, which means in a narrative medium alive with moving, mind-stretching innuendos. Here too ideas are a kind of action, rising out of character under pressure of emotion and generating suspense because of what they promise or threaten. But most important of all, Mann has again found a way to eat his cake and have it: here too every detail is symbolic as well as real.

Not only does his hero this time practice an art which is a paradigm of all art, and therefore of his own. His career (like Mann's, as we will see) duplicates in the sphere of art the essential characteristics and the twentieth century culmination of German *Kultur*. And it does so because of what they have in common. Mann tells us this himself — and makes clear how the novel's staggering complexity is unified — when he explains why the still unpublished writing on Schönberg which he received from his musical mentor Theodore Adorno was exactly what he needed.

> What I appropriated from it in order to portray the whole cultural crisis, in addition to the crisis in music, was the fundamental motif of my book: the closeness of sterility, the innate despair that prepares the ground for a pact with the Devil. Moreover, this reading nourished the musical conception which had long been my ideal of form, and for which this time there was a special esthetic necessity. I felt clearly that my book itself would have to become the thing it dealt with: namely a musical composition.[3] (*Story*, 64)

He is telling us that the Faust legend, always visible through the "transparency" of the two subjects, would be a metaphor for the personal experience underlying them both and that, as a source of leitmotifs, it would enable him to carry further than ever his "technique of musical interweaving" (*Letters*, 495) by which a unifying core of meaning and feeling is kept before us all the time.

So Mann's twentieth century Faust is also a product of medieval Germany and also finds his normal human powers inadequate to his ambition. Like the other, he conjures up the Devil, signs a pact with his blood, gains "XXIV years" of "genius-time" by giving up his fellowship with human beings, is borne through the depths of ocean and space, and dazzles the world with feats of (musical) magic. Finally, there comes a moment in this version too when the moral self which had been silenced by lust for glory makes itself heard again and Faust seeks to renege on his bargain. As we know, he can't. Instead, Mann's composer writes a cantata called *The Lamentation of Doctor Faustus*, in which *his* Faust, like the original, refuses to repent as a kind old man advises. And then the composer, also like the original, confesses his wickedness to assembled friends and gives up his soul. In fact, as Adrian Leverkühn represents Mann's most open confession of the sinister root of the artist-character, the novel is his own *Lamentation of Doctor Faustus*.

I have said that every real detail is also symbolic. Since the sheer amount of the real has become so enormous, we can't hope to do justice here to the vast web of the novel's meanings. What we can do is explore the idea underlying them all by following the clue of the Devil. And first we must note how the daemonic character of Mann's protagonist determined his choice of a narrator, and how this narrator uncovers, as the foundation of his story, the non-supernatural reality to which the word "daemonic" refers.

2. The Narrator as the Other

As we know, Mann's artist has always been posed against an other — the bourgeois more simply devoted to life — to whom he was drawn but from whom his fruitful defects cut him off. To convey that new sense of the horrors linked to those defects, Mann shows him this time through the other's eyes. This "biography" of the late composer is written by a childhood friend, whose name is Serenus Zeitblom, who became a teacher of Greek, Latin and the humanities, and who doubts his fitness for his subject because he is "by nature wholly moderate, of a temper . . . healthy and humane, addressed to reason and harmony," while in the sphere of genius, for all the world's noble associations, "the daemonic and irrational" must have a "disquieting share" (3-4). He has resigned from his school because of its outrageous treatment of Jewish colleagues, and once, thinking of the "reactionary evil" going on around him, he solemnly declares, like another *Zivilisationsliterat*, that the best weapon against the dangerous "folkish layer [which] survives in us all" is "literature . . . humanistic science, the ideal of the free and beautiful human being" (37-38).

But Mann's view of the other has also been driven to bedrock by twentieth century history. His bourgeois humanist, whose name suggests that he is a "flower of time" in all its accumulated wisdom, is now a Catholic, and one who takes pride in his heritage. Where the Jesuit Naphta served to highlight the danger of Catholic emphasis on the "absolute" over the claims of ordinary life on earth, Zeitblom reminds us that the "Christian-Catholic tradition" reflected (in the Middle Ages, and even before) a "serene love of culture untouched by churchly schism" (8). And Luther's Reformation, in which the Mann of World War I and *Reflections of a Non-Political Man* had read the "voice of God" as it spoke in the individual conscience, is seen by Zeitblom as "the revolt of subjective willfulness . . . against the objective bond," and Luther himself as one of the "backsliding types and bringers of evil," a cause of "endless blood-letting and the most horrible self-laceration" (88).

Then it turns out that this other has come strangely close to the artist he used to oppose. When the story arrives at World War I, Mann assigns to Zeitblom the outbreak of patriotism that produced his own attack on the *Zivilisationsliterat*, his feeling then that "everyday morals are outbid by the abnormal" (300) and that at last, in spite of their usual opposition, "state and culture might become one." And though, like his author, Zeitblom soon recovers from the brief intoxication, he has already revealed that humanism itself opens the way to such dangers.

Reporting on his friend's childhood introduction to the "equivocal" properties of nature through his father's scientific experiments, Zeitblom informs us that old Leverkühn got his chemicals from the apothecary shop long in the Zeitblom family and then being run by his own father, and that the shop was called "The Blessed Messengers." This is an early hint of the idea, which will return later in other ways, that God Himself is equivocal, and that the free inquiry into nature by which the humanist thinks to serve Him leads to darker realities than literary high-mindedness tends to expect. Moreover, for all his shrinking from such realities, Zeitblom loves the artist who dwells among them, loves him, as we will see, *because* he dwells among them, and even calls the life he is narrating "nearer to me, dearer, more moving than my own" (176). In short, as Mann has told us himself, what the novel will half hide and half reveal about the humanist and the artist is "the secret of their being identical with each other" (*Story*, 90).

This is why Zeitblom can express at the end his author's defining faith. He does so in the form of a doubtful question whether the youth of war-ravaged Germany could still understand what he had to teach: "the cultural ideas in which reverence for the deities of the depths blends with the civilized cult of Olympic reason and clarity, to make for a unity in uprightness" (505). This "blending" is an echo of the double blessing of Joseph, the "blessing from the heavens above and from the depths beneath" (28). And the concluding proviso of "uprightness" recalls the lesson Hans Castorp took away from his dream in the snow, that although the path to life-serving wisdom leads through the realm of death, "for the sake of goodness and love man shall let death have no sovereignty over his thought" (497).

But it is those "deities of the depths" our humanist-narrator will set before us throughout most of his friend's story. In fact, the novel is a continuing education in the timeless reality represented by the Devil.

3. The Reality of the Daemonic

To begin with, theology itself is shown to be dealing in realities. Explaining why he felt "choked" (87) by the theological atmosphere of the University of Halle, where he and his friend were students, Zeitblom makes it clear that this was not because the subject deals in exploded superstitions. If philosophy is "the queen of the sciences," then theology, he says, should rank even higher because the "most exalted goal" of "the inspired intellect" must be the "contemplation of the highest essence, the source of being, God and the things of God" (80-81). Once again Mann is using the language of religion in a way that insinuates its secular meaning. As "the highest essence, the source of being," God becomes a name for the ultimate objective of science itself, that is, for the unknown source of "All," the "Whole," the infinite complexity of nature. So Zeitblom can later grant that "liberal theology," turning religion into "moralism and humanity," grew more "shallow" as it grew more "cultured," and that the "conservative tradition" at Halle, remaining open to the world's dark realities, has preserved far more of "the true understanding of human nature and the tragic nature of life." But precisely this is the source of the humanist's discomfort, his feeling of the "uncanny." For the theology his friend is studying has been infiltrated by the "irrational currents of philosophy," the chief themes of which are "the non-theoretic, the vital, will or instinct, in short, the daemonic." And Zeitblom believes this infiltration was no accident. On the contrary, it is his view that theology, confronted by the irrational, "is in danger, by its very nature, of becoming daemonology" (90). As the study of the Whole, of "the sources of being," it tends to lead not to an order harmonizing with our own order-making minds, but to wild, non-human nature, both within man and outside him. [4]

So the characteristic Mann "overture" we get at the novel's beginning, an account of the influence on the composer-to-be of his parents, is actually a lesson in the irrational — or daemonic — character of nature and in what stands against it in human life. Jonathan Leverkühn, a farmer whose features seem to belong to a German of the late Middle Ages, whose eyes are blue, and who suffers from occasional migraine, is given to scientific studies which would once have been ascribed to a desire "to speculate the elements," a "leaning to the black arts." Among other things, Jonathan shows the boys pictures of blue-spotted butterflies — one, called Hetaera Esmeralda, will later give Adrian a name for the prostitute who will infect him with syphilis — whose beautiful azure is due not to pigment, but to the way light is refracted by the surface texture of their wings and strikes the human eye. ("So it is all a cheat?" Adrian's mother puts in, and her husband replies, "Do you call the blue sky a cheat?") On the shells of certain mussels he points out marks resembling oriental writing which he struggles in vain to read. At last, by "teasing ... [Nature] into manifestations, 'tempting' her," he shows them how certain chemicals sprinkled on sand at the bottom of a jar of water develop through "osmotic pressure" into a rich "vegetation" resembling mushrooms, trees, limbs and how these "pathetic imitations of life" are heliotropic, actually reaching toward the "warmth and joy" of the sun. "And even so they are all dead," the father says with tears in his eyes. This comically literal expression of the sinister "sympathy with death" that haunts *The Magic Mountain* makes his son burst into laughter. "Such weirdnesses," Zeitblom concludes, "are exclusively Nature's own affair, and particularly of Nature arrogantly tempted by man" (13-20).

Zeitblom gives the show away in his comment on Jonathan's attempt to read the marks on the shell. He knew even then, he says, that the attempt must fail because "Nature outside the human race is fundamentally illiterate — that ... is precisely what makes her uncanny" (17). He means that the distinct entities, categories and qualities we "read" in it, like organic and inorganic, life and death, and the lovely blue of Hetaera Esmeralda and of heaven, are all creations of the human mind. Nature itself, as the old man has been revealing and sympathizing with her, is a fluid chaos. And when Zeitblom adds that those "impish phenomena" emerge "particularly" when Nature is "arrogantly tempted by man" (20-36), he is referring not only to science, but to all our attempts to acquire nature's powers by artificial means—by alcohol, drugs, sadistic cruelty. This means he is also foreshadowing the Devil-pact by which the composer, grown impotent with "knowledge," will later seek to renew instinctual vitality by "tempting" nature forth in sex and disease. The father, as lover and teacher of Nature, has been exposed as an agent of the Devil. The migraine he passes on to his son, in whom it becomes a periodic agony, will show itself more and more as a sign and consequence of that sinister connection.

But there is more to say about nature than we hear from the blue-eyed father. It is hinted in the recurrence of the same blue color in the eyes of the heavenly child Adrian will later love and lose; in those of the violinist Rudi Schwerdtfeger, who seduces him into a brief homosexual affair and in whom the seducer's destructive narcissism mingles with a genuine reverence for excellence; and in those of Helmut Institoris, a weakling worshipper of mindless force who anticipates the Nazis. The heaven-color they share is a reminder that nature gives rise to good and evil alike. In fact, it is the source of all, the "source of being," which means it is a version of God, Whose dwelling place is the vastness our eyes domesticate as blue, and Who said, if we may add some evidence ourselves, "I form the light, and create darkness; I make peace, and create evil; I the Lord do all these things" (Isaiah 45:7).

As for the mother, what we learn from her is how the daemonic is resisted. Elsbeth Leverkühn seems at first to resemble Mann's earlier artists' mothers (including his own). She, too, as a black-eyed brunette, calls up ideas of the south, and she is responsible for her son's artistic gifts, her inherently musical temperament being evident in her unusually pleasing voice. But as in this novel the father's influence is on the side of art because he represents the primal chaos which is art's basis, the mother here opposes art. "Elsbeth never troubled about music, never so to speak 'professed' it" (22). Her musical gift showed itself mainly in the charm her voice added to her activity as wife, mother and mistress of the home, that is, to ordinary, healthy life. And when Adrian's great music teacher Kretschmar urges him to take up composition, as later when the young man is about to begin that work in earnest, she treats it as a danger from which she would save him. Not only does she manifest each time a mute opposition. We are pointedly told each time that her arm is encircling her son's head against her breast, a touch that gets its meaning from the fact that Adrian's migraine first appeared when, at fifteen (puberty), he began to "experiment" on the piano, and became a devilish torture in the time of his greatness. Since the mother's black eyes (as well as her musical voice) will be repeated in Marie Godeau, from whom the mature composer will briefly hope to win his own share of "human warmth," it is clear that the black of the mother's eyes is intended to remind us of those affections and responsibilities of our ordinary life on earth which could protect the artist from that fluid chaos, but from which he is fated to be shut out.

And yet not completely. For in Adrian's eyes, we are told, the black and the blue mingle and produce "a shadowy blue-grey-green iris with little metallic sprinkles and a rust-coloured ring around the pupils." To our narrator it is "a moral certainty" that this mingling "formed his taste in this matter or rather made it waver. For never . . . could he decide which, the black or the blue, he liked better. Yet always it was the extreme that drew him: the very blue, or else the pitch-black gleam between the lashes" (22-23). Of course, that mixture is a sign of a leaning to the Devil, of the daemonic detachment, the irony-that-goes-both-ways, which unites the artist with the mocker. We see this in the fact that exactly such eyes will belong to Rüdiger Schildknapp, a friend of whom Zeitblom will be jealous because he becomes Adrian's crony whenever the artist is most withdrawn from the human community, his companion in mocking laughter. But though these two are significantly alike, they are also significantly different. In Schildknapp the opposing elements (of earth and heaven) cancel each other out and the result is withdrawal from both. In the artist they retain all their force. In spite of his mocking laughter and his icy detachment, he is *drawn* to the black and the blue. He can love them. This conflict is the deepest truth of his nature.[5]

Still, the novel is Mann's confession that his artist is Faust and "brother" to monsters. To understand how this can be, we must now follow that clue of the Devil in his life story, in the German *Kultur* he was shaped by and in his music as it grew increasingly great and increasingly his own.

4. The German Artist as Faust

When Zeitblom meets his friend some time after Adrian has entered into the hellish pact, he finds him not changed, but only "more definitely that which he was" (159). In fact, the biography makes it clear that the composer was Devil-prone from the beginning. This was due, in part, to the culture into which he was born: his most advanced music will be "music of Kaisersaschern" (63). This ancient city, which was still medieval in appearance like Mann's own Lübeck, showed signs in Adrian's childhood of "a morbid excitement, a metaphysical epidemic, latent since the last years of the Middle Ages," and the same thing, we are told, is now emerging again as the new Germany "enthusiastically reenacts symbolic deeds of sinister significance . . . such, for instance, as the burning of the books and other deeds of which I prefer not to speak" (36-37). In short, Mann's artist is a product of the *Kultur* linking Luther and Hitler. That the humanist came from the same town means only that it was home to his Catholic tradition as well.

Then there is the more intimate world of Adrian's childhood and the strangeness of his later "return" to it. Remarking on the artist's tendency to remain "closer, not to say truer, to his childhood than the man trained for practical life," even though "his course is endlessly farther, wilder and more shattering to watch" (24), Zeitblom informs us, with a certain discomfort, that the home his friend chose to work in as an adult — the farm of a family called Schweigestill — would duplicate the abnormally cold pond of the first, its hill called Mt. Zion, the earthy stable girl who introduced Adrian to music in polyphonic folkish rounds, a barking watchdog, and even his father, mother and elder brother, though there is no second son in that family for "who would this second son have been?" (26). As with the stranger who directs Joseph to his brothers, Mann has deliberately violated realism to emphasize a meaning. And when Zeitblom admits that he "never cared for the phenomenon," this is a hint that the artist clings to his childhood, not out of sentiment, but because the forms in which "being" first appeared to him are his roots in the Whole, that Whole which tends toward the daemonic.

But it is in Adrian's "extraordinary gifts" that his nature most fully revealed itself. As a schoolboy, he mastered with ease subjects to which his teachers had devoted their lives, and developed an "arrogance" that disdained all tasks but the highest and most difficult, a tendency to laughter that seemed to his more sober friend an unhealthy, "orgiastic" escape from "life's manifold sternness" (84), and a chilling detachment from other human beings. "All about him was coldness — and how do I feel," Zeitblom exclaims, "using this word, which he himself in an uncanny connection once also set down?" (6) This "uncanny connection" we rightly suspect is with the cold-exuding Devil.[6]

Of course, there *is* a passion that goes with such coldness and such gifts: intellectual passion. Zeitblom shows us the form this takes in his friend — and so begins our education in the meaning of music in the novel — by reporting three moments of startled discovery. In the first Zeitblom realizes that the fifteen-year-old Adrian is "religious" when the boy explains why mathematics is his favorite school subject. Other subjects deny their "relative character," he says, but mathematics is concerned openly with "relations between things," and must therefore be "higher . . . universal . . . 'the true'. . . . Order is everything," he goes on. And then he quotes from Romans xiii, "For there is no power but of God" — and reddens. Immediately after this Zeitblom tells of an earlier "discovery, not to say unmasking." Embarrassed to be found one day making chords on a harmonium, the boy casually pointed out a "curious" fact: because a chord's key depends on the notes around it, its context, it has "of itself no tonality. Relationship [in music] is everything," he went on, "and if you want to give it a more precise name, it is ambiguity." Then (and again his cheeks are hot): "Music turns the equivocal into a system" (45-47). Finally, there is Adrian's response as a young man after listening to Beethoven. "There is something very odd indeed about this music of yours," he says — and his pretence of detachment fails to hide a "slight feverishness." It is "energy itself, yet not as idea, rather in its actuality. . . . That is almost the definition of God. *Imitatio Dei* — I'm surprised that it is not forbidden. Perhaps it is" (79).

It should be clear that all of this is confession. The art which turns the equivocal into a system is a metaphor for Mann's famous irony. For, as we saw in *Joseph*, this irony is a smiling "yes, but" to all who take what they see from the part as a vision of the whole, or who are unaware that time changes the meaning and value of a thing or idea because it changes their contexts. Music thus exemplifies Mann's own aspiration as an artist, an aspiration which perhaps "ought to be forbidden," to speak for and as the Whole. Now, we will see again here how love of the human saves his irony from nihilism. But what this picture of the artist as Faust is confessing is that, as theology may become daemonology, irony may indeed become nihilism and icy mockery of the human, and music, which is to say, art, the language of the Devil.

We learn more about the daemonic character of Adrian's development as a composer (though music is not named) in two ideas he picked up at the University of Halle in a philosophy class he shared with his humanist friend. The first is the theory of the pre-Socratic Pythagoras, who, regarding "All-Nature ... as Cosmos, as order and harmony, as the interval system of the spheres," taught that the world's "origin and existence," as well as "moral value," were determined by "number and the relations of numbers." Out of this conviction rose an ideal of authority uniting "the beautiful, the exact and the moral," and a community devoted to a "religious renewal of life," to "silent obedience and strict subjection" (93). That the idea of the Whole as an order ruled by number is linked to music has already been hinted. We have been told that Adrian placed over the piano in his student lodgings a copy of the "magic square" in Dürer's *Melancolia*, a square divided into sixteen smaller squares containing numbers which add up in every direction to 34, and so to the magic number 7. The meaning of this link emerges some years later when Adrian speaks of the effect of the musical "constellation" as if he were speaking of astrology. "Reason and magic," he says, "may meet and become one in that which we call wisdom, initiation: in belief in the stars, in numbers ..." (193-194). He means that the cosmic order our reason glimpses in the "relation of numbers" remains so mysterious in its bottomless complexity that for us it is one with the fluid chaos. Music is the expression of wisdom as irony precisely because it is the art in which number and magic—systematic human thought and the mysteries of nature which lie outside it—are combined.

The second idea—Aristotle's—is that form is the "moving unmoved ... soul of existence," urging it to "self-realization and self-completion," and that in the organic this soul is "the entelechy," that part of "the pure form of all being" which "guides" and "shapes the single manifestations." To Adrian this is a version of the religious idea that "the soul is from God," and is the individual's "angel," his guiding "genius." When Zeitblom recalls his prayer at this, "May thine own angel prove himself faithful and wise" (94), we understand that Adrian's—the artist's—confidence that he is serving God when he submits to his own "genius" may not always be well-founded.

In fact, Zeitblom has already told us his friend studied theology out of "arrogance" (80), the desire "to dedicate himself as an adept" to a sphere to which "the profane disciplines" (82) were subordinate. And what we learn from the two theology professors we meet next is precisely that the hidden self may turn devotees of God into servants of the Devil. One utters the devilish messages of the body, and the other those of the mind, and each becomes a permanent inhabitant of Adrian's imagination as an embodiment of what he teaches.

Ehrenfried Kumpf imitates Luther, even lecturing in his archaic, scatalogical style,[7] because he is himself an example of what for Mann is the eternal Luther type. That is, he is a "powerful personality," whose rejection of dogma is based not on reason, in which he tends to see the Arch-Deceiver at work, but on "a blithe and hearty trust in God" that is really a trust in his own appetites and impulses. These tell him that religion can go along with "healthy enjoyment" of the bodily pleasures, and of culture, provided it be German, with no trace of the "flatulent furriner." Whether or not he believes in the Devil's personal existence, his comic folksy nicknames for him show "a grim and reluctant recognition," and his lectures are evidence that for the theologian, especially one so "meaty," the Devil "belongs to the picture and asserts his complementary reality to that of God." So, after a certain rich dinner and much drinking and embracing of his plump wife, he points to a dark corner and cries, "There he stands . . . the mocking bird . . . the malcontent, the sad, bad guest, and cannot stand it to see us merry in God." And shouting "Apage!" (95-98) he flings into the corner, not an ink well, but a roll. For this foreigner-hating provincial the Devil is the Adversary suggested by his own "meaty" nature, and with his "blithe and hearty" self-acceptance, he is not likely to suspect that it is the Adversary who is in charge when he thinks he is serving God.

But Kumpf's way of suggesting the Devil's reality is "child's play," we are told, "compared to the psychological actuality with which [Eberhard] Schleppfuss invested the Destroyer, that personified falling-away from God." This last phrase is a clue to his message. As his name identifies him with the foot-dragging Devil, what he teaches is that the idea of God requires that of the Devil; they are the two sides of one coin. "The holy," he says, is "a constant Satanic temptation" because "vice did not consist in itself but got its satisfaction from the defilement of virtue, without which it would have been rootless." Then, too, since God gave man freedom so he could choose the good of his own will, freedom could only mean "the freedom to sin." Indeed, "if you listened to Schleppfuss," avoidance of sin would be a "diminution of the intensity of being." Finally, the idea we have of God's "All-sidedness" implies that the creature must be "made over to" sin because evil is required for "the wholeness of the universe" and because without it God's power "to bring good out of evil . . . could not reveal itself" (100-104).

This devil-agent's account of the mind's daemonism ends with his discussion of sex. He tells a painful story of a man who becomes impotent to all women but the one he loves and regains his potency when she is burned as a witch. This evidence of the power of the mind over the body corroborates "the reality of magic, of daemonic influence," and even of the "complex of experience" called the "evil eye," a "poison" (110) to which children are especially susceptible. (The idea will bear fruit in Adrian's final agony of guilt at the death of his nephew.) And though the tempter has granted it is theological superstition to think that "conjuring formulae . . . black arts . . . vices and crimes" can elicit from the Devil what is "only to be expected from God" (103), this is actually another hint that the Devil is God's other side, that God is responsible when those black arts work. He has thus suggested precisely the way his victim will soon take to enter into the Devil-pact, the way of "vice."

Vice shows itself, appropriately enough, as soon as the young man begins his adult life in the "world," that is, when he yields to his teacher's urging at last and joins him in Leipzig. He is promptly led astray into sexual temptation. The guide who offers to introduce him to the city turns out to be "a small-beer Schleppfuss," who takes him to a house with a brass railing "as bright as the fellow's badge and a lantern over the door, red as the felow's cap," in fact, into a "lust-hell." Zeitblom gives us the episode by way of a pseudo-playful letter from his friend about "what is afoot betwixt me and Satan," written in an archaic style imitating Kumpf's imitation of Luther. Adrian reports that in his acute embarrassment at the sight of the women, he had run to the piano and played the hermit's prayer from the *Freischütz* and then fled, but not before being touched on the cheek by "a brown wench . . . an Esmeralda." And the strange words "Pray for me" (141-142) appear amid the letter's casual jocularities. In the agitated analysis of the letter that follows, Zeitblom tells us that its medieval lingo is "parody as pretext" (145), that is, as a way of expressing with apparent detachment what is deeply felt (one key to Mann's own use of parody and playfulness). In fact, Adrian will fall into that same medieval language, though with diminishing playfulness, whenever he writes or speaks of "what is afoot" between him and Satan. And Zeitblom goes on to make clear the anecdote's symbolic meaning by an altogether realistic account of the effect on virginal genius when its "armour of purity, chastity, intellectual pride, cool irony" has been pierced by "soulless instinct." The "derogation into the human, and therefore also into the beast," is "mockingly debasing and dangerous" — dangerous not only because the gifted youth's imagination has been touched and enslaved, but also because "the proudest intellectuality stands in the most immediate relationship of all to the animal, to naked instinct," and is least given to the ordinary man's "veiling, ennobling" illusions. So he would "return to the place whither the betrayer had led him" (147-148).

When the deeply shaken humanist learns that a year later Adrian tracked down his Esmeralda to the hospital in Hungary where disease had taken her ("the hunted hunter found her out"), he is consoled by the fact that the "brown wench" had remained the object of his friend's desire. For when "instinct wears the face of a human being, be it . . . the most contemptible," there is always, he insists, "a trace of purifying love" (153-154). There was love in the woman, too, for Adrian reported that in her gratitude she warned him against herself before giving him what he came for. But it was neither lust nor love that drove the artist to her bed. It was the demands of his art, of his genius.

We have been told that he had resisted his teacher's urging to devote himself to composition because the "methods and conventions" of music, even when it moved him to tears, had become for him laughably predictable and *"good for parody only"* (134, emphasis Adrian's). And though he was won over by Kretschmar's reply, that his disgust with the outworn was only music itself expressing its need for "revolutionary progress" (135), we find that his first important work, *Ocean Lights*, was precisely a parody of outworn conventions, the "proud expedient of a great gift threatened with sterility by a combination of scepticism, intellectual reserve and a sense of the deadly extension of the banal." And he has begun to seek ways "to get for . . . the productive impulse . . . the necessary little ascendancy over the impediments of unbelief, arrogance, intellectual self-consciousness" (152). So, when Zeitblom asks what could have led Adrian to despise the woman's warning, he answers his own question in a way that clearly translates the Devil-pact into its secular meaning:

> Was it not also love, or what was it, what deliberate, reckless tempting of God, what compulsion to comprise the punishment in the sin, finally what deep, deeply mysterious longing for daemonic conception, for a deathly unchaining of chemical change in his nature. . .? (155)

This meaning of that act of sex is confirmed by the discovery Zeitblom now boasts of having made in his friend's music. It is that the theme which recurs in his work from then on, the note combination h (the German designation for our b), e, a, e, e-flat, is a cipher made of the key letters of the name he gave his prostitute, Hetaera Esmeralda. With this name he is acknowledging his music's debt to the Devil, to the forces of nature he had unchained in himself by that poisonous embrace.

As the reader may have recognized, the brothel episode, the later return to the prostitute and the syphilis that is to drive Adrian mad and kill him are taken from the life of Nietzsche.[8] But Mann took more than that. He has himself reminded us of a doctor's hint that Nietzsche deliberately sought out the disease. Then, Adrian will duplicate the philosopher's increasingly feverish genius, his descent into megalomania, his last years of helpless idiocy. And of course, we will recognize Nietzsche in the composer's ruthless psychological insight into the hypocrisies of virtue and his rejection of morality on behalf of creative vitality. These will reach their fullest and most brilliant expression in the voice of the Devil, who appears in Chapter 25. It is of course "no accident" that the two digits of this chapter's number add up to seven.

5. The German Artist's Devil

Adrian's dialogue with the Devil in Palestrina ranks in dramatic and intellectual power with those of Hans Castorp and Clavdia on Walpurgis-Night and Joseph and Potiphar's wife at the tragic climax of her lust. But what it immediately resembles is the Devil-dialogue of Ivan Karamazov.[9] Like Ivan, Adrian responds to his visitor with bursts of rage and contempt that are met by the knowing railery of an intimate — and for the same reason. The Devil is the voice of the Adversary in the self.

Not only does the composer go to Italy (with his crony in mocking laughter Schildknapp) after telling Zeitblom he wants to "hold speech alone with my life, my destiny" (209). We are told that before the humanist copies out for us the dialogue he had discovered set down in his late friend's handwriting, he fights off as madness the thought that his friend was not alone, insists Adrian himself had to know there was no one there, "notwithstanding the cynicisms with which his interlocutor sought to convince him of his objective presence," and is left with the equally "horrible" idea that "those cynicisms, too, those jeerings and jugglings, came out of the afflicted one's own soul" (221). Finally, the composer, like Ivan, "proves" the Devil is his delusion by pointing out that the visitor keeps echoing what he has thought himself.

In fact, what gives the Devil his intellectual range, as well as his dramatic livingness and power, is precisely that he is the fully realized voice of a German artist of genius — of that part of him open to the fluid chaos of nature and beyond the reach of his civilized conscious mind. When he changes in appearance from a low-class thug to a knowing music critic to Professor Schleppfuss (referring, by way of explanation, to the "adaptation, mimicry . . . of Mother Nature" [228]), it is in order to look like the aspect of Adrian himself which has begun to be heard. The Devil's icy coldness which makes Adrian shiver and complain is, as we have seen, the artist's own. And when Adrian laughs at the Devil's absurdity in speaking in Kumpf's Luther-German in Italy, he replies first that the composer's pride should rather insist, "Where I am, that is Kaisersaschern," and then that Italy had long been the object of "German romantic wander-urge and yearning" (226). With this second remark Mann reminds us not only of himself, starting his career in this very town of Palestrina, but of Goethe. For it was Goethe who went to Italy — and also for two years — to establish contact with his own nature in freedom from the restraints of civilization.

Every thrust and parry of this dialogue conveys some aspect of the meaning or the psychological reality of the German artist's battle with his Devil-self. But three idea-clusters are fundamental and cast their light backward and forward over the whole story.

We learn first that what that artist has in common with the political dreamers whose dreams were fulfilled by the Nazis is an element of German *Kultur* that has obsessed Mann all his life, its profound attraction to illness and death. Thus the Devil's remark about Nature's "mimicry" leads, by way of a reference to butterflies, to Adrian's diseased Esmeralda, and that to Bismarck's idea of the Germans as needing "half a bottle of champagne to reach their normal height" because they are "gifted but halt" and seek to overcome "paralysis" by "hand-over-head illumination." And he reveals that Adrian's half-bottle of champagne, syphilis, will bring illumination in precisely the German ways. First, by placing death in view it liberates him from moral scruples and wins the Devil's reward. Having been sold enough time—"let us say, XXIV years"—a man who knows it must end can "astonish the world as a great nigromancer with much divil's work." The payment of course is that "at the end he is ours." Then, in addition to that death-inspired moral liberation, there is the inflaming fever Adrian will get from the "swarm of animated corkscrews" that came from the West Indies into Germany around "anno MD . . . shortly before Dr. Martinus," came along with "children's crusades . . . famine, war . . . nuns with stigmata" into a Germany that was "pure Kaisersaschern."

To be sure, disease in general inclines one to "the intellectual," to the irony and rebellion of "the free spirit against the bourgeois order." But there are certain types who find the condition especially congenial and seek it out. Adrian hears that the Devil's "little ones" rise into the brain at the invitation of the hospitable "cell fluid of the pia," by "osmotic pressure," that all depends "on the disposition, the readiness, the invitation" and that some people are more qualified than others to practice "witch-craft." So the artist from Kaisersaschern is drawn to those "little ones" as a source of "the archaic . . . the genuine old primeval enthusiasm unparalyzed by thought," and will indeed find that marvelous "osmotic growths *sine pudore* sprout out of the apothecary's sowing." For "the artist is the brother of the criminal and the madman" (229-237). By opening himself to the fluid chaos with that intoxicating moral freedom and self-admiration, the composer will be rewarded by beautifully life-like flowers of death.

As for the charge that these will be a product of illness and so not really true, the Devil scorns such destructive criticism. "Is not 'really' what works, is not truth experience and feeling? What uplifts you, what increases your feeling of power . . . damn it, that is the truth—and whether ten times a lie when looked at from the moral angle." For "life is not scrupulous—by morals it sets not a fart" (242). And the world agrees! Ideas born of illness are adopted by healthy youth and turn into culture, "which lives not on home-made bread alone, but as well on . . . poison from the apothecary's shop at the sign of The Blessed Messengers" (243). In this reminder that "poison" itself comes from the blessed realm, from God, and serves life—an example, too, of the novel's dazzling wealth of suggestive echoes—we must surely hear the author murmuring the same "He's right!" that was wrung from Dostoevsky at the hateful ideas of his Raskolnikov. For Mann has made this point before and will do so again.

The second of those idea-clusters traces out the implications of the first one in music. The Devil reminds his victim that because the conventions of traditional music have grown increasingly stale and "tonality and its dynamics" have lost the authority to determine "what is right and what wrong," composition has become a draining effort to supply what is missing by technique. It is now "a pilgrimage on peas," in which serious composers try "to persuade themselves and others that the tedious has become interesting, because the interesting has begun to grow tedious." As is right and proper, music (that is, art) has rebelled. It has turned "against the self-contained work" and "the self-glorification of form, which censors the passions and human suffering, divides out the parts, translates into pictures," and the result is, "Only the non-fictional is still permissible, the . . . untransfigured expression of suffering in the actual moment" (238-240).

"How high-mindedly he shits on art!" the composer breaks in. For whatever he must yield elsewhere to the Devil of his cynicism, *this* fruit of civilization he continues to value. But his Adversary, as if confident he will be helpless to disagree, goes on to explain why twentieth century art has to rebel against itself. It has grown impossible to accept art's pretense that its "prescribed and formalized elements . . . [are] the inviolable necessity of the single case" (241), the pretense, in other words, that the particular experience which gives art its contents must exemplify the general law embodied in its form, that form and content can be one. When all general laws — and so the forms art imposes on the chaos — have been exposed as sentimental, idealizing (bourgeois) simplifications, then nothing is authentic but the cries we utter, "the untransfigured expression of suffering in the actual moment."

Of course, the Devil has been expressing Adrian's own sense of art's paralyzing new difficulties only to spur him into action against them. He must "break through" the stale "culture" of his epoch. He must "dare to be barbaric," to leave behind "the humane . . . and bourgeois raffinement." Arriving thus at his deepest — his religious — meaning, the Devil has taken on the appearance of the daemonic theologian Schleppfuss, and he now reminds Adrian that when their talk began he had been reading Kierkegaard's *Either/Or*, in which Mozart's *Don Giovanni*, expressing the forces of amoral nature, proves that music is theological, as sin is. "Barbarism," he declares, will show "more grasp of theology" than a culture which has "fallen away from cult, which even in the religious has seen only culture, only the humane, never excess, paradox, the mystic passion, the utterly unbourgeois ideal" (243). The artist's "breakthrough" is the same as the Nazi's!

And yet. Though the Devil has insisted — with justice — that the artist had sought him out, it is also true that Adrian has been fighting him all along, fighting against the message of nature and death on behalf of humanity and life. So, in the dialogue's final phase, when his Adversary's arguments have grown impossible to resist, he is impelled to consider how he may yet escape damnation. He asks what hell is like in the hope, as the knowing Devil observes, that he will be induced to repent and break free. The Devil isn't worried. He freely describes what awaits his victims, the total inhumanity, the alternation between intolerable extremes of heat and cold, because he knows that this one, lusting for glory, will prefer all that to the "good safe average." But it turns out the Devil can err! When Adrian grasps at the idea — it is the

dream of Dostoevsky's Marmeladov — that despair of salvation might itself win
mercy, his Adversary makes two mistakes. Where, he asks, could the artist's
kind ever get "the single-mindedness, and the naive recklessness of despair."
And then, putting into "legal" form what already seems to belong to the artist's
nature, he announces the pact's final proviso. "Love is forbidden you, in so far
as it warms" (246-248). As events will make tragically clear, the artist may con-
sent to the proviso, but he can't be trusted to live by it. Adrian *will* love. He
will love — as we all do — what nature horribly destroys. And this will be quite
sufficient to bring him to despair. The arrogant Devil of the artist's cynicism,
though brilliantly right about so much, has misjudged the feeling man because
he can only see through love, and never know it.

All that is possible for Adrian now, however, is one last feeble gesture of
resistance. He mocks the Devil's stupidity in failing to realize that he was
betrayed by the very act of sex that brought them together. Not only does lust
partake of love, even if poisoned by him. It was for the sake of the work the
act was done, and "they say that work itself has to do with love." To this the
Devil's answer is the Nazi's. Having changed back into the thug, he bluntly declares that the world is sick of such "bourgeois nineteenth century" psychology
and that whoever "disturbs life" with psychology will henceforth be silenced by
"a crack on the pate" (249). The Nazi in Adrian's psyche knows well what brute
force can make of human beings and their subtle ideas. At last, promising
agonies that will be gladly endured as the condition of intoxicating bursts of
creation, and coldness that will be richly rewarded by its warming fires, the
triumphant Devil disappears and is replaced in his seat by the composer's
Devil-crony.

6. Daemonic Germany

The artist, we see, is daemonic in his lust for intoxication and greatness
and his cynical "jeerings and jugglings." What makes German politics daemonic
is that it is politics as art. This grows virtually explicit in Zeitblom's account
of his brief intoxication by patriotism during the first World War. "The psychological is always the primary," he says in this period. And though the war is
a "wrong," still, "we [Germans] must take it on ourselves" because of our need
for a "break-through" to the world out of our long isolation. Adrian grants that
in the realm of art "a real break-through is worth what the tame world calls a
crime." But to the new patriot "aesthetics [is not] a separate and narrow field
of the humane"; it is "at bottom everything" (306-308). Long ago Adrian had
scorned (like Nietzsche) the German tendency to "muddle together antithetic
principles of thought and life . . . using the coinage of the one in the sense of
the other" (84). Now, resisting "muddle" again, he mocks the delusion that Germany can join the world by conquering it. But it is precisely that muddling of
art and politics from which the German horrors will come.[10]

The whole development — seed and flower — is sketched for us in advance with a grimly playful openness during a certain political discussion among theology students, the "Winfried Circle." A student appropriately named Deutschlin affirms the unique youthfulness of the German spirit, its nearness to "the sources of life," its "religious" loyalty to "the natural and daemonic side of being." In his view this "mighty immaturity"—vide Luther—gave Germans the courage others lack to "shake off the fetters of an outlived civilization, to dare . . . to plunge again into the elemental," and will in the future "vouchsafe . . . [the world] still some renewal, some revolution" (117-118). This dreamer of German dreams even arrives at the formula "national socialism." He has insisted that the legitimacy of the State rests on its "honor and dignity," and not on its mere "usefulness," and that its "transcendental foundations" made it "independent of individual valuations." Now he declares that because people are no longer fooled by "the empty word 'freedom,'" there remain "just these two possibilities, of religious submission and religious realization: the social and the national." When another student objects that the "myth" of the "national" and the "warrior" arising out of the breakdown of old certainties and "the search for new forms of 'order'" is not only arrogant and spurious, but dangerously open to the daemonic, Deutschlin replies, "Well, and? Daemonic powers stand beside the order-making qualities in any vital movement" (124).

We will see in a moment how such aesthetic politics took its next steps toward the Nazis. But it is worth noting that the extension of the aesthetic into "everything" is at the bottom of the tragic lives of the Rodde sisters.[11] For the Munich home in which the composer found lodgings is that of a woman who had come to "the art-metropolis" and created a salon for "the artist or half-artist world," ostensibly for her daughters' sake, but actually driven by her own "never satisfied love of life." It seems at first that the moral chaos of this "house-broke Bohemia" affects only the younger daughter Clarissa, an untalented actress who kills herself when her chance of love and marriage is destroyed by a seducer who takes pleasure in the pain he inflicts. But then it turns out that the bourgeois conservativism of her sister Inez was only a feeble "defense mechanism" (196-197). The wonderfully excruciating painfulness of her story comes precisely from the explosion of the repressed against an extreme version of its antithesis. Inez marries a proper middle-class professor with a passion for blond German manliness intensified by his own physical insignificance, begets two daughters who become, like her rich home, unloved emblems of her middle-class prison, and falls ragingly in love with the violinist Rudi Schwerdtfeger, who loves only himself and his art. At last, rejected by him, she joins a circle of painted, drug-taking lesbians. The suicide of Clarissa and the moral decay of Inez dramatize the rampant daemonism—that is, aestheticism—which counteracted the Weimar Republic's brief promise of German "normalization."

We are introduced to Germany's pact with the Devil—"the new world of inhumanity" it will enter to fulfil its dreams of greatness—in Zeitblom's account of two gatherings of German intellectuals. In the first a brilliant and ugly

"polyhistor," Chaim Breisacher, comically overleaps the old-fashioned conservativism of the other guests at a musical salon. With what Zeitblom tells us is
a Jewish sensitivity to changes in the Zeitgeist, he attacks "bourgeois liberal
standards" on behalf of a revolutionary return to the archaic. In music, he
prefers the old "monody" to the "part-music," the "harmony," that replaced it,
and after that "the great and only true art of counterpoint, the cool and sacred
play of numbers" in the old vocal polyphony, to the "prostitution of feeling"
displayed by that "harmonist" Bach, and carried even further by composers like
Palestrina. Polyphony, he says, had been "miserably weakened by their regard
for the harmonic factor, for the relation of consonance and dissonance." We
will soon arrive at the cultural significance of these musical developments,
which the novel has already prepared us to understand. Here it is enough to
note that Breisacher is just as startlingly extreme a conservative in religion. For
him Solomon and David were liberals who undermined "the metaphysical
power of the folk" by the "twaddle" of "enlightenment." To replace the national
god by "an abstract and generally human god in heaven," and to treat the
bloody, god-forcing sacrifice of "genuine folkishness" as a symbol and of less
value than "gratitude and humility," was to turn "religious reality" into "weak
water-gruel." No genuine folk religion, he concludes, deals in sin and punishment in the "ethical" sense.[12] Zeitblom remembers withholding out of tact the
reminder that Moses himself regarded sacrifice as secondary to "obedience to
God and the keeping of His commandments," and realizes as he writes that this
liberal's tolerance of the intolerant was "the mistake of our civilization"
(279-284).

But it was in the new ideas that accompanied the "far-reaching . . . laxity"
of Germany after the war that Zeitblom saw "the epoch of bourgeois humanism," his "spiritual home" (352), actually coming to an end. He tells us about
his encounter with them in the "Kridwiss Circle" in the middle section of
Chapter 34, which is placed between two sections that deal with Adrian's great
work the *Apocalypsis cum Figuris*. So Mann not only emphasizes the connection
of this work and those ideas, but puts both into the one other chapter whose
numbers add up to seven. For together they cost the horrified humanist "a good
twelve pounds in weight" (362) because they represent the full emergence of
German daemonism.

The "circle" consists of people like a literary historian who evaluates
writers in racial terms, as "blood-and-soil" products of the Reich, and a poet
whose one poem ends with "Soldiers . . . I deliver you to plunder—the World!"
These people take satisfaction in "the enormous loss of value" of the individual
in this period, scorn the democratic republic as ephemeral and applaud Sorel's
idea (in *Réflexions sur la violence*) that the atomized masses of Europe can be
reunited only by war, and their political energy activated only by "mythical
fictions, devised like primitive battle cries . . . fables, insane visions . . . which
needed to have nothing to do with truth . . . in order to be creative . . . and
. . . to prove themselves dynamic realities." If this requires from intellectuals

a new *"sacrificium intellectus,"* the reward will be that they will thus rejoin the community. The humanist's hesitantly offered objection that truth, "even the bitter truth," might be more useful to people than lies, which "destroyed from within . . . the basis of genuine community," is regarded as "idealism" that has been thoroughly exploded. For they all know that free thought is a delusion, that thought begins with hidden assumptions imposed by force, open or disguised. "Freedom," we hear, "was given to thought that it might justify force" and force must again create "a firm ground under the feet." Nor would the new tyranny rule out the surrender to "personal fantasy" (363-369) any more than that of the Church had done.

It is Chaim Breisacher who reveals the hidden goal of this "deliberate rebarbarization." Commenting on the high-sounding reasons of hygiene by which the new order would justify the elimination of "the unfit, the diseased and weak-minded," he observes (to emphatic agreement) that they would be rationalizations. The real reason would be to wipe out the "humane softness of the bourgeois epoch" (370) and so to prepare humanity for the wars and revolutions that would bring back the savage values preceding Christian civilization. [13]

We have been catching glimpses from the novel's beginning of the monstrous fruit of this "revolutionary reaction." In Zeitblom's increasingly passionate outbursts about what is happening in Germany as his work nears its end, the voice of Mann himself blends with that of his narrator. Not just the war, he says after the Allied invasion of Italy has brought into view the "madness and despair" of defeat, but *"we* are lost: our character, our cause, our hope, our history." And in spite of his "grief and sympathy," he welcomes the defeat out of hatred for "the vicious violation of the truth, the cheap, filthy backstairs mythology, the criminal degradation and confusion of standards" that corrupted all that was good in his country. "For liars and lickspittles mixed us a poison draught and took away our senses. We drank—for we Germans perennially yearn for intoxication—and under its spell . . . we committed a superfluity of shameful deeds, which must now be paid for" (175). When an Allied general forces the citizens of the art-city Weimar to file past the crematoria in which Germany's aesthetic politics arrived at their fulfillment, Zeitblom/Mann breaks into agonized curses on the corruptors of a once decent people, who, out of docility and the willingness to live by theory, "went to school to Evil" and, "as Luther put it, 'took on its shoulders' immeasurable crimes" (482).

But what torments him most is what has been revealed about his own culture. Is not "everything German" henceforth subject to "mistrust," he exclaims, "even the German mind and spirit, German thought, the German Word . . . ?" Is not "the state of mind" which gave rise to the Nazis "stamped upon the features of our greatest, the mightiest embodiments of our essential Germanness?" (481-482). At last, remembering what his country was like on the day in 1940 when his friend was being buried—she seemed "about to gain the world by virtue of the one pact she was minded to keep, which she had signed with her blood" — he describes her "today" as the figure in Michelangelo's *Last Judgment*, "clung round by demons, a hand over one eye, the other staring into horrors" and falling "from despair to despair." And he ends his tale, "When, out of uttermost hopelessness — a miracle beyond the power of belief — will the light of hope dawn? A lonely man [in German *Mann*] folds his hands and speaks: 'God be merciful to thy poor soul, my friend, my Fatherland'" (510).

So Mann joins the artist with his Fatherland in guilt. For proof of their kinship we turn now to the work which led his current *alter ego* to risk damnation.

7. Music as the Language of the Devil

In order to "make the reader see . . . [music] as Adrian did" (70) Zeitblom reports in detail the four public lectures by his teacher which begin his serious education in the art. It turns out that Wendell Kretschmar, though brilliantly "real" in his passion for music and in his learned account of its Western developments, is another agent of the Devil. For not only is he the organist of Kaisersaschern. As music's spokesman in the novel, he speaks for non-verbal, "illiterate" nature, and so, like that other champion of nature Peeperkorn, he finds it hard to express himself in words; his lectures are often interrupted by painful and hilarious explosions of stuttering. (The stuttering grows worse in the presence of Adrian's mother!) It tells us something, too, that, driving his pupil hard, he calls the health he may be risking a "philistine, not to say cowardly value," which has little to do with "mind and art." And finally he insists that music is a "stunting specialization" unless studied along with "other fields of form, thought and culture" (71-72) — that is, in its relation to the Whole — and so points Adrian toward the theology which will become daemonology. In fact, his lectures are a seductive inducement to his pupil to express in music the daemonic developments of twentieth century German *Kultur*.

This grows clear in his opening lecture, which answers the question, Why does Beethoven's late Piano Sonata in C minor, Opus 111, have only two movements? The reason is that in these two movements were concluded and transcended the music of bourgeois culture, which, over the last 500 years, had replaced that of the church, of "cult." The distinction between the "harmonic subjectivity" of the former and the "polyphonic objectivity" (53) that preceded it will remain a key element of the composer's thought. As he later explains it to his friend, in the "real chord" of true polyphony "each one of its component parts becomes a voice part" in which we "do honor to the part as implied in the single chord-note," while the chord that is not "the result of part-writing," that is created for harmony's sake to express the composer's feelings, we must "rather . . . despise as subjective and arbitrary" (74). What Opus 111 shows is what happened in the soul of "greatness" when it was confronted by — and the word emerges out of a climactic burst of stuttering—"death." The result was an "abandonment of self . . . an objectivity tending to the conventional," in which the "merely personal . . . outgrew itself" and "entered into the mythical, the collectively great and supernatural" (53). In other words, the idea of death, diminishing the individual, enhances the value of what makes him one with the race and links him to the supernatural Whole.

Of course, Mann is intentionally reminding us of his own myth-novel of the artist as a servant of God. But—to say it again—his tale this time is that of the artist as Faust. We are now made aware that the same development—which in music moved away from the harmony that expresses individual feeling and back to the choral polyphony of the church—can also lead to the Devil. So Zeitblom will later refer to Wagner's "word-tone drama," which Adrian has called the inherent goal of German music, as an expression of "nature-daemony" (164). And though Adrian's own goals will go beyond Wagner, what will unite his "quasi-ecclesiastical music" (178) with the Nazi regime is that both sought to express the "nature-daemony" in the human animal by a return to cult, in which the individual is submerged in the collective. Zeitblom will make this clear in his account of what he heard after World War I in the proto-Nazi Kridwiss Circle. The development of Adrian's later works to oratorio and cantata "agreed very precisely," he will say, "with the derogatory judgment [being passed on] . . . the position of individualism . . . in the world. It was . . . a state of mind which, no longer interested in the psychological, pressed for the objective . . . the compulsory, and . . . laid on itself the pious fetters of pre-classically strict form" (372). It is this sinister meaning of choral polyphony that Kretschmar develops in his second lecture.

Describing Beethoven's painful labors on "the Credo with the fugue" of his *Missa solemnis*, his struggle to show he too could produce contrapuntal music in the old "strict style," the lecturer makes another distinction that Adrian will remember. It is a distinction between "cult epochs," when music was part of "divine service," and "cultural epochs," when it grew separate and autonomous, the latter, in his view, only a passing episode in music's history. After the lecture, Adrian draws its moral. The reason for Beethoven's difficulties, he tells his friend, was that the "elevation [of art] into the individually and culturally self-purposive had laden it with an irrelevant solemnity . . . a pathos of suffering." He begins to speculate on the return of music to a role "more modest, happier . . . in the service of a higher union"—that is, of "cult." To Zeitblom's protest that "the alternative . . . to culture is barbarism," the boy replies in a way that foreshadows Deutschlin's later "Well, and?." He rejects Zeitblom's "culture" as mere "civilization" given over to "technique and comfort." True culture, he says, is naive and unconscious and might not only accept, but even require "many a colorful barbarism." And he concludes that "the homophone-melodic constitution of our music [is] a condition of musical civilization—in contrast to the old contrapuntal polyphone culture" (59-60).

In the third lecture, "Music and the Eye," we are told that the character of a musical work can often be "read" by the knowing from the printed score. This prepares us for the name-cipher to be hidden in Adrian's music as a hint of its debt to the prostitute whose disease joined him to the Devil. But it reminds us, too, that musical notes may express something other than themselves. In fact, "music's deepest wish," the lecturer says, is "to be perceived and contemplated as pure mind" (61). So we are ready for Zeitblom's later "readings" of the composer's works as expressions of the demon-ridden mind that links him and his country.

It is in the final lecture, which, we are told, made on Adrian the strongest impression, that the kinship of his future music and his country's politics is most clearly foreshadowed. As an example of how music "is at any moment capable of beginning at the beginning . . . bare of all knowledge of its past cultural history, and of creating anew" (63), Kretschmar tells the story of an uneducated eighteenth century religious fanatic named Johann Conrad Beissell, who left Germany for America and, as head of a new religious sect in Pennsylvania, began to set hymns to music in a style of his own invention. This style, to which Adrian will later refer as an influence on his own, was born when Beissell "decreed" that the notes which belonged to the common chord at the center of any key should be "masters" and assigned to the accented syllables of a text, and that the other notes should be "servants" and assigned only to the unaccented syllables. Then, after devising for all possible keys "chord tables" which enabled anybody to write tunes, he made up for that rigidity in the treatment of individual notes by a rhythmic freedom given to the "master" accented syllables, which could be as long or as short as the syllables required. And this account of what may be called musical dictatorship is followed by a report of the unearthly beauty of sound Beissell elicited by dehumanizing his choir. They sang in falsetto with mouths hardly open and lips hardly moving, and their voices, with the help of the hall's low ceiling, produced "peculiar and moving" tones that were less like human voices than like "delicate instrumental music" which "hovered angelically" (65-66) over the heads of the audience.

We are told that after the lecture the two friends "made merry over . . . this backwoods dictator with his droll thirst for action," who behaved "stupidly with reason" — i.e., who acted out "rational" theories stupid in their premises. But "even while he mocked," Adrian preserved "the right, not to say the privilege, of . . . keeping a distance, which includes in itself [along with "half-admiration"] the possibility of . . . conditioned agreement." The humanist sees "arrogance" in such "ironic remoteness" and even a danger to the soul's health. But he confesses that it was just this arrogance which aroused his "fearful love" (67). What we know of the daemonic underlying that arrogance — that is, the sense of an "inborn" or natural merit which is above morality — helps us see why. The privilege the artist reserves to himself is that of staying open to the "non-theoretic, the vital, will or instinct," to the fluid chaos of nature. Though the humanist is fearful of nature as "illiterate" and indifferent to humane values, he is helpless not to love the artist who keeps us in contact with it because it is also the source of the vitality of those values, and indeed, of life itself.

The composer enters into his Devil-pact during his friend's year of war-service, and what Zeitblom finds when they meet again — in the man and in his music — foreshadows the career that lies ahead. Adrian is setting to music a passage from Dante about the damnation of the unbaptised "good and pure." When Zeitblom shows his distaste for such "incomprehensible justice," such a "rejection of the human," he is answered with a "look" that is "something new," though he is to see it again: "Mute, veiled, musing, aloof to the point of offensiveness, full of a chilling melancholy, it ended in a smile with closed lips, not unfriendly, yet mocking, and with that gesture of turning away so habitual, so long familiar to me" (162-163). It is the look of one who has entered into intimate relations with "the sources of being" and knows what most of us are protected from knowing by our usual dreams and theories. What he knows will lead, both in the texts he chooses to set to music and in the music itself, to a rejection of the forms of civilization.

The texts are all cynical or heartbroken exposés of the inhuman reality — in the psyche or outside it — which refutes our dreams of meaning and value. They are works like Blake's "A Poison Tree" and "The Chapel of Gold," Keats's "Nightingale" and "Melancholy" Odes, *Love's Labor's Lost*, which mocks both the "natural man" and his lofty opposite. Most shockingly we see that reality in the contrast between two works written just before World War I, Adrian's setting for a poem out of Klopstock's *Spring Festival* called "The Drop to the Bucket" and the one-movement symphony *Marvels of the Universe*.

In the first the poet has deliberately refused to "fling himself into the ocean of the worlds" in order to "hover [over] and adore" the drop-like earth, and the music conveys the coming of the Deity after a storm "in hushed murmurings" and with "the bow of peace" (265). This work's spirit of "humble glorification" is so different from the "luciferian sardonic mood" of the next, its "sneering travesty of praise" which mocks not only the universe, but its own medium, "the cosmos of sound" (274), that the two might seem to be by different minds. But Zeitblom tells us he realized later that the first was actually a preparation for the second, an advance "plea to God, an atonement for sin, a work of *attritio cordis*." For the symphony does enter that "ocean of worlds." It expresses in music the mind-defeating vision of the universe insinuated by modern science. This is the vision to which Adrian claims he has been led by "an American scholar named Akercock" (266-267) in the course of Faust-like journeys with his "mentor" to the depths of the sea and among the stars. Zeitblom assumes he is jesting, that he acquired the vision from books, but it is the composer who is closer to the truth. For the name Akercock, like the German Capercailzie[13] it was chosen to duplicate for readers of English, is a nickname for the Devil. And whether or not the artist believes in the Adversary's literal reality, we have to take as simple realism this hint of the anti-human, the daemonic, implica-

tions of modern science. For in the sea, Adrian says, he gratified the "itch . . .
to look at the unlooked at" (268), silencing the irrepressible guilt with the principle that science is above all moral concerns and must be free to go as far as
it can in every direction. And among the stars, already separated by unimaginable light-years of space and still exploding apart unimaginably faster than the
fragments of a bursting shell, he learned about magnitudes that Zeitblom is
surely right to take as a blow to humane values. Such "devil's juggling," he says,
undermines not only the "civilizing process born of reverence," but also the
"proud consciousness" that man is more than a "biological being," that he
belongs to "an intellectual and spiritual world" and can arrive at ideas "of truth,
of freedom, of justice. . . . In . . . this reverence of man for himself," he concludes, "is God; in a hundred milliards of Milky Ways I cannot find him."

To this the artist gives the Devil's answer, which is to say, the answer of
"physical nature." It is that this "monstrosity" of a universe is the inescapable
"premise" and "soil" of the moral, and to deny it shows a medieval resistance
to the science humanism claims to respect. In fact, Adrian "had it on the best
authority" that life was "the product of the marsh-gas fertility of a neighboring
star" carried to earth by "cosmic projectiles or . . . radiation pressure," so that
homo Dei himself, "together with his obligation to the spiritual," was a "flower
of evil." The symphony that issued from such ideas contributed to a view of
Adrian's work as "a virtuosity antipathetic to the artist-mind, a blasphemy, a
nihilistic sacrilege" (272-275), charges roughly similar to those that have been
brought against his author's.

Two apparently contradictory attitudes to form result from that corrosive
Devil's knowledge: on the one hand, a barbaric rejection of form, and on the
other, a slavish submission to it. But to understand this development it will
help us to look first at an apparent contradiction in the novel's use of the terms
"subjective" and "objective." Kretschmar's lectures taught that devotion to the
subjective (the "merely personal") belongs to the humanistic culture of "civilization" which replaced that of "cult," with its emphasis on the "conventional," the
"collectively great and supernatural." In this context the subjective is what is
sacred to the humanist, and the objective is an external power that enslaves it
and despises the achievements — of life and art — born of its free expression. But
we have seen too that Zeitblom regards Luther's work as "the revolt of subjective willfulness against the objective bond," and the cause of "endless blood-
letting and the most horrible self-lacerations" and that it is the Devil who
celebrates "feeling," "self-admiration," "what uplifts you, what increases your
power . . . whether ten times a lie looked at from the moral angle" (242).
Adrian himself (before his "pact") replies to Deutschlin's Luther-like scorn of
the Church by declaring that "even as she is today" the Church provides "the
objective disciplining of religious life" required to save it from "subjectivist
demoralization . . . a chaos of divine and daemonic powers . . . madness" (119).
In *this* context the "objective" represents not what crushes the individual's free
intelligence but its finest flower, those "forms" of civilization — moral distinc-

tions the chief of these — by which a subjectivity which risks destroying life is controlled and made to serve it.

We have encountered this idea in Mann's work before. It is the point of Joseph's great defense of "divine reason" against Pharaoh's tendency to seek guidance in "fits," his idea that "civilized life" requires that the "traditional" (or "typical" or "mythical") — what issues from the biological subjectivity common to all — be controlled by the "I [which] is from God and . . . is free" (937). Now, as the forms evolved by the free I to control what issues from the depths were discarded by Germany's twentieth century political daemonism and were replaced by others in which those depths took control, the same thing will happen in Adrian's music. Rejecting both humane objectivity and humane subjectivity, his music will in one development mock and dissolve form, and in another, bring back, from below the reason, a form of inhuman rigidity. This is why Zeitblom's descriptions of the formal aspects of his friend's work are not only dramatically alive, but intelligible, whether we know music or not. They are revelations, moving and painful, of the state of his soul.

Adrian announces that rejection of form himself when he shocks the humanist with the idea which, in his battle with the Devil, he called "shitting on art." "The work of art . . . is a fraud," he says. "It is something the burgher wishes there still were." For "at the present stage of our consciousness, our knowledge, our sense of truth," the "conscience of art" rejects "pretense and play," consigns music's traditional goals and methods to "the kingdom of the banal," and finds "genuine and serious" only "the very short, highly consistent musical moment." Zeitblom wonders as he listens "what strain . . . intellectual tricks . . . ironies" would be necessary to save art "and to arrive at a work which as a travesty of innocence confessed to the state of knowledge from which it was to be won" (180-181). His words here point straight to Adrian's version of *Love's Labor's Lost*, which Zeitblom, admiring and saddened, will call an "arrogant travesty . . . a tense, sustained, neck-breaking game played by art at the edge of impossibility" (218).

This development emerges full-blown in the "barbarism" of the first of Adrian's two greatest works, the *Apocalypsis cum Figuris*. For the work shows itself as precivilized in abandoning the tempered scale, which corrected nature's sound intervals — its "raw, primitive features" — and enabled man "to win from chaos a musical system." The work arrived at "pure music," that is, music free of the spirit's intervention, by way of whispering and antiphonal speech, the "mere noise" of tom-toms and gongs, a frequent glissando, not only with instruments, but in human howling. Then, too, like nature in the father's experiments, it violates bourgeois culture's categories and distinctions. It expresses the spiritually lofty by means of dissonance, reserves "firm tonality" for "the world of hell" and makes voices sound like instruments and vice versa. Finally, it recalls Beissell's "master" and "servant" notes in replacing traditional rhythm with the "flexibility" (373-376) of speech. Where all this is heading we learn soon afterward from a chamber work which is pure "musical prose," for

it has "no thematic connections, developments, variations, and no repeti-
tions.... Of traditional forms not a trace" (456).

But the composer's abandoning of the forms evolved by the free spirit is
accompanied, as I said, by the development of a kind of anti-human form. "We
need a system-maker [like Beissell]," he tells his friend one day, "a teacher of
the objective and organization, with enough genius to unite the old-established,
the archaic, with the revolutionary." And the reason he gives is the Devil's,
which he had once resisted. It is that "in an age of destroyed conventions and
the relaxing of all subjective obligations . . . freedom begins to lie like a mildew
upon talent and to betray traces of sterility," and subjectivity, grown impotent,
may find new powers in "constraint . . . in subordination to law, rule, coer-
cion." Of course, such constraint is not necessarily an attack on the subjective
and its values. Adrian reminds his friend that the subjective itself must produce
form — "crystallizations of living experiences" — to do the job of "organization"
without which "there is nothing, least of all art." Thus even in the work of
Brahms and Beethoven, where the form is "absorbed by the subjective," we see
how "subjectivity turns into objectivity." We find a "development or working
out" of themes in which there is at last "nothing unthematic left" and "one can
no longer speak of a 'free style'" (189-191). But this suggestion that art itself
tends toward the control of freedom and feeling recalls what Zeitblom has
already said about the darker side of that necessary process. He saw in Adrian's
two final masterpieces a union of the "declamatory expressiveness" of composers like Monteverdi and Buxtehude in their treatment of the "Bible word"
and "the intellectual passion for austere order, the *linear* style of the Netherlands
composers." This combination of "heat and cold," in which the "objective
blushes with feeling," gave him the impression of a "glowing mould" and
brought home to him "like nothing else . . . the idea of the daemonic" (177-178).
In short, art itself tends toward the daemonic, and not only because it is rooted
in the primal chaos, but because its drive to form puts humane feeling and
values in second place.

This effect of the break-down of old conventions has its culmination in the
rigid formalism of the Schönberg invention Mann borrowed for his composer,
the 12-tone scale. The Brentano lied "*O Lieb Madel*," with its five-note Esmeralda theme, had brought him near the "strict style" he sought, the "complete
integration of all musical dimensions, their neutrality towards each other due
to complete organization." But he has decided that five notes are too few and
limiting. His plan now, he tells his friend, is to use all twelve notes of the scale.
"Words" made of these notes could become the organizing principle, no note
recurring until all the others have sounded, and each fulfilling a function in the
structure of the whole. "Impoverishment" would be avoided by reversing or
rearranging the letters of the 12-note word, as in double or triple fugues. The
fact that any note gets its meaning and function from "its place in the basic
series or its derivatives" would not only guarantee "indifference to harmony
and melody" but would constitute "a rejuvenation of the worn-out by the con-

stellation," a way of mixing the progressive and the regressive that reflects "the equivocalness of life itself" (191-193). So the daemonic artist has rejuvenated the worn-out by an organization that is not a "crystallization of experience," but, like the regime of the Nazis, is imposed arbitrarily, ruthlessly, from outside.

But here again we must say "and yet." Our narrator has given us more than one glimpse of how, for all his necessary daemonism, the artist also resists the Devil. And in the composer's last and greatest work — as in the chapbook — Faust will declare, "I die as a good and as a bad Christian." In fact, even as the novel uncovers the timeless, secular meaning of the artist's Devil-pact, it is doing the same with his persistent loyalty to God, and with a comparable wealth of nuances and complications.

8. The Artist as a Servant of God

It is to convey the source and meaning of this other loyalty that Mann has woven into his story a number of references to Anderson's fairy tale of the "sea-maid." As Adrian tells the tale to his friend, it is out of love for a *dark-eyed* human prince that the *blue-eyed* mermaid braves the "raging whirlpools" of the sea-witch and begs her for human legs. For his sake she accepts the knife-pains they cost her, hoping "perhaps to win, like human beings, an immortal soul" (343). What she represents has already been suggested by the Devil, who offered to bring her to the composer's couch. He likened Adrian's agonies of migraine (inherited from his father, intensified by the illness he got from the prostitute and endured "with pleasure and pride for . . . [the delights of genius] he has so much enjoyed") to the "pains which the little sea-maid . . . had in her beautiful human legs she got herself instead of a tail." Moreover, he deliberately united the two metaphors when he assured the composer that his "sense of . . . power and splendor will more and more outweigh the pangs of the little sea-maid" (243, 386). These pangs are a version of the artist's painful labors to turn his own nature-wildness into art, and art, even if it issues from his daemonic depths, is also born (as Tonio Kröger knew) of the artist's yearning to be accepted by the "others" — the "bourgeois," the human. Art comes not only from the fluid chaos of nature, but also from the love of human beings, and it is this love that is the meaning of the artist's loyalty to God.

Of course, we are not permitted to forget that Faust remains a bad Christian, as well as a good one. The sea-maid's love of the human is not spared the composer's usual irony. During a terrible bout of that migraine — which led to a period of great creativity and coincided with the post-World War I collapse that led to the devilish "creativity" of Germany — he talks to his friend about his "sister in affliction." And here he ascribes her "sentimental infatuation for the two-legged world of men" to her "cult" of a statue that fell into the sea — "obviously by Thorwaldsen," that is, obviously the human idealized — which led to an "hysterical overestimation of the upper world and the immortal soul."

Absurd, he says, to prefer an immortal soul — that is, an eternity of sentimental idealization — to being simply "the foam on the sea, as Nature wills." Better to have "tenderly drowned" her prince then to make "her fate depend . . . on his stupidity," especially since he would probably have loved her more with her fish-tail — that is, as half an animal — and since, as half-animal, she had her own "complete and charming organic reality, beauty and inevitability" (344). Still, in spite of his ironies, Adrian can't help identifying himself with this self-betraying nature-creature in her "absurd" love of the human. (We have seen before how nature — the daemonic — betrays itself, in the love begotten by lust.) So at the end we hear the composer-Faust "insanely" confess that he has mated with the sea-maid and that their union produced a son of flesh and blood whom he had loved in defiance of the Devil and then killed at the Devil's command.

In Adrian's life-story what draws him away from the Devil of inhuman nature and his own will is called the "world." And here too there are complications. On the one hand, we find the "cosmopolitan" artist defending the "world" against the "provincial conceit" of German *Kultur*. So at Halle he responds to Deutschlin's claim that the German is more capable than others of rebirth because he is closer to nature by reminding him that "rebirth was once called *renascimento* and went on in Italy. And 'back to nature' . . . was first prescribed in French" (118). And as we know, he is similarly ironic against Zeitblom's World War I German patriotism, which thought it could join the world by conquering it. On the other hand, Zeitblom observes that his friend feels less "at home" in worldly little Switzerland than in provincial Germany. And though he insists that it is mere "German provincial conceitedness . . . to deny depth to the world," yet it is a "world depth," and to be born to "the provincial — and thus so much the more uncanny — depth of Germany" is also "a destiny" (179).

In fact, as Adrian's steady musical progress begins to bring him and the world together, we are shown, in his relations with three "seducers," how it would draw him away, not only from his provincial isolation, but from his genius. The first is the violinist Rudi Schwerdtfeger, whom we meet early persuading the composer to return to a party, and who completes the process thus begun with a two-fold "conquest" (415): he draws the composer into a homosexual relationship, winning the privilege of the "*du*" which was hitherto Zeitblom's alone, and he gets Adrian to write for him a violin concerto Zeitblom calls "the apotheosis of salon music" (410). Moreover, we are told he won that "*du*" during a visit to the castle of a rich and noble admirer of the composer, the Baroness von Tolna, who, like Tschaikovsky's Mme. von Meck, was ready to offer him the wealth of the world, provided they never meet.[14]

Then, in the French-strewn monologue of Saul Fitelberg, a virtuoso creation, funny, profound and utterly alive, we see both the seductive world and what opposes it. As an "international business man and concert agent," he has come to the "retreat where genius created and suffered" — so he respectfully puts it — in order to snare the genius and make a killing. But in him the shrewd worldliness of "the little Jewish boy" who rose to prosperity and culture out of "lousy Lublin" by beating the world at its own game is mixed with a speed and subtlety of awareness and with unworldly spiritual values that are equally Jewish. So, though he frankly tempts the composer with Satan's promise to Jesus "to bear you on my mantle through the air and show you the kingdoms of the earth and the glory of them . . . [and] to lay them at your feet," he assents at once to the refusal he intuits, and to its implied scorn for the world. For he not only sees where they come from — the "old-German" character expressed in Adrian's music, the "pride" that regards his *"destin"* as "something unique and . . . sacred." He also sympathizes with them, and precisely as a "human being," or "more specifically" as a Jew who has "the Old Testament in my bones" (397-407). And having noted that the composer seems to be living in a duplicate version of his Kaisersaschern home, just as he, Fitelberg, still carries Lublin in his own depths, he arrives at the idea of the kinship of Germans and Jews which we heard from Mann's Goethe in *The Beloved Returns.*

Though the German's character, "essentiellement anti-sémitique," has forced the Jew to become international, they are akin in their mixture of "arrogance and a sense of inferiority," in "the ressentiment [they share] of the serious-minded against the salon world," and above all, in their religiousness. Just as the German composer (Bruckner) turns music-teaching into a "priestly office," the Jews remain "a priestly people, even when we are minaudering about in Parisan salons." For that reason — this is the ground of his final (vain) appeal — "the Germans should let the Jew be the mediateur between them and society, be the manager, the impressario." Otherwise, "with their nationalism, their pride, their foible of 'differentness,' their hatred of being put in order and equalized, their refusal to let themselves be introduced into the world . . . , they will get into . . . real Jewish trouble, je le jure" (406-408). In short, the German's unworldliness is a sign of his kinship with the "priestly" Jew, even as his provincial, brutal, daemonic version of it marks the vast difference between them.

With the third of those "seducers," we see how the world can show itself in a loved human being. As Adrian explains at the end in his mad Faust-confession, he yielded to the blandishments of the violinist because he thought that loving a male would be only a minor betrayal of his Devil-pact. But that irregular and partial approach to the human takes him further than he intended. Led by Rudi into the world, he meets the woman he wants to marry. Zeitblom's vivid description of Marie Godeau places before us a woman whose "sympathetic" beauty is perfectly convincing. But as he explains the grounds of her appeal for his friend, he suggests too, and at last makes explicit, what she represents. He finds it easy to see her as Adrian's "life-partner" because of her black eyes, her musical voice, the impression her directness conveys of the "capable woman." And to these hints of her similarity to the composer's life-serving mother, Zeitblom adds plainly that it was "the world" that came near to him in her, and that drew him out of his "recluse state" and "his own world of musical theology, oratorio, mathematical number-magic" (423). As we know, these three aspects of the German artist's world are precisely what links him with twentieth century German *Kultur*: its daemonic theology, its subordination of the individual in the collective, and its "magical" or non-rational ways of thought. It is because the woman is a human being whom he loves, and by whom he is in real danger of being drawn away from himself and his own will, that the Devil ruthlessly intervenes.

We catch our first glimpse of the Devil's opposition in the fact that the artist's rebellion through love seems strangely half-hearted. He courts the woman in a way that keeps throwing her and the helplessly flirtatious violinist together, and it is Rudi he sends to her with his proposal. True, he persuades the reluctant violinist to do him the service by insisting that it is for his art, as well as himself, that he seeks "human warmth," and that the other is wrong to think it is "only out of inhumanity I am what I am" (436). But when Rudi "betrays" him by winning the woman for himself and thus brings about his own murder at the hands of the wildly jealous Inez Rodde, Zeitblom is left with a suspicion so terrible he cannot at first bring himself to divulge it. Like Ivan Karamazov unconsciously arranging the murder of his father by Smerdyakov, the Devil-ridden artist has brought about what his conscious mind deplores. He has used Rudi to rid himself at once of the two representatives of the "world" who had threatened his precious isolation and self-will. And what is striking — Dostoevskian — in this account of the Devil's triumph is the fact that both the artist's love and his need to destroy it are perfectly genuine.

But it is in the conclusion of the novel's human drama — Adrian's greatest love and the terrible agony of its loss — that Mann's Faust arrives at the "single-mindedness" the Devil thought impossible for him and turns most completely against his master. With an adored grandson as his model, Mann has created in Adrian's five-year-old nephew Nepomuk — or Echo, as he pronounces his own name — a child who is "real" enough, if exceptionally sensitive. But he too belongs to the novel's meaning. His function is to make clear the relationship between the love of human beings and the idea of God.

We find, to begin with, that the blue-eyed Echo does not come from the "world." To the pastor his precocity of compassionate awareness makes him seem "a child of God," and Zeitblom regards him as an example, like the child Jesus, of "'the child' on earth," that is, of an innocence which seems to come to us as "envoy" and "message-bearer" (464-467). The message he brings is put darkly into words in six antique prayers the composer and his friend hear the child recite, wondering but preferring not to ask where he had learned them.[15] These prayers say that whoever lives by God's commandments has God in himself; that man's sins are trifles to God, Who can smile and pardon; that man builds on the "rainbow" when he barters "heavenly bliss" for "earthly joys"; that though no good deeds can save those "born for hell," those who are not can touch evil and remain blessed; and finally, that "whoso for other pray, Himself he saves that way." All of this can be "translated" into secular language, but it may be enough to note here that the prayers are a way of relating human life to the Whole (or nature or "the source of being") and that the key to them all is in the first. This tells us, in effect, that human goodness and God's are the same, which is to say that God is the name of the human dream that the Whole is good.

As for the concluding "theological speculation" of praying for others to save oneself—so odd, Adrian says, in a pious child—its meaning emerges when he asks the humanist, "Surely, the unselfishness is gone so soon as one sees it is of use?" He is also asking for an opinion of his own "calculation" on the saving power of despair. The answer he gets recalls Joseph's defense against that charge by Pharaoh's mother. It is that the child "turns the thing into unselfishness so soon as he may not pray only for himself, but does so for us all" (471-472). Zeitblom means that humanity's inescapable brotherhood turns such apparent selfishness into its opposite. The artist, too, however self-absorbed, cannot "pray"—or despair of salvation like Marmeladov and so (perhaps) win it—"only for himself, but does so for us all."

What the artist has risked by this extremity of human love for the bearer of the human dream comes to pass in an equally extreme demonstration of the way such love is punished. He must endure the same faith-destroying horror—the torture and death of the child—that led Ivan Karamazov to give back his ticket of admission to God's universe. And not only does the blameless child die in agony; he dies of spinal meningitis, a disease in which, as in Adrian's, the brain is attacked by the Devil's "little ones" and the victim shrieks and squints "as though he were possessed." At the peak of his ordeal, as Frau Schweigestill, "ever loyal to the 'human,'" is holding him in her arms, Adrian cries out to his humanist friend, "This is no place for you. Cross yourself," and then, though he madly laughs at the Devil's inability to kill the soul, which remains with him, "Take him, monster . . . hell-hound . . . scum, filth, excrement!" At last, against Zeitblom's horrified protests, he speaks of the susceptibility of children "to poisonous influences" (475-478) and thus confesses that the Devil's instrument in all this has been himself.

The composer's guilt at his nephew's death is hard to believe as part of the "realistic" story. Still, whether or not the feeling is literally justified, there may be reason enough for guilt in the fact that he has always been—partly—in league with what killed him. For the sake of his art he let this negation—partly—rule his mind as it ruled utterly the minds of those other seekers after power and beauty, the Nazis. In fact, Mann's account of the child's agony, though brilliantly written, seems to break through the artistic surface and become painful like something real because it is an exceptionally harsh reminder of how all our loving and dreaming are mocked by Devil-Nature. It certainly prepares us, in any case, for the composer's announcement to his friend after the death: "It is not to be. . . . What we call the human, although it is good and noble . . . [and what] human beings have fought for . . . [and] the ecstatics exultantly announced . . . will be taken back. I will take it back" (478). He will take back, he explains, "The Ninth Symphony." It is because his No to Beethoven's exultant celebration of the human is a genuine *lamentation* that his *alter ego* Faust can claim he dies a good Christian, as well as a bad one. And Zeitblom's account of his friend's great work, summing up the accumulated wealth of the novel's experience and thought — and even describing the novel's artistic character and effect as he describes those of the cantata — brings us the deepest implication of Mann's unifying idea.

Before turning to that work, it is worth noting that the artist's Faustian doubleness shows itself in two others which come before it. In the first, a musical farce for puppets made out of the story of Gregory, the "holy sinner" of the *Gesta Romanorum* (and of Mann's next novel), the human and the daemonic are equal in force. On the one hand, its "intellectual charm" is "not without a trace of malice and . . . travesty, springing . . . from a critical rebound after the swollen pomposity of an art-epoch nearing its end" (319). On the other, its cartoon-like directness comes from the composer's desire for the "redemption" of an art in danger of dying unless "she were to find her way to the folk, that is . . . to human beings." It is interesting that Zeitblom, though moved, now resists this abandonment of the arrogance he once saw as daemonic. His comment here is not only that he loves it, but that the artist has a right to it, and that such lowering of art to "the folk" is a "murder of mind and spirit." But the contradiction is only on the surface. For he rejects arrogance when it is scorn of the human, and defends it when it is devotion to spirit. It is precisely by remaining on the height, Zeitblom says, that art can serve people best "in the long run" (321-322). Of course, in his idea that art murders spirit by mocking its pomposities we detect Mann's gentle smile at a characteristic simple-mindedness of the right-thinking.

The second is the oratorio based on Dürer's woodcuts, the *Apocalypsis cum figuris*. Though, as we have seen, this work goes all the way in its "barbaric" rejection of form, the words it sets to music are such Biblical texts as Ezekiel's awful announcement that "an end is come . . . it watcheth for thee" and Jeremiah's "We have transgressed, Thou has not pardoned . . . Thou hast slain, Thou hast not pitied" (357-360). Far from being "soulless" (as Zeitblom has heard it called), the work is "a fervid prayer for a soul" (378). Far from mocking the idea of God, it expresses God's terrifying judgment on human evil.

But it is in the *Lamentation of Doctor Faustus* that the artist's resistance to the Devil shows itself most clearly and tragically. Our narrator comes to the subject, he tells us, in April, 1945, when Allied advances in the west have begun the destruction of Nazi Germany. And noting how strongly these times *in* which he writes are linked to the period *of* which he writes, he tells us that Adrian's final work was written in 1929 and 1930, years which were the last of his "rational existence" and the beginning of the "harms" which were to overwhelm Germany. "We children of the dungeon" dreamed thereafter, Zeitblom says, of "a hymn of exultation . . . to celebrate the dawn of a free Germany, freed by herself." But now "only this can avail us, only this will be sung from our very souls: the *Lamentation* of the son of hell, the lament of men and God, issuing from the subjective, but always broadening out and as it were laying hold of the Cosmos; the most frightful lament ever set up on this earth" (485). And though this introductory characterization of the work ascribes it to "the son of hell," it has also darkly hinted at something else. We will find that the cantata is linked to Echo and both are linked to the creative, God-making role of the human imagination.

The key to the cantata's form is the "echo-effect," the "variation principle," for the work is "a mammoth variation piece of lamentation ... negatively related to the finale of the Ninth Symphony, with its variations of exultation," in which one 12-tone setting of one 12-syllable text ("For I die as a good and as a bad Christian" — *"denn ich sterbe als ein böser und guter Christ"*) is "the basis of all the music ... and is responsible for the identity of the most varied forms" (487). The music for these twelve syllables is governed, Zeitblom reminds us, by that letter-symbol from Hetaera Esmeralda, that is, by that expression of "the bond and the vow, the promise and the blood pact." But here the pact is not recalled with coldness or cynicism. "Alas, it is not to be!" These words "speak in every note and accent of this 'Ode to Sorrow.'" True, the cantata's Faust, like the original, rejects the advice of "the good old doctor" that he save himself by repentance. But he does so because he despises the "positivism of the world ... the lie of its godliness." It is his "proudly despairing 'No' ... to false and flabby middle-class piety" (490), which means that it is a rejection of the pretense of piety by one who deeply respects the real thing.

How hope can rise out of this darkness — for it will, though it will be only a "hope beyond hopelessness" — is not easy to see, and Zeitblom's account of the subtle process is nearly, though not quite, opaque. He begins by pointing out two paradoxical effects in the music. One is the emergence of the "subjective" out of form that is "strict to the last degree," and that "no longer knows anything unthematic." The "deep diabolic jest," he says, is that "just by virtue of the absoluteness of the form the music is, as language, freed." Having determined the form in advance, the composer can, in the actual composition, "yield himself to subjectivity." The second paradox comes from the fact that the cantata's echo-like variations, which link it to the music of the seventeenth century and Monteverdi, provide a "resumé" of music's many "'characters' of expressiveness." And because they are now under "conscious control" and "refined to fundamental types of emotional significance" (487-488), the deeply personal lament emerges by way of what is common to us all.

Zeitblom has already suggested the meaning of "lament" in his friend's great work. "What we have here," he has said, is a "lament of the most painfully Ecce Homo kind[16] — the *Lamentation* as expression itself; one may state boldly [he goes on] that all expressivism is really lament; just as music, so soon as it is conscious of itself as expression at the beginning of modern history, becomes lament and *'lasciatemi morire'* [let me die], the lament of Ariadne [the human] to the softly echoing plaintive song of the nymphs [nature]." In fact, the "echo-effect" has here become a version of that "echoing" lament, and so an expression of that fundamental meaning of music itself. For "the echo," he says, "the giving back of the human voice as nature-sound, and the revelation of it *as* nature-sound, is essentially a lament: Nature's melancholy 'Alas!' in view of man, her effort to utter his solitary state"[17] (485-486).

We now understand the role of Echo, the beloved child who seems to bring from beyond this world the great human dream, that the universe is not a fluid chaos, but a beneficient order. In him that dream of God is echoed back to us as "nature-sound," that is, as a message from the universe itself. He is thus a living embodiment of the act of imagination that Abraham performed in the covenant which humanized God and uplifted the human to the divine. Of course, it is because that dream is horribly refuted by Devil-Nature that the *Lamentation* takes it back. But we know that this work was begun before the child's coming. The artist understood long ago that the dream was a delusion. What was added by that climactically agonizing demonstration of the Adversary's power was despair. And out of that despair came the artist's — the human being's — paradoxical triumph. For the "echo-effect" of the human imagination does not cease. If man's hopeful dream must be given up, his music, which is to say, his art, takes its place. It is now art which, "issuing from the subjective," lays hold on "the Cosmos," comes back to us as "nature-sound" — "Nature's melancholy 'Alas!' in view of man" — and so mitigates our solitary state. And then it does more.

A sentence before the last one asks, "When, out of uttermost hopelessness — a miracle beyond the power of belief — will the light of hope dawn?" With these words Mann reminds us of the "change" that takes place after the cantata's final note, when "above the reason . . . it touches the feelings" (490). It is not a diminution of its "irremediable anguish." It is only what happens when "despair achieves a voice." And pointing to the "artist paradox" that makes "expressiveness — expressiveness as lament — . . . the issue of the whole [apparently anti-expressive] construction," he asks if we may not "parallel with it another, a religious one, and say too (though only in the lowest whisper), that out of the sheerly irremediable hope might germinate? It would be but a hope beyond hopelessness, the transcendence of despair . . . the miracle that passes belief." And asking us to listen with him to the "high G of a cello" which ends the work in a "pianissimo-fermata" dying away into "silence and night," he affirms that in that silence "the voice of mourning is no more. It changes its meaning; it abides as a light in the night" (490-491).

So Mann arrives, even in his great lamentation, at hope for his country and his artist. He grounds it first of all on despair, which shatters daemonic pride and reminds us we are human beings; and then on the human power of which art is the great exemplar. When all is lost, unforeseeable renewal can come, like a gift of grace, from the power to express what we feel.[18]

Notes

1. The ambiguity of that "it" is in the German too, which reads: "*Fern sei es von mir, den Ernst der Kunst zu leugnen; aber wenn es ernst wird, verschmäht man die Kunst und ist ihrer nicht fähig.*" But the idea gets clear enough when first the Devil and then Mann's artist make the same point. "Now only the nonfictional is still permissible," the Devil says, ". . . the . . . untransfigured expression of suffering in the actual moment" (240). It's true that the Devil dismisses external factors as insignificant in this development. For him it rises out of the nature of art. But he exaggerates. Our narrator will show us that the artist's work *is* affected by his life.

2. Because of the vast increase in the quantity and complexity of his materials, as well as the nakedly personal confession the novel often became, Mann seems to have been far more worried than usual that he might be misread. It was to prevent this that he gave us his own account of the novel's key ideas, its sources and its methods in *The Story of a Novel*. Two of his essays that also shed light on the novel are "Germany and the Germans," which was written while he was still working on it and makes explicit its ruling idea, that "wicked Germany is merely good Germany gone astray" (*Addresses*, 64); and "Nietzsche in the Light of Recent History," which shows the view he had of Nietzsche when he used him as a model for his composer. (The latter essay is discussed in the last chapter.)

3. *Story of a Novel* acknowledges many of the novel's debts to scholars, but above all the help Mann got with its music from Theodore Adorno, whose combination of literary sensibility and philosophic and musical learning he found peculiarly congenial. That Mann succeeded in writing of music in a way the professional musician could respect, if not always agree with, I have been assured by the composer David Stock.

4. Mann's idea of the daemonic is close to Goethe's. In his autobiography (v. 2, 422-425) Goethe speaks of it as that "in nature which manifests itself in contradiction, and which therefore could not be comprehended under any idea, still less under one word." It is neither good nor evil, but gives rise to both, and in human beings it shows itself in "tremendous energy" which the "masses" find irresistibly attractive.

5. Schildknapp is a comic version of our artist, "artistic" not in the power to give real existence to the possible, but in being "a roué of the possibilities" (220) — in toying with them — and refusing to commit himself to the actual. So, as an Anglophile who despises things German, he scorns his own roots; he is a translator rather than a poet; and he is a sponger, living off others and evasive when they need him. As for the symbolism of eye-colors, this recurs all through the novel. Once we are told that on a fateful outing with the woman he loves, the violinist and his Devil-crony, "Adrian had under his own eyes the whole range of blue and black and like-colored ones" and that the day "stood in the sign of this constellation, perhaps ought to stand in it, that the initiated might recognize therein the real idea of the excursion" (427).

6. The boy Adrian defends his "arrogance" by citing Goethe's phrase "inborn merits," in which the poet sought to "divorce from the word 'merit' its moral character and, conversely, to exalt the natural and inborn to a position of extra-

moral desert" (84). We are thus invited to see, even in Goethe, a seed of the evil to come, the monster-making idea of an aristocracy entitled to "extra-moral desert."

7. It would be easy to find fault with Lowe Porter's sometimes clumsy and unconvincing use of archaic English to suggest Mann's Luther-like German. But one responsibility of the critic, as Gide remarked, is to distinguish between what matters in a particular work and what does not. The clumsiness of her archaic English doesn't matter because it conveys well enough what Mann intended by his Luther-German.

8. *Last Essays*, 144-146. I might add that when his first symptoms appear, Adrian seeks medical attention from two doctors who are soon removed, one by dying and the other by being arrested. And since the Devil will claim it was he who sent them and took them away, we must conclude that the doctors were sickly or shady types because Adrian sought them out in a "street directory" (156)—that is, carelessly—not wanting to be cured. That would keep the episode "realistic." Still, it could be said that this—and also, as I have said, the spooky duplication of Adrian's childhood home in his later one—shows Mann deliberately breaking through his "realistic" surface, as he did with that "stranger in the field" in *Joseph*. Does it matter? Not to me. The sacrifice of aesthetic logic is slight, peripheral and playful, and the reality of all that matters is undiminished.

9. "During this particular phase of my life, under the sign of *Faustus*, I was greatly drawn to Dostoevsky's grotesque, apocalyptic realm of suffering, in contrast with my usual preference for Tolstoy's Homeric, primal strength" (*Story*, 125). In fact, there will be more echoes of Dostoevsky in what follows.

10. The following is from a novel by Hitler's propaganda minister Joseph Goebbels and was quoted first by Paul de Man in his essay "Kant and Schiller," and then by Jonathan Culler in "Paul de Man's War and the Aesthetic Ideology": "The statesman is an artist, too. The leader and the led [Fuhrer und Masse] presents no more of a problem than, say, painter and color. Politics are the plastic art of the state, just as painting is the plastic art of color. This is why politics without the people, or even against the people, is sheer nonsense. To shape a People out of the masses and a State out of the People, this has always been the deepest intention of politics in the truest sense." *Critical Inquiry*. Summer, 1989, p. 782.

11. The Rodde sisters, as Bergsten says (19), are "truthful and ruthless portraits" of Mann's sisters, both of whom were suicides. (That he set forth the tragic facts so candidly may be due to that same new "seriousness" about life's actual horrors, the feeling that art must now let them be seen in their nakedness.) Their mother also bears certain resemblances to his own, and little Echo, who comes in near the end, is taken from a beloved grandson. But these are only the life-models he used that were closest to himself. Many other characters in the novel are modeled on actual people, for instance, Frau Schweigestill, Schildknapp, Professor Kumpf, Breisacher and other members of the Kridwiss Circle. See Bergsten, 19 et. seq.

12. For Mann's model for Breisacher, see fn. 6, p. 232.

13. About Capercailzie, too, see Bergsten (53).

14. After I completed this chapter, Reed (392, fn. 72) and others brought to my attention an essay by V. A. Oswald, "The Enigma of Frau von Tolna" in *Germanic Review* 23 (1948), in which a case is made for seeing in the Baroness von

Tolna, who continues to be Adrian's secret benefactor to the end, the prostitute Adrian had "loved" in spite of her warning. The idea carries conviction at once and wonderfully enriches this part of the story.

15. Mann tells us in *Story* that they come from a collection of 13th century sayings called *Wisdom* (218).

16. As Bergsten observes, this suggests an identification of the composer with Christ. In fact, there are other such references in the novel. Christ's "Why hast thou forsaken me?" might well be the basic lament Mann has in mind.

17. As I noted earlier (in connection with Abraham's role as a kind of Newton), Mann's idea of the role of the human imagination in creating the reality we see is more and more the conclusion of science at its furthest reaches. In Timothy Ferris's *Coming of Age in the Milky Way*, the point is made in a passage that startlingly echoes Mann's metaphor of the echo. Ferris reminds us that, according to Werner Heisenberg's "indeterminacy principle," one "can learn either the exact position of a given particle or its exact trajectory, *but not both*" (286) because our instruments for determining each alters the other. Later Ferris quotes the physicist John Wheeler: Though we once believed that "the world . . . exists 'out there' independent of any act of observation," we have learned that in fact the world we see is "brought into being by the experiment that the observer chooses to make, that is, by the kind of registering equipment he puts into place." For instance, if he had used different equipment, "the experimenter would have ended up with a different story for the doings of the electron." Reality is what we add to the record after such experiments. "In the real world of quantum physics," Wheeler emphatically concludes, "*no elementary phenomenon is a phenomenon until is is a recorded phenomenon*." And here, contemplating the origin of the universe, Ferris joins Thomas Mann: "We are left, then, with an image of genesis as a soundless and insubstantial castle, where our eyes cast innovative, Homeric beams and the only voices are our own. Having ushered ourselves in and having reverently and diligently done our scientific homework, we ask, as best we can frame the question, how creation came to be. The answer comes back, resounding through vaulted chambers where mind and cosmos meet. It is an echo" (365-366). *Coming of Age in the Milky Way*. New York: William Morrow, 1988.

18. Writing to Kerenyi, Mann said: "As soon as music at the start of its modern history . . . had emancipated itself into expressivity, it became lamento and *Lasciatemi morire*." A few lines later: "And yet a work, though it be one of despair, must in its essence be grounded in optimism, in a faith in life — and it is a strange thing about despair: it always carries in itself the transcendence of hope" (Kerenyi, 151).

Oscar Wilde came to have a view of the centrality of "lamentation" in human experience and of the healing power of expression that was very close to that of Mann in this novel. "The secret of life is suffering," he wrote in *De Profundis*. And in a letter to "Robbie," "Mere expression is to an artist the supreme mode of life. It is by utterance that we live" (*Works*, 865 and 893). It is worthy of note, too, that Wilde's critical essays show his view of art and the artist to be very close to Mann's.

CHAPTER NINE

The Holy Sinner

"Underneath all the jokes I am very serious about the religious core of the legend, the idea of sin and grace. My life and thinking for a long time now have been dominated by the idea; and really, is it not pure grace that it should be granted me, after the exhausting work on *Faustus*, to bring off this merry little book?" (*Letters*, 621)

The following study of *The Holy Sinner* (1951) was published in a magazine before Mann's death. I use it here, shortened but essentially unchanged, because it still represents my view of the novel and because Mann wrote me a letter about it which gave me the courage to undertake this book.[1]

To join this chapter to the others, however, it's worth noting that Mann wrote *The Holy Sinner*, and also *The Confessions of Felix Krull* which came next and completed his life's work, in a kind of recoil from *Doctor Faustus*. We get a hint of his need for something else in Zeitblom's view of Leverkühn's musical farce on the same "holy sinner." He called it a "travesty," slightly malicious, of art's "swollen pomposity" in this epoch, and an attempt to revive an art that was dying because it had cut itself off from "the folk," from "human beings." "Swollen pomposity" may not quite be Mann's opinion of what his own art had arrived at (though he knew well it was other people's). But he did say: "Comedy, laughter, humor, seem to me more and more the soul's salvation. I long for them after the minimal portion of them in *Faustus*." And when he read the American reviews of *Faustus*: "If I keep my strength, I'll throw them *Felix Krull*, which consists of nothing but pranks, so that at last they'll stop regarding me as a *ponderous philosopher*" (*Letters*, 535, 564).

Another point more important. In spite of Mann's remark about "grace" quoted above, the novel's real subject is a larger vision, of which its "grace-abounding" (5) end is only a part. Mann hints at this himself on his last page. His monk-narrator warns the reader there not to count on such a gift if he goes on living as "a jolly sinner." "First spend seventeen years on a stone," the monk says, "and...you will see if all that is a joke!" (336). He means that what we get is not entirely unconnected with what we are and what we do, though

God — or the infinite complexity of the Whole — may indeed present us with blessings we could never have counted on or known how to earn.

Here, then, reduced to essentials, is that earlier study.

The Holy Sinner is a very funny novel and a reminder that Thomas Mann is a very funny writer. This is a fact to which we don't do justice if we talk only of his celebrated irony. True, most of his humor comes from his ironic doubleness of vision. But his irony emerges so often as humor because this joke of another side to things, which makes some of us bitter, delights him. He has a tenderness, and even a relish, for the human mixture.[2]

That the novel was so persistently amusing misled a number of its first reviewers. For them it lacked meaning because it seemed a mere "parody" of Mann's usual concerns or "complacent" about them. Such readers understood the novel "too quickly." In fact, most of the pleasure it gives is precisely intellectual. And while something like parody and something like complacency make for a good deal of the fun, to use the words pejoratively is to have missed the point, since these effects are part of it.

What *The Holy Sinner* aims to show is that holiness and sin are necessary to each other, and that the godlike foreknowing author — knowledge, in short — can hardly take evil as "seriously" as the ordinary man must because he sees, even as his simple humanity shrinks from it, the good which it makes possible. But there is another reason for our author's lack of "proper" gravity about those moral opposites. It is that for him the conception of life which, together, they represent is fundamentally arbitrary, an imposition on indifferent nature, from whose point of view it can sometimes look terribly silly. These two ideas are the theme of *The Holy Sinner*, of which, however, as will appear, there is much more to be said. In fact, though it may well have provided its author with relaxation after the profound philosophic labors of *Doctor Faustus*, the novel is a deliberate extension of Mann's characteristic insights into areas he had never before so thoroughly explored. Every development provides the intellectual thrill of a double awareness: that of its deep familiar roots and its startling new blossoms.

The novel retells a medieval story taken from the *Gesta Romanorum* and a poem of Hartmann von Aue, a story of incest far more extravagant than that of Oedipus.[3] Its hero is the issue of sin to begin with, his parents being a Prince and the sister he loved far too well. Brought up by a fisherman who found the little cask in which his penitent parents set him afloat, he comes back to his own land by chance, finds his mother, now the Queen, at war with a wicked Duke she has refused to marry, kills the Duke and himself wins her for a wife. From this depth of sin he rises to the papal throne when, having discovered the awful truth and had himself chained to a rock for 17 years of penance, he is proclaimed by a voice from Heaven the holiest man in Christendom and the late pope's successor. The fame of his sanctity brings his mother to Rome. She confesses, is absolved and recognized, and is made an abbess of a religious order; and so both are restored to honor as their story ends.

In the *Gesta Romanorum* each tale is followed by an "application" or moral which turns it into a Christian allegory. Of this one we are told that the father of the incestuous brother and sister is Christ, Who gave the human soul, His daughter, to its brother, the flesh, their son is "all mankind," the Duke is the Devil, and so on. And though a recent editor has stripped all that away as an excrescence on the pure narrative, for Mann the old story *is* full of Christian meaning; it is precisely the relationship of Mann's obsessive themes to insights embodied in Christianity that his version is designed to uncover.

But the fact that the tale is so perfect a vehicle for both that it need hardly be changed at all presents the novelist with his major aesthetic problem: how to get us hidebound realists to accept a medieval tale of Christian miracle? To solve the problem he not only brings it closer to us, making its characters and their crises "real"—this we would expect. He also brings us closer to it by loosening our allegiance to the modern literary convention of realism. This is one of the two chief reasons for the monk who is his narrator and for the "rambling" reflections with which this monk introduces his story.

The convention is attacked head-on: Mann pointedly begins with the story's "grace-abounding end," the miraculous ringing of the bells of Rome. "Who is ringing the bells?" it is asked. And the answer is *"the spirit of story-telling,"* a spirit which is "as air," "abstract," "not subject to distinctions of here and there." We are thus reminded at the start that any story, for all the tricks by which it tries to appear "natural," is essentially miraculous. "Reality" is as clay in its hands, to be molded to the spirit's purposes. "And yet," the narrator goes on, "he [the spirit of story-telling] can gather himself into a person . . . and be incarnate in somebody who speaks in him" (4-5)—and this somebody now introduces himself. He is Clemens, an Irish monk with all the limiting particularity of any actual person (we glimpse at once his funny jealousy, as an Irishman, of the Roman authority). To say that the spirit is "embodied" in him disturbs our monk, however, for the body is the domain of Satan. On the other hand, it is also "the vehicle of the soul and God-given reason, without which these would be deprived of their basis, and so one must regard the body as a necessary evil" (8-9). We shall soon learn that this remark has more than one connection with the novel. What is pertinent here is that it is another step in that instruction in the mysteries of art with which Mann finds it politic to begin. The "necessary evil" of the body is in this case a metaphor for the particular narrative conventions through which the spirit of story-telling must operate, but which are not identical with it, which, indeed, work against it by limiting the freedom which is its essential nature. The implication is clear that though we must use a particular convention, we must not forget it is only a "vehicle," nor reject what the spirit may have to offer by other means.

So throughout the story we find the monk slyly discrediting the realistic convention by which he makes his story convincing. "What know I of knighthood and venery," he interrupts his own vivid and enthusiastic description of the young prince's education. The technical terms "which I use with such apparent ease," he goes on, "I have just picked up. But so is the way and the spirit of story-telling which I embody that all it tells of it pretends to have experienced and to be at home in it" (24). With realism itself thus shown to be mere trickery, the miracles to come should find us less stiffly "modern" in our response to them.

But we are still not done with the monk's rich first pages. He points out that the spirit of story-telling, though it has submitted in him to the limiting of incarnation, is at least embodied in a monk, Clemens (mild, gentle), one who has "put off," along with his original name of Morhold (place of death), his fleshly self. In him, therefore, the spirit "has preserved much of that abstraction which enables it to ring from all the titular basilicas of the city at once." And he gives two examples of this "abstraction." First, his manuscript is not dated — he would make it impossible to say that it takes place at one time and no other. And second, it is written in a fluid mixture of languages (these are "Latin, French, German, or Anglo-Saxon," and we do, in fact, meet scraps of each later on) which will "become one — in other words, language. For the thing is so, that the spirit of narration is free to the point of abstraction, whose medium is language in and for itself, language itself, which sets itself as absolute and does not greatly care about idioms and national linguistic gods. That indeed would be polytheistic and pagan. God is spirit, and above languages is language"[4] (10). Have we not been told that the monk is here an artist, a man detached to some degree from the desires and fears in which he deals, his point of view deeper than common, more "spiritual"? And do not these two examples of the tale's "abstraction" define precisely the abstraction to which the artist aspires, timelessness and universality? We are to find, indeed, that just as these characters are recognizably human and hence possible always, so their story's meaning, though here expressed in medieval Christian idioms and symbols, can also be expressed by the "languages" of other cultures and religions. To think differently is, pagan-like, to bow to the mere vehicles — idols which last a while and go — not to the Truth which they all attempt, with only partial success, to embody.

I said there was another reason for this preface, as well as for the monk it introduces. These pages serve too as a characteristic Mann overture, foreshadowing the developments to come. That whole business of the distinction between spirit and body — or rather, of the relationship between them — is also a way of describing the novel's plot, and is pertinent both to its concern with art and its concern with Christianity. And this is the second function of Mann's medieval narrator. Just as in his character of story-teller he shows how art works, undermining our faith in those conventions which the tale must violate, so, as a monk, he gives us the tale's Christian meaning. He thus unites in a single person the novel's double intention.

Before we explore this intention directly, however, we must examine how Mann performed his second task, that of bringing these medieval characters closer to us. For it is naturally his understanding of them that will determine what he discovers their fate to mean. (It will also, of course, reveal the permanent human significance of the Christian "language" in which the monk describes it.) His method is chiefly to expose the additional, the hidden, motive for every act. It is simplicity we find archaic; with a warring mixture of motives we are instantly at home. So the dying father of the incestuous brother and sister turns out to have left his daughter unmarried because he too had loved her more than he should, rejecting all her suitors as if they were hated rivals. Just such a rival, indeed, had the son, her brother, become, a fact the young man is aware of, if not "on top [where] the soul pretends," then "underneath, where truth abides in quietness" (328)—a phrase used during the climactic confession, but pertinent throughout. For he dreams revealing dreams of the father's terrible animosity.

In Mann's version Gregor (as he is called) does not have to wait for the discovery of his birth to feel beneath his apparent relatedness to those about him something that divides him from them, something both sweet and bitter as it both raises him above them and sinks him below. For his high and sinful birth has its counterpart—or result—in certain "gifts" which make him awkwardly different from others and which make not only his "father's" life as a fisherman seem impossible to him, but even that of cloistered scholar, the life proposed by the abbot of the monastery where he is educated. He dreams of knighthood—of winning love and glory by rescuing the distressed. When he leaves the monastery to seek his real parents and by such knighthood to redeem their sin, this comes less as the simply "logical" decision of the legend than as the realization of presentiments and wishes.

As for the mother-son incest, that unfortunate accident turns out to have been no accident at all, but a fate secretly willed by both. This awful guilt is exposed first darkly in certain ambiguities that enrich from its earliest moment the narrative of their relationship, and then plainly at the end where the Pope and the Duchess (the queen of the old tale) confess their deepest secrets. The many little signs that he was her son which she had failed to recognize—though they had alarmed her and started memories of bliss and pain—their meaning *had*, in fact, been grasped "underneath," and it was her sinful desire for her own flesh and blood that both prevented conscious recognition and made the pretended relationship so wondrously sweet. Nor was the son less guilty, as the great Pope is to pain her by firmly insisting. Reason alone would have had to tell him that she *could* have been his mother. But feeling, he says, had made it unmistakable from the beginning.

Such mixtures, such ambiguities, occur throughout the novel. But it is in the character and fate of Gregor, the holy sinner, that we find the particular mixture that leads us most directly to its theme. An early statement of it comes when the Duchess, thanking her young champion for his conquest of her enemy, points out what seems a contradiction between his thought and his behavior. "Wherein does the humility and abasement of the Christian draw the courage, nobility and presumption of the knight?" "Lady," he replies, "all bravery and every daring emprise to which we dedicate ourselves, and on which we set our all and uttermost, springs from the knowledge of our guilt, springs from the fervid yearning to justify our lives and accordingly before God to redeem a little of our debt of sin" (192). This explanation of Gregor's behavior, which makes it hard to know whether he should be blamed for his sin or given credit for his bravery and holiness, is a central formula in the novel, not only stated explicitly a number of times, but clearly defining the very plot. We know that if there had been no sinful birth to be discovered, he would never have left the monastery on that journey leading to the papal throne (indeed, he would not have existed). When, married to the Duchess, he becomes an especially good Duke, it is "only because he so urgently needed to be" (213). And when the mother learns that the Pope is her son, she exclaims, "Grigorss, poor darling, . . . how ruthlessly you must have done penance, for God to have set you so far above us sinners" (332). Thus even his ultimate holiness is linked to a penance made especially severe because of a sinfulness especially black.

And this holiness is even further compromised. For the Pope it is — "underneath" — a thing welcomed not merely as the necessary counterweight to all his sins, but also as the tool of a selfish motive. Mann's hero, no less than that of the old tale, sets out on his fateful journey in order to redeem the sins of his parents. And his first words when, on that desolate rock, he is given the great name of Pope and with it the keys to the gates of heaven, the power to bind and loose, are "Sweet parents, . . . I will loose you" (295). Moreover, "has he not become so great a Pope," it is later asked, "in order that his fame should penetrate everywhere and so to her ear as well?" (319).

So, with the mixture at work in Gregor, we reach the first stage in our grasp of the novel's theme. But if we are thus led to "see through" the good to its dark other side, we are not left in mere cynicism. For this double nature of the Pope not only compromises his greatness, it also belongs to it — it is itself the source of the peculiar wisdom which makes him a blessing to his people. Our first example of this occurs immediately after his descent from the rock. Mann has taken from his sources the fact that the wife of the fisherman who chained the pilgrim there had persuaded her surly husband to shelter him. But the modern novelist reveals that when the man gladly does the harsher deed it is out of spite, a spite aggravated by the suspicion that his wife's generosity was due to Gregor's good looks. And lo, when the fisherman's wife kneels before the Pope seventeen years later, she confesses that her husband had been right. "Wantonness was at the bottom of the good I did you, depraved lost soul that I am." At this, in a decision foreshadowing many others of which we are to be briefly told, the new Pope willingly pronounces the words, "Absolvo te." For "seldom," he says, "is one wholly wrong in pointing out the sinful in the good, but God graciously looks at the good deed even though its root is in fleshliness."

Now this "Christian" forbearance engenders problems — as we are instantly reminded. "The woman was blissful," the monk observes. "I suspect she derived from his absolution leave to feel still a little love for him in fleshly wise" (299).

Forgiveness of sin, that is, can sometimes work like toleration of it. Nevertheless, since "no one was worthy, and he himself on account of his flesh most unworthy of his dignity," the Pope chose thereafter to take the risk of "enforcing the divine mercy in cases where the Deity would scarcely have come on it by Itself" (308). For he believed that

> one should lighten the sinner's load, that remorse might be sweet to him. Justice is hard and horny-handed, while the world of the flesh needs indeed firmness, yet gentleness. If one so zealously pursue the sinner, one may well bring more harm than healing. Too rash a penance laid upon a seeker for grace may make him lose heart, not bear it and again renounce God, spoilt as he is by the Devil, whose service he in reverse remorse takes up again. Accordingly it is statesmanlike to make mercy go before justice, since it creates the right measure in the life of the spirit, by which means the sinner is saved and the good is constantly preserved, that the honour of God may wax mightily in the Roman Empire. (312)

Here, then, is a theme for this novel, "entertaining" though it is, and one which surely justifies its "complacency," its lack of full seriousness, about its appalling sins. The gifts with which the chosen ones shed blessings on the rest of us are born out of weakness—they could not have become our fruitful superiors if they had not felt painfully the reverse—and the guilty awareness of their weakness is an essential element of their greatness. A theme, I said, for even this must submit to its author's irony, which will carry us deeper. But before we descend, let us pause to examine what the student of Mann will already have noticed: the fact that in the holy sinner, no less than in his monkish narrator, we find Mann's eternal artist, of whose character and fate the story is a kind of parable. It is, I think, no coincidence that the chapter devoted to the greatness of the Pope and the blessings he brought should end with the observation that, while part of his authority was due to his knowledge, part was due also to the fact that he was "very beautiful to look upon, as children of sin, for whatever reason, often are." For "he . . . is gladly hearkened to, whom one loves" (312-313). As Dr. Johnson—and not only he—observed long ago, it is the artist's business too to "instruct by pleasing." Moreover, Mann had showed us before that such pleasure is a fruit of "sin" in that it comes from the lawless realm of desire and feeling—the artist is one afflicted with knowledge of this, a knowledge he shares with his happier ordinary brothers in beautiful form. At any rate, the story of Gregor abounds in evidence of this hidden identity.

There is first the fact that the sin which gives him birth (a sin fruitful at once, we are pointedly told, as his grandfather's virtuous marriage had not been for years) and which, in his monstrous marriage, leads on to his final glory, is at bottom the sin of excessive self-love. Mann has changed the old tale precisely to enforce this view of its incest, for he has made the guilty brother and sister twins,[5] and he has explicitly named the evil mating self-love more than once. Elsewhere he had already spoken of the love with which the artist can regard his very hand. And in "The Blood of the Walsungs," the incest of a pair of twins is a kind of substitute for art, growing out of the same dangerous soil. Artistic sensibility there ends in sterile and destructive self-indulgence because self-love is not balanced by that love for the "others" which, in Mann's view, the artist needs in order to rise above mere Bohemianism and to grow productive. So the self-absorbed Tonio Kröger discovered long before that it was his yearning toward the healthy blue-eyed "bourgeois" that would make him great.

There is above all Gregor's character, which any reader of Mann must instantly recognize. He is the familiar dreamer, gifted and lonely, irritating others with a superiority which he makes even more offensive by trying charitably to hide it, melancholy at last with a sense that even with his "rightness" — that is, his gifts, so shady in their origins — "it was quite distinctly not right" (114), and longing for a glory he needs in order to assuage his guilt. Again we are reminded of Tonio Kröger, who becomes an artist because for him "there is no such thing as a right way" (*Stories*, 98) and who, pained to find that an officer he had been prepared to respect wrote verses, cried, "I ask you: a lieutenant! A man of the world! He surely did not need to...." (109)

It is not only in the awkwardness of his superiority, however, but also in its nature that Gregor resembles the artist. He is one who "came better off with his weakness than others with their strength ... because he understood better than they did how to pull himself together" (114-115). To this power of concentration is added another, of which we learn when he conquers the Duchess's evil wooer, here a Duke named Roger. Instead of simply chasing and killing him, as in the old tale, he makes him a prisoner, that his power might be useful to the Duchess. And he does so by a trick which involves using the enemy's own strength to entangle him and then gripping the other's sword in one hand, though the weapon draws blood. The aptness of this struggle as a symbol for the life of art — and for more — will be examined further on. It is enough now to observe that this power of "pulling himself together" beyond the average and this "firm-holding hand" become Gregor's leitmotifs, the phrases recurring again and again. For along with the ambition born of his guilt, these are essential characteristics of productive genius.

Finally, when Gregor first learns he is not the fisherman's son, he cries, "Since I know who I am not, only one thing avails: the journey after myself, the knowledge of who I am" (139). He soon discovers his exalting and humiliating birth, and his journey becomes a struggle for redemption. But are not both motives involved in the fate of the artist? We hardly need, in order to see the bearing of the first, to remember Mann's own observation in the preface to his *Stories of Three Decades* that works of art are "stones on that harsh road we must walk to learn of ourselves" (viii). And the bearing of the second motive the whole story has made clear. The artist, as Mann has always shown him, is divided from the "others" by a self-consciousness which is born of extreme self-love and which means inferiority, as it makes for awkwardness in ordinary living, and superiority, as it makes for knowledge. And his achievement, in which he shares his hard-won knowledge with those others by making it easy to take, by making it beautiful, is also due in large part to the desire to atone for his guilty difference and to win their love.

The fact is, for this master of the leitmotif, his recurring artist-protagonist is the leitmotif that unifies his entire *oeuvre*, and it functions in the same way as the device does within the novels. In these it is a phrase which first rises naturally out of a particular context and then recurs in others where it takes on a more general significance. This, we know, is a source of Mann's ironic humor. When the Pope, for instance, decides that a bastard can become a bishop, "if the illegitimate one was a true and religious man, and godly, and of firm-holding hand" (309), we recognize in that phrase a memory of his youth and we smile to see through the pretense of impersonal wisdom. And yet we see more than the lowly personal origin of the generalization; we see also, with a small shock of insight, the general meaning of what began as personal. Just so do we see through the present tale of good and evil to Mann's familiar ideas about the artist, but with a smile not wholly ironical, for we have also learned these ideas can take in much more than we thought, their personal basis only guaranteeing the felt validity of the rest.

It remains for us to descend to rock bottom. In addition to the theme we have already found—that of the fruitful interrelationship of good and evil—there is that other "opposition" I have mentioned, an opposition which is prior. Before we can have good and evil at all, we must impose a spiritual scheme on the chaos of nature, who is herself supremely "indifferent." "He was a man and she a woman and so they [mother and son] could become man and wife, for that is all that Nature cares about," the monk tells us, "desperately" trying to justify the pair whose love and need have won his "Christian" sympathy. But "my spirit cannot find itself in Nature; it rebels," he goes on. "She is of the Devil for her indifference is bottomless" (206). No, spirit cannot leave them simply man and woman, it must give them names—mother and son—and thereby replace their joyous innocence with notions of sin, and with pain. When the mother and son learn their "true" relationship and she in horror utters it by name, he shudders and holds up his hand. "Mother, desecrated one," he says. "Speak not so plainly. But yet do so, I understand why thou dost. We shall speak expressly and name things by name to our chastisement. For to tell truth, that itself is chastisement" (228).

But this naming of things is also absurd. And of this absurdity Mann playfully reminds us—such is his mastery of his ideas and his art—at the very moment when it is causing its most moving anguish and exaltation. Here is another serious reason for his lightness and especially for his "kidding" at those climactic moments about the tangle of relationships which the sinful-fruitful matings have produced. "Since the father is the brother of the mother," the knight Eisengrin reproachfully explains to the first incestuous pair, "he is uncle to the child, and the mother, since she is the father's sister, is its aunt and fantastically carries her little nephew or niece about in her womb. Such a disorder and confusion have you unthoughted brought into God's world!" (51) But what has happened after all? A young male and female occupying adjoining beds have responded "naturally" to the "natural" promptings of the flesh. And they have had such fun! And they are so ready to be happy with the baby that results! That confusion, which grows even more laughable when the nephew-son marries his aunt-mother, and ends, with the question of what to call *their* children, in "the defeat of thought" (229), that ridiculous complication is not inherent in the act, but comes out of man's mind and would not exist if we would only leave the blissful pair unnamed. This is what that "kidding" is meant to tell us.

But if man's naming of things, which enables him to distinguish and relate them (in spite of nature's indifference), can look silly, and if that silliness can becloud with guilt and anguish an otherwise delightful experience, there is one thing more to be said of it. Without it there is no need to concentrate our powers, no need to struggle toward redeeming greatness. Without it Gregor would never have been Pope.

As for the spiritual scheme which makes possible the foolishness, guilt and triumph of this novel, the monk names it for us in his rueful observation that the aged Duchess, despite her sufferings, remained handsome and proud of gait, "the nobility of the flesh strangely asserting itself against the abasement of the soul by reason of Christian consciousness of sin" (317). But we have not yet arrived at Mann's ultimate audacity. When Gregor cries out that he is a "monster," set off by his birth from all mankind, the abbot thus reassures him: "But no . . . you are *a child of man*, and a very dear one, even although not in the regular order. God is full of wonders. Very well can *love* come out of evil, and out of disorder something ordered for the best" (144-145, emphasis mine). Then, when the royal mother addresses heaven in a prayer on the eve of her marriage to her son, she prays not directly to God, with whose perfect justice she does not stand well, but to Mary, Queen of Heaven — to a picture of the Annunciation, where also a woman is on the eve of a most irregular union. She speaks in verse , as do certain other characters at moments of passion, as though poetry — art — were a device for throwing dust into the eyes of reason. And her prayer sounds strangely like a demand for special consideration, on the startling grounds that Mary must have a special sympathy with her sin:

> For thou art of the Highest child, as are we creatures all, and yet art thou His mother mild and thus He all must do that she doth say, and her obey. Somewhat thou ow'st to me, with woman's guile I said, that thou with God shouldst aid since He for sinner's need in thy pure womb came in and thee His mother made. Had never no one sin committed, ne'er had been what God with thee hath done, nor hadst thou everlasting praises won. (201)

Finally: "A new task . . . have I to set your soul, but a merciful one," the Pope tells his mother at the end. "It is to grasp the three-in-oneness of child, spouse and Pope [i.e., father]" (332-332). And surely there, if not before, the shocking parallel should leap into light. Not only is this novel about the human habit of imposing a spiritual scheme on the indifferent chaos of nature; and not only is it more particularly about the scheme known as Christianity. *The Holy Sinner* is a secular version of the story of Christ, and the meaning of both stories is the same.

For is not Jesus the Child and — as He is God — the Spouse and the Father of Mary, Queen of Heaven? And though He is of high birth (none higher), is He not a child also of sinful humanity, without whose sin He would never have been born, and whose guilt He suffers his frightful penance to redeem? What, moreover, is the distinguishing character of His greatness? It is precisely Gregor's "bold way of enforcing the divine mercy in cases where the Deity would scarcely have come on it by Itself" (308). This is a purpose understandable enough in view of His own questionable, mixed nature, and His "natural" desire to save His own parents. But if His holiness is partly "selfish," like Gregor's, it has also Gregor's justifying result. This is "to create the right measure in the life of the spirit," to mitigate for feeble man the crushing absoluteness of pure Deity, lest he despair — as well he might — and fall back entirely into the arms of the Devil.[6]

And does not this justification apply to art as well? Both art and Christianity exist to save us from the dominion of nature, of passions uncurbed by human law. These have their own joys, and even "dignity," but their realm, finally, is one in which the spirit of man cannot abide, for it is a realm of chaos. Yet the peculiar value of both art and Christianity is that while each stands firm against the chaos, they do not turn their backs on it completely. How should they? Not only would it be inhuman, for the human partakes of it; but each grows out of that chaos and lives on it — nature and passion are their "basis" and provide them with their special task.

And here we are ready to see that in one respect at least the tale's old commentator had been exactly right. That hotheaded ruler whom Gregor fought with over — or for — the Duchess, and whom he conquered by holding firmly to the man's naked sword, Mann too has seen him as the Devil. Indeed, if the woman represents humanity, both in the divine incest and in the novel (where, in her fleshly weakness, she speaks out for nature, or prays for indulgence of it, and where, at the end, the flesh retains its dignity in her in spite of the soul's abasement), and if Gregor represents Christ (holiness born of sinful man, whose guilt He redeems), who *else* would Roger be? For he was "a prince," the monk remarks, "such as for my life I cannot bear, a shameless fellow. Even at fifteen years he had a pointed beard, eyes like burning coals, eyebrows arched like his moustache, and was tall, hairy, quarrelsome and gallant, a cockerel, a heart-breaker, a dueller, a devil of a fellow, to me quite unspeakable." No woman "less than fifty" was safe from this "cock and stallion," whose lust for the Duchess, however, was the great motive of his life and who wished, we learn finally, to "increase his realm by adding hers" (78-79). That Gregor made him a prisoner because as such his power could be useful to the Duchess is another detail from the old tale that here acquires meaning. Religion, too, of course, would only harness the passions, not kill them, for it is they which give heat and energy — and even birth — to its higher purpose. And how does the Son and Champion of humanity fight his lawless Adversary? Brought into being because of sin and for sin, He knows the Devil well enough to turn his own strength and weapons against him, though He must undergo the risk of intimate contact with them, must hold the sword firm in His bleeding hand. Exactly the same is true of the artist, that dealer in the passions, who uses their dangerous power to ensure a triumph which means their conquest and control. And so it is not strange that our narrator, our good artist-monk with his feelings always comically mixed, should have preferred, as he frankly confesses, to write of the sinful brother-sister pair, rather than of another he might have chosen, saintly from the beginning.

No meaning! *The Holy Sinner* is at least about the absurdity, the tragedy and the glory of Christianity and of art. And the rest of what it means I must leave to others.

Notes

1. At the urging of friends, I will risk the unseemliness of sharing Mann's letter with my readers for the sake of the interesting glimpse it gives of his view of his novel.

The letter is from Switzerland ("Kilchberg am Zürichsee, Alte Landstrasse 39") and is dated "23 v 54."

Dear Mr. Stock,

You made me quite happy by your fine essay on the "Holy Sinner." It is undoubtedly the best analysis and exegesis of the novel I ever read. I am very grateful for your receptiveness because the little thing is especially close to my heart and I am often remembering with a certain tenderness the time when I wrote it in Pacific Palisades, California. It was a *good* time and I was amused in a rather deep and uncommon sense of the word. Now, your review has something sensational for me because you are the first American critic who calls my books "enjoyable", "humoristic", "funny" instead of "ponderous" and "pompous" which are the two epithets mostly given to them. What a terrible misunderstanding! I feel quite redeemed by your discovery which must be an enormous surprise to all your colleagues. I assure you: in the German original these books are still more funny than in English. My desire and goal is to entertain and I am fully in sympathy with my pope Gregor when he answers to his mother and wife at the end of their colloquy of confession: "Wir taten

es, um Gott eine Unterhaltung zu bereiten." ["We did it to provide God with
an entertainment."]

Cordially yours
Thomas Mann

Of course, Mann was right. The novel is funnier in German, as I discovered
soon after reading the translation. But it's funny enough in English.

2. Some years after writing that I found the following remark by Mann quoted
in *Thomas Mann: A Chronicle of His Life*: "I feel a bit bored when criticism defines
my work absolutely and completely through the concept of irony. . . . I am always
pleased when one sees in me less an ironic writer than a humorous one" (250).

3. Though a note at the novel's end tells us it is "based in the main on the verse
epos *Gregorious vom Stein* by the Middle High German poet Hartmann von Aue (c.
1165-1210), who took his legend of chivalry from the French," Mann says in a letter
to Hermann J. Weigand that he got his idea from "the story of Gregorius (in its
most primitive form, to begin with, that of the *Gesta Romanorum,* the form in which
Leverkühn also made its acquaintance)" (PMLA, v. 87, no. 2, March, 1972, 306).
Still, a reading of the von Aue poem will show that Mann did indeed base his story
on it "in the main," for there the characters take on the humanity and depth of feeling that clearly prepare the way for Mann's account of them. That rather than kill
the wicked Duke Mann's Gregor captures him and forces him to make reparations
to the wronged Duchess also comes from von Aue (143), while the passage by Mann
on the great Pope's merciful judgments which I quote further on is, in part, a virtual paraphrase of the corresponding section of the old poem (214-215). The edition
of von Aue's poem I refer to provides, on pages facing the original German, a charming and affecting translation into English verse by Sheema Zeben Buehne.

4. There is a meaning in this that is pertinent to Mann's own career. He seems
to have copied the first sentence of this quotation from his foreword to the one-
volume edition of *Joseph and His Brothers* (xiii), where he thus defended himself from
the charge that his language, all mixed with foreign elements, was no longer
German. "Really?" this novel comments. "Behold, then, how much further I dare
go in the same direction. We shall see who is master, language or the human
mind."

5. That it was Mann who made Gregor's parents twins is true according to
my present knowledge, at least. Of course, it doesn't matter where the detail comes
from—its *meaning* is now Mann's.

6. At this point in the argument, certain intelligent readers of my study have
recoiled—as if the audacity were my own and not Mann's. So here is a bit more
evidence that Mann intends us to see such a parallel. First, when the abbot (of the
cloister Agonia Dei) learns from the tablet that the baby he has found is "brother
and nephew and niece of its own parents," he reflects: "God has made our sin His
own agony, sin and cross, they were one in Him, and above all He was the God
of sinners. He therefore had consigned this stateless little scion to His stronghold
of God's Passion as a state and status" (104). Is it to mean nothing to us that the
sin of Gregor's parents, too, becomes his agony, and that "God's Passion" becomes
his "state and status"?

Second, when Gregor, no more inclined to shirk his coming agony than Christ had been, runs after the fisherman who was about to leave him behind, he too staggers under the instruments needful for that agony — a leg-iron to chain him and a ladder to raise him up. "Carry it," cries the pitying fisherman's wife of the ladder, "as the Lord Christ His Cross" (141).

Lastly, here is something to put beside the Duchess's ambiguous prayer. It is a poem uttered by Gregor shortly after his penance has ended and his glory begun.

> Shall I find my life's black story
> Turn to lustre in Thy glory?
> With what wonder do I see,
> Lord, Thy heavenly alchemy.
> Clear the flesh's shame and pain
> Back to purity again.
> To the spouse and son of sinning
> Highly from the Highest winning
> Leave for earthly need where'er
> To open Paradise's door. (301)

Since Christ, as a Son of fallen humanity, is necessarily a "son of sinning," and since Mary is the spouse of her own Son (Christ and God being One), and indeed, in spite of the Virgin Birth which guarantees her personal purity, is human and a daughter of Eve, how can we fail to grant the double application of all the rest of this verse?

But the clincher is in what Mann wrote to Professor Weigand on April 29, 1952. Having observed that his monk-narrator's gentleness to his hero's sin comes from a "dim notion" that incest had always been a privilege of kings and deities, he goes on, "All mythology teems with marital unions of brothers and sisters, sons and brothers. And such minglings extend from the Near East down to the Christian mystery of the Mother of God. Not for nothing does Sybilla [the sinner's mother-wife-daughter, addressing herself to Mary] pray: "Thou of the Highest child, mother and bride" (*Letters*, 641).

CHAPTER TEN

Confessions of Felix Krull, Confidence Man: The Early Years

"One effect of the drama, said Plato, is that through it a man becomes many, instead of one; it makes him lose his proper personality in a pantomimic instinct, and so prove false to himself. Aristotle might reply: True; he passes out of himself, but it is through the enlarging power of sympathy.... He quits the narrow sphere of the individual. He identifies himself with the fate of mankind." (S. K. Butcher)[1]

Felix Krull (1954) might well seem an unlikely work of fiction to have been written by a philosophic novelist in his old age. The autobiography of a con-fidence man, and one who, in spite of a reference to time spent in prison, tells his life-story as if it were that of a lofty success destined to triumph by his gifts, the novel is a parody of the self-important, self-adoring artist — of Goethe in his autobiography, to begin with, but inevitably and deliberately of Thomas Mann as well. Moreover, it is the gayest, swiftest and funniest of his novels, and the most openly and happily sexual. True, the idea for the story came to Mann long before: he wrote Book I (about his hero's childhood) in 1911. True, too, that when he resumed the novel in 1951 (on the very page of manuscript where he had abandoned it), his view of its meaning had changed. Still, the old man went back to the story because it profoundly suited him. This is why he not only resumed the comically complacent tone, but also launched his hero on precisely the career that the earlier pages had promised. If reading the novel is for some of us like eating ice cream, this, I'm afraid, is a large part of the reason. It is the autobiography of a charmer whose driving motive is his desire for what we, as well as he, must call "the sweets of life," and whose distinctive gifts are precisely his exceptional potency in desiring and enjoying those sweets and his exceptional skill at winning them without slavery to a respectable job, by fraud and seduction. In short, though Mann does not degrade his subject and the pleasure he gives does not go bad, his novel is a kind of pornography.

On the other hand, since all the elements of a Mann novel rise out of and reflect its core idea, this slightly disreputable deliciousness, far from cancelling the possibility of meaning, is itself a clue to what the novel is about. So too are the cartoon-like vividness of its people and places, its humor, its rapid movement from one high point to another. Mann said himself that what "curiously stirred" him into going back to the forty-year-old fragment was the possibility of giving up his original emphasis on the "artist-bourgeois problem," which had been "outmoded by the Joseph," and telling the story "from the point of view of life's unity" (*Story*, 21). This he did, with his usual breathtaking thoroughness. But if that dominant idea of his later novels made his last one too, as he playfully complained, "degenerate into the Faustian mode and turn into a pilgrimage through infinity" (*Friendship*, 164), its chief function is to serve as the basis for another that is simpler and more fundamental, and that underlies the novel's fun. This final message of Mann's career (his career as a novelist — as we will see, the man himself had another word to add) is that the artist is a "Sunday child," for whom life is joy and whose happy labor it is to bring joy to his fellows.

1

What drew him to the story, both in 1911 and 1951, was that it could be one ever-deepening joke from beginning to end. To see how the joke works, it will be helpful to begin with a quick reminder of its "surface."

The great man's memoir opens with his childhood amid the luxuries his father gained by fraud — undrinkable champagne sold under an elegant label — and passes quickly to the father's bankruptcy and suicide. Too poor for school, the boy educates himself by "enthusiastic researches" in the streets of Frankfurt. This is not what everyone would call education, but "one must after all be of educable stuff," Krull sententiously observes, "in order to be educated" (71). Sure enough, the "passionately ambitious youth" picks up exactly what his career will require from Frankfurt's opulent shop windows, from the lingering glances of rich women, and from the accomplished prostitute Rosza in her "naughty school of love" (113). After his escape by fraud from the army service that would have postponed his adult career in the world comes a lively account of how he rises from humble beginnings as a hotel employee in Paris. This job among the rich had been procured for him by his artist godfather as work that was suitable to his gifts and that offered swift "by-paths" to fortune, though also, he was warned, "cul-de-sacs" he would have to avoid. Sure enough, we see him rapidly stealing and seducing his way to a prosperity that enables him, a waiter, to spend his hours of freedom impersonating a gentleman and being waited on by others. After he has firmly rejected as cul-de-sacs the passionate invitation of an English heiress he is serving at one table to father her child and of a Scottish nobleman he is serving at another to become his lover and heir, we see the waiter stumbling on the right by-path at last and fulfilling, with fairy-tale ease and completeness, his most extravagant fantasies. Not only does the wealthy young Marquis de Venosta beg Krull to take his place on the world tour by which his parents hope to prevent his marriage to Zaza, a Parisian soubrette. On that tour's first stop in Lisbon the false Venosta seduces two beautiful women at the same time, a mother and her daughter. And because the younger woman resists him and the mature one overawes and scares him, it is especially thrilling when the former gives herself up utterly at last in a first kiss, and the latter, indignantly commanding him to release the girl, leads him away to her bed. "*Hole! Heho! Ohe!*" the riper beauty is soon exclaiming in his arms. And as we leave our hero (forever, it turned out — and the first time I read the novel, I felt a real pang at the thought), "a whirlwind of primordial forces seized and bore him into the realm of ecstasy" (378).

The joke's realistic "surface" thus offers a good deal of entertainment in itself, as I've said. But as usual with Mann, our richest pleasure comes from below the surface, or rather from our sense of what is added to the surface by its dark or playfully obvious implications. And though in the novel these unfold simultaneously, like the harmonizing melodies of a fugue, the critic must perforce take them singly. We therefore begin with the idea that underlies all the rest, that is, by seeing how this secular con man, like that God-serving one Joseph, carried further Mann's exploration of his one "egocentric" subject.

2

What draws that subject naturally into the open, and adds to the story a characteristic wealth of psychological, moral and philosophic reflection, is that this fraud is richly gifted with the awareness of self and others his profession requires. To him the idea that the artist is a con man presents itself in reverse as the proud conviction that the con man is an artist. As the mature man tells the story of his "early years," we are therefore getting, in effect, a conscious meditation — with examples — on the nature of the artist and his work, and getting it by way of that continuous parody-echo, now of Mann's great model Goethe, now of Mann himself.

From Goethe's autobiography come Krull's stately complacency of manner, his tendency to high-toned generalizations, and even a few virtual quotations.[2] And from the Mann who made a point of the self-love that belonged to his talent, and who called his life "a happy, blessed life" because, in spite of troubles, "the foundation is, so to speak, sunny," and the artist, though "he deals with the absolute," is always entertaining himself and others with "a kind of child's play" (*Letters*, 373-376), comes Krull's bland references to his own physical beauty and to his parents' view of him as "a Sunday child" quite properly named Felix (happy). He echoes his author too when he calls his bad times merely "a cloud, as it were, through which the sun of my native luck continued to shine" (73). But of course, the real meat of the joke is in the way he delights all his life in "the glorious gift of imagination" which lifts him above the "dull and limited" others (8).

Not only does our hero play from childhood on the "game" of pretending to be what he is not—the frowning Kaiser, a violin prodigy (brilliantly manipulating his bow on greased and soundless strings), the officer, bullfighter and other types he models for his artist godfather, looking each one "to the life." When his "child's play" grows serious, it succeeds, he tells us, because it always has "a higher truth at its root" (31). Thus he gets out of a day of school by convincing not only his mother but a doctor that he is sick, and he can do so, he tells us, because, being "of finer stuff," he is on familiar terms with suffering and can create a "compelling and effective reality out of sheer inward knowledge . . . and the daring exploitation of my own body" (34). In short, Krull deceives as the novelist does, by expressing what is true to the human nature he shares with us all, if not to his particular self of the moment. And when he reports his brilliant (and hilarious) debut as an adult at his army medical exam, in which he pretends to want to be accepted by the army doctors while he ensures his rejection with horrifying, though false, epileptic explosions, it is hard not to think of *Buddenbrooks*, that other great beginning by which a creator of illusions freed himself from bondage (that of bourgeois life) while seeming to celebrate it. Certainly we have to think of the artist at his most serious. For we have been told that as his army examination came near, he felt the "happy nervousness" of one "about to test . . . [his] abilities in a great, indeed excessive enterprise"; spent hours in research because "talent requires knowledge," though it can "really assimilate," he knew, only what it demands in each instance to gain "the requisite substance"; felt a certain "apprehension" because he was determined to go "all the way, putting all the latent powers of . . . body and soul into the game" (82-83); and found at last that his long preparation and immersion in the task paid off in the moment of "creation" in a "somnambulistic" (87) readiness for every challenge and every opportunity.[3]

3

This joke will end by lifting the artist up, and very high indeed. But no reader of Mann will be surprised to find that it puts him down too. Thus the reason for our con man's life of fraud—what the aged Mann thereby confesses is the driving motive of the artist's career—is planted at the start in the frivolous messaged tinkled out when visitors press the doorbell of Krull's childhood home: the opening bars of Strauss's "*Freucht euch des Lebens,*" or "Enjoy life." And far from disassociating himself from his light-minded father's commonplace idea of life's pleasures, Krull makes a point of his appetite for them. So he loves

to consort with the upper classes and, indeed, scorns all revolutionary reform-
ers because he counts on his ability to win for himself the privileges reserved
for the lucky few. As for the pleasures of the senses, we begin to learn how much
they mean to our hero when he reports the first of his "dream-like forays upon
the sweets of life" (42), his schoolboy theft of some chocolate creams. For the
thought of those sweets awaiting him in his room brought about an "expansion
[tumescence?] of my whole being" that, he says, was "long familiar to me as
the result of certain private trains of thought." Then, assuring us he scorns
"lewdness" and will treat with proper respect "the most important and mysterious concern of nature and of life" (42-43), he makes it clear that his pleasure
in the chocolates is a daylight version of what he had long referred to in his
childish mind as "The Great Joy," or "The Best of All," of which all other joys
were faint foreshadowings.

It will turn out to be significant that this is a joy for which he is specially
gifted, displaying, even at his nurse's breast, "the most unambiguous evidence
of sensual pleasure," and at sixteen, in the arms of the voluptuous thirty-year-
old housemaid Genovefa, a talent for "the pleasures of love" that is "almost
miraculous" (44). For such talent carries him far beyond the usual boundaries.
After an oddly thrilling glimpse, on a balcony in Frankfurt, of a brother and
sister of the dark-haired Latin or Jewish type, both beautiful, he finds them
coming back to his mind again and again in "dreams of love, dreams of delight
and a longing for union." That he was aroused precisely by the "duality" of this
image, by its "charming doubleness," and this because he found in its "primal
indivisibility and indeterminateness . . . a significant whole blessedly embracing what is beguilingly human in both sexes" (76-77) is a point we will come
back to. Enough to note here that he is as far from conventional inhibitions in
sex as in the matter of chocolate creams.

Then, just as our con man-artist is frank to confess the primacy in his life
of sensual appetite, he doesn't scruple to present himself as a thief, or even a
pimp, taking "a reasonable share" of what his teacher Rosza earned from her
"paying customers." He does so boldly, rejecting all conventional moral labels,
because for one who is "a favorite of the powers that be," what determines the
meaning of an action is "not the what . . . but simply and solely the who" (41).
We must be careful, he warns us, not to "make the elementary mistake of
dismissing something living and specific with a general term" (112). And though
this warning is often in order (the meaning of an action — indeed, of everything — does depend on context), there can be no doubt that the morality he
draws from this truth is the very artist's morality whose dangers were exposed
with anguish in *Doctor Faustus*.

And yet. This novel is *not Doctor Faustus*. It is perhaps a defense against
that gloomy novel, the self-defense of the "sunny foundation" of Mann's artist-
nature. And this time, in the rich chord of his tale's innuendos, the negative
note tends to sink almost out of hearing.

4

To be sure, his idea was such a chord even in 1911, when he thought his con man's story was about the "artist-bourgeois problem." But then that negative note was of central importance. Suggested, he says, by "the memoirs of a Rumanian adventurer Manolescu" (*Stories*, vii), his idea was to show that the hidden sources of the artist's beautiful creations would appall the decent bourgeois. We can still see traces of this earlier "problem" in the teaching of Krull's artist-godfather Schimmelpreester (mold-priest), who declares that "nature . . . is nothing but mould and corruption and I am her high priest," and who points out that the sculptor Phidias was a thief and that if people "want talent" they'd better accept such "oddities" as "perhaps essential to it" (19). There is also the boy Krull's shocking discovery, when his father takes him backstage after a play, of the physical and moral ugliness of the actor who had charmed them all behind the footlights. "This repulsive worm," the boy thinks, "is the reality of the glorious butterfly" (27) in whom the audience saw its dream of beauty realized. Upon which the mature Krull corrects his youthful absolutism with the other side. Isn't the butterfly as real as the worm? he asks. And isn't it the actor's yearning toward the "yearning crowd" that drives him to perfect his art? Thus the younger Mann.

But the author of *Doctor Faustus* not only felt a hunger for humor and lightness; he also wanted to put aside for once the pathos in his view of the artist, and to show, with appropriate exuberance, that what is "wrong" in him may be outweighed by what is "right." It happens that the seeds for this were also planted in the forty-year-old fragment. We find them in the two "strange, introspective practices" which, along with his impersonations, enlivened Krull's boyhood solitude.

The first was his study of "the human will and . . . its mysterious, sometimes supernatural effect" (9). By concentrating his powers and banishing all other thought, he found he could bring the expansion and contraction of his pupils under voluntary control, an achievement which gave him a joy "almost terrifying" and made him shudder "at the mystery of man." The second was the game of shifting his point of view as he asked himself, "Which is better, to see the world small or to see it big?" He finds subtle advantages in each way of seeing. But what suits him best is not to stand above the world, like generals and statesman who aim to rule it, but rather to see it up close, for to him it is an "infinitely enticing phenomenon," and both the world and mankind are "great, glorious and significant, justifying every effort to attain some modicum of esteem and fame" (10-11). Most of Mann's final idea of the novel is latent in these two "introspective" practices. For: "he who really loves the world," he says later, bringing them together, "shapes himself to please it" (61).

What this implies is carried all the way when Krull insists on the "particular authority" of a certain priest who detected in his charming appearance "the immaterial yet nevertheless corporeal emanations of a child of fortune, a

Sunday child." The priest's idea that his charming physical appearance is
related to the non-physical can be believed, we are told, because he represents
a form of worship which "takes special account" of the "world of the senses"—
music, pomp of color and form, clouds of incense—in order to lead us beyond
that world. Presiding as he does over the "loftiest mystery of the church, the
mystery of Flesh and Blood" (57-58), he must know how the "corporeal" can
embody spirit. The implication is clear that when Krull was engaged in the
trick with the eyes which made him shudder at the "mystery of man," he was
performing that miracle in his own way. Of course, to give corporeal substance
to ideas is a practice engaged in by all mankind. But for the con man who loves
the world and shapes himself to please it is a conscious vocation. And in that
trick, as later in all the impersonations by which he recreated himself, he
demonstrated something even more thrilling.

When, after his army rejection, someone remarked that he might have
made a good soldier—and even risen to sergeant major—he felt a pang of
regret that he would never play that role. But this was a momentary error, he
tells us, because in spite of the "martial severity" his "strange life" has required,
"its primary prerequisite and basis has been freedom, a necessity completely
incompatible with any kind of commitment to a grossly factual situation." For
"if it is permissible to describe intellectually an emotional treasure as noble as
freedom," he goes on, "then it may be said that to live like a soldier, but not
as a soldier, figuratively but not literally, in short, to live symbolically spells
true freedom" (101). And this freedom is "noble" to the con man-artist because
it means he is not limited to the particular forms of our humanity in which ordinary folk are trapped who take them literally. His loyalty is to the inexhaust-
ible wealth of possibilities, as well as the endless changing and growing, which
constitutes our essential nature. As for "the real I" under his masquerades, he
tells us later that this "could not be identified because it did not exist" (224).
In fact, his is "the poetical character" described by Keats, which "is not itself—it
has no self—it is everything and nothing. . . . It has as much delight in conceiving an Iago as an Imogen."[4]

In the delightful dialogue with the marquis which ends in his taking over
the other's identity, Krull observes that it would be easier for him to become
a nobleman than for Venosta to become a waiter because "waiting is a trade,"
but "to be a nobleman is existence pure and simple" (222). That metaphorical
nobility now becomes literal! For to one who lacks a "real I" existence pure and
simple is his natural condition. So, when he hears himself called marquis for
the first time, he "shivered with joy at the thought of the equality of seeming
and being which life was now granting me, of the appearance it was now appropriately adding to the substance" (240). And if we add this "joy" to certain
dark earlier hints, we arrive at the strangest and deepest reason of all for the
"child's play" of imagination by which he pursued the sweets of life.

Remember, to begin with, "The Great Joy" which those sweets had
foreshadowed, even as the chocolate creams of the child. Then there was the

odd revelation he once made that it was only by taking Genovefa into his bed that he could be saved from the horrible depression he felt when he returned to real life after his thrilling hours of "dressing up" as his godfather's model. For this, he told us, was "the continuation and the logical conclusion of my brilliant evening among the costumes of my godfather's wardrobe" (45). Why do both his love of life's sweets and his masquerades find their "logical conclusion" in sex? This question was answered when he explained the effect on him of those glances he exchanged with rich women in the streets of Frankfurt.

With Goethe-like gravity, he began by "cautiously" inserting "a supplementary observation." The power of that "bit of slime embedded in a bony hole" to "bridge the chasms of strangenesses between human beings" is to be found, he said, in only one other activity, in "the opposite pole of human contact." Only in the glance and the embrace, "where there are no words," do we experience the truest happiness, that of "unconditional freedom, secrecy and profound ruthlessness," for all that lies between is "conditioned and limited by manners and social convention." In this social realm "the word is master," which begets "tame, mediocre morality" and is "essentially alien to the hot inarticulate realm of nature." And he insisted that though his memoir is a verbal enterprise, his "truest interest does not lie there," but rather in the "silent regions of human intercourse," where strangers come together in "dream-like wantonness" and return to the "wordless, primordial condition" (79). Our con man's "dressing up," which means the artist's play with plausible fictions, is his mind's way back to the "hot inarticulate realm of nature," just as sex is that of his body. And here we see why the "duality," the "charming ambiguity" of that male-female pair roused him to desire as no proper heterosexual love-object could. It was an invitation to freedom from the "tame, mediocre morality" to which society would confine him. It was an intoxicating glimpse of the "wordless, primordial condition" where all limits, conventions, taboos are dissolved.

Once again we think of *Doctor Faustus*. The "primordial condition" thus revealed to be the source and goal of the con man-artist's vocation is clearly the fluid chaos of nature represented by the Devil. But we must also remember once again that this is *not Doctor Faustus*. If the con man-artist's gifts are amoral in their essence, it appears, too, that they are rooted in the same soil as morality and so — as it were, naturally — bring the ethical back into his life.

5

To begin with, there is the sensitivity to the feelings of others that underlies Krull's power to imitate and seduce. He informs us once that his beauty, which he has claimed was the product of his will to please the world, is "only an external symbol of a deeper power — sympathy" (202), and that he could have won all his beauty seemed to bring him with this power alone. In fact, when the heiress and the noble lord are at our hero's mercy, he pities them and spares their feelings as well as he can. Then, as one who understands that desire gives life its bloom and fuels the will (and so the power) to charm, he ceased, after his "schooling" by Rosza, to waste it in frequent or too easy gratification. And later we learn that for him there were pleasures "finer and more subtle" than "the crude act, which is after all but a limited and illusory satisfaction of appetite."

But what chiefly gives the con man-artist's career the stamp of the ethical is the fact that he does his chosen work as work ought to be done. His "difficult and dangerous life" (46) is a life of self-discipline. "Everything I have accomplished," he solemnly declares apropos of the pretense of illness that freed him from school, "...has been the result of self-conquest—indeed, must be regarded as a moral achievement of a high order" (32). This is why he looks on the great performers of the Paris circus, Andromache the trapeze artist and her husband Mustapha the lion tamer, with profound "fellow-feeling." The woman, who used no net, "lavished upon art what others devote to love," and performed a *salto mortale* that was "impossible," that must be fatal without the most "precise calculations." The man forced those great representatives of wild nature to submit to a human will. And Krull responds to them, not with the "passive enjoyment" of the crowd, but as "a member of the profession," a fellow "entertainer and illusionist" who was also "born to act and to achieve" (185-191).

So, when Lord Strathbogie promises to fulfil his childhood dream by making him heir to the noble name, he refuses the offer because "a confident instinct within me rebelled against a form of reality that was simply handed to me, in addition to being sloppy" (215)—sloppy, that is, because it would be tainted by his status as the lord's former waiter and then as his plaything. Such immediate self-denial on behalf of the truer good, the good as he conceives it to meet his own standards, is, of course, already a moral act. It is at least the kind of morality that made a respectable, hard-working bourgeois out of Thomas Mann, however wildly he rioted at his desk.

But all this is still earthbound, as it were; it has to do with the con man-artist's way of relating to those around him and to himself. What caused the story to "degenerate" into a Faustian "pilgrimage through infinity" is the older Mann's compulsion toward "unity." The novel's joke begins to go "all the way" when the con man-artist enters on his triumphant career as a nobleman on the train to Lisbon. For it is there he meets the "starry-eyed" Professor Kuckuck, director of Lisbon's Museum of Natural History, who will later, through his wife and daughter, provide Krull with a supreme experience of "The Great Joy," and who will now teach him his kinship with the whole creation.

6

Here again we find Mann stating his ideas in all their complexity and scope in a way that keeps them quite sufficiently alive as fiction. Professor

Kuckuck's scientific survey of the birth and history of "Being" is like the account we received of Hans Castorp's "researches," a kind of poem of ideas—full of restrained feeling, eloquent, vividly concrete, and dramatic in its leaping suggestiveness. And the young man's response is an example, again as with Hans Castorp, of the thrilled *experience* of understanding. Thus what our hero learns from the professor is also part of the drama. On the one hand, it echoes and completes his developing understanding of himself, for he finds it "plucking at the inmost strings of . . . [his] being" (261). On the other, having illuminated what came before, it will have an effect on what comes after, fulfilling itself in the climax of feeling and insight that brings the novel to a close. Mann the performing magician doesn't fail to boast of this artistic effect in advance. After his tour of the museum, Krull thus explains his eagerness to rejoin the Kuckuck ladies, whom he had met and been dazzled by the day before: "I regarded the tour as a preparation for my reunion with mother and daughter exactly as Kuckuck's conversation in the dining car had been a preparation for this tour of inspection."

That the professor's role in the story is to lead Krull to a double fulfillment is hinted in his opening remarks, which point now in the direction of the body's hunger and now in that of the mind. He tells the false Venosta about his family, which includes a daughter named Zouzou (and so recalls Zaza, the real Venosta's beloved) and about the Portuguese people, whose racial mixture contains the blood of African slaves and whose eyes have "a certain melancholy animal look." Then he compliments the young nobleman on his planned "tour of inspection of this star and its current inhabitants," and this remark, which contributes to Krull's sense of his eyes as "star-like," gives our hero "a feeling of vastness and significance" that, as the talk goes on, intensifies to the point of fever. For moving quickly from "cultural history" to "geologic time" (257), the learned chatterbox presents Krull with three ideas about the great developments of Nature that the young man responds to with comically personal feeling.

The first was that all life on this planet, let alone the period graced by "the pinnacle of creation" man, is a fleeting episode amid the aeons. This, Krull declares, boyishly portentous out of sheer emotion, "predisposes me in favor of the same." And recalling that the old song's "Enjoy life" was followed by "while the lamp still glows," he says the professor has given it "a much profounder meaning" (251). The second is that Nature, as if aware time was short, was enabled to hurry along the development of its orders and genera by the "precious basic idea" of "the cohabitation of cells." Joining together "bits of primeval life" in ever increasing numbers, it arrived at "living designs of a higher order . . . great individuals—in short . . . flesh and blood." At a reference to certain untenable excesses (the dinosaur), Krull *defensively* drags in the god Hermes, to whom he was once likened by an infatuated literary lady. But when Kuckuck grants that in man, as idealized in the god, Nature hit on the "golden mean," he arrives at the idea Krull finds most exciting of all, that in rising to that "pinnacle," life has left nothing behind. We see this not only in our similarity to the apes. The human arm—even a woman's lovely arm—is a version of the primordial bird's "hooked wing," our eyes and skin resemble the pig's, our brain the rat's, and "the whole animal world . . . strikes us," the professor concludes, "as humanity disguised and bewitched" (265).

But this is only the beginning. Krull hears that there were three "descents" or "spontaneous generations" in which what had been was repeated with "something . . . added" (264-265). Before man emerged from the animal, the organic came out of the inorganic, and at the beginning of all, Being came out of Nothingness. The professor shows what he means in an account of how Being celebrated its "tumultuous festival in the measureless spaces which were its handiwork" that expresses the latest developments out of Einstein's special and general theories of relativity. It seems that both time and space were brought into existence by the explosion of matter out of the nothingness that had preceded it, and that matter, like time, is without "general validity," which is to say, is relative to other things. Moreover, all of Nature's variousness issues from one source. Anticipating the Grand Unified Theory (GUT to insiders) for which scientists are still looking, Kuckuck declares that "the whole of Being, known as Nature, everywhere in everything . . . was one," was "a unitary system." It is because the same "elementary particles" make up both "Life, this fine flower of Being," and "the inanimate world" that "the boundary line between . . . [them] was indistinct" and the inorganic, as in sulphur flowers and ice ferns, keeps taking on "the deceptive appearance of life." (The very lesson and the very examples we heard from that old devil-agent Jonathan Leverkühn!) And the same is true of Being and Nothingness. For the atoms which constitute Being were themselves made up of elements that "occupied no definite position in space and did not have a definable mass as any reasonable body should." Thus, not only did "Nature in all its forms" remain "collective" and those forms continue "to exist side by side—star cloud, stone, worm and Man." Nothingness too was always part of the picture because "Being was formed from Not-Yet-Being and passed into Hardly-Still-Being" (267-269).

Long ago, we remember, those chocolate creams brought about an "incomparable expansion of my whole being" (42) and called into Krull's mind "The Great Joy" as the child had begun to know it. Now he tells us that the hand holding his demitasse began to shake because of "a feeling of expansion that almost burst the limits of my nature" and that, "strange as it may sound" (272), was identical with the same "Great Joy." Our hero had understood that it was in himself, as the "pinnacle of creation," that all those forms lived on! His feeling was that of "The Great Joy" because it united him with the same "hot inarticulate nature," the same "wordless primordial realm" to which he was led both by life's sweets and by the liberating imaginative play of "dressing up."

At last, plucking again, as he had been doing all along, at the "inmost strings" of Krull's being, Kuckuck himself adds to his vision of "life's unity" both the note of "joy" and the note of "sympathy." Having casually observed that it was earth's "joy and labor" (267) to spin on its axis and circle the sun, he returns to that significant phrase in his conclusion. "To give man and me, the Marquis de Venosta, our due," he declares that though everything in the world of man and Nature remained present and even the finest could therefore sink back "drunkenly into barbarism," yet something was added to man too. What distinguished him from the animals was that very "knowledge of Beginning and End" which had predisposed Krull in favor of life and deepened his appreciation of the old song. And out of this knowledge of the "transitoriness [that] . . . lent all existence its worth, dignity and charm" came the beautiful discovery that the oneness of joy and labor is the very law of existence. For it meant that "the whole of Cosmic Being," unlike the Nothingness it came from, was eternal process, motion, change. Since it is only in such labor that it exists, labor has to be joy. "Being was joy and labor, and all Being in space-time, all matter, partook, if only in deepest sleep, in this joy and this labor." It is this perception that "disposed Man, possessor of the most awakened consciousness, to universal sympathy. 'To universal sympathy,' Kuckuck repeated . . . and he looked at me with his star-like eyes" (270-271).

So the nature of the con man-artist turns out to be a version of the all-containing universe itself. The joyful labor of art is now revealed to be the human form of the force that keeps the whole of Being in motion. And since Being is one family and this family is moving to an end, how else would its son and heir and "most awakened consciousness" regard it, if not with "universal sympathy"?

Which doesn't mean our hero will cease to pursue those "sweets of life." On the contrary, it is only now, in the Lisbon adventure that comes next, that he can go after them with a consciousness fully awakened.

7

Explaining his eagerness to rejoin the ladies after his museum tour, Krull tells his conductors, the professor and his assistant, "Very often great charm is to be found in brother and sister. But mother and daughter, I feel free to say, even though I may sound a trifle feverish, mother and daughter represent the most enchanting double image on this star" (301-302). This leitmotif of the double image will keep connecting the Kuckuck mother and daughter with that brother-sister pair in order to tell us why they too set Krull sexually aflame. And that the tour brings into his mind the image representing the "hot inarticulate realm of nature" where all boundaries and all "tame and mediocre morality" are cancelled tells us that realm remains life's and mankind's longed-for native country. For the tour completes the vision of the dining car by *showing* that Nature left nothing behind. Krull is introduced to all his organic forebears: the earliest, who lived in the sea or crawled out of it; the monstrously varied family of animals; the shaggy creature squatting beside the fire who, though weaker than the others, was already aware (Krull is certain) that he was "of finer clay"; the "eccentric" who painted on cave walls imaginary versions of the animals his fellows were hunting; and at last a worshipper lifting flowers to the sun, that is, a thinker about the Whole. Like the splendid antlered deer in the museum entrance hall, who is both "crowned king of the forest" and, as a ruminant, a "crowned cow" (293-300), man has remained the animal he was even while soaring far above it.

After that thrilling talk in the dining car Krull had had a strange dream. He was splashing through the Milky Way on the skeleton of an extinct tapir and amid a crowd of yellow-skinned, dark-haired people, one of whom was both Zouzou and Zaza. To the crowd's derisive laughter, he was thrown from his bucking mount and soon found himself "crawling on all fours" and dragging after him a long, liana-like stem. And because Kuckuck had compared the traveling nobleman to a sea lily, a plant which breaks away from its roots and becomes a swimming animal, he wondered, as the dream ended, whether he was an animal or a plant. Now, if not before, we understand the dream — and also those references to the animal quality in the Portuguese racial mixture. That Krull was riding on a figure of death among an exotic people, one of whom is both the mistress of the real Venosta and the titillatingly possible mistress of the imitation, and ended the dream "on all fours" and perhaps an animal tells us that Lisbon will be for Krull what Egypt was for Joseph. It reminds us of Joseph amid those other death- and animal-worshippers — which means, too, of Hans Castorp amid his fellow devotees of the loving and dying animal flesh, and of that over-disciplined dreamer of animalistic orgies, Gustave von Aschenbach.

What had been darkly hinted comes fully into the open in the great bullfight scene that triggers the novel's explosive conclusion. For this is a "somber celebration" to these people, and the bull they await with an "air of consecration" is "a visibly irresistible concentration of procreative and murderous force, in which earlier, older peoples certainly saw a god-animal, the animal-god" (368). Nor are such "Egyptian" rites alien to Christianity. As the professor observes, the blood of a victim-god, always part of mankind's "pious popular ceremonials," made a "connection between the sacrament of communion and the festal, fatal drama" (373) of the bullfight. Given all this, we should have no difficulty recognizing Senhora Kuckuck, whose "racial arrogance . . . had an animal quality about it," who "terrified" as well as "strongly attracted" Krull because of her "almost forbidding majesty of demeanor" (304), and who seemed to him, as he glanced back and forth from the surging bosom of the "regal Iberian" to the "living statue" of the *toiro* and his victim, "one with the game of blood below" (371). This is another version of Mut, the wife of Potiphar, who, at the climax of her lust, confronts that earlier version of Mann's artist as Isis, lust's very goddess.

But if Mann's last novel is not *Doctor Faustus*, neither is it *Joseph*. In this treatment of his eternal subject it is not sex his artist-figure defends himself against, but chastity! Like his Goethe, but with less guilt, Mann now celebrates the worm. For it is Zouzou's resistance that provokes our hero to his great confession of faith. "However fair and smooth the skin," she quotes at him, "stench and corruption lie within" (350). Which doesn't mean she is any the less an "Egyptian." On the contrary, she is ripe for defeat even before he speaks because her resistance is that of the Puritan who dwells on the body's hidden repulsiveness to fight off a powerful lust. It is precisely the way she keeps angrily acknowledging Krull's beauty even as she fights it that makes the seduction so funny and so titillating.

In fact, though his story will remain unfinished,[5] we can be pretty sure that his reply to Zouzou's attack on that "Best of All" completes Mann's theme, his idea of what the con man represents. For Krull speaks as a champion of "life's unity," and of the "precious basic idea" by which Nature serves it. Zouzou's rejection of the "joy without which there can be no life" is "sinful," he says, a "blasphemy," an attempt to "spoil the game of life" that is "entirely Devilish." Though he has to grant that Nature herself separated human beings by making them repulsive to each other, she broke her own law, he reminds her, when she gave birth to the miracle of love. Lifting men and women above the "classifications" that divide them, this miracle changes their loathing to delight—as Krull shows in comic and brilliantly evocative detail—and fills them with "the yearning desire to touch" (366-367). Indeed, the same "precious basic idea" can be seen at work when people shake each other's hand. Underlying all the forms of social civility, it makes a community of the human race.

Of course, as we would expect from Mann, this self-defense of his final *alter ego* comes to us pointedly undermined. We smile at the way Krull, naively pompous, invites Zouzou to notice the "nobility" of his language. He is amusingly diminished too when he parades as his own the lofty ideas about "Being" he picked up so recently. Above all, we are reminded that his self-defense is that of a con man who can't marry the girl even if he should want to because, as he once realizes, his life's "delicate ambiguity . . . ruled out any such excursion into reality" (305). This is why, as he speaks, he passes over with obvious discomfort the admission that children alone can make the union of lovers complete. "At best," he admits, "I could set myself the goal of seducing her" (349-350)—precisely the darker reality that brought the "searing pain" of guilt to Goethe. But here, by way of conclusion, we must add a final "and yet."

And yet—though Krull's defense of the "joy of life" is not in the least disinterested, it is, as we have seen, grounded in the nature of all "Being." Moreover, the con man-artist seduces in order to give pleasure as well as receive it. If the pleasure has its source and its goal in the "hot inarticulate realm" where ordinary morality is cancelled, still, mutual pleasure, not crime, is his object. Finally, Krull does, after all, leave Zouzou unharmed. That delicious kiss with which she surrenders (a kiss he is justified in boasting must fill the reader with envy) is all he will get from her; the climactic experience of "The Great Joy" which ends the tale of his "early years" takes place in her mother's arms and does no harm at all.

Granted, the happy ending may be another example of the Sunday child's good luck. Since he did want to seduce a girl whom he couldn't marry and who was promised to another, it's clear that crime *is* among the con man-artist's possibilities. But this means only that Mann's view of his eternal subject remains double. It seems just as clear that he now wants us to see why its dark side might very well go into the subordinate clause, as it were, and its bright side into the main one. For if his artist is a confidence man, whom it would be a dangerous error to take literally, his deceptions are images of truth. If he is unfaithful to some, it is out of sympathy for all. And if he does at times offend, and even outrage, by playing at lives we others must take seriously, it is this playfulness to which we owe the gift he brings us: joy.[6]

Notes

1. S. K. Butcher, "Aristotle," in *The Proper Study: Essays on Western Classics*. Ed. Quentin A. Anderson and Joseph A. Mazzeo (New York, 1962), 188.

2. Goethe tells us once that he could pass himself off in his boyhood for a speaker of French because of his "natural gift" for picking up its "sound . . . , movement, accent, tone and all the other outward peculiarities" (*Truth and Poetry*, 71). Krull boasts that because of his ability to pick up sounds and gestures exactly, "I didn't need to learn a foreign language in order to seem to be master of it" (142). Later, reporting that he fooled even a doctor into thinking him too sick for school, he echoes Goethe on professional experts when he observes that doctors, like the members of other professions, are mostly "empty-headed dolts," ready to see what is not there and to deny the obvious, and are therefore less likely to plumb the body's subtle mysteries than the untrained "connoisseur" who loves it.

3. He says here again that his performance, though a product of "calculation," was "by no means a lie" and that he already knew some of what he acted out from "true and deep experience." "Should we not," he asks, ". . . be able to command the timely and useful manifestation of our own precious experience?" And though his frightful grimaces came from "emotional experiences" of lust, torment, rage which he may not yet have felt, the impersonation called them up in his soul "in premonitory and shadowy fashion" (96).

4. *Letters of John Keats*, Ed. Sidney Colvin. (London, 1935), p. 184.

5. Interviewed in the presence of his wife by Frederic Morton, Mann offered a glimpse of what was to come. "In the second volume I shall put Krull through some matrimonial and penitentiary episodes ["Don't make them sound so synonomous!" the Frau Doctor interrupted] and finally into a kind of retirement in London where he writes his memoirs" (*New York Times*. June 5, 1955, 33).

6. As we finish here our account of Mann's novels, it may make the picture more complete to set down, if only in a footnote and in gist, what Mann was saying in the more celebrated of the novellas that followed *Death in Venice*, works for which my concentration on the philosophic novels and what led up to them left me no place. It will be understood that, as with my treatment of the novels, the gist I set down is not synopsis, but interpretation.

Disorder and Early Sorrow (1925) is about a history professor who takes refuge from the disturbing novelties of the Weimar Republic in the settled, orderly past which is his subject and in the "timeless" experience of father-love. Dismayed by his five-year-old daughter's "crush" on a young man at a party, he consoles himself with the thought that it will pass. But he has had to recognize that the turbulence from which he withdraws into history is life, which made the real past very different from "history," and which will sooner or later take his darling away from him.

Mario and the Magician (1929) dramatizes the nature of fascism in another of Mann's humanly defective artist-types. This time it is a humpbacked performing magician, who, shut out of life's ordinary joys, gets his own back by his hypnotic power over the crowd, tramples spitefully on the feelings of a healthy young peasant who embodies all he lacks and is destroyed by the explosion he provokes of outraged human dignity.

The Transposed Heads: An Indian Legend (1940) is a delightful parable of the irreconcilable conflict between romance and reality. When a young woman's longing for the brawny friend of her wise, soft-bodied husband leads the men, in a tangle of passions, to kill themselves by cutting off their own heads, and a miracle restores the head of one to the body of the other, the wife's joy at having in her lover, the best of both gradually fades as marriage and regular life turn the lover's body soft, and the husband's body, grown brawny in its exile, becomes the object of her illicit desire. Along the way to the tale's funny-tragic conclusion, Mann's richest thought enters the story as our Indian narrator's playful innuendos, that is, without diminishing its humor, drama or charm.

In *The Tables of the Law* (1944) Mann did with the story of Moses — more swiftly, less richly, but masterfully just the same — what he had done with that of Joseph: he grounded it in psychological reality. We are shown the imperious inner compulsions that underlay the struggle of Moses with Pharaoh for the release of the Jews and then, during the years of desert wandering, with the Jews to make them worthy of their covenant with God. Moses emerges as the great dreamer and creator of morality, and his difficult triumph in imposing it on a people forever sliding back toward the Golden Calf — and the freedom of the beast — is shown to be a version of the eternal conflict between the human animal and his creative, humanizing mind. As the curse Moses ends by pronouncing upon mankind's bestiality becomes, between the lines, a clear condemnation of its twentieth century embodiment in the Nazis, it tells us, too, that the Nazis' hatred of the Jews was the rage of the beast against the moral law that would force him to be human.

The Black Swan (1953) joins *Felix Krull* in its (mainly) positive view of nature and sex. It is an account of the strange effects of the love of an elderly woman for a boy in his twenties. Though this love seems at first to have restored, in a surprising and thrilling renewal of menstruation, her sexual youth, the evidence turns out to mean something else. Love has apparently caused, "through heaven knows what process of stimulation" (139), a cancerous ovarian growth. The story's tone, playfully "romantic" in keeping with the character of its heroine, changes to icy detachment in the talk of the surgeons over her open abdomen of the terrible reality it has been hiding. And yet this "unmasking" is not the final note. It is followed by the woman's heartfelt plea to her daughter not to say that "Nature" had cruelly deceived her. The younger woman is an abstract artist who feels that "Nature" is no longer available as a subject, which, for her, is true enough: being lame, she has spent her life without experiencing sexual love. But as a passionate devotee of "Nature's" ever-returning spring, the mother asks her: "How should there be spring without death?" For "death is an instrument of life," she says. "If for me it took the guise of resurrection, of the joy of love, that was not a lie, but goodness and mercy" (140). What the tale has compressed into that swift transition to death from life at its most intense — in passionate love — is the process that does in fact make a unity of the two, but a unity that sets life in the center. And in the woman's error, and her defense of it, we see the permanent opposition between nature's deadly chaos and the feeling-inspired, life-serving human imagination.

CHAPTER ELEVEN

Final Views

> "[W]hat I have called the new . . . humanism in my essays . . .
> was a new approach born of suffering to the idea of man . . .,
> a new feeling of sympathy with and awe of human ex-
> istence. . . ." (*Letters*, 630)

> "Your last question, about the 'real purpose' of my work, is
> hardest to answer. I say simply: Joy." (*Letters*, 328)

If *Felix Krull* is the last word of the novelist, the man left a final message of his own. It is to be found in the essays brought together after his death in their English translation in *Last Essays* (1959): "Nietzsche's Philosophy in the Light of Recent History" (1947), "Fantasy on Goethe" (1948), "On Schiller" (1954) and "Chekhov" (1954). A brief look at each will tell us what he was thinking at the end about "human existence" and his own vocation.

We might consider first, however, the kind of essays Mann wrote. *A Sketch of My Life* tells us that "Goethe and Tolstoy" (1922), "The German Republic" (1922) and "An Experience of the Occult" (1924) were "offshoots" (95) of *The Magic Mountain*, and we know that others accompanied *Joseph* and *Doctor Faustus* as well. But though these, and indeed most of Mann's essays, were written to convey more or less directly the ideas underlying his fiction, it is worth adding that they are also, just as much as the fiction, an expression of the whole man, that is, of feeling as well as thought. This is why he rejected the German tradition of setting the "creative author" (*Dichter*) apart from and higher than the "writer" (*Schriftsteller*) and reminds us (in *Sketch*) of what he wrote on the subject in his 1929 essay "Lessing." That distinction was an example, he said there, of the tendency to value the unconscious mind over the conscious. But "an art whose medium is language" is necessarily "a critique of life," since it not only "creates," but "names, . . . characterizes, . . . passes judgment." Moreover, "The enthusiasts of simplification forget, or do not observe, how the conscious and the unconscious dovetail into each other in the productive; or how much of the naive, the unconscious — of the daemonic, to use their own sinister and darling word [but it is Mann's darling word!] — enters into and determines all conscious action" (192). The artist, he is telling us, wrote the essays, too.

219

So his literary criticism is mainly about writers he loves, and he refuses
(often explicitly, as in his essay on Kleist's *Amphitryon*) to forestall and chill his
personal responses with the scholar's parade of background material and
received opinions.[1] So in spite of the subtlety — the unrelaxing *intelligence* — that
presides over all and lengthens his sentences, his prose is always direct, lively,
passionate, varying in tone and emphasis like a living voice. Even more important, his essays tend to be dramatically organized, the underlying theme hinted
in apparently casual opening observations, developed in a crescendo and
brought to a conclusion that is a genuine climax of feelingful thought. Finally,
just as in his fiction, we can always see through his various subjects, though
these are brilliantly illuminated, the author himself carrying further his eternal
project of self-realization.

What emerges from the rich body of Mann's critical prose (including
Reflections of a Non-Political Man) is that the writers who hit him where he lived
were all leading him to the deeper implications of his own divided nature. And
as that conflict had issued in a reconciling idea of the "human," these last essays
are all attempts to express the judgment on his four great subjects of "humanity
itself."

1

The object of "Nietzsche in the Light of Recent History" is to convey
Mann's final view of the Nietzschean "aestheticism" he had espoused in his
youth. He now sees it as identical with Nietzsche's "glorification of barbarism" — vigorous action propelled by instinct and uninhibited by that consolation of weaklings, morality — and this, he tells us, was not peripheral to his
philosophy, but an essential part of it. For the "major premise" of this "most
uncompromising aesthete in the history of thought" was that "life can be
justified only as an aesthetic phenomenon" (172). His soaring thought was not
to be held down by "pedagogic responsibility" or any concern for "how his doc-
trines would work out in practice, in political reality." Indeed, in spite of his
scorn for "theoretical man," he was himself that man "*par excellence*," his ideas
quite without any real connection with "that beloved life which he defended
and hailed above all else" (174-175).

Mann cites evidence that Nietzsche often knew better than he preached,
cherished intellectual freedom and excoriated as "suicidal drunkenness" the
"peculiar vices of the Germans," their rejection of reason on behalf of "romantic
passion." And he grants that Nietzsche belonged, along with Kierkegaard,
Bergson and others, to the revolt against the Enlightenment's overvaluation of
reason, and that such a correction was needed. But what is "eternally
necessary," he now insists, "is the correction of life by mind — or by morality,
if you will." For we who "have made the acquaintance of evil in all its
nauseating forms" have learned that an "aesthetic ideology is absolutely unem-

powered to meet the problems we must solve" (176). Not only is it rather mind than unreflecting life — "instinct," "selfishness" — that needs our protection; it is just as true that morality, far from opposing life, is its necessary "prop." This is why "the Jews, thanks to their morality, have proved themselves good and persevering children of life. They have, along with their religion, their belief in a just God, survived millennia, while the profligate little nation of aesthetes and artists, the Greeks, vanished very quickly from the stage of history" (163). And on Nietzsche's belief that "there is no authority before which life might be ashamed," Mann comments, "Really not? We have the feeling that there is one after all, and if it is not morality, then it is simply the spirit of man, humanity itself assuming the form of criticism, irony and freedom, allied with the judging word" (161).

Mann doesn't — couldn't — repudiate altogether a thinker he had once found so stirring. He ends by attempting to isolate the element in Nietzsche that may well have been the deepest reason for his youthful emotion and will always be precious. It is that Nietzsche was a humanist in spite of himself. It was to elevate man that he proclaimed the death of God, and in spite of "grotesque error," he served the "humanitarian ideal, a religiously based and colored humanism which, out of depths of experience . . . , includes all knowledge of the lower and daemonic elements of man's nature in its homage to the mystery of man" (177). If it is possible at all to achieve "the new order" we need, the "new relationships, the recasting of society to meet the global demands of the hour," this will have to come from "a new feeling for the difficulty and the nobility of being human." Such a feeling can't be created by laws or institutions, but we can perhaps be helped toward it by "poets and artists," and by artist-philosophers like Nietzsche, whose life-work "demonstrated" that such saving wisdom must first be "experienced and suffered" (177).

In "Fantasy on Goethe" Mann sketched directly the Goethe he had dramatized in *The Beloved Returns* nine years before. We meet again the "spoiled darling" of Nature; the reactionary "autocrat" who, believing in "innate merit" (109-110), displayed traces of the German's brutality to inferiors, but who also united "the folk-oriented Teutonic temper" with "the Europe-oriented Mediterranean temper . . . , genius with rationalism, lyricism with psychology" (123); the thinker whose ironic doubleness went all the way in opposing directions and ended in "serene betrayal of mutually exclusive points of view, one to the other" (129); and with all this, the "seducer," who, in spite of "penitent guilt feeling," is "forever amorous and will not tie himself down" (130).

But the conclusion of Mann's final portrait of his great model is that Goethe's "notorious paganism was . . . predicated upon the profoundest revolution, or rather mutation, that man's conscience and attitude toward the cosmos has ever undergone" (126). Though he occasionally thought otherwise, it was he who saw "some divinity in all suffering" (126) and made "renunciation" his general theme, as "freedom" was that of Schiller. It was he whose self-portraying characters, all "scoundrels and weaklings," were "by way of compensation ... candidly human, human in the extreme" (129). And it was he who ended by becoming the champion, first of the human in all its wealth of possibilities, and then of the various, cooperative human community its development required, of "the world." In fact, the older Goethe got and the more his works were regarded as "world literature" (the term *Weltliteratur* was his invention), the more pronounced became "his personal tendency to universalism" (136) and the more he valued reason and looked forward to humane social change. So the aged Goethe was thrilled by such "global, technological, rational matters" as a canal to join the Pacific and Atlantic Oceans, and by America's freedom from the "dead rot" of outlived times; and this, Mann says, is really the same Goethe who warned us in *Wilhelm Meister's Apprenticeship* that "stupidity" was far more dangerous than "intelligence," though preferred because the latter "generates discomfort" while stupidity is "only ruinous," and ruin comes later. The essay's last sentence gives us Goethe's life-long message precisely as "words ... directed against death and in support of life: 'In the end the only way to move is forward!'" (136-140).

Mann's aim in "Schiller" was to show how that same goal was arrived at by the writer Goethe saw as the great other to himself. We get first the contrast he had set forth in "Goethe and Tolstoy" between nature's "spoiled darling," whose work seemed to flow unforced out of personal experience, to whom success came easily, and who lived long, and the younger man, whose work was a strained effort of will in the service of ideas and ideals, who had to struggle for a secure place in the world, and whose sickly body gave out at the age of forty-six. But Mann reminds us, too, that these "opposites" knew and intensely valued each other. For all the ambivalence in Schiller's love for the luckier man, he revered what Goethe had done, and even more the work that lay ahead, and was mostly successful in rising above envy. And though Goethe had his own ambivalence, this settled after Schiller's death into a stubborn resistance to all criticism of his friend (even his own) and a passionate conviction of his greatness. It was the greatness, he hints in a lyric in *Faust*, of Hercules, who, though not a god, rivaled the gods by his power to will and do. Schiller became for Goethe the genius who "left behind, remote and shadowy, / What fetters all of us: the ordinary [*das Gemeine*]!" (84). In his gloss on "*Gemeine*" Mann again defines that old polarity: "It is the whole natural world, seen from the point of view of the mind and of freedom. It is attachment, dependence and obedience, not will and ethical emancipation. It is what Schiller called the naive." And though Goethe regarded Schiller's rejection of all this as "overdoing the categorical imperative" and thought that "the idea of freedom was literally the death of him" (85)—the relentless moral will leading to fatal overstrain—he was amazed at its "phenomenal results" and of course profoundly grateful for the receptivity that spurred him to finish *Faust*. So "this splendid friendship was ... a league between intellect and nature" (85), and the friend who survived answered his daughter-in-law's complaint that Schiller was "boring" with, "You are all too wretchedly earthbound for him" (90).

This remark, "by which we are all called to account," becomes the key to Mann's view of Schiller's current importance. "The element of 'Schiller'" which our "social organism" now requires, Mann says, is indeed his power to rise above the "earth"—but to do so in the sense of the "Public Announcement of the Horen" he set down for his new periodical. Schiller spoke there of lifting people's minds above enslaving "petty concerns" and political controversies to those "loftier and universal matters which are purely human" and timeless, to those interrelated ideals of "truth and beauty" which lead to "decency, order, justice and peace" (90-91). Nor is this dream of "universality, pure humanity," an aesthete's flight from life. On the contrary, it was for the sake of life, to free the soul from "anxiety and hatred," that Schiller rejected nationalism. "The most important nation is a mere fragment," he said, "and worthy of our support only if its progress meant also the progress of mankind." The objection to this—it was Carlyle's—is that it is too abstract to engage human sympathy. But we have seen the fruit of that loyalty to the concrete called nationalism. After two world wars, in a time when "rage and fear and unreasoning hatred, panic, and a wild lust for persecution ride mankind," the human race, Mann says, must return to Schiller's idea of "humanity," of "the honor of mankind and the widest possible sympathy." If not, "it is lost, not only morally, but physically as well" (93).

"Chekhov" was finished a month or so earlier than "Schiller," but it rightly ends the book. For the latter is a call to battle. This is a confession of the uncertainties that forever dog our hopes, and it is clearly intended to linger in the mind.

Again we find that what has moved Mann in his subject is what relates it, illuminatingly, to his own thought. Here it is the "modesty" that for him belongs to Chekhov's greatness, both as an artist and as a human being. Mann admits he had misunderstood this at first. He had regarded Chekhov's avoidance of the "long wind" as a sign of his inferiority to those creators of "the monumental epic" (Balzac, Tolstoy, Wagner) he himself hoped to emulate. But he had come to realize that "in the hands of genius" brevity can rival the epic's "fullness of life" and even surpass it in "artistic intensity," since the epic is "bound occasionally to flag, to lapse into venerable dullness" (179). Then he had begun to see that modesty in Chekhov's loyalty to his profession of medicine and to science and reason, in his attentiveness to the real needs of human beings, and in his impatience with the great Tolstoy's lordly way of rising above them. And what hit him hardest was the fact that Chekhov's "self-doubt as an artist" embraced literature in general. In the face of the Russian people's suffering, he regarded his growing literary fame with "skepticism and a stricken conscience," and began to ask himself, "Am I not fooling the reader . . . since I cannot answer the most important questions?" (181).

In fact, the inner development Mann sketches for us is shown leading Chekhov to the question that haunted Mann himself from the beginning of his career: What is the value for life of the artist's superior awareness, of the

knowledge it is his nature to acquire and share? The question is starkly posed
in Mann's favorite Chekhov story, "A Tedious Tale." In this a famous old
scholar and "Excellency" begins to find the respect he gets "absurd" because he
realizes that his ideas are mere responses to "outer circumstances" or "symptoms," and that his life, lacking a "spiritual center," is "meaningless." When his
niece, in "confusion and despair" about the "shipwreck" of her own life, asks
him, "What should I do? Just one word . . ., I implore you," he can only
answer, "Upon my honor and conscience . . . I don't know" (189-190).

    Of course, Chekhov's stories and plays are full of characters who do
have answers and pour them out in endless talk about how life should be lived.
But "the artistic function" (190) of such talk, Mann reminds us, is to provide
targets for irony. "The truth about life, to which the writer should be in duty
bound, devalues his ideas and opinions. *This truth is by nature ironical* (191)." And
it is this that underlies Chekhov's unease. For though he insisted, when reproached for his detachment, that it was up to the reader to supply "the ethical
point of view," Mann's view is that it was his own gloomy helplessness the old
scholar had expressed in that "I don't know." And here Mann asks (he, of all
people!): "If the truth about life is by nature ironical, then must not art itself
be by nature nihilistic?" This is the challenge that he had struggled with all his
life and that is still being levelled against his work. The answer he discovers
in Chekhov and through him is a final version of the one he had arrived at for
himself.

    It begins with the word "nevertheless." Though Chekhov is convinced that
the work of artists like himself is a kind of frivolity in the face of human suffering, "nevertheless, they go on working to the end"; and that "'nevertheless,'"
Mann says, ". . . must have a meaning, and so give a meaning to work as well."
They go on working, he believes, because work, and especially literary work,
contains within itself "something ethical." This is partly the discipline it imposes and the community it offers with all who labor and are not "parasites,"
but there is something more important. Mann finds it in a critic's observation
that Chekhov's increasing "mastery of form" was connected with a new attitude
to his time, a "deepening awareness of what is condemned by society and dying,
as well as that which is to come" (192-194). As we know, this is a formula for
Mann's own sense of things. He had said in *Reflections* that artistic form itself
is ethical insight, and in *Joseph* had defined the goal of such insight in exactly
the same way. But no rousing tributes to art follow this defense, either from
Chekhov or from Mann. Instead, Mann goes on to report how useless the Russian writer found that "deepening awareness," his persisting sense that "life is
an insoluble problem" and that even the material progress he loyally supported
left fundamental evils untouched. The "honorable sleeplessness" (197-198) of an
heiress in one of his stories, guilty because of the wealth she hasn't earned, was
what all his work expressed. It's true that Chekhov dreamt, as his end came
near, of human beings "proud, free, active," and living at last a life that was
sensible and just. But Mann leaves it an open question whether this was a

dying man's delusion or whether, if it was more than that, "the passionate longing of a poet can actually ater life" (202).

In fact, Mann ends by confessing his "deep sympathy" for that "honorable
sleeplessness." He too, he says, in the face of humanity's permanent question,
"What am I to do?" can answer only, "Upon my honor and conscience, I don't
know." The most he can offer is the modest "nevertheless" of his last sentence:
"Nevertheless, one goes on working, telling stories, giving form to truth, hoping darkly, sometimes almost confidently, that truth and serene form will avail
to set free the human spirit and prepare mankind for a lovelier, worthier life"
(203).

2

And now, having acknowledged the final message of the man, we are entitled to return to the story-teller. It is of course the stories — absorbing, funny,
dramatic, moving — that matter most, which is to say, the life his fiction reflects
and possesses, not its ideas. "The power to appreciate life and what life brings,"
he said himself, "is the artist's chief and fundamental power; for to be an artist,
a writer, does not mean to think something about things, but to make
something of them" (*Order*, 257).

And yet we have seen that Mann's pleasure-giving art is itself full of meaning. It is the embodiment and expression of the wisdom that lies deeper than
ideas. In fact, the remark about "making" goes on, "And to make something
of [things] . . . means, again, to think something into them." He is reminding
us that art is life transformed by the artist's own way of feeling and seeing, by
what he is. This is the process by which Abraham arrived at a conception of
the Highest worthy of mankind's devotion. Because "God's mighty properties"
were also in Abraham and "the power of his own soul . . . interlaced and melted
unconsciously into one with Him," he "recognized them" and "by thinking
made them real" (*Joseph*, 251). Moreover, this process — the working of the
imagination — is not only exemplified in the art of Mann's novels; we have seen
that it is also their subject. Mann's career of self-exploration is a gift to us all
because it shows the artist's work as a paradigm of that fundamental activity
of the human mind. And though he went all the way in exposing its difficulties,
its dangers, and indeed the horrors for which that activity has been responsible,
these were not, we saw, the whole story. Just as important was his recurrent,
high-spirited demonstration that it is a kind of joyful play amid the endless
wealth of our possibilities and that it makes a human habitation out of the chaos
of the world.

Notes

1. The quotation that heads Chapter One is relevant here.

BIBLIOGRAPHY

First Editions of Mann's Chief Works in German

Der Kleine Herr Friedman. Berlin: S. Fischer Verlag, 1898.

Buddenbrooks. Berlin: S. Fischer Verlag, 1901.

Tristan. Berlin: S. Fischer Verlag, 1903.

Fiorenza. Berlin: S. Fischer Verlag, 1903.

Königlicher Hoheit. Berlin: S. Fischer Verlag, 1909.

Der Tod in Venedig. Berlin: S. Fischer Verlag, 1913.

Das Wunderkind. Berlin: S. Fischer Verlag, 1914.

Betrachtungen eines Unpolitischen. Berlin: S. Fischer Verlag, 1918.

Herr und Hund, Idyll. (Contains also *Gesang vom Kindchen.*) Berlin: S. Fischer Verlag, 1919.

Wälsungenblut. Munich: Phantasus Verlag, 1921.

Bemühungen. Berlin: S. Fischer Verlag, 1922.

Rede und Antwort. Berlin: S. Fischer Verlag, 1922.

Bekentnisse des Hochstaplers Felix Krull: Buch der Kindheit. Stuttgart: Deutsche Verlags-Anstalt, 1923.

Der Zauberberg. Berlin: S. Fischer Verlag, 1924.

Unordnung und frühes Leid. Berlin: S. Fischer Verlag, 1926.

Kino. Berlin: S. Fischer Verlag, 1926.

Pariser Rechenschaft. Berlin: S. Fischer Verlag, 1926.

Deutsche Ansprache: Ein Appel an die Vernunft. Berlin: S. Fischer Verlag, 1930.

Die Forderung des Tages. Berlin: S. Fischer Verlag, 1930.

Mario und der Zauberer. Berlin: S. Fischer Verlag, 1930.

Lebensabriss. Berlin: *Die Neue Rundschau*, July 7, 1930.

Goethe als Repräsentant des burgerlichen Zeitalters. Berlin: S. Fischer Verlag, 1932.

Joseph und seiner Brüder.

    I. *Die Geschichten Jakobs.* Berlin: S. Fischer Verlag, 1933.

    II. *Der junge Joseph.* Berlin: S. Fischer Verlag, 1934.

    III. *Joseph in Ägypten.* Vienna: Bermann-Fischer Verlag, 1936.

    IV. *Joseph, der Ernäher.* Stockholm: Bermann-Fischer Verlag, 1943.

Leiden und Grösse der Meister. Berlin: S. Fischer Verlag, 1935.

Freud und de Zukunft. Vienna: Bermann-Fischer Verlag, 1936.

Ein Briefwechsel. Zürich: Dr. Oprecht & Helbling AG, 1937.

Schopenhauer. Stockholm: Bermann-Fischer Verlag, 1939.

Achtung, Europa! Stockholm: Bermann-Fischer Verlag, 1938.

Die schönsten Erzählungen. (Contains *Tonio Kröger, Der Tod in Venedig, Unordnung und frühes Leid, Mario und der Zauberer.*) Stockholm: Bermann-Fischer Verlag, 1938.

Das Problem der Freiheit. Stockholm: Bermann-Fischer Verlag, 1939.

Lotte in Weimar. Stockholm: Bermann-Fischer Verlag, 1939.

Die vertauschten Köpfe: Eine Indische Legende. Stockholm: Bermann-Fischer Verlag, 1940.

Deutsche Hörer. Stockholm: Bermann-Fischer Verlag, 1942.

Das Gesetz. Stockholm: Bermann-Fischer Verlag, 1944.

Doktor Faustus: Das Leben des deutschen Tonsetzers Adrian Leverkühn, erzählt von einem Freunde. Stockholm: Bermann-Fischer Verlag, 1947.

Neue Studien. Stockholm: Bermann-Fischer Verlag, 1948.

Die Entstehung des "Doktor Faustus": Roman eines Romans. Berlin: Suhrkamp Verlag, 1949.

Goethe und die Demokratie. Amsterdam: *Die Neue Rundschau,* Summer, 1949.

Der Erwählte. Frankfurt am Main: S. Fischer Verlag, 1951.

Die Betrogene. Frankfurt am Main: S. Fischer Verlag, 1951.

Altes und Neues: Kleine Prosa aus fünf Jahrzehnten. Frankfurt am Main: S. Fischer Verlag, 1953.

Bekenntnisse des Hochstaplers Felix Krull: Der Memoiren erster Teil. Frankfurt am Main: S. Fischer Verlag, 1954.

Versuch über Schiller. Frankfurt am Main: S. Fischer Verlag, 1955.

Nachlese: Prosa 1951–1955. Frankfurt am Main: S. Fischer Verlag, 1956.

Briefe, v. 1, 1889–1936; v. 2, 1937–1947; v. 3, 1948–1955 und Nachlese. Frankfurt am Main: S. Fischer Verlag, 1961–1965.

Briefe an Paul Amman 1915–1952. Lübeck: Schmidt-Romhild, 1959.

Thomas Mann an Ernst Bertram, Briefe aus den Jahren 1910–1955. Pfullingen: Neske Verlag, 1960.

Thomas Mann-Robert Faesi, Briefwechsel. Zürich: Atlantis Verlag, 1967.

Thomas Mann-Karl Kerenyi: Gesprach in Briefen. Zürich: Rhein-Verlag, 1962.

Thomas Mann, Briefwechsel mit seinem Verlager Gottfried Bermann-Fischer 1932–1955. Frankfurt am Main: S. Fischer Verlag, 1975.

Thomas Mann-Alfred Neumann, Briefwechsel. Heidelberg: Schneider, 1977.

Thomas Mann-Heinrich Mann, Briefwechsel: 1900–1949. Frankfurt am Main: S. Fischer Verlag, 1984.

Briefwechsel mit Autoren: Rudolf Georg Binding.../Thomas Mann. Frankfurt am Main: S. Fischer Verlag, 1988.

Thomas Mann-Agnes E. Meyer, Briefwechsel: 1937–1955. Frankfurt am Main: Fischer, 1992.

Tagebücher, 1918–1921, 1933–1934, 1935–1936, 1937–1939, 1940–1943, 1944–April 4, 1946, May 28, 1946–December 31, 1948, 1949–1950. Frankfurt am Main: S. Fischer Verlag, 1977–1991.

The Editions of Mann's Work in Translation Used for This Book

Fiction

Buddenbrooks. Trans. H. T. Lowe-Porter. New York: Vintage Books, Random House, 1973.

Royal Highness: A Novel of German Court Life. Trans. A. Cecil Curtis. New York: Alfred A. Knopf, 1939.

The Magic Mountain. Trans. H. T. Lowe-Porter. New York: Modern Library Edition, Random House, 1955.

Stories of Three Decades. Trans. H. T. Lowe-Porter. New York: Alfred A. Knopf, 1936.

Joseph and His Brothers. Trans. H. T. Lowe-Porter. New York: Alfred A. Knopf, 1948.

The Beloved Returns. Trans. H. T. Lowe-Porter. New York: Alfred A. Knopf, 1940.

The Transposed Heads. Trans. H. T. Lowe-Porter. New York: Alfred A. Knopf, 1941.

The Tables of the Law. Trans. H. T. Lowe-Porter. New York: Alfred A. Knopf, 1945.

Doctor Faustus: The Life of the German Composer Adrian Leverkühn as Told by a Friend. Trans. H. T. Lowe-Porter. New York: Alfred A. Knopf, 1948.

The Holy Sinner. Trans. H. T. Lowe-Porter. New York: Alfred A. Knopf, 1951.

The Confessions of Felix Krull, Confidence Man: The Early Years. Trans. Denver Lindley. Modern Library Edition. New York: Random House, 1965.

The Black Swan. Trans. Willard R. Trask. New York: Alfred A. Knopf, 1954.

Non-Fiction

Reflections of a Non- Political Man. Trans. Walter D. Morris. New York: Frederick Ungar, 1983.

Three Essays. (Contains "Frederick the Great and the Grand Coalition," 1915; "Goethe and Tolstoy," 1922; and "An Experience of the Occult," 1923.) Trans. H. T. Lowe-Porter. New York: Alfred A. Knopf, 1929.

A Sketch of My Life. Trans. H. T. Lowe-Porter. New York: Alfred A. Knopf, 1960.

Past Masters and Other Papers. Trans. H. T. Lowe-Porter. Freeport: Books for Libraries Press, 1968.

Essays of Three Decades. Trans. H. T. Lowe-Porter. New York: Alfred A. Knopf, 1947.

Essay in *I Believe: Personal Philosophies of Certain Eminent Men and Women of Our Time.* New York: Simon and Schuster, 1939.

Listen, Germany! (Twenty-five Radio Messages to the German People over BBC.) New York: Alfred A. Knopf, 1943.

Order of the Day. Trans. H. T. Lowe-Porter, Agnes E. Meyer and Eric Sutton. New York: Alfred A. Knopf, 1942.

"In My Defense." *Atlantic* (October, 1944): 100–102.

"What is German?" *Atlantic* (May, 1944): 78–85.

Addresses Delivered at the Library of Congress, 1942–1949. (Contains "The Theme of the Joseph Novels," 1942; "The War and the Future," 1943; "Germany and the Germans," 1945; "Nietzsche in the Light of Contemporary Events," 1947; "Goethe and Democracy," 1949.) Library of Congress: Washington, D.C., 1949.

"The Years of My Life." *Harpers Magazine* (October, 1950): 251–254.

Introduction to a chapter of *Buddenbrooks* in *The World's best.* Ed., Whit Burnett. New York: Dial Press, 1950.

The Story of a Novel. Trans. Richard and Clara Winston. New York: Alfred A. Knopf, 1951.

Last Essays. Trans. Richard and Clara Winston and Tania and James Stern. New York: Alfred A. Knopf, 1959.

Mann's Letters and Diaries

Letters. Trans. Richard and Clara Winston. New York: Alfred A. Knopf, 1971.

Letters to Paul Amman: 1915–1952. Ed. Herbert Wegener. Trans. Richard and Clara Winston. Middletown: Wesleyan University Press, 1960.

The Hesse/Mann Letters. Ed. Anni Carlsson and Volker Michels. Trans. Richard Manheim. New York: Harper and Row, 1975.

An Exceptional Friendship: The Correspondence of Thomas Mann and Erich Kahler. Trans. Richard and Clara Winston. Ithaca: Cornell University Press, 1975.

Mythology and Humanism: The Correspondence of Thomas Mann and Karl Kerenyi. Trans. Alexander Gelley. Ithaca: Cornell University Press, 1975.

Thomas Mann's Diaries: 1918–1921, 1933–1939. Trans. Richard and Clara Winston. New York: Harry N. Abrams, Inc., 1982.

Secondary Works Cited or Recommended

Aue, Hartmann von. *Gregorius the Good Sinner.* Bilingual Edition. Trans. Sheema Zeben Buehne. New York: Frederick Ungar, 1966.

Bergsten, Gunilla. *Thomas Mann's "Doctor Faustus": The Sources and Structure of the Novel.* Trans. Krishna Winston. Chicago: University of Chicago Press, 1969.

Bloom, Harold, Ed. *Thomas Mann* (Modern Critical Views). New York: Chelsea House, 1986. (See especially essays by P. Heller, H. Hetay, L. Nachman and A. S. Braverman, M. Price, N. Rabkin, I. Traschen.)

Burgin, Hans and Hans-Otto Meyer. *Thomas Mann: A Chronicle of His Life.* University, Alabama: University of Alabama Press, 1969.

Cunningham, Raymond. *Myth and Politics in Thomas Mann's "Joseph Und seiner Brüder."* Stuttgart: H. D. Heinz, 1985.

Ettinger, Albert. *Der Epiker als Theatraliker: Thomas Manns Beziehungen zum Theater in seinem Leben und Werk.* Frankfurt am Main, New York: P. Lang, 1988.

Ezergailis, Inta M., Ed. *Critical Essays on Thomas Mann.* Boston: G. K. Hall & Co.,

1988. (See especially essays by K. Hamburger, P. Heller, E. Murdaugh, R. Peacock, H. Weigand.)

Ginzberg, Louis. *The Legends of the Jews*. (Vols. I and II.) Philadelphia: The Jewish Publication Society, 1909 and 1910.

Goethe, J. W. von. *Truth and Poetry from My Own Life*. Trans. John Oxenford. London: George Bell and Sons, 1897.

_____. *Faust*. Trans. Walter Arndt. Norton Critical Edition. New York: Norton, 1976.

_____. *Goethe's Werke in zwei Bänden*. Munich: Droemer Verlag, 1951.

Hamburger, Käte. *Thomas Manns Biblischer Werk: Der Joseph-Roman, die Moses-Erzählung, das Gesetz*. Munich: Numphenburger, 1981.

Hamilton, Nigel. *The Brothers Mann*. New Haven: Yale University Press, 1979.

Hatfield, Henry. *Thomas Mann*. New York: New Directions, 1962.

_____. *From The Magic Mountain: Mann's Later Masterpieces*. Ithaca: Cornell University Press, 1979.

_____. Ed., *Thomas Mann: A Collection of Critical Essays*. Engelwood Cliffs: Prentice Hall, 1954. (See especially essays by A. von Gronicka, H. Hatfield, M. Van Doren, H. Weigand.)

Heller, Erich. *Thomas Mann: The Ironic German*. South Bend: Regnery/Gateway, Inc., 1979. (Rpt. of edition of 1958.)

Heller, Peter. *Probleme der Zivilisation: Versuch über Goethe, Thomas Mann. Nietzsche, und Freud*. Bonn: Bouvier, 1978.

Hirschbach, Frank R. *The Arrow and the Lyre: A Study of the Role of Love in the Work of Thomas Mann*. The Hague: Nijhoff, 1955.

Holtz, Barry, Ed. *Back to the Sources: Reading the Classic Jewish Texts*. New York: Simon and Schuster, 1984.

Kahler, Erich. *The Orbit of Thomas Mann*. Princeton: Princeton University Press, 1969.

Kaplan, Abraham. "The Jewish Argument With God." *Commentary* (October, 1980): 43–46.

Koopmann, Helmut. *Der Schwierige Deutsche Studien zum Werk Thomas Manns*. Tubingen: Niemeyer, 1988.

Lewisohn, Ludwig. *Goethe: The Story of a Man*. New York: Farrar Straus, 1949.

Lukács, Georg. *Essays on Thomas Mann*. Trans. Stanley Mitchell. New York: Grosset and Dunlap, 1965.

Mendelssohn, Peter de. *Nachbemerkungen zu Thomas Mann*. 2 vols. Frankfurt am Main: Fischer Taschenbuch Verlag, 1982.

Morton, Frederic. "A Talk with Thomas Mann." *New York Times* (June 5, 1955): 5, 32–33.

Nieder, Charles, Ed. *The Stature of Thomas Mann*. New York: New Directions, 1947. (See especially essays by J. Bab, A. F. B. Clark, A. von Gronicka, E. and K. Mann, M. Mann, H. Slochower.)

Reed, T. J. *Thomas Mann: The Uses of Tradition*. Oxford: The Clarendon Press, 1974.

Reich-Ranicki, Marcel. *The King and His Rival*. Trans. Timothy Nevill. Bonn: Inter Nationes, 1985.

Schiller, Friedrich von. *Two Essays: Naive and Sentimental Poetry and On the Sublime.* Trans. Julius A. Elias. New York: Frederick Ungar, 1966.

Scholem, Gershom G. *Major Trends in Jewish Mysticism.* New York: Schocken Books, 1961.

————. *On the Kabbalah and Its Symbolism.* Trans. Ralph Manheim. New York: Schocken Books, 1969.

Speiser, E. A. *The Anchor Bible: Genesis.* Trans. E. A. Speiser. New York: Doubleday, 1964.

Swales, Martin. *Thomas Mann: A Study.* London: Heinemann, 1980.

Thomas, R. Hinton. *Thomas Mann: The Mediation of Art.* Oxford: The Clarendon Press, 1956.

Winston, Richard. *Thomas Mann: The Making of an Artist (1875–1911).* New York: Alfred A. Knopf, 1981.

Weigand, Hermann. *The Magic Mountain: A Study of Thomas Mann's Novel Der Zauberberg.* Chapel Hill: The University of North Carolina Press, 1965. (Rpt. of edition of 1933.)

————. "Thomas Mann's Gregorius." *The Germanic Review*, XXVII, February and April, 1952.

Vaget, Hans. *Thomas Mann: Kommentar zu samtlichen Erzählungen.* Munich: Winkler, 1984.

Wolf, Ernest A. *Magnum Opus: Studies in the Narrative Fiction of Thomas Mann.* New York: P. Lang, 1989.

INDEX

236   Index